TY COBB, BASEBALL, AND AMERICAN MANHOOD

Praise for *Ty Cobb, Baseball, and American Manhood*

"Tripp's stunning account of Cobb as a mythic player and manager is a complex glimpse into a tormented personality." —***Publishers Weekly***

"In this biography, Tripp skillfully links Ty Cobb's life and baseball career to broad social patterns, particularly a muscular form of masculinity. With the examination of Cobb through the lens of masculinity, Tripp blends and illustrates an analysis of white American masculinity with a chronicle of an American sports legend." —***CHOICE***

"Tripp's book is one of the best recent studies not only of baseball but of southern and American masculinity as well. . . . On every page Tripp displays a thorough command of the scholarly literature on baseball and on American history more broadly. Anyone who wishes to better understand American masculinity and the appeal of baseball in the early twentieth century should consider Tripp's measured, persuasive reading of Ty Cobb." —***Journal of Southern History***

"Tripp engages an intriguing conversation about the impact of prominent sports figures in the formation of masculine culture in early twentieth-century America." —***Essays in History***

"Readers interested in late nineteenth and early twentieth-century masculinity, baseball, race, or celebrity culture will find [Tripp's] engaging writing style and authoritative analysis valuable. Instead of forcing Cobb into either/or categories, Tripp's greatest contribution to the legacy of Cobb is showing how he was the logical outgrowth of late nineteenth-century Southern American manhood, for better or worse." —***The Journal of American Culture***

"Tripp's work is a nice complement—and a refreshing, different view—to the volume of works about Ty Cobb." —***The Sports Bookie: A sports blog by Bob D'Angelo***

"An exemplary work of cultural history. With engaging prose, impressive research, and an admirable amount of historical empathy, he gives us the definitive treatment of Ty Cobb and his place in American popular culture. I enjoyed this book immensely." —**John McMillian**, author of *Beatles vs. Stones*

"A judicious corrective to the many myths surrounding Ty Cobb, and above all, a book that embeds this fascinating star in the context of his times and the game he played so well. Tripp has grasped an essential truth about Cobb as a man obsessed with near-perfection and greatness, both of which he attained at times, but shaped by the values of the South and his family. Both a learned and moving portrayal of Cobb that will recast him in a positive light." —**Thomas W. Zeiler**, author of *Ambassadors in Pinstripes: The Spalding World Baseball Tour and the Birth of the American Empire*

"A provocative portrait of a player who was both a catalyst to baseball's emergence as the nation's game and its most reviled warrior. This perceptive book is about notions of manhood and honor during troubled times, and how they played out on and off the field." —**Rob Ruck**, author of *Raceball: How the Major Leagues Colonized the Black and Latin Game*

"A wonderfully full-scale, analytical treatment of the tempestuous hero in his own times and in his own terms, Steve Tripp explains how Cobb came to represent a popular, nationwide version of aggressive manhood at the very moment that it was under a massive assault." —**Benjamin G. Rader**, author of *Baseball: A History of America's Game*

"Steven Tripp's compelling book is the first work to place Ty Cobb fully in the context of his times. The result is much more than a biography. Here is a rich and nuanced study of how the culture of manhood shaped the making and meaning of one of the greatest, and most controversial, players who ever lived." —**Louis P. Masur**, Distinguished Professor of American Studies and History at Rutgers University and author of *Autumn Glory: Baseball's First World Series*

"A first-rate biography of one of the most interesting characters in all of sport. It is also an excellent social history of America at the beginning of the twentieth century. The great Detroit Tigers outfielder stepped onto the national stage just as the United States came of age as a political, economic, and military juggernaut. Best of all, Tripp weaves it all together—our national pastime, a gifted athlete, a troubled man, and a defining moment for American masculinity. Ty Cobb, baseball and turn-of-the-century America come to life in these pages." —**Elliott Gorn**, Loyola University Chicago

"In this fresh and fascinating approach to Ty Cobb, Steve Tripp's critical and yet sympathetic analysis moves beyond basic biography to explain baseball's first celebrity and perhaps most controversial player. Tripp tells a compelling story of a complex man and by contrasting the conflicting values of the rural American South into the expanding cities of the North like Cobb's adopted Detroit, we learn about both sport and the changing values of the modernizing twentieth-century United States. This is an important book for students of sport and of American history." —**Orville Vernon Burton**, professor of History at Clemson University and author of *The Age of Lincoln*

TY COBB, BASEBALL, AND AMERICAN MANHOOD

Steven Elliott Tripp

ROWMAN & LITTLEFIELD
Lanham • Boulder • New York • London

Published by Rowman & Littlefield
A wholly owned subsidiary of The Rowman & Littlefield Publishing Group, Inc.
4501 Forbes Boulevard, Suite 200, Lanham, Maryland 20706
www.rowman.com

Unit A, Whitacre Mews, 26-34 Stannary Street, London SE11 4AB

Copyright © 2016 by Rowman & Littlefield

All rights reserved. No part of this book may be reproduced in any form or by any electronic or mechanical means, including information storage and retrieval systems, without written permission from the publisher, except by a reviewer who may quote passages in a review.

British Library Cataloguing in Publication Information Available

Library of Congress Cataloging-in-Publication Data

Names: Tripp, Steven Elliott, 1956- author.
Title: Ty Cobb, baseball, and American manhood / Steven Elliott Tripp.
Description: Lanham, Maryland : Rowman & Littlefield, [2016] | Includes bibliographical references and index.
Identifiers: LCCN 2016004996 (print) | LCCN 2016015725 (ebook) | ISBN 9781442251915 (cloth : alk. paper) | ISBN 9781538119112 (paperback) | ISBN 9781442251922 (Electronic)
Subjects: LCSH: Cobb, Ty, 1886-1961. | Baseball players--United States--Biography. | Baseball--Social aspects. | Masculinity in sports.
Classification: LCC GV865.C6 T75 2016 (print) | LCC GV865.C6 (ebook) | DDC 796.357092 [B] --dc23
LC record available at https://lccn.loc.gov/2016004996

∞ ™ The paper used in this publication meets the minimum requirements of American National Standard for Information Sciences Permanence of Paper for Printed Library Materials, ANSI/NISO Z39.48-1992.

Printed in the United States of America

In memory of my mother,
Jeanette Elliott Tripp

CONTENTS

Preface	ix
Acknowledgments	xiii
Prologue	xvii
1 Becoming Ty Cobb	1
2 The Game	41
3 "The Professional Teach"	79
4 Honor	107
5 The Players' Ethic	163
6 Fans	223
7 "The Most Unpopular Popular Man in Baseball"	255
8 Cobb in the Age of Ruth	293
9 Protecting a Legacy	355
Selected Bibliography	381
Index	393

PREFACE

Several years ago—more than I care to remember—I decided to write what I hoped would be an instant gratification sort of an essay: an analysis of how Ty Cobb's ethic of honor informed his behavior. Almost immediately, I realized I could not make sense of Cobb's behavior without first understanding more about the social and cultural contexts in which he thrived, especially the values and ideals of the other participants in Cobb's many on- and off-field dramas—namely the players and fans who served as both his adversaries and audience. This posed a problem, however, because few scholars had paid much attention to either group. As a result, my little project turned into a big project and my quest for instant gratification evaporated. In all, this manuscript has taken me about twice the length of the average major league baseball career to prepare. Ironic, eh? Not that I'm complaining. Cobb captivated me from the start; he was a remarkable and complex individual.

Before beginning, I need to come clean about a few matters regarding presentation and emphasis. First, this is not a biography per se. Rather, this is a work of social and cultural history. Although I provide biographical information about Cobb, beginning with his childhood and youth in rural Georgia, I do not try to offer a year-by-year chronicle of his baseball exploits or his life more generally. Nor do I examine every facet of his life; for example, I pay scant attention to his private life. Readers interested in such matters would do well to consult one of the many excellent traditional biographies. Instead, I opted for a more analytical approach that gives primacy to questions of causation, contexts, and consequences. One of these questions is why Cobb acted as he did. That is, why was he willing to sacrifice almost everything—health, friendships, popularity—to be the best player in the game? Remarkably, few Cobb biographers have examined this issue with any sort of systematic rigor. Most have feebly resorted to psychological interpretations of dubious diagnostic validity. They claim Cobb was either paranoid, bipolar, manic-compulsive, or some combination of all three. The problem with such interpretations is twofold. First, those who have made these assertions have absolutely no expertise in psychiatry. Second, the interpretations are ahistorical in that they hold Cobb to standards of emotional normality that may not have existed when he was at his peak in the early twentieth century. I rest my analysis on the firmer ground of what we actually know about Cobb and his era. I suggest Cobb's childhood in the rural South played a formative role in his later public behavior. Specifically, I argue the men in Cobb's life—his father, two grandfathers, neighbors, and friends—modeled a standard of manhood that placed primacy on family honor, personal autonomy, nerve, and will. These values remained central to Cobb from childhood, through his baseball career, and beyond.

A second question that receives considerable attention here concerns Cobb's remarkable and enduring popularity. At the height of his career, a period that began in 1907 and lingered into the early 1920s, Cobb was easily the most popular player in the game. Why was this so? How did this combative and egocentric Southerner from the backwoods of Georgia become professional sport's first true national celebrity? Why did the sporting public, that is to say working- and middle-class urban men, find this mercurial man-child so captivating? More than any single player, Cobb turned baseball into a national game—a sporting event that captured the public imagination. Along the way, he delighted, enraged, alienated, entranced, and at all times fascinated and entertained fans and journalists alike. How he did this and what his story tells us about broader social and cultural currents in American life is a primary focus of this work. I am also interested in the flipside to this question: why did so many of his peers, both teammates and opponents, detest Cobb? To answer this, I examine the work culture of early twentieth-century ballplayers. Ultimately, this means I devote as much attention to fans, players, managers, and the press as I do to Cobb himself. Cobb was a fascinating individual in his own right, but he becomes even more so when placed in the social and cultural milieu of early twentieth century America. That is what I try to do here.

Years ago, when I first started this project, I told an archivist very familiar with Cobb (I'm sorry; I can't remember his name) what I planned to do. He sighed and replied, "Well, finally, someone is asking the right questions." Now that my work is completed, I hope I also provided the right answers.

ACKNOWLEDGMENTS

My journey to Ty Cobb and early twentieth-century baseball began with a National Endowment for the Humanities Summer Grant in which I first began to explore the mindset of post-Reconstruction Southerners. I never imagined my intellectual journey would lead to Cobb and baseball, but somehow that is what happened. A former student, Angela Newcomb, helped me to do much of the initial research on Cobb. Her findings piqued my interest and inspired me to continue. I shared my early research in a variety of different forums. Two proved especially beneficial. I am especially grateful to the incisive criticisms of two anonymous readers for an article I published in *The Journal of Social History*. Thanks, too, to the *Journal*'s editor, Peter Stearns for his early encouragement. I am also grateful to James Gates, Library Director of the National Baseball Hall of Fame and Museum for giving me an opportunity to share my ideas at the Hall's Twenty-First Cooperstown Symposium on Baseball and American Culture (2009). The paper, "Ty Cobb and the Culture of Honor," was accepted for publication in *The Cooperstown Symposium on Baseball and American Culture, 2009–2010* anthology by McFarland & Company, Publishers, Inc. Perry Bush of Bluffton University and A. Kristen Foster of Marquette each read early drafts of some of my work and offered both helpful criticism and enthusiastic support—both of which I desperately needed as I ventured into new territory.

Thanks to the archivists at the Baseball Hall of Fame in Cooperstown, New York, the *Sporting News* in St. Louis, Missouri, and the Ernie Harwell Sports Collection at the Detroit Public Library for sharing their Cobb materials with me. Of course, I could not have done any of this without the excellent work of Grand Valley State University's library staff, especially the very good people in Interlibrary Loan who tracked down a number of obscure documents for me to peruse.

Thanks to Jon Sisk of the publishing house of Rowman & Littlefield and their anonymous readers for their support. And to my agent Henry Thayer of Brandt & Hochman Literary Agents for his encouragement as I entered—tentatively this time—the very foreign world of commercial publishing.

I am deeply grateful to the chairs of the history department for their assistance as I worked on this project—James Smither, Gretchen Galbraith, and William Morison. All three indulged my academic interests by allowing me to develop and teach courses that enabled me to think more broadly and deeply about the topics connected to this project—sports history, masculinities, and popular culture. I am very grateful. Thanks to the largesse of the university, I was able to take two sabbaticals during the process of completing this project. Both were invaluable: the first enabled me to lay the groundwork for this ambitious project; the second enabled me to complete several chapters. I hate to think how onerous this task might have been without the opportunity to focus solely on my research for extended periods. Sabbatical is an absolute necessity in our line of work.

I realize it often sounds insincere to thank one's students for their inspiration, but in this case, it's especially warranted. I wrote this book—in part—in response to their complaints that many of the books I've assigned over the years are much too dry. Thus the challenge—to write something that even an undergraduate might want to read. To my former students who chance to read this, I am honored that you picked this up and I sincerely hope it is up to your critical standards. The cumulative impact of talking to you—my students—about reading and writing history has been transformative. You have helped me to clarify my thinking about writing, to become a more intentional and self-aware writer, and to strive to constantly improve. Thank you for that.

ACKNOWLEDGMENTS

My greatest debt is to my family. My father Marv Tripp instilled in me a love for learning, especially about history. In recent years he has also discovered a love for writing and I have enjoyed talking to him about the challenges and rewards of putting thoughts to paper. I am also grateful to my brother Tom and my sister Cynthia for their continued support and love.

No one in my immediate family gives a wit about Ty Cobb or baseball. But that's okay. Our family is a blending of diverse and sometimes discordant interests—history, the environment, nuclear physics and engineering, and opera. Somehow, we have made it work and have learned to encourage one another even when we don't understand just what it is we're encouraging. In this case, my wife Elise endured my soliloquies at the dinner table as I tried to think through some notion or other, long hours alone in the evening as I typed away on my desktop, and countless restless nights as I lay awake fretting over the best way to present some portion of my argument. Being married to a nocturnal writer cannot be enjoyable, but Elise has been amazingly compassionate. I am very grateful and love her deeply. I also owe her one heck of a vacation. I am also exceedingly thankful for my children, Nathan and Hannah. Somewhere in the process of my writing this book, they grew from teenagers to adults. Like their mother, they have endured my absences and absent-mindedness. Also like their mother, they remind me every day of life's riches. Both are treasures. I am infinitely prouder of them than anything I can type onto a computer screen.

Probably no person has been as important to my intellectual development as my mother, Jeanette Elliott Tripp. As a child, she read to me every night—beautiful stories and deeply moving poems that heightened my love for the English language. As a youth, she helped me with my homework, drilling me with flash cards and spelling words. When I started to write essays for history and English classes in high school, she insisted on typing them. Truth be known, she continued this practice through my undergraduate years at Berkeley. When my father wondered if she didn't have enough to do as a full-time elementary school teacher, my mother just smiled and said, "I don't mind. Besides Steve always writes such interesting papers. I like reading them." Thinking back, I suspect my mom was a very easy sell. Even so, her unwavering enthusiasm inspired me to find a career path in which I could continue to write. That was just one of the many things my mother gave to me.

She was a remarkable woman. She devoted her professional life to teaching inner-city kids in Oakland, California, and her private life to raising her three children, "spoiling" them, her husband, and just about anyone who walked into her home. As a teacher and as an individual, she was the best role model a person could have. This book is dedicated to her memory.

PROLOGUE

On the night of August 29, 1905, eighteen-year-old Ty Cobb sat on a bench in the empty lobby of the Michigan Central Terminal in downtown Detroit. It was late. He was nervous and confused. Cobb had just arrived by train from Augusta, Georgia, to play ball for the Detroit Tigers. He had expected someone from the ball club to meet him when he arrived. But here he was, alone. Perhaps the club thought his arrival so inconsequential that it was not worth their bother. Perhaps they figured a man old enough to play ball should know how to navigate a city the size of Detroit for himself. Regardless, the fact remained, Ty Cobb was in the largest city he had ever been in and he did not know what to do or where to go.

The train ride had been an ordeal. The 700-mile trip from Augusta to Detroit should have taken thirty hours, but Cobb missed connections along the way, prolonging his trip by a day-and-a-half. He had never been north of the Mason-Dixon Line and never been to a city larger than Atlanta. He was a boy from rural Georgia. His birthplace was a community so remote and lonesome that the local folks dubbed it "The Narrows." His backcountry Southern accent was so thick that the Northerners he met along the way had trouble understanding him. Everything struck him as new and different. When the train stopped for several hours in Cincinnati, he used the opportunity to stretch his legs and play tourist. His first real exposure to a Yankee city left him ill at ease. The city's size overwhelmed him. Years later he could still remember how small and insignificant he felt: "the extensiveness of it . . . so many houses stringing out mile after mile." He wondered at the "limited chance a single individual would have in such a place." Though he was excited for the opportunity to play in the Big Leagues, the sights and sounds of Cincinnati sobered him: he suddenly realized that he was about to confront a society and culture vastly different than anything he had encountered in the small towns and byways of the Deep South.

In fact, Cobb's disorientation ran deeper than the mere bewilderment of being alone in a big and distant city late at night. Recent traumatic events weighed on him as well. Three weeks earlier, on the night of August 8, Ty's mother, Amanda, shot his father, William, twice at close range with a revolver, killing him almost instantly. She claimed it was an accident, that she had mistaken him for a burglar when she heard him entering the house through an upstairs window. Few believed her. Neighbors whispered that William had tried to sneak into the house so he might catch his wife with her lover. There was even some talk that Amanda—or perhaps the unidentified lover—had shot William intentionally.

Ty grieved for his father, the only man he truly admired. William had been a highly admired man in the tiny town of Royston—newspaper editor, teacher, county school commissioner, former state senator. It was natural for people to talk when bad things happened to important people. Ty must have known that this could easily erupt into something ugly, destroying not only William's memory but the memory of every good thing associated with the Cobb name. Ty had respected and loved his father with an intensity that may have bordered on idolatry. In the coming days, months, and even years, he would feel his loss intensely. But not now; as he sat fidgeting in the terminal, he told himself that he had no time for sentiment. As the eldest son, he had to face the strange and daunting responsibility of replacing his father as the male head of the family. He fully understood what he needed to do. First, he had to silence the awful rumors by demonstrating his faith and devotion to his father's killer, his mother. He had no choice in this matter: family honor demanded it. Second, he needed to show by word and deed that the Cobbs were unbowed by this horrible tragedy, that they were still a worthy and respectable clan.

Cobb realized the road to family redemption would have to run through Detroit. Becoming a successful major league ballplayer might enable him to make enough money to keep the family afloat financially and pay for Amanda's legal counsel. This meant he would need to make the most of this opportunity as a big league ballplayer. But what sort of an opportunity was this? The club had purchased his contract for a paltry $750 because they were desperate: injuries had left the club with only two healthy outfielders. They gave Cobb no assurances they would keep him once their regulars got better. It was the 29th of August; there were only six weeks left in the season. What could he hope to accomplish in so short a period? He had played well at Augusta, leading the league in hitting, but that was in the "Sally," the South Atlantic League. This was the American League. He had talked to enough former Big Leaguers to know that minor league success was just that—a minor success. In no way would it compare to the challenges he would face in the Big Leagues.

So here he was an eighteen-year-old kid alone in a big city. He was scared. "Nothing was familiar," he told sportswriter Al Stump, his collaborator for his final autobiography, composed just months before he died. "I didn't know anyone between the train depot and the boondocks. Hell, I didn't even know where the Tigers' ballpark was located."[1] Once he realized no one from the club was coming to meet him, he decided to find a place to stay for the night. It was a week night, so respectable working people had long since retired to their homes, leaving the heart of the city to the usual cast of sporting men and women who frequented the many downtown bars, pool halls, and whorehouses. They must have viewed him as a pathetic specimen, a young bewildered man-child with the look of a bumpkin wandering about cumbersomely clutching his only possessions—a suitcase, a uniform roll, a glove, and a few prized bats.

Cobb was lost. Unable to find a decent hotel at that late hour, he settled for a lodging house situated above a cheap burlesque joint. "Definitely on the third-class side" he later recalled. Sleep would not come easily on this night. As he lay in his bed, his thoughts must have turned to what would await him when he reported to the Tigers the next morning. He had less than two years of professional experience as a ballplayer. Whatever excitement he felt as he anticipated playing in his first big league game the next day was dampened by the stern reality that he would have to prove himself quickly if he hoped to stick with the club. It had been that way at every other stop he had made along the way. Teams wanted players who produced. If he could not produce, they would let him go. His one great chance would come to nothing. Cobb may have been young, brash, and naïve about many things, but he had been around enough to know that this might be his one opportunity to establish himself as a big league player.

No doubt, he thought of his father. A year-and-a-half earlier, he had found himself in a similarly forlorn state when the Augusta team unceremoniously released him only a week into the season. Crushed, he called his father to ask what he should do. Though his father disliked baseball, he told Ty exactly what he needed and wanted to hear: "Don't come home a failure," he said; that was not the Cobb way. Cobb must have wished he could have that conversation again, but that was impossible: his father was dead. All Ty could do now was remember his father's words and commit himself to living up to them.

Many years later Cobb confided to Stump that he was "nervous and anxious" that first night. But when it came time to describe that first night in his autobiography, he refused to be so revealing; instead, he instructed Stump to state only that he was "apprehensive." And then he added this for good measure: "I don't believe I looked, or felt, like too much of a rube." After all, he insisted, the Cobbs "were people of position and property in the South." Blood will tell, as Southerners used to say.[2]

Ty Cobb would make his way in the world by living up to his family name and its legacy. No matter what, he would remain true to the values and ideals that had been instilled in him as a child of the South, as a child of William Cobb. True, he needed to learn his way around town. He would admit to that. And yes, he needed to elevate his game to become a successful ballplayer. But he was not about to change his basic principles. They were as much a part of who he was as his blond hair and his hot temper. So far as he was concerned, they were superior to anything anyone in the North could teach him. He felt no need to conform to the values of this strange new environment. He would become a man on the major league ball fields of America, but he would do so on his terms, the terms of his native South. He was confident that his upbringing as a Cobb would be enough to ensure his success in Detroit.

Did it ever. For over twenty years Ty Cobb was the game's preeminent star, a player so dominant that when he finally retired after twenty-four years in the majors, nearly all agreed he was the greatest player in the history of the game. His contemporaries described him as the consummate player—fast, smart, courageous, daring, driven, graceful. Fans adored watching him. And the records he set, 131 in all by the time he retired, included most games played, most plate appearances, most base hits, most total bases, most extra base hits, most doubles, most runs scored, most stolen bases in a season, most steals of home, most batting titles, most consecutive batting titles, highest lifetime batting average. When he retired, aficionados and players alike lamented his passing—aware that they would never see his like again. His feats on the bases were such, some of the best players in the game could only watch in disbelief. "I don't blame any young ballplayer who looks at the records Cobb set and refuses to believe them," White Sox catcher Ray Schalk remarked. "If I hadn't played against that devil, I wouldn't believe them myself. And most of the time it was even hard to believe the things you actually saw him do."

Yet as an elder Cobb looked back on his life in baseball, he fairly seethed with bitterness. He claimed to have played the game following the ethic of honor; "the honorable way is the only way" was his personal code. Yet the public knew nothing about this. All they knew of Ty Cobb was that he was a "spike-slashing demon of the diamond with a wide streak of cruelty in his nature." Public memory had turned against him. "The fights and feuds I was in have been steadily slanted to put me in the wrong," he complained. Enough was enough. Diagnosed with advanced prostate cancer and acute kidney disease—the pain so searing he could only beat it down with a daily dosage of a fistful of painkillers washed down with a quart of bourbon—he would execute his final act of vindication. He would tell his story, candidly revealing how the ethic of honor had informed his behavior at each turn. Now as he faced death, he would appeal to the ethic one last time, confident it would serve him as well now as it had nearly sixty years earlier when he had first arrived in Detroit as an anxious young man eager to leave his mark on the world. "There comes the moment when a man must speak—not in rebuttal, and certainly not in anger, but as a simple duty to himself and those who carry his name," he said, adding with a tone of finality, "My critics have had their innings; I will have mine now."[3]

When Ty Cobb came north to play with the Detroit Tigers, he brought with him a change of clothes and the tools of his trade. But he brought more than that. He brought a distinctive social orientation and worldview that was unique to the turn-of-the-century South. And he brought a burning desire to reclaim his family's legacy by living up to what he believed that legacy entailed—their superiority as people of position and property. The story of Ty Cobb is in large part the story of a man determined to retain his values in an alien and often unwelcoming world. How he did this and how his peers and baseball fans across America responded to his efforts make for one of the epic stories in American sports history. Cobb did not just set baseball records; he helped shape American sporting culture for the next century and beyond.

NOTES

1. Al Stump, *Cobb* (Chapel Hill, NC: Algonquin Books, 1994), 103. As other Cobb biographers have explained, Stump was neither an accurate nor an honest chronicler of Cobb's life. Still, he did have access to Cobb and Cobb—at least for a time—entrusted Stump with helping him tell his story. As with every source of questionable veracity, I have used Stump only when other sources corroborate his writings. For critics of Stump, see: William R. Cobb, "The Georgia Peach: Stumped by the Storyteller," *The National Pastime* (2010) http://sabr.org/research/baseball-peach-state (accessed August 24, 2015); Tim Hornbaker, *War on the Basepaths: The Definitive Biography of Ty Cobb* (New York: Sports Publishing, 2015), 282–85; Charles Leerhsen, *Ty Cobb: A Terrible Beauty* (New York: Simon and Schuster, 2015), 380–402.

2. Stump, *Cobb*, 103; Ty Cobb with Al Stump, *My Life in Baseball* (1961; repr., Lincoln, NE: Bison Books, 1993), 21.

3. Cobb, *My Life*, 19–20.

I

BECOMING TY COBB

Ty Cobb loved baseball for many reasons. He loved that it was a game that compelled him to marshal all his resources—physical, mental, psychological, and emotional—to compete and succeed. He loved that it was a thinking man's game, a game of strategy and nuance. He loved the steady and unrelenting war of nerves created by individual competitions—hitter against pitcher, hitter against fielder, base runner against infielder, base stealer against catcher. He loved the camaraderie of team membership. He loved the game's combative nature, the intensity of competition, especially in the heat of a pennant race. It was like war, he proclaimed, and he reveled in it. He loved that he was the game's best player and its most popular draw. He loved the cheers of the crowd when he pulled off a daring heist of home or scored from second on an infield single. He even loved the boos and catcalls he received at every ballpark—save his own—as he strode up to the plate.

Enveloping all these reasons was the most essential reason of all: Ty Cobb loved baseball because it was a man's game. If it was not, nothing else would have mattered. "Baseball," he declared in his final autobiography, "is a red-blooded sport for red-blooded men. It's no pink tea, and mollycoddles had better stay out." What made baseball such a manly enterprise? For starters, it encouraged aggressive and unrelenting rivalries. It was a "contest and everything that implies, a struggle for supremacy, a survival of the fittest," he asserted. Indeed, ruthless competition inundated every aspect of the game. "Every man in the game, from the minors on up is not only fighting against the other side, but he's trying to hold onto his own job against those on his own bench who'd love to take it away." To his way of thinking, the fiercely masculine nature of the game made it the great American pastime. "Why deny this? Why minimize it?" he asked in near disbelief. "Why not boldly admit it?"

The most essential attribute of Ty Cobb, the trait that defined him more than any other, was not his intellect, his speed, or even his infamously mercurial temper; it was his manhood. Ty Cobb delighted in his manhood and admired the manhood of others. It is even safe to say that he loved men more than he loved women. He was not homosexual, but he was certainly homosocial. That is, he much preferred the company of men to women. In media interviews and in public writings, including his multiple autobiographies and memoirs, he rarely discussed the women in his life and when he did his tone was either dispassionate or dismissive. This was true whether he spoke of his mother, his sister, his two wives, or his two daughters. That is not to say that he was misogynist; extant evidence does not allow for such an assertion. Rather, he simply enjoyed the company of men so much that he saw little need to cultivate intimate relationships with women. During his baseball playing days, he competed with men, gambled with men, traveled with men, dined with men, and conversed with men. In the off-season, he seemed to make a point to stay clear of the feminizing domesticity of home and family as much as possible. As a result, he never developed much of a relationship with any of his five children. His oldest daughter Shirley Cobb Beckworth remembered her father was often indifferent and short-tempered. "As a baseball player, he had a great record," she allowed, "but as a man, as a husband and father, he didn't have much of one." The problem, she concluded, was that he really "didn't have time for his children." Even when alone, he engrossed himself in the lives of men—by reading military histories and biographies of his heroes, all of whom were men—Napoleon (his personal favorite), Lee, Jackson, and Washington.[1]

Cobb's preference for the company of men was hardly abnormal given the culture in which he grew up. While historians generally agree that middle-class Northern culture became more feminized during the late nineteenth century as women gained greater influence beyond the household, Southern culture retained stronger male and female spheres due to the continued dominance of patriarchy. Southern men might agree with Northern men that women were far more pious and pure than men, but this compelled very few to follow the advice of women. Rather, Southern men brazenly adhered to a culture of honor that celebrated such masculine values as courage, indifference to pain (whether their own or someone else's), competitive aggression, and physical strength.[2] Ty Cobb developed an intense and abiding devotion to this culture. In time, he came to epitomize it.

Cobb encountered this culture at an early age. Born in 1886 in the remote farmlands of northern Georgia, Cobb grew up surrounded by a special breed of men—strong, assertive, willful, and occasionally cruel white men. They were also exceedingly troubled. The older ones—those who were born before the Civil War—had experienced firsthand the horror of war and military defeat, followed by the humiliation of black emancipation and Yankee rule. By the end of the century, most had rebuilt their lives, but they remained defensive and combative, determined to prove the ultimate rightness of their Lost Cause and to reclaim at least a portion of their former glory. They looked to the past for both inspiration and solace. While military defeat and Yankee occupation forced them to accept the new realities of late nineteenth-century industrialism, most were reluctant to do so. They had experienced enough change and wanted to preserve as much of the past as they could, even as the world advanced around them. In this, they were the ultimate conservatives.[3]

Their sons often saw things differently. They had not experienced the war firsthand, or if they had they could scarcely remember it, but they did experience something almost equally traumatic—the shame of their defeated fathers. They responded with a mixture of admiration and disappointment. They respected their fathers for what they had tried to accomplish and for the power, authority, and splendor they had once enjoyed as planters and patriarchs. Even though they had never experienced the idyll of the Plantation South, they appreciated its allure—a time and place in which white men exercised their full birthright and enjoyed the fruits of their absolute authority. But they were not tied to the past as their fathers were: these sons were young and eager to make a world for themselves. They looked to the past for inspiration, but they understood that it could never be re-created, at least not in its entirety. Growing up amidst decay made them realists. The South needed to change, they said. The only way to ward off further shame and humiliation was to rebuild the South into something new, stronger, better. This second generation became the apostles for a New South. Follow us, they said, and we will reclaim the dignity, purpose, and authority of our fathers. We will do it by becoming masters again—masters of technology, industry, finance, and labor. That was their mantra—their cure for all that ailed the South.[4]

Ty Cobb was a member of the third generation. Growing up, he learned what it meant to be a man by observing and interacting with both his rebel grandfathers and his progressive-minded father. All were powerful and charismatic men, leaders in their respective communities. The young Ty Cobb took notice. A good portion of the man Ty Cobb would become emerged from his interactions with the men of his youth. His journey toward manhood began with the man he admired most—his father.

In many respects, William Herschel Cobb personified the changing ideals and commitments of progressive Southern whites of his generation. As an educator, he embraced one of the basic tenants of New South ideology—that universal public education (universal for whites, at least) would lead the South to a new age of economic expansion and political enlightenment. William himself exemplified the transformative possibilities of a formal education. The first-born of a family with a moderate-sized farm near Murphy, North Carolina, in the Appalachian foothills, William was determined to gain a college education—a remarkable feat for a man of humble means in the postwar South, as most boys rarely went to school beyond eighth grade. After attaining the equivalence of a high school education at a local boarding school, the Hicksville Academy, he set out on his own, crossing into the sparsely settled farm country of northern Georgia. There, he took on a variety of jobs, including general laborer, bookkeeper, and schoolteacher. By 1884, he was working for Captain Caleb Chitwood, a Confederate military hero, cotton farmer, and the most prominent citizen in the tiny community the locals called "The Narrows." Situated in the upper Georgia Piedmont on the southernmost edge of the Great Smoky Mountains, the hamlet was extremely isolated, even by the standards of the late nineteenth-century rural South. Consisting of about fifty or so farmers and their families, the community offered no postal service, no rail lines, and no general stores. The only access residents had to the outside world was a furrowed road that led to the small towns of Cornelia to the north and Baldwin to the south. William Cobb's new neighbors preferred it this way. Local lore has it that the people who settled the region shortly after the close of the Civil War chose the locale because they thought its isolation might enable them to escape the intrusion of Yankee rule so they could nurse their wounds and make a new start. Although The Narrows might not have been the ideal spot for an ambitious man like William, he soon found reason enough to stay— Caleb Chitwood's beautiful oldest daughter Amanda, seven years William's junior. The two married in February 1886 at the Chitwood home and stayed in the area for the next two years, in part because Amanda almost immediately became pregnant with their first child—a boy they named Tyrus Raymond. Ty, was in fact born at the Chitwood home, a thirteen-room structure Ty termed "a plantation."[5]

The birth of a son apparently inspired William to fulfill his career aspirations. Within a year, he enrolled at North Georgia Agricultural College in Dahlonega, Georgia, thirty miles west of The Narrows. The school was just fifteen years old, employed only a handful of teachers, and graduated only about a dozen students each year. The education William obtained there could not compare to that which he might have received had he been able to afford a premier college like the University of Georgia or the University of North Carolina, but it furthered his love of learning and enabled him to become a teacher, one of the most accessible professions open to a man of limited means. Perhaps equally important to the ambitious William, an advanced education made him an exceptional figure in the foothills of the southern Appalachians. He made the most of his distinctive achievement. Eager to let folks know that he was a man of learning, he took on the title of "Professor," always wore suits to display his professional status, peppered his speech with quotations from the ancients, and tailored his manners according to the most popular self-help books of the era.[6]

For the next several years, William helped raise the family (which soon included another son, John Paul, and a daughter, Florence), taught school in several small towns, and completed his college degree, graduating at the top of his small class in 1892. During this time, he was something of an itinerant educator as he searched for a permanent locale to establish himself. Finally, in 1897, after stops in several small towns in northern Georgia, William settled his family in Royston, a village of no more than 600 residents, in Franklin County. Why Royston? The region's economy was probably an important factor. Franklin County's demographic and economic growth portended well for a young professional on the make like William Cobb. From 1880 to 1890, the county's population increased by over 25 percent from 11,453 to 14,670 and would increase another 20 percent during the next decade. Economically, the county joined the rest of northeast Georgia in an era of commercial agricultural expansion. From 1880 to 1900, the value of all farm produce nearly doubled. Henceforth, Franklin County would be one of the more prosperous farming counties in the state.[7] Royston itself may have been a small community, but it possessed some important amenities—a railroad station, cotton mills, a hotel, and—as of 1895—a large two-story brick schoolhouse that was "modern for its time" according to a local historian. By the early 1900s, Royston had become an important regional cotton and fertilizer market. William probably saw potential in Royston and its environs. It wasn't a city, nor even a large town, but William understood this might be to his advantage. He must have realized he could make a name for himself much easier here than in a larger community. In Royston, he would be a fairly unique and valuable entity—a bookish college-educated man. He possessed skills and talents a small town on the rise needed.[8]

Once settled, William worked to make a name for himself in the community. He joined the Royston Baptist Church and served as its Sunday School superintendent. He became a Mason, the town's most select fraternal organization, and ascended to the degree of Master. Somehow, he also found time to write for the town's weekly newspaper, the *Royston Record*, and became its editor in 1905. He even served a term as mayor. In his ever-growing list of public roles, William made public education a pet cause. His commitment to education was sincere, but it was also politically astute. By the turn of the century, many Southern politicians had embraced education reform as a surefire way to marshal votes among both Southern progressives and poorer whites.[9] William's advocacy of public education attracted the interest of the local Democratic Party. In 1900, they invited him to run for the Georgia Senate. He served one term, working to help create the state's tax-supported county school system. Upon leaving the senate, he helped establish the new system in Franklin by serving as the county's first school commissioner. Thus empowered, he quickly became one of the region's most prominent citizens, described by friends as "a good man, a strong man, an honest man with honest convictions, with courage to express and strength to defend them." With an influential position that sent him all over the county, he might easily return to politics if he so desired. Indeed, Ty later claimed that some political insiders saw William as a future candidate for governor.[10]

William was ambitious not only for himself, but also for his children. He was especially eager to see his eldest son make good. His was a typical expectation of Southern fathers. Just as he had advanced the family's fortunes by his various pursuits, he expected his eldest son to do likewise. As Ty matured, William kept a close eye on his academic and social progress and tried to instill in his son the same drive and self-discipline that had set him apart. When Tyrus was in his early teens, William encouraged him to consider his career options. Apropos to his rising ambition, William suggested careers that would enhance the family name—law, medicine, or perhaps the military. At the very least, William expected his son to seek an advanced degree and enter a profession. He desperately wanted Tyrus to be a man of learning and a man of consequence in society, perhaps even become a leader in the South's transformation to modernity.[11]

Yet even as William embraced modernity and encouraged his son to do the same, he remained deeply connected to certain values and ideals of his region's past. He neither challenged nor questioned the South's system of racial segregation. He invested his meager savings in land with a dream, perhaps, of becoming a gentleman farmer or planter. By the time Ty neared adulthood, William owned over 100 acres of tillable bottom land and leased it to black sharecroppers to grow cotton. He kept a fine house, one of the biggest in town, and hired a handful of African American servants, including a "mammy" to help his wife manage the household. In other words, he followed the examples of traditional upper-class Southern society.[12]

Another indication of William's attachment to traditional Southern culture concerned the name he chose for his first-born—Tyrus. A student of ancient history, William admired the story of the ancient Phoenician island city of Tyre which had resolutely defended itself against a number of invading armies during its storied past. Only the massive army of Alexander the Great was able to conquer it after a long and terrible siege. When Alexander finally broke through, he ordered that the entire Tyrian army be put to death and all its citizens sold into slavery. From a Southerner's perspective, the similarity between the history of Tyre and what the South had endured in war and Reconstruction could not be plainer. William's choice of Tyrus as a name revealed his allegiance to the cult of the Lost Cause, a growing cultural movement that hoped to keep alive the dream of Confederate nationalism through public rituals and—as in the case of William's choice of a name for his first-born—private acts. Like the ancient Tyrians, William hoped that his progeny would fight the righteous fight against unwelcome invaders.[13]

Then there was the matter of William's obsession with lineage. William may have decided to settle in Georgia rather than stay in North Carolina because the Cobb name carried more weight in Georgia. The Cobbs of North Carolina were hill people and lived in relative obscurity; conversely, the Cobbs of Georgia were people of elite status. Some had even become great public figures. These included Howell Cobb, a former Speaker of the House of Representatives, governor of Georgia, and Secretary of the Treasury, and Thomas Reade Rootes Cobb, codifier of Georgia law and a general in the Confederacy who died gallantly at the Battle of Fredericksburg. Because the North Carolina Cobbs were only distantly related to the Georgia Cobbs, William grafted his family onto the Georgia Cobb family tree. This was more than just good politics. It was an attempt on William's part to change the family's identity—to give it a much nobler lineage than it had previously enjoyed. William even raised his children to think of the Georgia Cobbs as their close kin and models to emulate. Such admonitions suggest William was deeply influenced by another aspect of traditional southern life—the ethic of honor. A complex term, honor meant many things to Southern whites, but at a very basic level it was, as historian Edward Ayers has stated, "a system of values within which you have exactly as much worth as others confer upon you." This was primarily a familial system; that is, the man of honor was expected to uphold the status—or name—of his ancestors. Failure to do so would bring shame to both the individual and the family. In his final autobiography, Ty recalled that he learned at a very young age and "all too well" that he would be expected to live up to the standards set by the "twenty-seven Cobbs" who had "achieved varying degrees of note in the law, military, medical, mercantile, and agricultural fields," no matter that they were only distantly related.[14]

William further revealed his connection to the past in his organization of his household. If William's deeds are any indication, he saw himself as something of a traditional patriarch. His choice of a young bride enabled him to set himself up as the near exclusive voice of authority in the household. In an era when Victorian women assumed considerable control over the domestic affairs of the household, including household management and child-rearing, Amanda's life is noteworthy for the utter lack of impact that she seemed to have on domestic matters, at least as Ty remembered her. Conversely, William Cobb dominated Tyrus's recollections of his early life. In his autobiography, Ty recalled his father's opinions on those matters that weighed most heavily upon him as a child, but remembered almost nothing about his mother's views. Ty noted that his father detested baseball, believing it to be a waste of time that attracted unsavory types—gamblers, rowdies, liberty men, and other such lowlifes. Conversely, Ty said nothing about his mother's view of baseball. When it was time to choose a career, Ty recalled that William tried to influence his options, but he made no comments about his mother's wishes for his future. In his final autobiography, Ty described his mother as a "woman of warmth, grace, and strength." That was about as much as he wrote about her in any of his other autobiographical writings. Apparently, Ty wanted his readers to believe her influence upon him was negligible.[15]

According to Ty, William was an austere and unrelenting taskmaster. "In a paternal-filial relationship," Ty recalled late in life, "my father held me down, withholding acceptance of me as the man I yearned to be." Although Ty claimed that he tried desperately to please his father, nothing seemed to work: "He was critical, very strict, and I couldn't reach him." When Ty was just fourteen, William expected Ty to have "formed some definite lifetime plan." That Ty had not done so frustrated the father to no end. His attitude, Ty recalled, was "Quit fooling around and settle down to some serious work."[16] William became especially irate when Ty disobeyed him—a common occurrence once Ty reached adolescence. One incident, in particular, brought matters to a head between authoritarian father and miscreant son. When Ty was about fifteen, he committed what William must have considered to be the most unthinkable of acts: he traded several of his father's precious books at the local dry-goods store in exchange for a new baseball glove. By now, William had come to believe that baseball was the cause of all Ty's vices. But to steal books for the sake of baseball? To William that was an abomination. As Ty remembered it, William ushered him into his library, sat him down, and urged him to give up ball and perhaps consider a West Point appointment. When Ty refused, William decided it was time to teach Ty a lesson in humility and subservience. He ordered Ty to take over ten acres of the family's land for the remainder of the summer. Any self-respecting white man understood exactly what William had in mind. William believed Tyrus would become a pariah to the family if he persisted in playing ball, a "muscle-worker" rather than a gentleman. Well, if this is what Ty wanted, William would give him the lowest form of muscle work imaginable: cultivating cotton behind plow and mule. This was no work for the son of a prominent citizen. This was "nigger" work at worst, "poor white trash" work at best. Ty felt the humility keenly. "He had negroes to work it," after all. So far as Ty knew, "no Cobb had ever done such mean and grimy work" before. Yet here he was: "I was a Cobb and stuck behind a mule that broke wind when the breeze was the wrong way. I resented it deeply." Whenever a certain young woman happened to pass by, he looked for a place to hide so that she would not see him "in overalls doing manual labor."[17]

Although Ty probably did not realize it, William had an objective beyond humiliating his son. Like a traditional Southern father of the nineteenth century, William hoped to instill certain character traits in his male children. Beyond wanting Ty to be disciplined and ambitious, he also wanted him to be independent—an autonomous, confident, and self-directed man. The biracial nature of Southern society influenced Southern fathers' thinking. Only a generation or so removed from slavery, Southern whites understood independence and assertiveness to be defining attributes of whiteness, dependence and submissiveness attributes of blackness. Southern whites believed it was as simple as this: whites mastered others; African Americans mastered no one, not even themselves. The young man who lacked the requisite initiative and will risked being compared to African Americans, akin to social death to race-conscious Southern whites. It also might make him appear too feminine, a "sissy" in fact. William could not dare let his male progeny meet either fate; like most white men, he wanted his first-born son to be an emblem of Southern white manhood.[18]

At the same time, William also believed that Ty needed to be mindful of those in authority, especially his authority as family patriarch. There was, of course, some contradiction in these aspirations, so much so that child-rearing in the South must have been exceedingly difficult at times as parents grappled with the best way to help their children to be both fiercely independent but also dutiful to them.[19] Occasionally, a father devised a plan that responded to all necessities. William's decision to make Tyrus a plowboy for one summer may have been one such occasion. Commanding Ty to do field work would force him to respect William's power and authority. At the same time, however, William probably also hoped humiliating Ty would make him that much more determined to resist doing such work in the future. In other words, William wanted Ty to show subservience to him, but also to resolve to escape subservience in the future. Quite likely, William hoped the punishment would serve as a rite of passage. Ty claimed that once he resigned himself to the task, William's attitude toward Ty changed. For once, Ty confided later, his father "fully accepted" him. William even told Ty that he looked "manly" because fieldwork had put more muscle on his once narrow frame. Thereafter, William sought Ty's opinion on diverse matters ranging from the purchase of farm animals to the most advantageous way to market their cotton. Ultimately, the punishment strengthened their relationship as each gained new respect for the other. Because of incidents like this, Ty grew to revere his father. "My father was a greatest man I ever knew," Ty remembered. "He was the only man who ever made me do his bidding." In the patriarchal South, this is exactly the way it was supposed to be.[20]

William understood that because he wanted to instill a strong will in Tyrus, he could not use such strong-arm methods too often. To do so would negate his desire to see Ty grow up as an assertive, independent, and determined man. Indeed, the summer William forced Ty to farm was one of the few times he wielded his absolute authority over his miscreant son. Even then, he bent just enough so that Ty retained some control over his affairs. Shortly after William ordered Ty into the fields, Bob McCreary, the catcher-manager for the local ball club, the Royston Reds, paid a visit. McCreary was one ballplayer William respected: a fellow Mason who came from a prominent local family. McCreary asked William to let Ty continue to play for the team and personally assured William that he would keep Ty away from saloon culture and sporting types. Finally, McCreary gently suggested to William that perhaps Ty would be more obedient if William ruled with a lighter rein. William took McCreary's advice by allowing his son to resume his avocation—so long as he did his work in the field first—or (as we shall see) found someone to do it for him.[21]

Fearful that naked force might break Ty's spirit, William resorted to other means to nurture Ty's will and independence even as he tried to steer him toward a specific life course. Most often, William appealed to reason to convince Ty to abandon his youthful games for more serious endeavors. A letter written in January 1902 to Ty while he was visiting his grandparents in the mountains of North Carolina was typical of William's efforts to appeal to Ty's "better angels." After commending Ty for his love of the great outdoors, William offered a few general comments on the role formal education plays in enhancing one's appreciation of the natural world. Using the same lofty language that earned him the title of "Professor," William observed, "to be educated is not only to be master of the printed page but be able to catch the messages of star, rock, flower, bird, painting, and symphony." He continued, "It is truly great to have a mind that will respond to and open the door of the world to all the legions of thoughts and symbols of knowledge and emotions that the whole universe around brings to us." No reproach. No condescension. Just a simple statement of fact in hopes that this alone might sway his son to recognize the value of education. Next, William turned to Ty's moral conduct. He urged Ty to demonstrate self-mastery by conquering his anger and "wild passions." Rather than fall victim to "the demon that lurks in all human blood," he encouraged Ty to "be under the guidance of the better angel" of his nature. Once he succeeded, William offered, Ty would be "ready and anxious and restless to arise and reign." Some have interpreted William's remarks as a pointed criticism of Ty's past misdeeds. His lack of specific accusations coupled with his reliance on rather familiar phrases, however, suggests that William's intent was more general than specific: he simply meant to remind Ty of the importance of self-mastery. Ty took no offense at his father's statement. He carried this letter with him throughout his life and often showed it to reporters as a way to give credit to his father and to offer proof of his own genteel upbringing.[22]

William was more direct the night he learned that Ty had contracted with the Augusta Tourists of the South Atlantic League to try out for a spot on their team. It was the spring of 1904 and Ty was only seventeen years old. His action must have troubled William greatly. Even so, William did not impose his will on Ty. Although the two argued for several hours, Ty claimed that William listened to his every word without once losing his temper. "He was as austere as ever," Ty recalled, "but he gave me his complete attention." William tried to reason with Ty, telling him "You are seventeen years old and this is the decisive moment for you." He then repeated his concerns about baseball—that it was full of "a riffraffish type of men who drink and carouse and lead a pointless life." "With eyes that bored through you," he again cautioned Ty that if he failed to develop his mind, he "would become a mere muscle-worker" the rest of his days. Ty remained adamant, interjecting "I just have to go" each time his father paused. Finally, William relented: "You've chosen. So be it, son. . . . Go get it out of your system." Years later, Ty remarked that his father had little choice but to let him go, since he would have run away if William tried to stop him. Perhaps so, but William still got what he wanted—a son who was willful and independent enough to stand up for himself. According to one contemporary account, William took great pride in the headstrong son he helped raise. A childhood story goes, when Amanda expressed concern that young Ty was "too impulsive and strong willed" for his own good, William proudly exclaimed, "Don't mind that boy; he'll get along all right. He's a law unto himself." By modeling his own fierce independence and by raising his son to act likewise, William had sown the seeds for his own heartbreak.[23]

If William felt he had lost the battle when Ty decided to play professional ball, he still held out hope to win the war. What mattered most to William, even more than book learning, was that Ty grow up to be a true man according to the values and ideals of the South. William articulated this aspiration for his son in one of the last bits of advice to Ty. That advice came in a short phone conversation between father and son shortly after Ty left home to play ball. Just two days into his first season, Augusta released Ty. Desperate and depressed, Ty turned to his father for advice. He told him that he had heard that a semi-pro team in Anniston, Alabama—some 230 miles away—might need an outfielder. He wondered if he should try out for that team. William responded, "Go after it." And then, "I want to tell you one thing—*don't come home a failure.*" When Ty recalled this moment in his autobiography, he italicized the final five words. For good reason: they were loaded with meaning. Although William gave Ty his blessing, he also meant to offer Ty a poignant lesson in honor and manhood. Essentially, William told Ty that now that he had left home, he must assume the responsibilities of adulthood and behave accordingly. To William this meant that Ty should not think of returning until he had succeeded. William wanted Ty to show some resolve and determination. He believed a man who would slink home after a single failure was no man at all. Home could not serve as a refuge from the world. In addition, William meant to impress upon Ty that he needed to defend the family's honor. To return home would shame not only Ty but also the Cobb family. Conversely, if he waited until he had achieved his goal to return home—that is become a professional ballplayer—he would bring honor to all. Ty absorbed the advice. Later, he remarked that he interpreted his father's response as a "sanction" of his "quest for success," that is, a validation of his desire for manhood and honor. This emboldened Ty. He came away from the conversation with "more determination in me than even he knew." He was so excited he shivered when he hung up. By William's standards, he had raised Ty well.[24]

Ty Cobb idolized his father. To the youthful Ty, William Cobb exemplified mastery, authority, will. William was everything Ty hoped to be in a man. Yet in all Ty's writing about his father, he never described their relationship as being particularly close. William was a stern taskmaster. "Fun" was not a word Ty associated with his father. For that, Ty looked to others. One such person was his paternal grandfather, William's father, John Cobb. For the young Ty, John Cobb was an endless source of adventure and excitement. Once Ty was old enough to travel by himself, he made regular summer and winter sojourns to Murphy, North Carolina, roughly 100 miles by rail, to see his grandparents. Ty loved spending time there. John Cobb's fierce independence and rascality appealed to Ty's own rebellious streak. While Ty's father could be remote, intimidating, and hard-to-please, his grandfather was warm and gregarious. Early on, Ty realized that he fit in much more easily with the free-spirited culture of the Appalachian backcountry than the austere surroundings of his father's academic world. Ty's frequent visits to his paternal grandparents played a fundamental role in his maturation toward manhood and further inspired him to find a path in life that would offer him greater independence, adventure, and freedom of expression.

The men and women who lived in the North Carolina Piedmont were fiercely protective of their personal autonomy. Most were ancestors of humble immigrants from North Britain and Scotland whose chief attribute may have been a stubborn pride. It may also have been their greatest asset in carving out a livelihood in the rolling hills and valleys of the backcountry. There, they settled into subsistence-first agriculture as a way to retain their personal independence. This desire for independence also made them singularly egalitarian—at least in so far as whites were concerned—and democratic. For this reason, they often resented the planter-elites of the Eastern Seaboard who they denounced as haughty, conniving, and antagonistic. Because the region remained sparsely populated, frontier traditions survived well into the late nineteenth century.[25]

John Cobb epitomized the distinctive culture of the region. Born in 1832, the son of a farmer and sometimes Methodist minister, John lived his entire life in the Appalachian foothills of Georgia and North Carolina. Although his neighbors understood he held certain views that were contrary to their traditions they respected him because of his strength of character and overall good sense. Before the Civil War, he showed his disdain for the affectations and power of the lowland planters by embracing antislavery. Yet when war came, he followed most young men of his generation and joined the Confederate cause. He served in Company C of the 39th North Carolina Infantry for less than a year and then returned home to look after his new wife Sarah and—within a year—his newborn son, William. Leaving the military was not wholly remarkable as many young men of the South developed a rather casual view of military service. This was especially true of young men who came from the upcountry. Independent men like John simply could not abide taking orders from anyone, especially officers who came from the planter class. After the war, John continued to show his disdain for the old planter class by joining the Republican Party. This, too, was not unusual. Many North Carolina upcountry whites who felt oppressed by the ruling class joined the Republican Party. Termed "Scalawags" by white conservatives, they joined ranks with former slaves and Yankees to push for democratic reforms including greater state support for public education. The coalition lasted until 1870 when Democrats appealed to white supremacy to attract whites from the Republican Party and regain power. John's precise political views are not known, but it is likely he agreed with his neighbors on the most essential issues, including the issue of race. After the war, John Cobb became an exceedingly popular figure in his community and even gained a reputation as a just and careful arbiter in local disputes. Had John Cobb diverged from his neighbors on the vital issue of white supremacy, they would not have trusted his judgment in other matters. Instead, locals traveled from miles around to ask John to mediate everything from family disputes to boundary feuds. Folks even took to calling him "Squire" Cobb, an honorific title that reflected his stature in the community. John Cobb was independent in mind and independent in spirit. He raised trotting horses and ate steak for breakfast. While others relied on him for counsel, he placed a premium on personal autonomy. He grew most of what the family ate and hunted for the rest. He crafted the household furniture with crude tools. His wife Sarah Ann was equally resourceful. Throughout their married life, she made clothing from homespun, dyed the garments herself, ticked the comforters that the family slept in, and became the community's "practicing healer" because of her skills in homeopathic medicines.[26]

Ty admired his grandfather almost as much as he did his father. He especially appreciated his grandfather's eloquence and keen logic when he argued with his four college-educated sons during family discussions. "It became evident to me," Ty recalled, "that book-education wasn't everything." Inspired by his grandfather, Ty slowly began to realize that he need not follow in his father's footsteps, that he could demonstrate the same independence as his grandfather: young Ty first entertained the notion of making baseball a career while staying with his grandparents. Far more than the bookish William, the squire introduced Ty to the world of Southern white men. He took Ty on hunting trips and exposed him to the inside of a courthouse, places where Ty could observe men participate in activities that required some of the essential traits of manhood—assertiveness, boldness, and force of will.

During one visit, eleven-year-old Ty traveled with his grandfather to the county seat, where he had been summoned to be foreman for the local grand jury. One defendant took exception to the squire's decision and decided to take justice into his own hands. He grabbed the squire by the shirt and threatened him. In response, John calmly told Ty to get behind a courtroom desk. Once Ty was out of harm's way, the squire whipped out a pocket pistol and told the man to leave the courthouse. Order restored. Or nearly so. Before the man made it outside, Ty ran up to him and kicked him in the knee. On their way home, the squire told Ty that he should not have acted so rashly, but that he appreciated the kick nonetheless. That was just like his grandfather. He was nearly always kind and encouraging, far different from the stern and relentlessly demanding William. When ten-year-old Ty confessed to his grandfather that he had been suspended from school for hitting a classmate, his grandfather only shook his head.[27]

Hunting was an integral part of traditional male culture—a form of recreation that enabled men to act with boldness, nerve, and authority. So, for that matter, was storytelling. The squire proved to be a champion of both. On quiet evenings as they whiled away the hours, he regaled Ty with tale after tale of his exploits as a tracker and marksman. Before long, Ty was convinced that his grandfather was as deft a backwoodsman as Davy Crockett and Daniel Boone. John Cobb did his best to pass on his skills to his devoted grandson. Ty readily absorbed the squire's frontier orientation toward life. "Grandpa was an opportunist," Ty recalled, "a trait I was later alleged to have displayed on the diamond." The older Cobb often roused Ty in the middle of the night so the two could track down some wild animal that his grandfather's hunting dogs had sniffed out. In time, Ty began to smuggle his own dog, Old Bob, on board the train when visiting his grandfather—an act forbidden by the railroad company—so that he would have a hunting companion of his own. This sort of disrespect for authority may have angered his father, but it greatly amused the squire.[28]

For all their differences, John and William Cobb, the two men most responsible for shaping young Ty's understanding of manhood, had much in common. Both were Southerners, after all. Each wanted Ty to be independent, strong-willed, and a credit to the family name. Equally significant, each hoped Ty would settle down and obtain a formal education beyond grade school. In fact, the squire valued education almost as much as William. Amidst the upheaval of war and Reconstruction, John had still seen to it that all four of his sons and one of his daughters had gone to college—a remarkable feat for the era. Still, Ty resonated with the squire's rough-hewn style far more than he did his father's stoic and reserved deportment. Ty respected his father and was inspired by his many bits of advice, but he often found himself resisting his father's efforts to mold his behavior. Conversely, he willingly followed his grandfather's example. Ultimately, contact with his grandfather helped Ty to embrace a more visceral and physical style of manhood than his father would have liked.

One other group galvanized Ty Cobb's conception of manhood and his preference for strong rugged men. This was his peer group—the boys and young men he associated with in school and on the streets and ball fields in and around Royston. In the late nineteenth century rural South, the world of boys was a world unto itself. Traditionally, Southern parents gave their sons considerable freedom because they wanted to encourage them to develop an independence of mind and a willful spirit. In addition, the late nineteenth-century establishment of public schools throughout the South gave same-age boys more time and greater opportunity to bond with one another. Ty benefited from the ascendance of the public school system in a more personal way. His father's role as an advocate for public schools in the Georgia State House in Atlanta and then as county school superintendent kept him away from home—and thus out of Ty's business—for days and sometimes weeks at a time. Finally, the very patriarchal nature of the Cobb household helped Ty gain greater autonomy and personal freedom. Since Amanda seems to have had little influence on Ty, Ty felt free to do as he pleased. Like many Victorian mothers, Amanda may have wanted to keep Ty close to hearth and home so she could impart her moral leanings through a mother's love, but there's no evidence that Ty listened to her.[29]

In the social space provided by these changes, Ty and his friends fashioned a world for themselves that enabled them to practice for the adult world they would someday enter and to simultaneously escape from it. On the one hand, they learned many of the essential skills that would help them to be successful and well-adjusted adults, including camaraderie, sociability, loyalty, and the spirit of competition. On the other hand, many aspects of the boy culture that Cobb enjoyed with his friends were more in keeping with a traditional model of manhood that ran counter to the dominant Victorian culture that influenced male behavior in the North and West. These boys embraced a culture that encouraged extreme risk-taking, physicality, aggression, and even violence. When Ty and his friends left their homes to play with one another, they temporarily broke free from the domestic restraints that stifled their nearly inexhaustible quest for thrills and adventures. Wherever they played, boys created a world that was uniquely their own.[30]

From an early age, Ty craved companionship with boys his own age. One of his "first clear-cut memories" was of riding in a buggy with his family as they moved from Commerce to Carnesville. With his feet dangling from the back of the buggy, he carefully wound yarn around a small core to make a baseball. Later he asked the local saddle maker to make a cover so that it might resemble the real thing. It was worth the trouble, he reasoned, because a "new kid in town who owned a hittable ball could overcome social obstacles faster than the boy who didn't." This may have been Ty's introduction into boy culture. His craving to be one of the boys would only grow from there and leave a lasting impression. Ty recalled that from a very young age, he "hungered for competition" and felt an overwhelming need to prove himself as a "real man."[31]

No doubt, this appetite was whetted by a certain class of men who wandered in and out of town. These were not respectable men like his father or even rough-hewn mountain men like his grandfather, but a rough and tumble lot of farmers in from the countryside, loiterers and loungers, and rootless working men. On Court Days, lazy Saturday afternoons, or when there was a break in their work schedule, these men congregated in town to partake in the coarser forms of male culture—drinking bouts at the saloon, assignations at the whorehouse, contests of strength, skill, and stamina, baseball matches between rival communities, and gambling contests of all sorts. Living in town gave Ty ample opportunity to see these men on a regular basis. It must have been an eye-opening experience. Watching these men argue on street corners, stumble out of the saloon, organize impromptu wrestling matches, or heckle actors in a traveling show introduced Ty to the bravado that certain men exhibited whenever they congregated. He was probably most fascinated by the way they goaded one another to take risks. In contrast to the stoicism and self-control exhibited by his father, these men were all about bluster and show. As historian Ted Ownby has observed, turn-of-the-century male culture "was a culture of intense pleasure and pain, pride, and shame."[32] The young men about town goaded one another to take another drink, make another bet, or tell a more prodigious lie. They cursed loudly, fought boldly, and insulted one another prolifically. Ty did not want to live a life of indolence like these men, but he must have been intrigued by their brashness and competitive spirit just the same. Here was Ty's first major challenge in life: how to prove himself in this visceral world of men while retaining the respect of his father. Resolving this conundrum would remain an issue for Ty for much of his adult life.

Visceral needs came first.

Ty demonstrated a competitive edge at a very young age. He won a sprinting race at the Franklin County Fair one year and kept the blue ribbon pinned to his shirt for months. In one oft-cited incident, he beat up a fellow classmate because the boy's error had led to the defeat of the boys against the girls in a classroom spelling bee. His desire to excel was palpable. Joe Cunningham, Ty's next-door neighbor and best friend, recalled, "You could see it the moment you set eyes on him. . . . He was always driving and pushing and pushing, even in grade school." So great was his hunger to dominate, that if no contest presented itself, Ty made one up. Bob McCreary, the manager of the Roosters, recalled that "he was always thinking of new things to try." Once, at the local swimming hole, McCreary recalled, Ty said that he could hold his breath underwater longer than anyone. "We all lasted maybe a minute, while he was still down there."[33]

And then there were Ty's dozen or so near death-defying risks. This was something of a ritual for these young men. Tradition held that to risk one's life in defense of one's reputation was the highest act of honor a man could perform. For this reason, many Southerners gravitated toward athletic competitions that involved some form of high stakes gambling, believing that to risk one's fortune for something as trivial as a card game or a horse race reflected courage and resolve, both key components of manhood. Youths had little property to gamble, so they sometimes gambled with their lives. In Royston, no boy took more risks than Ty. He once bet his friends that he could tight-rope walk across a wire cable suspended over the town's main street. As it turned out, this was one of Ty's safer youthful games. "Someone, probably Ty," McCreary recalled, "invented the crazy trick of laying on a railroad track and being last to roll off before the locomotive got there. He didn't lose that one often."[34]

At times, Ty's risk-taking took on a violent edge. Here too, Ty's inclinations reflected broader societal patterns. Violence permeated turn-of-the-century Southern male culture. Race lynchings were clearly one aspect of this, but so were Southern men's attraction to certain kinds of sporting events. Many of the men who congregated on Main Street gravitated toward dangerous athletic competitions that underscored the capriciousness of life and the certainty of death. In back alleys, saloon basements, and remote farms, they bet on cockfights and dog fights. As participants, they enjoyed bare-knuckle brawling, all forms of wrestling matches, greased pig chases, gander pulling, and hunting expeditions that often degenerated into orgies of killing. At these events, men experienced violence as energizing, cathartic, liberating, and even fun.[35]

No evidence links Ty to animal blood sports beyond hunting, but sources do reveal that Ty engaged in various forms of fisticuffs on a regular basis. Writing for *Baseball Magazine* in 1912, sportswriter Howell Foreman claimed that the boyhood Ty was a "chronic, continual scrapper." Foreman contended that "a day without at least three fights was as dull to the youthful Ty as a contest for the bean-bag championship."

> When his animal spirits rose to concert pitch and he was too thoughtful of the Caucasian race to pummel the countenance of a white boy, he used to vent his spleen on the ebony "pickaninnies" of the surrounding plantations. More than one incident is told of how Ty avenged a stolen watermelon or missing chicken.

Though Foreman's rhetorical style suggests he may have been more interested in mythmaking and playing off regional stereotypes than relating actual events, other sources confirm that Ty enjoyed the primitive thrill of physical combat. McCreary recalled that as a young teenager, Ty could outfight all his peers and many older boys at "catch-as-catch-can," an unrestrained folk game, popular among adolescent boys in the rural South. Joe Cunningham, Cobb's best childhood friend, recalled the two began to scrap almost as soon as they met. Bud Bryant, another childhood friend, remembered Ty as being a very combative companion. "Oh we had some fights, toe-to-toe stuff. He'd win one, next time I'd get the best of it. You couldn't make the little bastard stay down. Born to win." Such battles were common for men of honor in the making.[36]

Races, fisticuffs, daredevil feats: these were great fun, but nothing satiated Cobb's desire to replicate the swagger of the men on Main Street like baseball. He embraced the game with a passion. By eleven or twelve, he devoted nearly all his leisure hours to playing ball with other children his age. A few years later, he joined the local semi-pro team, the Royston Reds, holding his own against players who were two to three to several years older than he was. Here, at last, he found an opportunity to prove his manhood through the fierce competition of the town men. As he recalled, "in town ball—pitted against older boys and men," he finally had "the chance to become more than another schoolboy and the son of Professor Cobb." He loved playing with these older boys and developed an "intense respect" for the way they carried themselves on and off the field. He consciously tried to imitate them, adopting for himself their swagger and nonchalant bearing.

He later admitted that their influence "developed in me the characteristics that got me into so much early trouble in the big league" and "mystified me so at the attitude of my team mates."[37]

The game of baseball, as Southerners played it, offered Ty and his peers ample opportunity to enjoy their combative yearnings. According to Foreman, the informal games of Ty's youth often ended in a "battle royal" with the losing team taking vengeance upon the winners.

> The battle . . . that followed was too red with hot blood to be described in this cold, black ink. And after all the weapons of the game had been beaten to pieces upon the heads of the fighters, the worsted side would retreat to the yells of "Hump! Hump!" followed by a mountain of rocks—in separate pieces."

More mythmaking to be sure, but again other accounts confirm that Ty and his companions made baseball an extremely violent game. Young men wove brutality into the game—sometimes in extremely dangerous ways. Ty recalled that one of the informal rules of town ball as it was played in the South allowed for "soaking." This practice allowed de-

Figure 1.1. A very young Ty Cobb (seated at the far left) elevated his baseball skills by playing with older boys on the Royston Reds ball club. He also became exposed to a more visceral and competitive style of manhood by observing how his teammates comported themselves. *Source:* Courtesy of Ernie Harwell Collection. Detroit Public Library.

fenders to retire a base runner by nailing him with a thrown ball. According to Ty, defenders often aimed for the head since this offered the added bonus of disabling a player. When Ty made the Royston Reds as a scrawny fourteen-year-old infielder, his older teammates decided to toughen him up by hitting an onslaught of line drives at him during infield practice. Ty had never faced anything as difficult as this; the "screaming liners and grounders that could knock out teeth" he later recalled. Not wanting to jerk his head away for fear it would look like an act of cowardice, he had no choice but to stay down and try to scoop up as many as he could.[38]

The violence and risk-taking that seemed almost endemic to Southern boys' life served important social functions for those who participated. From an early age, Southern white boys learned that there was no greater status in the South than to be an independent adult white male. Once they reached adolescence, many boys yearned to achieve that status but often found themselves stifled by their powerful patriarchal fathers—just as Ty had been. In response, Southern boys looked to their own peers to gain the status denied them by their parents. In this quest, they gravitated toward games and dares that allowed them to test their strength, courage, fortitude, and decisiveness—that is to say their burgeoning manhood. Pitting themselves against one another allowed them to measure their maturation and establish a pecking order.

In addition, acts of aggression and daring allowed Southern male youths to connect with the pride and honor of the South's storied past. Though two generations removed from the Civil War, they felt keenly the meaning of Confederate defeat upon the South's economy, its social stability, and its self-esteem. Yet they also grew up at a time when the lore of the Lost Cause was beginning to find a place in Southern popular culture and public life. As children, they heard their parents and grandparents tell stories of family members' gallantry, watched them erect monuments to Confederate heroes, and walked with them to the cemetery on Decoration Day to honor loved ones who gave their lives to the cause. When eulogizing Confederate soldiers, parents and grandparents often held them up as the embodiment of Southern manhood. This point was not lost upon the youth of the South. Yet these same youths had few opportunities to display such heroism and valor. Sports offered one of the few ways in which they could test their courage and gain honor among their peers. For this reason, sports became increasingly popular among Southern youths and young men in the first decades of the twentieth century. Southern boys took a special liking to baseball and football, sports that offered them ample opportunity to display grit and manly aggression.[39]

Ty found ready accomplices in his various pursuits. Although Ty may have been more determined than most of the other boys, they all craved competition that enabled them to gain status. Be it a dare, a fight, or a game, they joined him willingly. Had Ty not been able to make a living out of one of their leisure pursuits, he probably would have grown up just like the other boys. That is, he would have learned to channel his aggression into mostly harmless leisure activities. Instead, he turned to professional baseball. He was fortunate that professional baseball stimulated and encouraged many of the same values that had governed his youth. One consequence of this is that baseball allowed him to hover in a kind of extended adolescence. On the ball field, Ty tested his mettle, defended his honor against all comers, meted out vengeance, and proved his manhood through exhibitions of daring and intrigue. As a youth, Ty had agonized over a suitable career—one that would enable him to attain the status of his ancestors, please his father's desire for respectability, and satiate his own needs for excitement and personal freedom. For over twenty-five years, Ty Cobb enjoyed the rare privilege of having found the perfect place for himself. He became not only the best player in the game, but one of the most popular Americans of his era and a symbol of manhood that others would emulate for decades.

Ty Cobb enjoyed something close to an idyllic childhood. He had a coterie of good friends. His parents and grandparents were people of property and status. He was surrounded by people who encouraged and supported him. Then, suddenly, a tragedy of unfathomable proportions catapulted Ty into the status he had coveted for so long—manhood. On August 8, 1905, at around 11:00 PM, Amanda Cobb shot her husband William dead from her bedroom window as he stood in the yard. Ty was just over 100 miles away in Augusta at the time. He learned of William's death the next morning.

Until that moment, Ty's life was very much on the upswing. He was enjoying the best of times doing the thing he loved most—playing professional ball for the Augusta Tourists of the South Atlantic League.

Sixteen months after the team had unceremoniously released him during the first week of the season, he had rebounded to become their star player. He led the circuit in hitting and ran the bases with an abandon that drew cheers, even in opposing ballparks. As good as things were going, the future looked even better. The *Sporting News*, the self-proclaimed "Bible of Baseball," had taken notice and was beginning to give him ink. In addition, a number of major league scouts were keeping an eye on him. One team in particular, the Detroit Tigers, seemed about ready to purchase his contract. Any day now, he expected to be summoned by one of the major league clubs. His life was beginning to take shape—exactly as he had dreamed it might.[40]

Ty Cobb had done a considerable amount of growing up during those sixteen months since he had left home to play professional baseball. The transformation had been slow and painful, but nearly everyone who knew him was impressed by how much he had matured. Playing for the semi-pro team in Anniston had helped him restore his self-confidence after Augusta released him. At Anniston, he established himself as one of the league's best hitters, batting over .300 for the season. Still, it was only a semi-pro league, hardly Ty's idea of the pinnacle of success. He desperately wanted back into the Sally League, but to get there he knew he would have to do something to get their attention. Being a good ballplayer did not seem to be enough. Anniston box scores were not published outside Alabama. When the weekly newspaper did mention Cobb, the stories invariably misidentified him as Cyrus Cobb. To draw attention to himself, he decided to commit a bit of subterfuge. During lonely evenings in Anniston and on the road, he wrote dozens of letters to regional newspapers in Memphis, New Orleans, and Augusta using a variety of aliases. Each one raved about an obscure outfielder for the Anniston Steelers, one Ty Cobb. His most influential target was Grantland Rice, sports editor for the *Atlanta Journal*. Rice fell for the trick: in his regular column, he described Cobb's play in favorable terms. He wrote, "Over in Alabama there's a young fellow named Cobb who seems to be showing an unusual amount of talent." Remarkably, the little blurb helped convince management of the Augusta Tourists to give Cobb another shot. By mid-August, Cobb was back with the Tourists under new manager, Andy Roth. Sadly for Cobb, it was not a fairy-tale ending—at least not yet. The young outfielder was still overmatched by the more experienced Sally League pitchers and hit only .237 in less than forty games to finish out the season.[41]

Perhaps because he was a rare hometown product and thus something of a fan favorite—very few Southerners played professional baseball in the early 1900s—Augusta retained Cobb's rights for the next season. He very nearly blew this opportunity, too, by starting slowly and acting immaturely. He hit poorly and on the rare occasions he got on base, he ignored his "coachers" and ran on his own. Obstinate as ever, Cobb still wanted to run wild like the boys back at Royston played the game. Players and management hated it, but not the fans. They loved Cobb because he was entertaining and because his cocky gameness resonated with their understanding of masculine behavior. For his part, Cobb was having the time of his life, despite his still-low batting average. Intuitively, he was learning to exploit his opponents' weaknesses with split second decisions. This is what had worked in Royston and even at Anniston—to take daring risks when others least expected it. By his view, Roth's "by the book approach" was unmanly and disrespectful of his individuality. Roth, for his part, believed Cobb needed to learn discipline. After Cobb was thrown out in yet another failed act of daring on the base paths, Roth fined him and sat him on the bench for two days. When Cobb returned only to defy Roth's instructions again, the manager fined and benched him a second time. Apparently, Cobb was the only player Roth believed needed a tighter rein. Otherwise, he ran a very loose ship, so much so that the still young and impressionable Cobb began to follow the lead of some of the more worldly veterans. Had Roth remained manager, he probably would have released Cobb, leaving his baseball future very much in doubt.[42]

Instead, Cobb got lucky. In April, Augusta's brain trust brought in thirty-six-year-old reserve outfielder and sometimes manager George Leidy. Ownership appointed Leidy captain and asked him to help Roth bring order to the team. Within a few months, the owners decided Leidy might as well simply replace Roth and named him manager. Neither Roth nor Leidy helped the Tourists win very many games, but Leidy did succeed in one area in which Roth had failed: he got Ty Cobb to listen to him. Rather than try to bully and browbeat Cobb into submission as Roth had done, Leidy gently cajoled Cobb to rely a bit more on brain than instinct. At first, Cobb resisted his would-be mentor. As he had done with Roth, he tested Leidy's patience at every turn. In the middle of a game in Savannah, a hungry Cobb decided to take a bag of peanuts with him into the outfield so he could enjoy a midgame snack. When a fly ball came his way, Cobb tried to keep hold of the peanuts as he fielded the ball. Predictably, he lost control of both and a run scored. That evening Leidy suggested that Cobb accompany him on a trolley ride out to a local amusement park. As they sauntered along, Leidy took advantage of the young player's discomfiture to coax him into listening to him. Gently, but emphatically, Leidy talked to Ty about the rigors of making baseball a career. Mostly, he tried to impress upon the young outfielder that he could go as far as he wanted, so long as he worked hard to make the most of his talents. He "drew castles in the air," Cobb later recalled, as he described the advantages of a big league career. Leidy told Cobb he could be better than 99 percent of the other hitters in the game and make big money doing it. Travel. Fame. It was all there for Cobb if he applied himself. Cobb listened. Leidy's quiet demeanor, his reputation as a keen judge of talent, and his persistence finally affected a change in Cobb that no other manager or player had been able to accomplish. Years later, Cobb described his relationship with Leidy in the language that bore witness to Cobb's rural Southern roots—the language of honor. Although Leidy had never made it beyond the low minors, Cobb revered him as the voice of wisdom and truth. In fact, Ty looked upon him as a surrogate father, perhaps even the father that he wished he had always had—patient, understanding, and approachable. Thereafter, he treated Leidy as a sort of wizened old patriarch. "Every word of this from the kindly old gentleman burned into me," Cobb stated. "I knew he was right." To the young Cobb, Leidy's was the only opinion that mattered because he was the authentic voice of experience.[43]

For the next several weeks, Leidy helped Cobb work on his hitting and his mental approach to the game. They spent hours working together. Cobb later claimed that he learned nearly all of his skills and tricks from Leidy, including bunting, placing the ball, hitting behind the runner, sliding, and thinking at least an inning or two ahead of the game. Perhaps most important, Leidy helped Cobb bridle his passions so that he could make the most of his talents. Cobb recalled that before Leidy got to him, he had been undisciplined on the bases and in the field, so much so that his greatest attributes—his speed and energy—acted as liabilities. Leidy taught Ty to think before he acted, to use his skills for some greater goal than to draw attention to himself. Leidy's hold on Cobb was so complete that he even instructed him on how to eat, advising him "that too much food in the stomach will make you ill when taking up exercise." Some years later, Cobb paid Leidy the ultimate tribute, observing the obscure minor league manager was "the reason I made good in the majors." Leidy's tutelage began to show results as the season progressed. From a .230 hitter in the spring, Cobb's average climbed to a league-leading .326 by the beginning of August. Just as important, he had become a terror on the base paths, with a league-leading forty stolen bases. "I began to find myself," is how Cobb put it.[44]

As Ty Cobb slept in on the morning of August 9, all seemed right. His star was rising. He was adored by the hometown fans of Augusta. He had found a mentor who appreciated his genius and encouraged his ambitions. Detroit kept getting good reports from their scouts about the positive impact that Leidy was having on Cobb. Things were breaking his way.

Then it all changed with news from home that his father had been murdered, shot in his own yard the night before. Even worse, his mother Amanda was the killer. The story as it came out was indeed sad and disturbing. On Tuesday evening, August 8, 1905, William Cobb left home, telling his wife that he planned to be out of town for a few days. Such trips were not unusual for William; as county superintendent, he was often away from home. Ty's two siblings, Paul and Florence, were staying with friends, leaving Amanda home alone. For reasons that remain unclear, William returned just a few hours later. We have only Amanda's testimony offered before the Coroner's Jury to explain the sequence of events. She claimed that she was lying in bed at about 11:00 PM when she heard some sort of rustling outside her window. Fearing an intruder, she grabbed a pistol she kept near her bed, went to the window, pulled the curtain to the side, aimed at the form she saw in the yard, and fired once. A minute or so later, she fired again. Hearing no more noises, she peered out the window and into the darkness. There she saw her husband lying on the ground in a pool of blood. Neighbors rushed to the scene and found William with two bullet wounds—one in the abdomen and one in the head—but still breathing. A doctor was summoned, but it was no use. William was pronounced dead at 1:30 AM.[45]

This was Amanda's story. More sensational rumors—widely circulated among the locals and published in newspapers throughout the region—offered a far more sordid tale. Neighbors suspected that the thirty-four-year-old Amanda had taken a lover who had arranged to be with her that night. According to the gossipmongers, William suspected the truth about his wife and had doubled back so that he could catch her. But Amanda—perhaps accompanied by her lover—was ready: she murdered William to silence him. Adding another level of deception to it all, some claimed local law enforcement aided Amanda in hiding the truth in order to preserve William's good name and to protect the Cobb children and Amanda's Chitwood kin from shame. According to some biographers, most of the Cobbs' Royston friends knew all about this, but refused to give names. For Tyrus, the rumors—whether true or not—must have added to the trauma of an already horrific event. Thereafter, he refused to speak publicly of his father's death.[46]

Ty never recorded what happened once he arrived in town, but it must have seemed like a whirlwind of events—each one as tragic as the next. William was buried on the eleventh. The next day the local county sheriff arrested Amanda and the justice of the peace set her bail at $7,000. She immediately posted ten percent of the bond to avoid jail time; even so, she must have been an emotional wreck. At the age of eighteen, Tyrus found himself the head of the family—its sole breadwinner and its public face. For a young man sensitive to status issues and jealous of the family name, it was an abrupt and horrible awakening to the realities of adult life. Unfortunately, he had little time to absorb these events, much less cope with his own grief. He had to return to his career. Five days after his father's death, Ty was back in Augusta patrolling the outfield. Less than three weeks later, he was on a train to Detroit to begin his major league career. He never spoke of the matter with any of his new teammates or the Tigers management. Whatever grief, anguish, and anger he suffered, he suffered alone.

Many self-appointed Cobb aficionados have suggested that William's untimely and tragic death unhinged Ty emotionally. Famed New York sports columnist Paul Gallico claimed the "traumatic experience of his father's terrible death" left Cobb "a highly neurotic individual." He further proposed that Ty's "admission that he never got over his father's death is all any modern psychiatrist would ask for in plumbing the causes of [his] illness." Gallico believed Ty coped with his father's death by constantly trying to prove his worth to him. As a result, he played with a kind of uncompromising urgency and frenetic energy that often boiled over into violence. In Gallico's view, "Cobb brought a fury, cruelty, and viciousness, heretofore unencountered" in baseball. It was a vicious circle, the more unbending and obsessive he became in his drive to succeed, the more players and fans hated him. The more they hated him, the more vicious he became. Others have largely followed Gallico's lead, including some of Cobb's most widely read biographers. Al Stump, Cobb's co-author for the final autobiography, quotes Gallico when he covers this episode in his fact-challenged biography of Cobb. Richard Bak, author of two of the most recent and sympathetic biographies of Cobb, opines, "the damage to Ty's psyche can only be guessed at," but suggests that it must have been extensive. Bak then speculates that Cobb suffered from a bipolar disorder, brought on in part by the death of his father. Others have been more cavalier, rifling off descriptions like "maladjusted," "nasty, mean-spirited, bullying, vicious," "bordering on the abnormal," "ruthless, even cruel," "a crude misanthrope," and "a man driven by internal demons that left even his sanity in question" to describe Cobb's professional behavior.[47]

This theory of Cobb's insanity makes two bald assertions that deserve greater scrutiny: that the incident dramatically affected Ty's subsequent behavior; and that this incident, more than any other, pushed Ty's already fragile mental health over the edge. As for the first assertion, there is little compelling evidence to suggest Ty's behavior changed markedly after his father's death. Well before William died, Ty showed a penchant for violence and a thirst for competition—just like every other white Southern boy of his generation. Ty may have been more competitive than most and perhaps even more violent, but he displayed these tendencies well before his father's death.

As for the second point, biographers should be cautious when making psychological assessments. Charles Alexander observed in the preface to his exhaustive study of Cobb that many Cobb biographers "have tossed around terms like 'paranoid' and 'psychotic' as if they had real meaning outside a clinical context." We can extend this argument even further. One of the chief problems with labeling a historical figure as psychotic or abnormal is that it imposes a static conception of mental health across time and space. Social and cultural historians blanch at such a technique, holding that what a late twentieth-century urban middle-class intellectual defines as normal may not have been shared by early twentieth-century small town Southerners. Thus the insanity argument turns out to be ahistorical. It also tends to be monocausal, ascribing all explanations for Cobb's behavior to his presumed mental instability set off by a single event in his life. Ultimately, both mistakes rob historical inquiry of the truly engaging and provocative questions regarding causation. Rather than asking whether Cobb was insane—which is nearly impossible to ascertain as Alexander rightly observed—it would have been more enlightening if Cobb's biographers had examined the values, ideals, and social constructs that informed his behavior.[48]

Ty Cobb interpreted his father's death using the only tools at his disposal—namely the ideals and values that he absorbed from the people who mattered most in his life—his father, grandfather, friends, and other childhood acquaintances. In other words, he intuitively turned to the Southern folkways that informed so many of his ideals. These taught the young Ty Cobb that life itself was capricious. Mortality rates may have improved in the decades since initial settlement, but dangers lurked everywhere in the isolated agrarian communities of the South. Some of the dangers were natural. Neither modern medicine nor modern technology could halt the sometimes-fatal consequences wrought by encounters with diseases, severe weather, or poisonous or rabid animals. In an age before antibiotics and vaccines, even minor flesh wounds could turn deadly. In addition, rural Southerners faced a host of man-made dangers. Industrial and farm machinery exposed workers to gears and levers and blades that crippled and killed. In fact, death was a fundamental feature of Southern life and culture. White Southern men prided themselves for their ability to not simply face down death with courage and fortitude. Indeed, they often resorted to violence and dangerous risk-taking for no other reason than to prove their ultimate mastery, bravery, and control. Grown-ups often engaged in violence of a much deadlier nature. Travelers in the South often commented on Southern whites' confrontational nature. One historian has observed, Southerners "have long been quick to take offense, quick to go to war, and when at war, quick to mount a direct assault." They were also quick to turn death into a kind of sadistic theater, as when they lynched blacks.[49]

The closeness of death nurtured a fatalistic worldview among Southern whites that was unique in the United States. More than any other group, Southern whites developed a deep appreciation for the capriciousness of life, the inevitability of death, and the immutability of nature. Southerners' attraction to blood sports like cockfights, dog fights, and gander pulls reflected this. Watching animals fight valiantly but bloodily to the death satiated their desire to observe violent confrontations and confirmed their understanding of nature—that it was merciless, brutal, and unyielding. White Southerners understood that they could never truly conquer nature, but they could control it, albeit fleetingly. Hunting trips offered one such opportunity to do so. During these excursions, Southerners engaged in veritable killing orgies in which they seemed to indulge in a primal blood lust. Apparently, these were compensatory affairs, allowing men to demonstrate their power and ability to conquer nature by controlling the quarry's passage to death. Violent confrontations against one another allowed Southern whites to go ever further in their quest to control nature. Bloody affairs with knives or even bare hands gave Southerners an opportunity to demonstrate self-mastery in the face of death. No, they could not defeat nature, but they could confront it on their own terms and show that they were not afraid of it and would fight against it to the end.[50]

This is the cultural context in which Ty Cobb coped with his father's death. William's death touched Ty deeply. Ty said it stayed with him forever. His best friend Joe Cunningham concurred. "It was always on his mind that his father would never see him in action," Cunningham observed. And yet given Southerners' conception of death and its close proximity to their lives, Ty could hardly have been too shocked by what had occurred. In Ty's world, violence happened; good people died young; death could happen at any time to anyone. Thus, William's death confirmed Ty's very Southern understanding of how the world operated. It was brutal, unrelenting, and uncaring. Recall Ty's description of baseball as a "red-blooded sport for red-blooded men . . . a contest and everything that implies, a struggle for supremacy, a survival of the fittest." Cobb might have applied this description to nearly any aspect of the human experience. His was a distinctively Southern orientation toward life, as indelible as the stains of Georgia red clay on his baseball uniform. William's death did not create such a brutal understanding of the world; it simply confirmed it. [51]

William's death was upsetting enough for Ty. Compounding the problem was the way in which he died. Traditionally, Southern men hoped to die an honorable death. By this they meant that they wanted to demonstrate their manhood even in death. The only way to do this was to face death without fear in a last heroic struggle. But William was shot by his wife sneaking into his own house. At best, it was a tragic case of mistaken identity. At worst, William had been brutally murdered by either his wife or his wife's lover. In either case, William died defenseless and vulnerable. Where was the honor in that? Regardless of the actual cause of death, so long as rumors persisted that William had been shot in a failed attempt to catch his wife, he was as good as disgraced in the community's eyes. Southerners placed a premium on appearances; to many, William's actions in the minutes preceding his death looked very much like those of a desperate man trying to reestablish control of his wife and his house. William's failure to do so meant that he had lost everything that he had struggled to attain. William's death not only left Ty fatherless; it also diminished the Cobb name. To a Southerner like Ty, this was just as bad.[52]

Thus, the circumstances of William's death left Ty, as the oldest male heir and now man of the house, in a particularly difficult position. On the one hand, he had to preserve the integrity of his family by clearing his mother of any wrongdoing. That was the immediate concern. Hiring a team of lawyers for Amanda's impending trial for manslaughter was an enormous gesture for a family that had just lost its breadwinner. Yet it was not enough. Ty had to help Amanda restore her reputation and thus the family name. To do this, he had to show all interested that the Cobb family believed her alibi and stood by her. At her trial held later that fall, Ty stood by her. Once she was acquitted, he never mentioned the ugly affair again. Amanda lived with Ty at various times until her death at the age of sixty-five. When she died, Ty had her buried in the Cobb family plot in Royston, next to the man she killed.[53]

This was all for the good, but Ty wanted to do more. He wanted to preserve the name of his father and simultaneously fulfill his father's dream of lifting the North Carolina Cobbs to an elite status. But how could an eighteen-year-old hot-tempered ballplayer do this? Ty might not have been able to imagine it during those fateful days in August 1905 when he came home to bury his father, but baseball ultimately became not only his salvation, but also his father's. Ty always saw the sporting events he participated in as an extension of his quest for honor. With his father's passing, however, that quest gained a new urgency. George Leidy had begun the process of encouraging Ty to take the game of baseball more seriously. William's death gave him further motivation. From this point on, baseball became very much an affair of honor for Ty—family honor. Ty believed his father outlined his creed in that tattered letter Ty carried in his wallet all those years. "I claim that I lived up to his creed," Cobb wrote in his final autobiography. "I *know* that I did." Yes, he had played the game fiercely, "with every ounce of fight I had—'ferocious' is an adjective I won't quarrel with." Nevertheless, he professed to have acted from the noblest of intentions, even when he retaliated. After all, his father had given him that bit of advice as well. "The honorable way is the only way," he said, paraphrasing his father's counsel. Cobb believed the proof of his devotion to his father's ideals was manifest in the success he achieved as a ballplayer and as a businessman. "I do not believe The Maker would have allowed me to do so much had I violated my father's creed," he asserted.[54]

Ty Cobb was impassioned and sincere when he made these statements, though not particularly self-aware. Yes, he followed his father's philosophy, but this was not the only person who influenced the way he played the game. The values and ideals that informed his behavior on the field and off during his two dozen years in the majors, his "creed" as he called it, were the product of the associations he made as a child in rural Georgia and the one horrible incident that forever altered his life.

NOTES

1. Don Rhodes, *Ty Cobb: Safe at Home* (Guilford, CT: Lyons Press, 2008), 66, 67.

2. On Southern male culture, see Ted Ownby, *Subduing Satan: Religion, Recreation, and Manhood in the Rural South, 1865–1920* (Chapel Hill: University of North Carolina Press, 1990); *Southern Masculinity: Perspectives on Manhood in the South since Reconstruction*, ed. Craig Thompson Friend (Athens: University of Georgia Press, 2009); Elliott J. Gorn, "'Gouge and Bite, Pull Hair and Scratch': The Social Significance of Fighting in the Southern Back-

country," *American Historical Review* 90 (February 1985): 18–43. My understanding of Cobb's devotion to the ethic of honor parallels that of Benjamin G. Rader. See Rader, "'Matters Involving Honor': Region, Race, and Rank in the Violent Life of Tyrus Raymond Cobb," in *Baseball in America and America in Baseball*, eds. Donald G. Kyle and Robert B. Fairbanks (College Station: Texas A&M University Press, 2008), 189-222. Nina Silber, *The Romance of Reunion: Northerners and the South, 1865–1900* (Chapel Hill: University of North Carolina Press, 1993), 20–22, 152–56, 172–78 succinctly contrasts Northern and Southern conceptions of masculinity. Gail Bederman, *Manliness and Civilization: A Cultural History of Gender and Race in the United States, 1880–1917* (Chicago: University of Chicago Press, 1995); John F. Kasson, *Houdini, Tarzan, and the Perfect Man: The White Male Body and the Challenge of Modernity in America* (New York: Oxford University Press, 2001); Thomas Schlereth, *Victorian America: Transformations in Everyday Life* (New York: HarperPerennial, 1991); John Pettegrew, *Brutes in Suits: Male Sensibility in America, 1890–1920* (Baltimore: Johns Hopkins University Press, 2007); E. Anthony Rotundo, *American Manhood: Transformations in Masculinity from the Revolution to the Modern Era* (New York: Basic Books, 1993), 247–83 examine what middle-class men perceived as the growing feminization of American culture in the late Victorian era.

3. For analyses of the "Lost Cause," see Gary W. Gallagher and Alan T. Nolan, eds. *The Myth of the Lost Cause and Civil War History* (Bloomington: Indiana University Press, 2000); Gaines M. Foster, *Ghosts of the Confederacy: Defeat, the Lost Cause, and the Emergence of the New South* (New York: Oxford University Press, 1987); Edward L. Ayers, *The Promise of the New South: Life After Reconstruction* (New York: Oxford University Press, 1992), 310–38; Charles Reagan Wilson, *Baptized in Blood: The Religion of the Lost Cause, 1865–1920* (Athens: University of Georgia Press, 1980); Bertram Wyatt-Brown, *The Shaping of Southern Culture: Honor, Grace, and War, 1760s–1880s* (Chapel Hill: University of North Carolina Press, 2001).

4. On the emergence of the New South, see C. Vann Woodward, *Origins of the New South, 1877–1920* (Baton Rouge: Louisiana State University Press, 1951, 143–157); Ayers, *Promise of the New South*.

5. Tim Hornbaker, *War on the Basepaths: The Definitive Biography of Ty Cobb* (New York: Sports Publishing, 2015), 4–5; Charles Leerhsen, *Ty Cobb: A Terrible Beauty* (New York: Simon and Schuster, 2015), 23–24, 28–33.

6. Hornbaker, *War on the Basepaths*, 4–5; Leerhsen, *Ty Cobb*, 29–30; Charles C. Alexander, *Ty Cobb* (New York: Oxford University Press, 1984), 9–12.

7. Historical Census Browser, Georgia, 1870–1910, Geospatial and Statistical Data Center, University of Virginia Library. http://mapserver.lib.virginia.edu/ (Accessed August 4, 2013).

8. Anna Belle Little Tabor, *History of Franklin County* (Carnesville, GA: Franklin County Historical Society, 1986), 372–77.

9. Ayers, *Promise of the New South*, 412–13, 417–18; Woodward, *Origins of the New South*, 400–406.

10. *Carnesville (Georgia) Advance*, May 18, 1900, 3, August 17, 1900; *Carnesville Advance*, August 11, 1900; *Carnesville Advance*, September 2, 1905; Ty Cobb, with Al Stump, *My Life in Baseball* (1961; repr., Lincoln, NE: Bison Books, 1993), 34.

11. W. H. Cobb to Tyrus, January 5, 1902 (photocopy), Ty Cobb materials, Baseball Hall of Fame Archives, Cooperstown, New York.

12. Cobb, *My Life in Baseball*, 32–33.

13. Cobb, *My Life in Baseball*, 33.

14. For explanations of Southern honor, see Edward Ayers, *Vengeance and Justice: Crime and Punishment in the 19th-Century American South* (New York: Oxford University Press, 1984), 13. For the importance Southerners placed on lineage in the ethic of honor, see, Steven M. Stowe, *Intimacy and Power in the Old South: Ritual in the Lives of the Planters* (Baltimore: Johns Hopkins University Press, 1987), 128–32; Bertram Wyatt-Brown, *Southern Honor: Ethics and Behavior in the Old South* (New York: Oxford University Press, 1982), 65–67, 118–25; Wyatt-Brown, *The House of Percy: Honor, Melancholy and Imagination in a Southern Family* (New York: Oxford University Press, 1994); Kenneth S. Greenberg, *Honor and Slavery: Lies, Duels, Noses, Masks, Dressing as a Woman, Gifts, Strangers, Humanitarianism, Death, Slave Rebellions, The Proslavery Argument, Baseball, Hunting, and Gambling in the Old South* (Princeton: Princeton University Press, 1996), 58; Gorn, "Gouge and Bite," 42; Cobb, *My Life in Baseball*, 32.

15. Cobb, *My Life in Baseball*, 34. On the patriarchal nature of the Southern family, see Wyatt-Brown, *Southern Honor*, 50–51, 61–66, 117–25; Stowe, *Intimacy and Power*, 110–14, 128–32, 152–53, 199–201; Lorri Glover, *Southern Sons: Becoming Men in the New Nation* (Baltimore: Johns Hopkins University Press, 2007); Ayers, *Promise of the New South*, 182–86. On Victorian men's child-rearing strategies, see Rotundo, *American Manhood*, 31–74.

16. Cobb, *My Life in Baseball*, 37, 43. On nineteenth-century Southern child-rearing practices of boys, see Glover, *Southern Sons*, 51–82; Wyatt-Brown, *Southern Honor*, 138–56; Ayers, *Promise of the New South*, 182–86; Stowe, *Intimacy and Power*, 180–82, 199–201.

17. Cobb, *My Life in Baseball*, 33–34.

18. A number of historians have examined white Southerners' commitment to independence, mastery, and personal autonomy. See Frank L. Owsley, *Plain Folk of the Old South* (1949; repr., Baton Rouge: Louisiana State University Press, 1982); Glover, *Southern Sons*, 139–46, 175–79; Stephanie McCurry, *Masters of Small Worlds: Yeoman Households, Gender Relations, and the Political Culture of the Antebellum South Carolina Low Country* (New York: Oxford University Press, 1995), 37–91; David Hackett Fischer, *Albion's Seed: Four British Folkways in America* (New York: Oxford University Press, 1989), 311–20, 687–96.

19. Glover, *Southern Sons*, 25–36; David Hackett Fischer has noted that it was even more difficult for the child: Fischer, *Albion's Seed*, 311.

20. Cobb, *My Life in Baseball*, 42–43; Al Stump, *Cobb* (Chapel Hill, NC: Algonquin Books, 1994), 48; Al Stump, "Ty Cobb's Wild Ten-Month Fight to Live," *True* 14 (December 1961); repr., Jeff Silverman, ed., *The Greatest Baseball Stories Every Told: Thirty Unforgettable Tales From the Diamond* (Guilford, CT: Lyons Press, 2001), 67.

21. Cobb, *My Life in Baseball*, 43–45; Stump, *Cobb*, 44–45: Leerhsen, *Ty Cobb*, 46–47.

22. W. H. Cobb to Tyrus, January 5, 1902.

23. Cobb, *My Life in Baseball*, 43–45; "Who is Ty Cobb and Why," *Baseball Magazine* 8: 5 (March 1912), 9.

24. Cobb, *My Life in Baseball*, 46–47.

25. Fischer, *Albion's Seed*, 605–782; Owsley, *Plain Folk*, 90–132; Altina L. Waller, *Feud: Hatfields, McCoys, and Social Change in Appalachia, 1860–1900* (Chapel Hill: University of North Carolina Press, 1988).

26. Cobb, *My Life in Baseball*, 32–34; Stump, *Cobb*, 33; Leerhsen, *Ty Cobb*, 29; 1860 United States Manuscript Census, Union County, Georgia, p. 18; 1870 Manuscript Census, Cherokee County, North Carolina, p. 16; 1880 Manuscript Census, Cherokee County, North Carolina, p. 16. For North Carolina politics during the Civil War, see Paul D. Escott, *Many Excellent People: Power and Privilege in North Carolina, 1850–1900* (Chapel Hill: University of North Carolina Press, 1985). For the overwhelming prevalence of racial antipathies in the late nineteenth-century South, see Leon Litwack, *Trouble in Mind: Black Southerners in the Age of Jim Crow* (New York: Alfred A. Knopf, 1998); Joel Williamson, *The Crucible of Race: Black-White Relations in the American South Since Emancipation* (New York: Oxford University Press, 1984), 180–223.

27. Cobb, *My Life in Baseball*, 34–35; Stump, *Cobb*, 33–35.

28. Cobb, *My Life in Baseball*, 35–36.

29. Fischer, *Albion's Seed*, 687–90; Glover, *Southern Sons*, 24–27; Rotundo, *American Manhood*, 32.

30. Rotundo, *American Manhood*, 32.

31. Cobb, *My Life in Baseball*, 17

32. Ownby, *Subduing Satan*, 13; Gorn, "Gouge and Bite," 42.

33. Stump, *Cobb*, 37; Alexander, *Ty Cobb*, 11; Leerhsen, *Ty Cobb*, 24; John D. McCallum, *Ty Cobb* (New York: Praeger Publishers, 1975), 4.

34. Rotundo, *American Manhood*, 34–37; Stump, *Cobb*, 37; Cobb, *My Life in Baseball*, 280.

35. On the violent nature of turn-of-the-century Southern society, see Ownby, *Subduing Satan*, 13–14, 53–55; Williamson, *Crucible of Race*, 180–223; Litwack, *Trouble in Mind*, 280–325; Woodward, *Origins of the New South*, 158–60; Wyatt-Brown, *Shaping of Southern Culture*, 270–95; Kris DuRocher, "Violent Masculinity: Learning Ritual and Performance in Southern Lynchings," in *Southern Masculinity: Perspectives on Manhood in the South since Reconstruction*, edited by Craig Thompson Friend (Athens: University of Georgia Press, 2009), 46–65. For the South's long tradition of violent behavior, see Dickson D. Bruce, Jr., *Violence and Culture in the Antebellum South* (Austin: University of Texas Press, 1979); Nicholas Proctor, *Bathed in Blood: Hunting and Mastery in the Old South* (Charlottesville: University Press of Virginia, 2002); Richard Nisbett and Dov Cohen, *Culture of Honor: The Psychology of Violence in the South* (Boulder, CO: Westview Press, 1996); Greenberg, *Honor and Slavery*, 13–16, 35–38, 62, 74, 122–132, 137–139.

36. Howell Foreman, "When Ty Cobb Was A Boy," *Baseball Magazine* (March 1912), 1–2; Stump, *Cobb*, 37–38; Leerhsen, *Ty Cobb*, 24–25.

37. Cobb, *My Life in Baseball*, 37; Ty Cobb, *Memoirs of Twenty Years in Baseball*, edited by William R. Cobb (Marietta, GA: Self-published, 2002), 12.

38. Foreman, "When Ty Cobb Was A Boy"; Stump, *Cobb*, 43, 46; Leerhsen, *Ty Cobb*, 35.

39. For the angst felt by many Southern white men as they came of age in the post-Reconstruction South, see Joel Williamson's treatment of Thomas Dixon in *Crucible of Race*, 140–79; Wyatt-Brown, *Shaping of Southern Culture*, 270–95; Ownby, *Subduing Satan*, 45–55. For the way sports entered into the South's culture of honor in the early twentieth century, see Patrick B. Miller, "The Manly, the Moral, and the Proficient: College Sport in the New South" and Andrew Doyle, "Turning the Tide: College Football and Southern Progressivism," in *The Sporting World of the Modern South* edited by Patrick B. Miller (Urbana: University of Illinois Press, 2002), 17–51, 101–28.

40. Alexander, *Ty Cobb*, 19–20.

41. Stump, *Cobb*, 57, 64–66; Alexander, *Ty Cobb*, 17–18; Cobb, *My Life in Baseball*, 48; Cobb, *Memoirs*, 22–24.

42. Stump, *Cobb*, 67; Alexander, *Ty Cobb*, 18; Cobb, *My Life in Baseball*, 48–50.

43. Stump, *Cobb*, 83–87; Alexander, *Ty Cobb*, 18–19; Cobb, *My Life in Baseball*, 31–33; Cobb, *Memoirs*, 24–28, 33.

44. Stump, *Cobb*, 83–87; Alexander, *Ty Cobb*, 18–19; Cobb, *My Life in Baseball*, 31–33; Cobb, *Memoirs*, 30, 33–34.

45. Leerhsen, *Ty Cobb*, 89–92; Hornbaker, *War on the Basepaths*, 17–19.

46. Leerhsen, *Ty Cobb*, 17–19; Hornbaker, *War on the Basepaths*, 89–92.

47. Condemnations of Cobb can be found in most general American sports histories and baseball histories. The statements offered above come from: Benjamin Rader, *Baseball: A History of America's Game* (Urbana: University of Illinois Press, 1992), 95–98; Steven A. Riess, *Touching Base: Professional Baseball and American Culture in the Progressive Era* (Urbana: University of Illinois Press, 1983), 25; Elliott Gorn and Warren Goldstein, *A Brief History of American Sports* (New York: Hill and Wang, 1993), 191; Harold Seymour, *Baseball: The Golden Age* (New York: Oxford University Press, 1971), 107; Ken Burns and Geoffrey C. Ward, *Baseball, Inning 2: Something Like a War*, DVD (Walpole, NH: Florentine Films, 1994).

48. Alexander, *Ty Cobb*, 6.

49. Fischer, *Albion's Seed*, 326, 697–702; Ownby, *Subduing Satan*, 13; Greenberg, *Honor and Slavery*, 87–114; Gorn, "Gouge and Bite"; Bruce, Jr., *Violence and Culture in the Antebellum South*, 196–211; Proctor, *Bathed in Blood*, 71–72; DuRocher, "Violent Masculinity," 46–60; Nisbett and Cohen, *Culture of Honor*; Ayers, *Vengeance and Justice*, 266–276; Wyatt-Brown, *Southern Honor*, 352–61; Litwack, *Trouble in Mind*, 280–325.

50. Ownby, *Subduing Satan*, 28–36, 76–87; Proctor, *Bathed in Blood*, 71–75, 111–115; Greenberg, *Honor and Slavery*, 87–114.

51. Stump, *Cobb*, 95; Cobb, *My Life*, 280.

52. Greenberg, *Honor and Slavery*, 87–114.

53. Stump, *Cobb*, 96; Alexander, *Ty Cobb*, 37.

54. Cobb, *My Life in Baseball*, 113–14, 280.

2

THE GAME

When Ty Cobb chose baseball as a career, it was less a conscious decision than a compulsion; he could not imagine doing anything else. Young men across America shared his passion. The same year that Ty made it to the majors, Richard "Rube" Marquard of Cleveland, Ohio, began to think seriously of a career in professional baseball. Born the same year as Cobb, Marquard was every bit as avid a fan of the game. "As far back as I can remember all I could think of, morning, noon, and night, was baseball," he later recalled. As a youth, Marquard had gained the reputation as the best amateur southpaw pitcher in the area. He was crazy, so crazy about the game that when a friend playing for Waterloo of the Iowa State League told him his team was short on pitchers, eighteen-year-old Marquard decided this was the chance he was waiting for. Without waiting to be contacted by the manager, much less receive traveling expenses, Marquard decided to make his way to Waterloo to try out. Marquard made the decision knowing his father might very well disown him. Frederick Marquard, a German immigrant, had worked hard to give his children an easier time in life than he had experienced as a first generation immigrant. Arriving in Cleveland at the age of ten with his father, a stonecutter, he had joined his father in the trade as soon as he was old enough to work. He also learned the skills of a butcher and for a time alternated between the two jobs. Wanting more for himself and for his family, he attended night school to learn the skills of maritime and stationary engineering. Upon passing the civil service exam, he settled into a desk job with the city.[1] His greatest ambition for each of his four sons was that they become educated so that they could get "good jobs," by which he meant white collar professional positions—the sorts of occupations that reflected respectability, status, and intelligence. He fumed when Richard demonstrated a decided preference to play ball rather than tend to his future. "I want you to cut this out and pay attention to your studies," Frederick warned. "I want you to go to college. . . . and I don't want any foolishness about it. Without an education . . . you'll *never* amount to anything." When Rube replied that he intended to play ball for a living, Frederick refused to believe that he could get paid for playing a game and wearing one of "those funny-looking suits." Obviously, Richard could not ask his father for train fare. With no other option, he lied to his father that he was going on an overnight camping trip, and bummed his way to Waterloo. It was the beginning of a professional baseball career that would last over a quarter of a century, including eighteen years in the majors.[2]

At about the same time, Walter Johnson, fresh out of Fullerton High School in Southern California, contracted to pitch with Tacoma of the Pacific League. When the team let him go after just a few games, he made his way to Weiser (pronounced Weezer), Idaho—a town of just over 1,300 residents, fifteen saloons, and an unspecified number of opium dens—to play ball for the town's semi-pro team. For nearly two years, he worked as a clerk for the local telephone company during the week and pitched for the Weiser Kids of the Idaho State League on Sundays and holidays. This was hardly the ideal locale to embark on a major league career, but somehow a scout for the Washington Senators happened upon him and signed him. He went on to win 417 games, second most in major league history.[3]

"Smoky" Joe Wood, a future star pitcher for the Boston Red Sox, showed a more audacious determination to play ball. When the all-girl barnstorming baseball club, the Bloomer Girls, passed through his hometown of Ouray, Colorado, the manager asked Wood if he would like to play for the team. Wood thought the idea crazy, but the manager reassured Wood that a few on the team "aren't really girls." For $20 and the thrill of playing pro ball, sixteen-year-old Wood donned a skirt and wig and played the infield for the team as they completed the season. A year later, he chose a more conventional course of entering professional baseball by signing with Hutchinson, Kansas, of the Western Association. A year after that, he made his big league debut for the Boston Red Sox.[4]

Cobb from Georgia, Marquard from Ohio, Johnson from California, and Wood from Colorado give testimony to the fact that baseball was not simply the national game but the avid obsession of young men throughout the country. Prior to the 1880s baseball's popularity had been largely confined to the Northeast. Beginning in the late 1880s, however, baseball fever burst forth throughout the nation. The extension of minor league franchises across the country gives some idea of the sport's growing popularity. In 1885, the Southern League and the California League organized, suggesting that both regions had both the fan base and the talent pool to support teams. By 1900 there were thirteen minor leagues, by 1904 twenty-three, by 1907 thirty-four. In 1913, there were 300 teams in forty-three leagues, employing roughly 5,000 professional players.[5] These organizations were often unstable, sometimes chaotically so. Leagues started and folded in a single year; franchises moved at midseason and sometimes simply quit before the season ended. Yet there was no denying the trajectory of organized baseball. It was expanding—seemingly everywhere.

By 1905, the *St. Louis Globe* could brag, "every city, town, and village in America has its ball team."[6] Or more. In 1910, Chicago offered two major league clubs, twenty-six semi-professional teams, and 550 amateur clubs. That added up to a grand total of nearly 75,000 players. On one summer Sunday in the Windy City, nearly 400,000 people spent the afternoon watching or playing the game in one of 278 venues. Nationwide the numbers were equally staggering. On a *weekday* in the early 1910s, some 543,200 fans watched professional games (those recognized under the National Agreement of professional teams). By this time, the paid admission to watch major league ball in any given year exceeded the adult population of the United States.[7]

Americans had been enraptured by sporting crazes before—marathon walking races, prize fighting, horse races—but none of these gave such a wide spectrum of American males an opportunity to participate in the sport. After work and on weekends, young men honed their skills, let off steam, and expressed their competitive desires. In the Lower Sacramento Valley of California, men from the small farming villages of Davisville and Dixon played one another over a dozen times each summer to claim bragging rights for the region. A decade earlier these folks had known very little about the rules of the game, but now everyone in the region seemed to be afflicted with what a local newspaper editor described as an "epidemic of baseball."[8]

More like a pandemic of fanaticism. Chicago Cubs infielder Johnny Evers observed the game was so popular that towns and cities gave their teams the same intense loyal support "that the cities of medieval Europe did to their chosen bands of warrior knights." Though a seasoned warrior himself, Evers claimed he could hardly comprehend the intensity of a community's loyalty for its team. "A close race between teams representing rival towns sometimes [creates] a condition not far removed from civil warfare," Evers noted.[9] Boys and men watched baseball, played baseball, and talked baseball. Increasingly, they also wanted to read baseball—to know more and more about the game and the stars who played it. To satiate this last desire, daily newspapers gave more and more space to the game, highlighting not only the doings of local teams but major league teams. By 1900 most metropolitan newspapers devoted a page to sports, giving baseball the most space when it was in season. By the end of the decade, metropolitan dailies expanded sports coverage to at least two pages six days a week with a whole section on Sundays. By this time newspapers added the musings of featured sports columnists two or three times a week. Some of these were syndicated in cities and towns across the country so that such early pioneers in sports journalism as Ring Lardner, Hugh Fullerton, Grantland Rice, Fred Lieb, and Tim Murnane gradually gained national followings as baseball experts. If that wasn't enough, three national journals appeared on the scene to offer more extensive coverage of the game. Francis Richter of Philadelphia established *Sporting Life* in 1883, hiring correspondents from across the country to cover all sports, but especially baseball. By 1886, weekly circulation climbed to 40,000. That year, Alfred Spink, a journalist and baseball executive founded the *Sporting News* in St. Louis, Missouri. This weekly focused exclusively on baseball and quickly gained a reputation for its thorough coverage of both the major and minor leagues. Within two years, it eclipsed *Sporting Life* in circulation (56,000) and advertising revenue. Indicative of its growing success, the journal increased in size by half in 1888, from eight to twelve pages, and acquired the nickname, the "Bible of Baseball." Finally, in 1908, these weekly journals were joined by a monthly magazine—publisher F. C.

Lane's *Baseball Magazine*. The journal featured articles from freelance writers, the editorial musings of its staff writers, and—on occasion—pieces purportedly written by major league players themselves. With these media outlets, the means were now available to turn baseball players into national stars and ultimately into celebrities.

Baseball historian Harold Seymour has observed that by the turn of the century baseball had become "ingrained in the American psyche." True, many sports vied for public attention during this new era of professional sports, but nothing satisfied like baseball. Prizefighting was illegal in most states and too closely associated with the unseemly underworld to gain widespread appeal. Golf and tennis were growing in popularity, but as future writer James T. Farrell remembered it, working- and lower-middle-class men denigrated both as games for "sissies." At the turn of the century, football was still identified with college life and thus smacked of elitism. Thus, baseball alone seemed to capture the popular imagination.[10] Moreover, many Americans were convinced that playing ball was an inimitable training ground for manhood. Leaders from a diverse array of scholarly and professional backgrounds made this claim. Theodore Roosevelt listed baseball as one of the "true sports" fit "for a manly race." Popular journalist and amateur psychologist H. Addington Bruce recommended baseball to all young boys because it would help them learn to think quickly under pressure, an essential skill in the "serious business of life." In *Training the Boy*, a popular advice manual for parents, philosopher William McKeever suggested, "no boy can grow to perfectly normal manhood to-day without the benefits of at least a small amount of baseball experience and practice." Novelist and former minor league player Zane Grey was even blunter. "All boys love baseball," he remarked. "If they don't, they're not real boys."[11]

Why such enthusiasm for baseball? Keen observers claimed the reason was simple: baseball taught uniquely masculine skills and virtues—the very skills and virtues that the next generation of leaders would need to govern and run America. Most obviously, baseball turned boys into men. Before he turned to westerns, Grey made his living writing stories about young ballplayers who invariably proved their manhood on the diamond. In one of his most famous novels, *The Short-stop*, an older player advises a young star to grow up and grow up quickly if he hopes to stay in professional ball:

You're too nice. Lots of boys are that way, but they don't keep so and stay in baseball.... Baseball is a funny game. It's like nothing else... When a professional puts on his uniform he puts on his armor. And it's got be bulletproof and spikeproof. The players on your own team will get after you, abuse you, roast you, blame you for everything, make you miserable, and finally put you off the team. This may seem to you a mean thing. But it's the way of the game ... But the main point I want to make clear to you is the aggressive spirit of the players who hold their own. On the field, ball playing is a fight all the time. It's good-natured and it's bitter-earnest. Every man for himself! Survival of the fittest! Dog eat dog!

To many early twentieth century men, Gray's words were more than romanticized sentiments. In his seminal *America's National Game*, dubbed baseball's "first Bible," ballplayer-turned-entrepreneur-and-journalist Albert Spalding argued, "Base Ball is the American Game *par excellence* because it requires Brain and Brawn, and American manhood supplies these ingredients in quantity sufficient to spread over the entire continent." Just so the point was not lost on his readers, Spalding enumerated all the qualities that made the game so uniquely American: "American Courage, Confidence, Combativeness; American Dash, Discipline, Determination; American Energy, Eagerness, Enthusiasm; American Pluck, Persistency, Performance; American Spirit, Sagacity, Success; American Vim, Vigor, Virility." Spalding scoffed at the notion that baseball might be descended from the British game of Rounders or—worse!—Cricket. It would be "impossible for a Briton, who had not breathed the air of the freed land as a naturalized American citizen ... who had no part or heritage in the hopes and achievements of our country, to play Baseball." Using far less jingoistic hyperbole (and far fewer capitalized letters), recreation advocate Henry S. Curtis agreed, suggesting that baseball, "perhaps more than any other game, trains in quickness of thought, in ready response to condition, in ability to grasp a situation and take immediate advantage of it." Playing ball on an organized team, Curtis suggested, was perhaps the easiest way to "engraft" national characteristics of courage, skill, and self-control upon the "rising generation." *Baseball Magazine* agreed. In a 1909 editorial, the journal asserted that of all sports, baseball best readied young men for the "hustle and bustle" of modern America. As in life, "every moment is tense with anxiety, lest something already gained be lost." Both were a "survival of the fittest, a submersion of the weak. Sentiment—altruistic principle and higher thought—enter not into it." Spalding loved this element of the game most of all. "Base Ball is an athletic turmoil," he claimed; "Base Ball is War!"[12]

In reality, most fans were not nearly as bloodthirsty as the vitriolic language they used to describe the game implied. The baseball establishment learned the truth of this the hard way as hundreds of thousands stopped attending professional baseball games because of increased violence—on the field and in the stands—during professional ball's wildest decade, the more-grisly-than-gay nineties. Prior to the 1890s, players usually relied more on verbal abuse and posturing than outright violence. That changed during the 1890s as the professional game turned increasingly brutal. The greatest perpetrators may have been the Baltimore Orioles, who mixed skill and brutality to become the most successful team of the era. In 1894, sports columnist Tim Murnane reported to the *Sporting News* that the Baltimore club played "the dirtiest ball ever seen in this country . . . ready to maim a fellow for life (in) just retribution for trying to stop them in their temporary flight." Even brawny power-hitting outfielder Sam Crawford was intimidated. "Let me tell you, after you'd made a trip around the bases against them you knew you'd been somewhere," he told oral historian Lawrence Ritter. "They'd trip you, give you the hip, and who knows what else. Boy it was rough." It was also successful. The Orioles won the pennant three straight years during the middle of the decade. What could other teams do but copy their tactics? By the end of the decade, every team in the National League rivaled the Orioles in what one old-timer termed "hoodlumism" and others termed "rowdyism."[13]

Fans often acted as maliciously as the players on the field. Perhaps taking a cue from their team, Cleveland fans gained an especially nasty reputation around the league. Cap Anson, no delicate orchid, called them the "Cleveland hoodlums." Journeyman infielder Joe Quinn told a Cleveland reporter—only half in jest—"it used to be that a player always saw that his insurance papers were right before coming to this burg. When with Boston I never came here without first writing farewell messages to my friends. After every game I would hustle to the telegraph office and send out the word 'safe' to my relatives." Not that dealing with fans from any city was particularly easy. Even home crowds could turn nasty. Anson, for example, called his own Chicago fans "the worst in the world" because of the "taunts and hisses" they hurled at him. Headlines in both the *Sporting News* and *Sporting Life* suggest that disruptions by fans were a common, near daily occurrence, throughout the league. Baltimore infielder John McGraw—who one reporter termed "a rough unruly man" with an "erratic brain" and a penchant for "contemptible methods"—claimed fans "egged the players on" toward "rowdyism." Fans, no less than the players, adopted the slogan of "win at any cost" and resorted to all manner of behavior to help the home team. During an exhibition game in Petersburg, Virginia, Oriole Hughie Jennings got into a scrap with one of the local nine. In defense of one of their own, fans swarmed the field, beat up two of the Orioles, and chased the rest of the team off the field. The players found refuge back at the hotel, but it was short-lived. When the mob discovered the Orioles' whereabouts, they stormed the hotel and plundered the place. Only the arrival of the police saved the players from further harm.[14]

Paying customers were not the only source of disorder for opposing teams. Especially for important games, throngs of partisans, including many adolescent boys, found special delight in waiting outside the park to abuse and torment the visiting team. Described by the press as "ruffians" and "hooligans," most of these fans were too poor to attend games regularly, but still hoped to express their loyalty to the team and contribute to their success. Such fans made traveling to and from the park a dangerous task for the visiting team. After an 1899 game in Louisville, waiting fans collected rocks, bricks, and dirt clods to throw at the Baltimore Orioles as they left the field. Police, presumably there to maintain order, "stood by . . . encouraging the cowardly lawlessness." Years later, McGraw recalled "running the gauntlet" from hotel to ballpark was merely part of the game, an aspect of the "never say die" attitude and intense devotion that permeated baseball in those days. With evident sarcasm, infielder Jimmy Austin recalled, "the ride from hotel to ballpark was always a lot of fun, . . . kids running alongside as we went past, with plenty of yelling back and forth" and "rotten tomatoes once in awhile" for good measure.[15]

Fans often gave umpires the worst of it. The notion that the umpire served the crowd as a source of popular derision was firmly in place by the 1890s as evidenced by this little ditty, first published in 1886:

Mother, may I slug the umpire
May I slug him right away?
So he cannot be here, Mother
When the clubs begin to play?

Let me clasp his throat, dear mother,
In a dear delightful grip
With one hand and with the other
Bat him several in the lip.

Let me climb his frame, dear mother,
While the happy people shout;
I'll not kill him, dearest mother
I will only knock him out.

Let me mop the ground up, Mother,
With his person, dearest do;
If the ground can stand it, Mother
I don't see why you can't, too.

Mother may I slug the umpire,
Slug him right between the eyes?
If you let me do it, Mother
You shall have the champion prize.[16]

Ernest Lawrence Thayer's "Casey at the Bat," first published in a San Francisco newspaper in 1888 and performed by comic vaudevillian De Wolf Hopper in New York later that year, also gave voice to the public's low estimation of the game's appointed peacekeepers:

From the benches, black with people, there went up a muffled roar, Like the beating of the storm-waves on a stern and distant shore. "Kill him! Kill the umpire!" shouted someone on the stand; And its likely they'd a-killed him had not Casey raised his hand.[17]

Umpires were vulnerable because they nearly always worked alone, often had to dress in the same quarters as the visiting team, had no power to eject players from the game until very late in the decade, and only rarely received more than moral support from the league's home office. National League president Nick Young claimed abusing the umpire was simply a part of the game. Trying to stop it would be a futile exercise:

> The difficulty arises as soon as the first ball is pitched. Magnates, managers, players, "rooters," and everybody who follow baseball, will sit down in the quietude of their homes and resolve to inforce [sic] the rules against unnecessary kicking at the umpire. There is something in the game that deadens good resolutions so far as the umpire is concerned, for as soon as the first ball of the contests starts toward the plate the umpire becomes the common enemy of everybody. Why I have seen gentlemen occupying high public offices under the Government jump up in the grandstand and shout to certain home players to "smash the umpire in the jaw and I will pay your fine."

The league could only do so much, Young asserted. Yes, the magnates "intend to sustain the umpire in the interest of fair play and clean sport," Young avowed, but "it is difficult for two men to view the same decision or play with the same result."[18]

Young was obfuscating. He possessed no real power because team owners, self-defined "magnates," wanted to retain all control for themselves. After witnessing a Pittsburgh player poke and grab an umpire during a game in Cincinnati without receiving so much as a fine from the league for his behavior, a correspondent for the *Sporting News* concluded league oversight was completely "farcical." "'Uncle Nick' (Young) is president in name only," the writer complained; "if he has any powers he has never been discovered in the act of exercising his authority."[19] Unfortunately, exercising authority was not really something that came easily to the National League president. A kindly sort, he was generally content to let the owners do as they pleased. Unfortunately, the owners were too disorganized, contentious, and egotistical to offer much assistance. Instead, most magnates enabled the rowdiest players by paying their fines—or worse. A sportswriter for the *New York Sun* claimed the "rowdy kickers" had come to dominate the National League because the magnates wanted it that way. "In striking contrast to the custom of fifteen years ago," the writer observed, "players who kick, fight, and are generally unruly are made either managers or captains."[20]

Journalists delighted in recounting the pomposity and arrogance of the club owners. As long as attendance remained robust and the league operated at a profit, their behavior seemed harmless enough. So what if the St. Louis owner Chris von der Ahe insisted upon running his team despite his limited knowledge of the game or that Cincinnati owner

John T. Brush was forever conniving to run the league or that New York owner Andrew Freedman was a ruthless penny pincher who alienated several of his star players because he refused to pay them market value? The fans and press could even forgive the congenial but ineffectual National League president "Uncle" Nick Young for his failure to keep the owners in check. Charitable writers often portrayed these self-styled "magnates" as loveable buffoons and comic relief: they were not the best guardians of the game, perhaps, but they were generally harmless.

That perspective changed during the late 1890s when attendance began to fall. National League attendance peaked in 1895 at 2,889,271; after that, it was all downhill, with an especially precipitous decline from 1899 to 1900 when turnout dropped to 1,822,587. Even the most successful franchises struggled to attract customers. Philadelphia had some of the most ardent fans in the game, leading the league in attendance in 1895, 1899, and 1900. Yet during that span of five years, turnout declined from a decade high 475,000 in 1895 to 389,000 in 1899 to 301,000 in 1900—a dip of 37 percent in five years. Other teams saw similar declines. In 1894, when Baltimore won its first championship, 328,000 fans came to watch them play, good for third best in the league. Two years later, when they won their last championship, only 249,000 showed up. By 1898, attendance was down to 123,000. The team was eliminated after the 1899 season, a victim of owner arrogance that led to fan indifference.[21] Boston supplanted Baltimore as the powerhouse of the National League during the late 1890s. In 1897, 335,000 fans watched the team as they won the championship. When they won it again the following year, 100,000 fewer fans showed up. Attendance declined again in 1899 as they barely attracted 200,000 fans even though they finished second with a .625 winning percentage.[22]

Attendance was miserable, but the bottom line was even worse. Only half the teams in the league made a profit in 1898. The following year, the league decided to jettison four of the weakest drawing teams—Washington, Louisville, Cleveland, and Baltimore—by buying them out for $110,000 and auctioning off the rights of the sixty-plus stranded players. The league hoped that contraction would create greater parity in the league and thus boost attendance by involving more teams in the pennant race. The magnates were so optimistic of this plan, they each agreed to use 5 percent of their gate receipts to pay off the $110,000 buyout. Instead, teams continued to lose money. According to a 1900 report, only Pittsburgh and Philadelphia ended in the black that year; all the others lost between $10,000 and $30,000. The league disputed the numbers, but they could not dispute the overall decline in the game's popularity.[23]

Professional baseball was in serious trouble. Those closest to the game were especially troubled that "mob rule" in the stands and rowdyism on the field was driving away a key demographic: the young professionals, clerks, salesmen, and other white-collar types who comprised urban America's new middle class. Baseball needed these men because they possessed the discretionary income and the leisure time to attend games regularly. A correspondent for *Sporting Life* bluntly asserted, "The strength and hope of the game is in men who are not professional sports, but substantial and respectable members of society." As the game deteriorated, however, these folks simply stopped coming. "Ladies and gentlemen rarely, if ever, go to the ball game now," the *New York Times* dolefully remarked. "Even the so-called 'rooters,' the persons who are proud of confessing in public that they regard hired baseball players as superior beings, are losing their love for the game." *The Detroit Free Press* agreed. "Bickering and brawls . . . all have a tendency to disgust the better class of patrons," the newspaper observed. As a result, they "are slowly being weaned away from the game they have so long followed." The future looked dire. "If the game is to be saved for decent people," *Sporting Life* warned, "two things are necessary. First, respectable people in the stands; second respectable men on the diamond."[24]

Sporting Life might have added, respectable men in charge. Many of those closest to the game believed the problem started at the top—with the owners themselves. As the National League lumbered toward insolvency, magnate incompetence could no longer be passed off as a burlesque sideshow. To save baseball, sportswriters set out to expose the owners as violators of the public trust. Acting much like their brethren the muckrakers, these journalists presented club owners as the sporting world's version of robber barons—with one caveat: these plutocrats were too incompetent to realize their selfish desires. The magnates may have seen themselves as baseball's Carnegies, Rockefellers, and Morgans, but they did not appear that way to most journalists. The owners "are as dumb as oysters," a *Washington Post* sportswriter asserted as he watched them quarrel, obfuscate, and bluster during a March 1899 league meeting. Francis Richter, editor of *Sporting Life*, offered an especially withering condemnation of league governance. "In the long history of the league, there has never been a time when the magnates have long used power wisely, generously, or even discreetly," Richter observed, "and there is no good reason for believing that they will profit by the bitter lessons of the past."[25] Even some high in the league hierarchy were becoming fed up with the owners' dysfunctional egoism. Harry Pulliam, secretary of the Pittsburgh club, complained, "the magnates cannot bring themselves to being honest with each other. Everyone of them wants a slight hunch over the other fellows, with the result that they are not quite on the level with each other." Ultimately, Pulliam concluded, "the club owners are too selfish ever to enact a rule of that kind and live up to it."[26]

This was only half of it. To sportswriters, the magnates were not just bad at business, they also made a pretty pitiable showing as men. For one, the magnates were poor providers. The true magnates of the era saw themselves as something like benevolent despots. Perhaps they deluded themselves, but these titans believed they served a public good even as they rode roughshod over smaller operators as well as their own workers. Baseball's magnates could offer no such pretense—not when they acted like squabbling children. On several occasions, contributors to *Sporting Life* reminded the magnates "to drop their childish quarrels and get down to business."[27] League president Nick Young may have gotten the worst of it. The press persistently questioned his manhood in a subtle, but ultimately more devastating manner. Journalists nearly always referred to Young as "Uncle Nick," reflecting an endearing familiarity to be sure, but also suggesting something a bit more sinister as well. As an "uncle," Young was no patriarch, no titan. Rather, the title suggested he was nearly irrelevant—the weak and dependent family member who never quite learned to stand on his own. When Young first took the position as president, his unassuming and kindly manner endeared him to the press. As the league's troubles mounted, however, many journalists became far more critical. By 1899, many condemned Young as wholly incapable of shepherding the league. "Nick Young is honest," a Pittsburgh scribe allowed, but then "so is a dead man."[28]

Dead. Hard to be less manly than that. But age seemed to be creeping up on all the magnates. And some saw this as a major source of the problem. The specter of rotting corruption permeated the league according to its harshest critics. No matter what sort of business acumen they demonstrated in their primary enterprises, when it came to baseball their orientation seemed more in line with the political intrigue of the royal court under the ancien régime than the modern corporation. Richter suggested that time had corrupted the magnates as much as their power. In a particularly caustic statement, he remarked that the magnates had grown so old that their only remaining passion was their "greed for lucre" and "the pursuit of base ball pelf."[29]

So were the magnates children or old men? It really did not matter. They were not doing the job and, as the century turned, it became increasingly clear that if major league baseball was going to regain legitimacy and stability, it would need a new leader, someone from beyond the dysfunctional management of the National League.

Enter Byron Bancroft "Ban" Johnson.

American League founder Ban Johnson had many virtues, but modesty was not one of them. *Detroit News* sports reporter Malcolm Bingay had occasion to hear Johnson speak on many occasions. Before long, he noticed that every speech Johnson made was pretty much the same. Each was "all about how he, singlehanded and alone, had made baseball a gentleman's sport, and it must be kept forever clean because sportsmanship spoke from the heart of America and he would lay down his life to save our beloved nation, at which point he would begin to cry."[30] Melodramatic perhaps, but Johnson did not exaggerate by much. He not only established the American League, he served as its first president, initiated reforms that dramatically increased baseball attendance, and forced the National League to follow suit. His rise to the lofty status of baseball savior was swift, but hardly surprising. He was a man of both great talent and great determination—so determined that one recent account has judged him a "monomaniac with a mission." That mission was to solidify baseball's place in American life by ennobling it as the national game. He believed the most certain way to do this was to draw the new middle class, the heart and soul of American progress and prosperity, to the ballpark.[31]

Byron Bancroft Johnson was born in 1865, the son of a prominent Cincinnati school administrator. His parents hoped he would become a minister, but as a student at Marietta College, he devoted more time to sports, especially baseball and boxing, than to academics. Upon graduating from Marietta, Johnson attended the University of Cincinnati's law school, but dropped out in his second year because he wanted to be closer to his true passion, baseball. He got a job as a sportswriter for the *Cincinnati Commercial Gazette*; within a year, he became sports editor. In this capacity, he gained an intimate knowledge of the inner workings of the National League's administrative establishment. Johnson was appalled by what he saw and let all Cincinnati know it. Among those who took notice was the Reds' manager, Charles Comiskey, who urged the faltering Western League to name Johnson president in 1893. Legend has it that this was all part of a plan that Johnson and Comiskey cooked up years earlier while drinking beer at a saloon near the Cincinnati ballpark: to bring the dysfunctional National League to heel by turning a minor league into a rival major league. Whether the story is true or not, Johnson acted as if this was his plan from the moment he took office. It was a daunting task. After all, the Western League was hardly a powerhouse when Johnson assumed the presidency. Less than a decade old, it had already gone through several presidents. Only a few of the cities in the league were attractive venues (Detroit and St. Louis); most were second tier at best (Topeka, Kansas City, Sioux City, Grand Rapids, Minneapolis, and Indianapolis). Johnson had his work cut out for him.

And work he did. As president, Johnson transformed the nature of league administration. Heretofore, Western League meetings may have been even more chaotic and unproductive than National League meetings as rival magnates spent much of their time trying to out-drink and out-bluster one another. Johnson had no tolerance for such shenanigans. "Our gathering had no refreshments," one of Johnson's early financial backers recalled. "As Johnson said: 'Boys we are here for business. Let us proceed.'"[32] Johnson was not a typical league president. Most were much like Uncle Nick—affable and innocuous souls who gained the position as a sort of reward for their devotion to the game. Johnson was something else entirely. In nearly every respect, he was Young's opposite. He was opinionated, bold, forceful, and young—having assumed the presidency when he was only thirty years old. While

Young sometimes sat sheepishly in the back of meetings, Johnson dominated meetings. He was an enormous fellow with a fat fleshy face that he accentuated by keeping his hair short and slicked tight to his skin. He filled the room with his large body, booming voice, powerful intellect, and brash personality. When challenged, he often resorted to pounding the table and barking, "That's the way I think it is, and that's the way it is." He was also a hands-on executive who threw himself into the minutiae of league matters.[33]

Most important, Johnson had a vision for professional baseball and worked systematically and tirelessly to see that vision become a reality. Essentially, Johnson wanted what the National League magnates claimed to want—to make professional ball reputable by ending rowdyism, eradicating even the slightest hint of corruption, and attracting respectable folks to the ballpark. The difference was that Johnson meant it and knew how to attain it. He placed umpires in complete control of the game on the field and supported their decisions almost without exception. In addition, Johnson worked to limit the power of his magnates so that the Western League would not go the way of the National League. When a team went up for sale, Johnson would only accept buyers who shared his vision for the league and would not challenge his authority. He chose a close circle of owners and managers to work with, among them Comiskey, who purchased the Sioux City franchise in 1894 (and promptly moved it to St. Paul) and Connie Mack, a former National League catcher who became manager and minority owner of the Milwaukee club in 1897. Once the league was on a stable footing and Johnson was secure in his position as president, he consolidated his power by requiring that all club owners hand over 51 percent of their stock for his direct safekeeping. In this way, he would be able to control franchise movements and discourage magnates from feuding. Within two years, Johnson's Western League was praised as the "strongest minor ever," second only to the National League in status.[34]

One of Johnson's greatest talents was that, as a former journalist, he understood and knew how to handle the press. Through speeches and interviews, he established the narrative that his league stood for clean ball. By 1899, he had created something of a cult following for himself—the young, energetic, and capable league executive "who stamped rowdyism out of the Western League." By the beginning of the 1899 season, the *Sporting News* and *Sporting Life* published rumors that

Johnson would replace "Uncle Nick" and thus save the National League from itself.[35] There was nothing to these reports; the last thing Johnson wanted to do was try to tame the National League magnates' egos. Even so, the rumors were important to Johnson: that he had gained such a reputation for baseball administration meant that he and his league were ready to challenge the National League as the sole major league.

For the next two years, Johnson acted methodically and decisively to confront and even supplant the National League. In October 1899, he changed the name of the Western League to the American League to give it a national scope. He then began what turned into a two-year process of moving franchises into National League cities by moving the Grand Rapids club to Cleveland and encouraging his friend Comiskey to move the Minneapolis club to Chicago. Johnson then boldly asserted, "The American League will be the principal organization of the country within a very short time. Mark my prediction." There was only one problem: the American League was a major league in name only; none of the eight teams could claim they had the talent to field a major-league caliber team. To correct this, Johnson and company had only one solution—raid the National League. For all Johnson's high-minded rhetoric, he understood that his league needed major league talent to be credible and the only way to get that talent was to steal players from the senior circuit. In this, Johnson and company benefitted from the arrogance of the National League magnates who so alienated their employees, the ballplayers, that dozens jumped to the American League. The list included nearly all the biggest names in the league, including Napoleon Lajoie, the reigning batting champion, and Cy Young, who had averaged twenty-seven wins a season for the past ten years. Nearly every team lost some of its best players. According to the *Spalding Guide for 1902*, the unofficial organ of the National League, seventy-four players jumped to the American League during its first two years—almost the equivalent of four team rosters. Johnson even recruited half the National League's umpires, who must have been relieved to finally work for a boss who offered them protection and support.

The American League's promise of cleaner play and more orderly grandstands coupled with the infusion of some of the National League's best talent enabled the league to make good on Johnson's prediction that the American League would eclipse the National League in attendance within two years. In the National League, attendance continued to fall, from 1,920,031 in 1901 to 1,683,012 in 1902; during those same years, American League attendance rose from 1,683,584 to 2,206,457. Those numbers persuaded the beleaguered National League that they had no recourse but to make peace with the new league. In early 1903, representatives from the two leagues met to hammer out a new "National Agreement." Under the new plan, major league ball would be governed by a new National Commission comprised of Johnson, the National League's new president Harry Pulliam, and a chair who would be chosen by the two league presidents. Johnson and Pulliam chose Cincinnati club owner August "Garry" Herrmann for this position. Pulliam was an able administrator, certainly better than Young but not Johnson's equal. Herrmann was affable and known for being a lavish entertainer, but otherwise unmemorable. Johnson easily dominated the other two. By force of personality, if nothing else, he pushed the National League to adopt the more professional policies and methods of his junior circuit. It was a slow process as many National League clubs continued to try to undercut Pulliam's authority, but there was no denying the trajectory of change: Johnson's vision was becoming a reality for both leagues.[36] The National League magnates may have resented Johnson for his arrogance, for wrecking their monopoly, and for stealing their players, but they could not argue with the bottom line. After 1903, major league baseball enjoyed an unprecedented era of prosperity as attendance increased to over seven million by the end of the decade.

In other ways, too, baseball solidified its place in American culture. At the end of the 1903 season, league champions met for the first "World Series"; after a year hiatus in 1904, it became a permanent fixture. From 1905 to 1912, revenues from the annual "Fall Classic" increased tenfold. It quickly became the most popular sporting event in the nation and would remain so for the next seventy-five years. A game so popular surely needed a history to match its grandeur, a history that would enmesh baseball to one of America's most sacred tenets—its exceptionalism. Spalding himself provided the impetus to perform this task. Responding to reports that baseball may have originated from the English game of rounders, Spalding suggested that a special commission of seven men "of high repute and undoubted knowledge of baseball" settle the issue of the game's origins. That the committee would conclude that the game was unique to America was a foregone conclusion. For two years, the committee members ruminated over the matter, though they conducted no original research. Finally, in 1907 the committee announced that the game had a single creator—one Abner Doubleday conceived of the game at Cooperstown, New York, in 1839. That the committee relied upon a single, uncorroborated source to make this argument bothered hardly anyone because it sounded so good—America's game invented in a picturesque country village by a man who would go on to become a Civil War hero. Though the story was hogwash, it really didn't matter. After the miserable Nineties, baseball had reclaimed its status as America's game.[37]

So everyone was happy: fans were happy because they could root for the home team in a safer, more pleasant environment. Magnates were happy because they began to make money hand over fist. The umpires were happy because they could now count on the backing of the league office. And the players were happy because salaries during the bidding war between the two leagues had skyrocketed after a decade of decline. Moreover, with two major leagues, chances of landing a job doubled. These were good times all the way around.

The only problem was that for the ballplayers the happiness did not last. At least not completely. Once the American League was established, its magnates proved every bit as tight-fisted as the National League variety. Together the two leagues colluded to reduce salaries across the board. Johnson, who had once claimed to be the players' ally, now told the players that the inflated salaries of the baseball war could not last forever. Prior to the 1905 and 1906 seasons, owners made a considerable fuss about holding the line. Although neither league adopted a strict salary structure as the National League had once done, an informal system seems to have prevailed for most teams whereby a few star veterans garnered impressive salaries, but everyone else saw their salaries decline to what average baseball salaries had been a decade earlier. According to one study, the average salary in the middle of the decade was about $2,500 for starting players and $1,500 for rookies. True, they made considerably more than steelworkers (perhaps $700 a year) or factory laborers ($600 a year), but it was hardly generous. Ballplayers received no wages through the six or seven weeks of spring training. They had no pension and no job security. If sick or injured, owners expected them to pay their own medical bills. This could lead to some dreadful experiences. Just ask Ty Cobb. As he prepared for his first full year in the major leagues, he came down with a horrible sore throat. He tried to play through it, but the pain and the fever would not go away. While traveling north at the end of spring training, the team stopped to play an exhibition game in Toledo. In agony, Cobb hunted up the hotel's house doctor who diagnosed his condition as an acute case of tonsillitis. He operated immediately, without aid of an anesthetic. He simply tilted Cobb back in his chair and began cutting with his "tonsil chopper." The procedure was a terrifying mess. Cobb's tonsils were so swollen, the doctor had to remove them in sections. The entire operation left him so weak from the shock and loss of blood that he needed a teammate's help to get back to his room. Though he was still sick and weak the next day, he arrived at the ballpark on time for the exhibition game. He had no choice; he feared if he did not show up, he would be replaced on the team. Later, Cobb learned the doctor was nuts and had to be committed to an asylum shortly after he had operated on him. The conditions that caused such harrowing incidents changed only slowly during the next several years. In 1909, the Tigers and several other teams began to carry accident insurance, but this was to protect the club from off-field calamities like train wrecks, not to provide protection for players who hurt themselves during a game.[38]

In many ways, ballplayers remained as vulnerable to the whims of the magnates as they had been a decade earlier. The reserve clause tied them to a team for the life of their career. Indeed, many teams began to abuse the system (at least from the players' perspective) by signing dozens of players to major league contracts and then assigning them to minor league teams—just in case they might need them. In addition, management still had many ways to punish players that raised their ire. According to one story, Frank Chance, player-manager of the Cubs disliked Cincinnati pitcher Jack Harper in large part because Harper had a bad habit of beaning Chance. Early in the 1906 season, Chance decided to exact his revenge: he traded for Harper and promptly cut his salary from $4,500 to $1,500. What's more, Chance refused to use his new player. Harper had been a fair pitcher up to this point in his career, twice having won twenty-three games in a season. Chance didn't care; he wanted to ruin Harper. He gave Harper only one opportunity to pitch for the rest of the season—a perfect inning to start a game. That was it; Harper never pitched again. He had no say in the matter and thus little control over his future. The same held true for all ballplayers.

As President Pulliam remarked that same year, "The ball player has no part in the making of the form of contract under which he plays. It is given him under the authority of the National Agreement."[39]

Players rarely felt safe to voice their opinions about the prevailing contract system. The few who did speak out—mostly star players whose value to the team was such they could voice their opinions more or less openly—hinted at the deep-seeded frustration and anger that nearly all players felt. In a remarkable section of his book on the mechanics of baseball, Chicago Cubs' second baseman Johnny Evers made the case that the power owners held over their players was simply un-American. "Understand in the first place that baseball 'law' is illegal, contrary to civil law, in direct violation of the Federal laws regulating combines" and—if that wasn't clear enough—"in defiance of the Constitution and of the Rights of Man." While recognizing that owners are entitled to some protection, Evers claimed the current system went too far. "Legally, the baseball player is a slave held in bondage," Evers complained. "The facts are indisputable and admitted." Quite an indictment. Then, realizing he had pressed the case too far, Evers backed off and affected a conciliatory tone. He interjected that the ballplayer "is the best treated, most pampered slave of history" and that "the majority of the players received just and equitable treatment." It was an ambiguous passage, but also remarkably revealing. So as not to run afoul of management, he tried to make a clear distinction between baseball law, which he saw as inherently unjust, and the owners, whom he presented as a benevolent and honest group. Tactfully, he obscured the obvious point: these same owners created the iniquitous law in the first place.[40]

Washington's star pitcher Walter Johnson offered an even more pointed—and personal—critique of baseball's contract system. After just his third full year in the majors, Johnson had already established himself as one of the game's best. In 1910, he posted league highs in starts, complete games, innings pitched, and strikeouts. His twenty-five victories, third best in the league, accounted for 38 percent of the hapless Senators' total number of wins. He also finished third in earned run average. Heading into the 1911 season, Johnson anticipated a substantial raise. To get it, he tried to negotiate with management all through spring training. Prominent stars Ty Cobb and Christy Mathewson, two of the highest paid players in the game, advised Johnson to stick to his guns. Cobb even encouraged Johnson to negotiate for a contract equal to his own—$9,000 a year for three years. Management refused to take Johnson's demands seriously and in fact ordered Johnson to leave the Senators' camp when he refused to sign. Johnson briefly considered holding out for the entire season, but thought better of it and signed for $7,000 a year for three years. It was a substantial raise from the $4,500 he had received in 1910, but it hardly matched his true value. Frustrated, Johnson boldly discussed the lowly legal status of professional ballplayers in an extended interview for *Baseball Magazine*. He began by asserting his worth. "I am one of the two great pitchers of baseball," he confidently asserted. And this was no egotistical hype. "I do not make my own rating," he remarked; "the press, which is the Blackstone of baseball players," made that determination. The other great pitcher of the game, Christy Mathewson, made $9,000 a year, so Johnson figured he could make at least $8,500 on the open market. Of course, that was impossible; the reserve clause meant that Johnson was stuck with the hapless Senators, seemingly for life. Like Evers, he likened his condition to slavery. "It may be a pleasant sort of slavery and organized baseball might not be able to exist without it" Johnson allowed, "but it is theoretical slavery just the same." Johnson claimed he was not bitter and "not making any complaint." Rather, he was just pointing out the obvious: "This is simply the direct application of the great intelligent American business principle of dog eat dog, the employer trying to get labor for as little as he can for his labor." Not bitter? Well, maybe just a little:

> You know the splendid basis upon which intelligent Americans, the greatest businessmen of the world, transact commercial affairs. The laborer asks so much, the employer offers so much. They agree to disagree. Then the employer tries to starve out the laborer, and the laborer tries to ruin the employer's business. They quarrel over a bone and rend each other like coyotes. . . . Our business philosophy is that of the wolf pack.

Johnson pitched for the Senators for the remainder of his extraordinary twenty-one year career. He retired with 412 wins, second only to Cy Young. During that span, the Senators finished in the bottom half of the standings more times than not. Finally, in 1924 and 1925, Johnson and the Senators broke through to appear in the World Series, winning in 1924 and losing in seven games in 1925. It had been a long wait for the pitcher known as "The Big Train." But what else could he do? The greatest pitcher in baseball had no other option but to endure.[41]

Fame and adulation offered some compensation—sort of. The American public was mad about baseball in the early twentieth century; as a result its best players ascended to a celebrity status that the previous generation of ballplayers had not experienced. For the first time, newspapers and sporting journals ran feature articles on the stars, complete with photos, descriptions of their lives beyond the playing field, and—of course—chronicles of their many on-field exploits. It was all great fun. Ballplayers clearly reveled in the special attention they received. For the first time, the best hotels opened their doors to ballplayers and restaurants that once shoved players "way back in the corner at the very end of the dining room"—as Sam Crawford recalled—now treated them as celebrities. Many used their growing fame to set themselves up in businesses that drew from their fan base. Star catcher Johnny Kling of the Chicago Cubs opened up a pool hall. Pirates' shortstop Honus Wagner opened a sporting goods store. Several took to vaudeville during the off-season, including New York Giants' pitcher Christy Mathewson, manager McGraw, and pitcher Rube Marquard. Advertisers loved celebrity endorsements and used ballplayers to hawk everything from breakfast cereal to business suits to cigarettes to soft drinks.

Yet even as fame boosted egos and provided extra sources of income, it also created a level of scrutiny and intrusion on private life that no one in the sports or entertainment fields had ever experienced. Celebrities themselves were not new to American culture. Since at least the mid-nineteenth century, various singers, actors, daredevil artists, and boxers had gained national recognition and mass followings.[42] But the baseball celebrity was different. From April through September and into October, baseball coverage dominated the sports news cycle and even infiltrated the front pages. As a result, early twentieth-century ballplayers received an unprecedented amount of attention. Naturally, it took some getting used to. When the ballplayer succeeded, he was adored by thousands, maybe millions. But when he failed, adulation often turned to anger and hostility. Fame was often fleeting, but infamy could last a lifetime—and then some. It was a hell of a life, *Baseball Magazine* observed. "The baseball player often labors under handicaps which would completely demoralize the average man," one article began. His is an "occupation that never lets up" as he must work even when "harassed by the most distressing mental anxiety." Fans could be absolutely heartless: "The ball player has only to remember that the crowd will make more noise over a three bagger with the bases full than they will if he were to overexert himself in the game and fall dead at its conclusion." They were also clueless: "With an entire disregard for the facts," fans persisted "in demanding the impossible" of players "who ought to be in bed." Or perhaps on the psychiatrist's couch.[43]

No one knew the consequences of public failure more than New York Giants' rookie first baseman Fred Merkle. During a late 1908 season game against their archrivals the Chicago Cubs, his base-running error cost the Giants a win and—as it turned out—the league championship. Although Merkle went on to have a long and productive career, he never lived down his blunder. His name quickly entered slang lexicon in baseball and beyond: "to pull a Merkle" became synonymous with performing a senseless or stupid act. The incident itself became known as "Merkle's boner." Forever after, Merkle was followed by jeers of "Bonehead." The incident so haunted him that he once told a reporter, "I suppose when I die, they'll put on my tombstone, 'Here Lies Bonehead Merkle.'" Fortunately, he was saved that indignity, but his obituaries did in fact harp on his costly miscue; all else remained secondary.[44]

Few players gained such infamy for their mistakes, but all lived with the pressure of needing to perform—and perform well—under the gaze of critical and vociferous fans and sportswriters. Coincidentally, the player who caught Merkle in his blunder was among the most articulate and honest about the anxieties associated with being a major league baseball player, Cubs infielder Johnny Evers. Writing for *Baseball Magazine* after his Cubs won the World Series later that year, Evers leveled with the public about the stress and anxiety players experienced. Pleading for a bit of compassion, Evers implored his readers to "think of what depends on each individual's work. If he makes a slip, ever so slight, he may lose the series, spoil the great work of his teammates . . . and throw away a snug little fortune for each of his fellow-players." Evers remarked, "The nervous strain is terrible." Fans, of course, only made matters worse. According to Evers, "The men who play the game, who are on the inside and who know what the strain is never question the man who errs." No, "it is the outsider, viewing things from a comfortable seat in the grand stand and knowing nothing of the real facts, who makes all the trouble."[45]

McGraw understood the dilemma all too well. As his Giants prepared for the 1913 World Series, the Little Napoleon confided to Cobb, "I wish my players would forget baseball, except during the games. But you can't get some of them to keep it out of their minds for a minute. They even dream about it, and most of them don't sleep well." The modern crush of journalism only made matters worse. Players, McGraw observed, "spend their time reading all the newspaper accounts and criticisms, and these bother them and keep them from composing themselves when they go to bed." In fact, downtime rarely helped. On long train rides or during idle hours before or after the game, players had far too many opportunities to be alone with their thoughts. Perhaps this explains why players often complained that the pressure was unrelenting. They could never completely escape replaying the previous game, anticipating the game to come, and wondering what tragedy might befall them tomorrow—"harassed by the shadow of possibilities," as one scribe put it. Stanley Coveleski, a Hall of Fame pitcher for the Cleveland Indians remarked, "I enjoyed playing ball, but it's a tough racket. There's always someone sitting on the bench just itching to get in there in your place . . . the pressure never lets up. Doesn't matter what you did yesterday. That's history. It's tomorrow that counts. So you worry all the time. It never ends. Lord, baseball is a worrying thing."[46]

Greater scrutiny and increased pressure to excel came from all corners. The methods management used to end rowdyism curtailed players' freedom and thus compromised a bit of their manhood. Off the field, teams began to establish stricter codes of conduct. Some required players to wear suits while traveling. Many teams hired private detectives to spy on players' off-field behavior. Most established an evening curfew; some managers, including McGraw, also required players to sign in at the ballpark each morning. Many imposed heavy fines for drinking, gambling, breaking curfew, and general insubordination—all in an effort to create greater team discipline and to present a public image of propriety.[47]

On the field, both leagues began to employ two umpires for each game in 1909. This meant fewer bad calls, but it also made it more difficult for players to rely upon long-practiced rule-defying tricks and stunts. Even more fundamental to the way the game was played, teams adopted what came to be called "inside" or "scientific" baseball, a more structured and deliberate approach to the game. Essentially, this new style promoted conservative offensive maneuvers—that is playing for the single run whenever the opportunity presented itself as opposed to swinging for the fences in hopes of producing an occasional big inning. Teams adopted a whole new set of "fundamentals" to succeed under this new system. At bat, they practiced the hit and run, the sacrifice bunt, place hitting, hitting behind the runner, and the double steal—relentlessly. In the field, infielders designed dozens of plays to cover every contingency and studied each hitter for weaknesses and tendencies. Baseball was now "soaked in strategy as never before, never since" according to baseball historian Bill James. Giants' outfielder Fred Snodgrass contended ballplayers of his era "played baseball with their brains as much as their brawn."[48] While true, they also had to give up a good deal of their personal autonomy to act in concert with their teammates. Even power hitters like Crawford, Lajoie, Wagner, and Joe Jackson were required to sacrifice, hit behind the runner, and place hit. The days of free swinging—or "heavy hitting" as it was then called—were over. Historian Robert Burk's assertion that inside ball "incorporated the lessons of Taylorism—of industrial time/motion studies and scientific management of production processes—on the ballfield" may be a bit of an exaggeration, but not by much.[49] The most successful teams operated with near-perfect precision, not unlike a machine. Indeed, the machine became a frequently used metaphor during the era, employed regularly by the press, managers, and players to describe how the most successful teams functioned.

This new strategy gave managers far greater control of the game than they had previously exercised. Heretofore, most managers had been more like player-coaches. They acted more like coordinators or facilitators than supervisors. As such, they were often closer to the players than they were to the owners. Now fewer and fewer managers played alongside their charges. This enabled them to devote their full attention to the managing of the team. In strict terms of labor relations, they removed themselves from the working class and joined the ranks of the managing class.⁵⁰ And manage they did. On most teams, managers now directed all the action and stated a clear preference for players who were more open to training, supervision, and instruction. In his insider analysis of the game, *Pitching in a Pinch*, Christy Mathewson (with ghostwriter John Wheeler) described the degree to which McGraw, the game's greatest exponent of inside ball, controlled his team. "The brain of McGraw is behind each game the Giants play," Mathewson told his readers. "And he plans every move" with an iron will, as "absolute discipline must be assured." Recounting the Giants' championship season of 1904, Mathewson stated, "Every play that season was made . . . by John McGraw through his agents, his manikins, who moved according to the wires which he pulled." By the end of the season, "his hands were badly calloused" from pulling those wires.⁵¹

Managers often supplanted star players as the objects of attention and adulation. Summarizing the 1909 season, Richter of *Sporting Life* praised Connie Mack for "building" and "handling" a "great fighting machine." Although the team was loaded with talented players, including three future Hall of Famers, Richter gave most of the credit to Mack because he "put the team together, drilled and developed it, and guided it skillfully over the rough places" until it operated "like a well-oiled piece of machinery." When the Giants won the pennant in 1911, *Sporting Life* gave most of the credit to McGraw. While noting that Christy Mathewson was a "tremendous asset," it was McGraw who "delivered the goods" by "maintaining the strictest discipline at all times and inspiring his men with the desire to win ball games." Sportswriters saw the disciplined handiwork of managers everywhere. When members of his St. Louis Cardinals helped rescue passengers aboard a wrecked train in Bridgeport, Connecticut, F. C. Lane of *Baseball Magazine* gave much of the credit to manager Roger Bresnahan because he had trained his men "to work with machine-like harmony and efficiency under a recognized leader." Befitting their status as the game's most valuable personages, managers—at least the most successful of the group—made more than the game's star players.⁵²

Granted, managers varied quite a bit in temperament, style, and administrative philosophy. Nevertheless, clear patterns emerged. A few took on an almost paternalistic persona. The most popular and successful of this type was the Athletics' Connie Mack. During the first fifteen years of the American League, his teams won six league championships, three of which went on to win the World Series. Players loved his gentlemanly demeanor because it reflected his underlying respect for them. He usually addressed players formally, as in "Mr. Collins" or "Mr. Plank." He rarely lost his temper and never cursed his players. When players made mistakes, he did his best to turn the incident into a teachable moment. Rube Bressler recalled, "He'd get you alone a few days later, and then he'd say something like 'Don't you think it would have been better if you'd made the play this way?'"[53] Although he was something of a prude, he tried not to become overly involved in his players' private lives, unless it hurt the team. Even then, he could be quite empathic. He once upbraided star pitcher Charles "Chief" Bender—a chronic boozer—in a hotel lobby after the pitcher tottered in from a night of heavy drinking, but this was the exception. More typical, he treated Rube Waddell, perhaps the most unruly player who ever played the game, as a wayward son, giving him dozens of chances to redeem himself. He expected players to be accountable to him, but also to themselves. If he learned that a player had spent the night carousing, he expected the player to own up to his transgression. If he did, that was enough for Mack; "I just wanted to let you know that I knew," he told more than one reprobate. If the player lied, Mack would get him off the team—as he finally did with Waddell. Jimmy Dykes, who played with Mack for fifteen years, could not recall Mack ever fining a player for breaking team rules. It simply wasn't his style; for one thing he realized that fining players often hurt the wayward player's family more than the player himself. He preferred to appeal to players' enlightened self-interest: "My notion was that ballplayers fit for the major leagues . . . would keep themselves in good physical condition as a matter of course," he remarked.[54]

Sitting quietly on the bench wearing a suit and his trademark straw hat, Mack struck many as being aloof and even detached. Sportswriter F. C. Lane observed, "Connie loves to sit back on the bench quietly and obscurely and direct the operations from a safe distance." He rarely appeared on the field, content to "let his men fight their own battles." His taciturn manner led one magnate to dismiss Mack as a phony: "Mack sits on the bench, twiddles his thumbs and looks wise while his men do all the work," Cubs owner Charles Murphy asserted. His players knew otherwise. Ever the systematic thinker, Mack met with his regulars after each game to assess their play and to plan strategy for the next contest. He gave his players meticulous instructions based on the voluminous records he kept of every player in the league. Although he allowed his players freedom to think on their own, this was only after they had been well versed in the Connie Mack School of Baseball. Mack's teams were always an extension of his personality and his baseball philosophy. As part owner of the Athletics, he had almost complete control over personnel. Once he had the players he wanted, he drilled and developed them from the beginning of spring training until the end of the season. And in at least one area, Mack assumed dictatorial power at all times—defensive alignments. He instructed his fielders to look at him before every pitch; if he thought they were out of alignment, he carefully directed them into position with the wave of his scorecard.[55]

Mack was at least kindhearted in his paternalism and offered his players a modicum of respect. Managers like McGraw of the Giants and George Stallings of the Boston Braves were often less considerate. Stallings, in fact, tried to motivate by shame. In 1914, he gained the appellation of "Miracle Man" for navigating the Boston Braves to the championship in what may still stand as the most amazing pennant run in major league history. On July 15, the Braves were in last place, ten games below .500, and eleven-and-a-half games behind the Giants. From that point on, Stallings' team won fifty-two of their final sixty-six games to overtake the Giants and win the pennant by ten-and-a-half games. To cap the improbable season, the Braves swept the heavily favored Athletics in the World Series. Stallings drove his men hard and made no apologies for doing so. "On the bench he is a czar," *Baseball Magazine* claimed. "His word is law and he must have his own way.... He admits that he terrorizes men who err and who fail to listen to his instructions." Another writer called Stallings a "brute driver," capable of "lashing" his men "to the quick with his writhing sarcasm." Infielder Jimmy Austin experienced Stallings first hand. "Talk about cussing! Golly, he had 'em all beat. He cussed something awful," Austin recalled of one of his encounters with Stallings.[56]

Stallings claimed that there was a method to his madness. Writing in *Colliers*, a few months after his shocking World Series triumph, he explained that he often "scolds" and "abuses" his players "to find out whether they are game." He found that if the player "has anything in him," he will try all the harder to make the grade. Conversely, "weakhearted" players often gave up because they believed their play was beneath the manager's notice. Stallings saw no reason to buoy their spirits, as he did not want quitters on his team. Sometimes Stallings cut right to the quick by challenging a player's manhood. After one of his outfielders muffed an easy fly ball, Stallings stormed after him, ordering him "Go out and take off the uniform. You are not man enough to wear it." Stallings later boasted, "the tongue lashing . . . drove him right out of the park."[57]

Stallings was a classic, but John McGraw was sui generis. In McGraw's system, one writer observed, "the manager is everything, the players are only a means to an end." McGraw had no patience for players who acted on their own. Too much individualism, he contended, "will kill any organization in the world. The result is what counts, and the only way to get it is by teamwork." True to his ethos, he once fined infielder Sammy Strang twenty-five dollars for hitting a home run. Why? McGraw had ordered Strang to lay down a sacrifice bunt. That the home run won the game made no difference to McGraw; he wanted his players to follow orders at all times. McGraw could also be ruthless and calculating when it came to personnel decisions. Shortly after defeating the Athletics in the 1905 World Series, McGraw marched into owner John Brush's office with a list of names he wanted the team to acquire—a list so extensive that it meant every position player on the team would be replaced. When Brush reminded McGraw that his team had just won the World Series, McGraw protested. "We won the championship . . . on Mathewson's pitching," he claimed, "not because of those men, but in spite of them and we need to rebuild from the bottom." He boasted to the press that his players' feelings rarely entered into his thinking. When a sportswriter asked McGraw for some background information on a new Giant, McGraw claimed ignorance. "I am not well-acquainted with my men. I seldom or never see them off the field. I know nothing about them outside their ability as players." He was lying. He knew a great deal about his players' private lives because he ordered his coaches to spy on them. On road trips, he maintained a tight regime, complete with a curfew, bed checks, and mandatory meals together so he could keep watch over what and how much his men ate. For home games, he regularly ordered his men to be at the ballpark by nine in the morning for a few hours of practice.[58]

McGraw's tirades may not have been as epic as Stallings's, but they were close. Outfielder Fred Snodgrass, who played seven years under McGraw, claimed that Little Napoleon was fairly tolerant of physical errors, but went into conniptions when players committed mental errors—any mental error. "I do believe he had the most vicious tongue of any man who ever lived. Absolutely!" said Snodgrass. Even when not screaming at his players, he knew how to keep them humble. Josh Devore was feeling pretty confident after his triple in the bottom of the ninth drove in the winning run—too confident according to McGraw. As the crowd cheered, the manager calmly strode up to the outfielder and remarked, "Gee, you're a lucky guy. I wish I had your luck. You were shot full of horseshoes to get that one. When I saw you shut your eyes, I never thought you would hit it." According to Mathewson, "this was like pricking a bubble" as Devore's "chest returned to size."[59]

As if high-handed managers were not enough, even the ball seemed to be against most ballplayers. Hitters complained it was "dead." It wasn't, but it was harder to hit. Rule changes had something to do with it. In 1900, home plate was reshaped from a twelve-inch square to its present five-sided figure measuring seventeen inches across. Then in 1901, the National League decided to count the first two fouls as strikes (the American League followed suit in 1903). These changes gave an obvious advantage to pitchers. Statistics help tell the tale. In 1900, the National League batting average was .279; by 1909, the major league average declined to .244. During the 1890s, 35 percent of all regulars hit above .300; during the 1900s, only 18 percent did. In 1900, teams averaged about five runs per game; by 1909, the number declined to about 3.5. The foul strike rule proved especially injurious to power hitting as batters became more defensive with two strikes; thus, the number of doubles, triples, and home runs declined by about a third and slugging percentage declined from .360 to .300.[60]

The first decade of the century may not have been the best time to be a batter, but it was a great time to be a pitcher. The major league earned run average fell from about 3.50 in 1900 to below 2.50 by 1909. Meanwhile, the number of shutouts per season doubled. As if the rule changes weren't enough to satisfy pitchers, they came up with a variety of less-than-legal tactics to further frustrate batters. Most obviously, they mauled the ball. Outright defacement of the spheroid was illegal, but this was one rule umpires never enforced—despite the greater scrutiny in most every other facet of the game. As a result, pitchers and catchers took turns scuffing and cutting game balls with everything from razor blades to emery boards to belt buckles. In addition, pitchers also did their best to soften the ball with a steady stream of tobacco juice between pitches. Some pitchers even pounded the ball against their spikes to soften it up. For good measure, pitchers darkened the ball by rubbing dirt into it before each game. Since teams used only about half a dozen balls in the course of a game, hitters were sometimes reduced to flailing at dark shadows by the later innings. Finally, pitchers doctored the ball with a variety of foreign substances to make it move in all sorts of unpredictable ways as it sped to the plate. When thrown by a true master, it was extremely difficult to hit. Some of the game's biggest winners during the era were spitball pitchers, including Jack Chesbro of the New York Highlanders, who won forty-one games in 1904, and Ed Walsh, who won forty in 1908 and compiled the lowest career earned run average of any pitcher in major league history with at least 1,000 innings. Walsh claimed he could make his spitter move in three different ways—down and away, straight down, and down and in. Symptomatic of the Dead Ball Era, Walsh's Chicago White Sox, the "Hitless Wonders," won the World Series in 1906 despite an anemic team batting average of .230 for the season, an on-base percentage of .301, and a slugging percentage of .286.[61]

Pathetic numbers to be sure—the worst in the history of the game for a championship team. So why didn't league officials do something to liven up the game? After all, it was an axiom as much then as now that offense draws the fans. In addition, major league baseball has never been averse to tweaking rules for the sake of higher profits. Nevertheless, neither club owners nor league officers saw much need to change the game, not with attendance steadily increasing. Moreover, club owners feared that more offense might lead productive players to demand more generous contracts and—as already noted—most owners were trying to hold the line on salaries. So far as they were concerned, fattening batting averages was against their economic self-interest. That baseball flourished under these conditions is a testament to the game itself.[62]

THE GAME

This is the context in which Ty Cobb began his major league career. The ball was dead, but the game itself was thriving. Thanks in part to reforms to curb rowdyism and in part to the continued maturation of the national sports media, more and more American men were becoming obsessed with the daily dramas of the professional game. One might even argue that the sport just needed a few new stars—that is players of exceptional skill who also possessed a bit of personal magnetism—for baseball to solidify itself as American men's favorite pastime. Yet for many ballplayers it was also a tumultuous time as players confronted the rapid changes that came with baseball's ascendance. This was a very difficult time to be a major league ballplayer, especially for someone as young, inexperienced, and headstrong as Ty Cobb.

Cobb played his first game on August 30, 1905, at Detroit's Bennett Park against the New York Highlanders. He was eighteen years old, not yet fully grown. He was so fair-skinned that even in the heat of summer, he wore long sleeves and turned his collar up to protect himself from the sun. The local scribes who tried to interview him could barely understand him. They had no problem understanding New York accents, Boston accents, Midwestern accents, far Western accents, and Irish brogues, but Cobb's Southern drawl was simply too foreign for their ears.

Before the game, manager Bill Armour sat with Cobb on the bench to calm his nerves and to offer some last minute advice. It was a kind gesture, but Cobb was too anxious and awestruck by his surroundings to digest whatever his manager had to say. "I barely heard Armour's soothing words," he later confessed. As he looked at the veteran players warming up in the expansive ball field, he suddenly had the revelation that perhaps he had "rushed things" a bit. Beneath his brash exterior, Cobb was just a scared kid, a thousand miles away from home, and still mourning his father's death.[63]

Cobb faced one of the league's best pitchers that day—right-hander Jack Chesbro of the New York Highlanders. The spitballer had won a still major league record forty-one games the previous year and was on his way to a respectable nineteen-win season this year. Cobb had faced spitballers in the minors, but no one as accomplished as this guy; he recalled Chesbro's pitches came to the plate like a regular fastball but then "took a diabolical dive under your bat." Cobb called it "the meanest delivery in the business." Batting fifth, he came to the plate for the first time in the first inning with two outs, a run in, and a runner on third. He swung and missed at the first pitch, took a called strike for the second, and connected on the third—a waist-high fastball—driving it into the gap between left and center for a clean double that easily scored the runner. Cobb had his first hit and his first run batted in. Besides that first at bat what he remembered most that day was the talent of the other players. "I'd never dreamed that men could field and hit so wonderfully," he recalled. "Such speed, class, style, speedy maneuvering, and lightning thinking! It seemed miles beyond anything I could ever do." He was equally impressed by the players' manly bearing. They went at it with "a red-eyed determination" that intimidated him more than a little.[64]

No one could have predicted it—leastwise Cobb himself—but within two years, this earnest young man would be the league's best hitter. In another two years, the press would proclaim him the best player in baseball; concomitantly, their fascination for all things Cobb would make him the game's first media sensation. By the end of the decade, he would dominate the sports page, gaining for himself a celebrity status unrivaled in the history of American leisure culture. Along the way, he also became the most controversial player in the game, sometimes loathed and detested, other times admired, respected, and even beloved.

Ban Johnson might have saved the professional game, but Ty Cobb gave the game a vitality and panache that it needed to thrive. At least that was the judgment of one of the game's leading experts—Charles Spink, editor of the *Sporting News*. Twenty-one years after Cobb's first game, Spink remarked:

> Cobb built the American League. In its earlier days when the league struggled with the pertinacity of a healthy infant that will kick in its crib and yowl for more experience, Cobb was a greater factor for arousing the baseball sentiment of the populace than any ball player of the league. . . . where Cobb played the crowd went. That is financial fact.[65]

As in all things, Ty Cobb did it very much his way.

NOTES

1. Obituaries, *New York Times*, December 18, 1945, 27.
2. Rube Marquard in Lawrence S. Ritter, *The Glory of Their Times: The Story of the Early Days of Baseball Told by the Men Who Played It* (New York: Perennial, 1966), 1–4; Larry D. Mansch, *Rube Marquard: The Life and Times of a Baseball Hall of Famer* (Jefferson, NC: McFarland, 1998), 13–15.
3. Henry W. Thomas, *Walter Johnson, Baseball's Big Train* (Lincoln: University of Nebraska Press, 1995), 1–32.
4. Joe Wood in Ritter, *Glory of Their Times*, 154–69.
5. Steven A. Riess, *Touching Base: Professional Baseball and American Culture in the Progressive Era* (Urbana: University of Illinois Press, 1983), 12–13.
6. Quoted in Harold Seymour, *Baseball: The Golden Age* (New York: Oxford University Press, 1971), 4.
7. John J. Evers, *Touching Second: The Science of Baseball* (1910; repr., Danvers, MA: General Books, 2009), 3.
8. David Vaught, "'Our Players are Mostly Farmers': Baseball in Rural California, 1850 to 1890," in *Baseball in America and America in Baseball*, edited by Donald Kyle and Robert Fairbanks (College Station: Texas A&M University Press, 2008), 8–31.
9. Evers, *Touching Second*, 3.
10. James T. Farrell, *Young Lonigan* (1932; repr., New York: Signet Classics, 2004), 145.
11. Theodore Roosevelt quoted in Michael Kimmel, "Baseball and the Reconstruction of American Masculinity, 1880–1920," in *Baseball History from Outside the Lines*, edited by John Dreifort (Lincoln: University of Nebraska Press, 2001), 55; H. Addington Bruce, "Baseball and the National Life," *Outlook* 104 (May 17, 1913), 103–107; Zane Grey, *The Short-stop* (New York: Grosset and Dunlap, 1909), 109, 112.
12. Albert G. Spalding, *America's National Game* (1911, repr., San Francisco: Halo Books, 1991), 2, 5; Henry Curtis, "Baseball," *Journal of Education* 83 (January 1916): 466–67; "Editorially: The Spirit of the Times," *Baseball Magazine* (October 1909): 2; "Editorials," *Baseball Magazine* (May 1916): 32.
13. Rader, *Baseball: A History of America's Game* (Urbana: University of Illinois Press, 1992), 67; Charles C. Alexander, *Our Game: An American Baseball History* (New York: MJF Books, 1991), 67; John J. McGraw, *My Thirty Years in Baseball* (1923; repr., Lincoln: University of Nebraska Press, 1995), 66–67; Seymour, *Baseball: The Early Years* (New York: Oxford University Press, 1960), 290; Bill Felber, *A Game of Brawl: The Orioles, the Beaneaters,*

and the Battle for the 1897 Pennant (Lincoln: University of Nebraska Press, 2007), 13–14; *Sporting News* (June 30, 1894): 2; Sam Crawford in Ritter, *Glory of Their Times*, 52; *St. Louis Republic,* May 27, 1894, 11.

14. Seymour, *Baseball: The Early Years*, 290; *Washington Post*, July 23, 1901, 8; McGraw, *My Thirty Years*, 82; Felber, *Game of Brawl*, 13.

15. *Sporting News* (September 2, 1899): 1; McGraw, *My Thirty Years*, 161; Jimmy Austin in Ritter, *Glory of Their Times*, 87.

16. The rhyme is provided in full in Seymour, *Baseball: The Early Years*, 338.

17. The website Baseball Almanac provides the original text of Ernest Lawrence Thayer's "Casey at the Bat." See Baseball Almanac, http://www.baseball-almanac.com/poetry/po_case.shtml (accessed August 25, 2015). Thayer's poem was first published in the *San Francisco Examiner* June 3, 1888.

18. *Sporting Life* (April 4, 1896): 2.

19. Seymour, *Baseball: The Early Years*, 291–292; *Sporting News* (November 4, 1899): 4; *Sporting News* (December 2, 1899): 4; *Sporting News* (December 9, 1899): 1.

20. *New York Sun*, January 13, 1898, 4.

21. Rader, *Baseball*, 70.

22. David L. Fleitz, *Ghosts in the Gallery at Cooperstown: Sixteen Little-Known Members of the Hall of Fame* (Jefferson, NC: McFarland, 2004), 206, 209.

23. *Sporting News* (October 13, 1900): 3.

24. *Sporting Life* (January 29, 1898): 9; *New York Times*, September 12, 1898, 6; *Detroit Free Press*, July 30, 1897, 7.

25. *Washington Post*, March 21, 1899, 8; *Sporting Life* (March 17, 1900): 2.

26. *Washington Post*, December 9, 1901, 8; *Sporting Life* (September 22, 1900): 1.

27. *Sporting Life* (December 30, 1899): 4; *Sporting Life* (March 11, 1899): 5.

28. *Sporting News* (December 9, 1899): 1; *Sporting News* (October 6, 1900): 2; *Sporting Life* (November 10, 1900): 8.

29. *Sporting Life* (March 17, 1920): 2.

30. Malcolm W. Bingay, "When Both Teams Won on the Same Error," *Baseball Digest* (October–November 1967): 21–22.

31. Norman L. Macht, *Connie Mack and the Early Years of Baseball* (Lincoln: University of Nebraska Press, 2007), 162.

32. Macht, *Connie Mack*, 163.

33. Robert F. Burk, *Never Just a Game: Players, Owners, and American Baseball to 1920* (Chapel Hill: University of North Carolina Press, 1994), 138; Seymour, *Baseball: The Early Years*, 308; Lee Lowenfish, *The Imperfect Diamond: A History of Baseball's Labor Wars*. Rev. ed. (New York: Da Capo Press, 1991), 71.

34. Burk, *Never Just a Game*, 138; Seymour, *Baseball: The Early Years*, 308–309; Lowenfish, *Imperfect Diamond*, 71.

35. *Sporting News* (September 16, 1899): 4; *Sporting Life* (October 14, 1899): 7.

36. Seymour, *Baseball: The Early Years*, 314; Alexander, *Our Game*, 78, 92; Rader, *Baseball*, 94.

37. Rader, *Baseball*, 82–87; Lowenfish, *Imperfect Diamond*, 71.

38. Ty Cobb, with Al Stump, *My Life in Baseball* (1961; repr., Lincoln, NE: Bison Books, 1993), 54–55.

39. Burk, *Never Just a Game*, 160–62.

40. Evers, *Touching Second*, 17–19.

41. Thomas, *Walter Johnson*, 80–81; Walter Johnson, "Baseball Slavery: The Great American Principle of Dog Eat Dog," *Baseball Magazine* (July 1911): 75–76.

42. On celebrities of the nineteenth century, see Paul E. Johnson, *Sam Patch: The Famous Jumper* (New York: Hill and Wang, 2003); Joy S. Kasson, *Buffalo Bill's Wild West: Celebrity, Memory, and Popular History* (New York: Hill and Wang, 2000); Christopher Klein, *Strong Boy: The Life and Times of John L. Sullivan, America's First Sports Hero* (New York: Rowman & Littlefield, 2013).

43. "Why Players Fail," *Baseball Magazine* (September 1913): 27; "Failure as a Factor in the National Game," *Baseball Magazine* (August 1913): 31.

44. Cait Murphy, *Crazy '08: How a Cast of Cranks, Rogues, Boneheads, and Magnates Created the Greatest Year in Baseball History* (New York: Smithsonian Books, 2007), 190–95, 240, 253–54, 294–95; *New York Times*, March 3, 1956, 20; *Chicago Daily Tribune*, March 3, 1956, B1; *Washington Post and Times Herald*, March 3, 1956, 11.

45. John J. Evers, "Do Players Lose Their Nerve?" *Baseball Magazine* (April 1, 1909): 42.

46. Ty Cobb, *Busting 'Em and Other Big League Stories* (1914; repr., Jefferson, NC: McFarland, 2003), 86; "Failure as a Factor in the National Game," *Baseball Magazine* (August 1913): 31; Stanley Coveleski in Ritter, *Glory of Their Times*, 123.

47. Sam Crawford in Ritter, *Glory of Their Times*, 51; Alexander, *Our Game*, 92.

48. Fred Snodgrass in Ritter, *The Glory of Their Times*, 98; Bill James, *The New Bill James Historical Baseball Abstract*. Rev. ed. (New York: Free Press, 2001), 73.

49. Burk, *Never Just a Game*, 173.

50. Burk, *Never Just a Game*, 171–72.

51. Christy Mathewson, *Pitching in a Pinch: Baseball From the Inside* (1912; repr., Lincoln, NE: Bison Books, 1994), 94–96, 127.

52. McGraw, *My Thirty Years*, 14; *Sporting Life* (October 9, 1909): 3; *Sporting Life* (January 13, 1912): 14; *Baseball Magazine* (September 1911): 36; Charles C. Alexander, *John McGraw* (New York: Penguin, 1988), 91, 119, 150, 195–96; Macht, *Connie Mack*, 259, 295, 378, 570. McGraw and Mack made as much as twice as much as their star players.

53. Sam Crawford in Ritter, *Glory of Their Times*, 121, 199; Jimmy Dykes in Donald Honig, *The Man in the Dugout: Fifteen Big League Managers Speak Their Minds* (Lincoln, NE: Bison Books, 1977), 275.

54. F. C. Lane, "The Greatest Manager in Organized Ball," *Baseball Magazine* (May 1913), 49; Dykes in Honig, *The Man in the Dugout*, 279–280; Macht, *Connie Mack*, 111–12.

55. Lane, "The Greatest Manager in Organized Ball," 53; *Sporting Life* (October 9, 1909): 1; Macht, *Connie Mack*, 282–85.

56. F. C. Lane, "How Much is a Star Worth?" *Baseball Magazine* (April 1913): 40; F. C. Lane, "Stallings: The Miracle Man," *Baseball Magazine* (February 1915): 65; Rube Marquard in Ritter, *Glory of Their Times*, 14; "Got Stung, Too," *Baseball Digest* (August 1952): 68.

57. George T. Stallings, "The Miracle Man's Own Story," *Collier's*, November 28, 1914, 7–10; "The Miracle Man: George Stallings was Two Persons," *Baseball Digest* (July 1949): 71–72.

58. McGraw, *My Thirty Years*, 10–12, 15; Lane, "The Greatest Manager in Organized Ball," 41–42, 52; Alexander, *John McGraw*, 232.

59. Bob Shawkey in Honig, *Man in the Dugout*, 172; Mathewson, *Pitching in a Pinch*, 113–114.

60. James, *New Bill James Historical Abstract*, 57, 75; Seymour, *Baseball: The Golden Age*, 122–26; Michael Bein, A Graphical History of Baseball, http://michaelbein.com/baseball.html (accessed August 26, 2015).

61. Rader, *Baseball*, 87; Seymour, *Baseball: The Golden Age*, 29–30; Alexander, *Our Game*, 90–91.

62. Burk, *Never Just a Game*, 170.

63. Alexander, *Ty Cobb*, 33; Cobb, *My Life*, 17–18.

64. Cobb, *My Life*, 18–19.

65. "Tyrus Raymond Cobb," *Sporting News* (November 11, 1926): 4.

3

"THE PROFESSIONAL TEACH"

Ty Cobb had a very good first game. Then he faltered. In the days and weeks that followed, he struggled to distinguish himself in all aspects of the game. By season's end, he had only a very modest .242 average to show for his forty-one games and 164 plate appearances. Fifty years later, Cobb expressed embarrassment at this early showing. He called himself a "walking study in faults"—a "scatter-brained runner" and an undisciplined hitter, particularly inept against left-handers. He realized that the game itself was much more ruthless than anything he had experienced in the minor leagues. "When the bell rang," Cobb realized, "I found myself involved in a duel by artists at the art of extracting every last inch of opportunity from every situation. And they went at it with a red-eyed determination I couldn't believe."[1]

When the season ended, he returned home, unsure if the Tigers would even renew his contract for the next year. This was a fretful time for the young man who would someday become resented for his arrogant swagger. For now, he was still just another young ballplayer of doubtful talent and meager experience. The only positive Cobb took away from his introduction to big league ball was that he had at least shown he was man enough to compete. He proved this by taking on one of the roughest, surliest veterans in the league, infielder Norman Arthur "Kid" Elberfeld of the New York Highlanders. Often referred to as the "Tabasco Kid" because of his hot temper, Elberfeld was a hardened, primal ballplayer, the sort who flourished in this desperate era. He washed his spike wounds with whiskey and gained a much deserved reputation for verbally and physically battering opponents and umpires alike. It was accepted as fact that Elberfeld was thrown out of more games than any other player of his era, though no one bothered to keep written records on such matters. The Kid proved he could take it as well as give it out: for seventy-five years, he held the record for being hit by pitches (165 times). No doubt, many of his opponents would have liked to have made that number much higher.

Cobb experienced Elberfeld's callousness a few games after his debut against Chesbro when he made an ill-planned attempt to steal second. Not only did he get a poor jump on the pitcher, but he tried to slide headfirst. Elberfeld was waiting for him, ball in glove, as Cobb snowplowed into the bag. The Kid took advantage of the rookie's vulnerability by giving him what players called "the professional teach." While applying the tag, Elberfeld slammed his knee straight down onto the back of Cobb's neck, forcing his face to scrape the infield dirt as he completed his slide. Laying awkwardly on the ground with Elberfeld's knee still grinding into him, Cobb feared the veteran infielder had broken his neck. Instead, the physical damage was fairly minor—bruises and scrapes on his forehead, nose, and cheeks. The bruise to Cobb's tender ego was much greater. Fans and players alike laughed and jeered as the embarrassed rookie stood up, dusted himself off, spit dirt out of his mouth, and stumbled back to the bench. Elberfeld had humiliated Cobb in front of his teammates, opponents, and the raucous crowd.

Years later, Cobb claimed the encounter with Elberfeld left him humbled, but unbowed. "I was much subdued," he said. Still, he had done his best to take it like a man, without "complaint or holler." He realized Elberfeld had made him pay "the penalty for being green." He vowed to learn from his mistakes. "I had run into a real big leaguer. I realized that he knew much of what I would have to learn."[2]

Cobb resolved to avenge himself—"to pay Elberfeld back in his own medicine for having roughed me up." Elberfeld's brutality taught Cobb that sliding headfirst put him at a distinct disadvantage because he was not only susceptible to injury but unable to respond to whatever action the fielder might make. Sliding feet first changed the dynamic. Watching veterans, including Elberfeld, Cobb realized that the runner could take the offensive, even when sliding. It was a revelation. If he came in with his "steel shining" he could take the advantage. Rather than let the fielder test his nerve, Cobb vowed to test the fielder's. Wisdom gained, Cobb waited to face Elberfeld again. In his next game against the Highlanders, Cobb stole second the first chance he had. Approaching the bag at full speed, he threw himself in the air, feet first and spikes high, hitting Elberfeld "just as hard as I could." As they collided, Cobb made Elberfeld absorb the force of the blow so he would be unable to make the tag. When the dust cleared, Cobb was standing on second while Elberfeld lay kicking on the grass. Cobb had himself a stolen base.

Cobb also had his first taste of major league revenge. Watching the man who had humiliated him sprawling on the ground pleased Cobb immensely. Still, that was not enough; Cobb also wanted Elberfeld's respect. As Cobb remembered it, Elberfeld realized the full import of what had transpired and responded with grace and magnanimity. The shortstop got up, gathered himself, and calmly went back to his position. In the process, he pointedly gave Cobb a look that said to him, "Well, you've learned something. You beat me to it that time and I've got nothing to say." Or perhaps Elberfeld even spoke to Cobb. As Cobb got older, he embellished the story with more and more details to enhance the drama. In two interviews conducted in the last decade of his life, Cobb recalled Elberfeld actually addressed him. In one, Cobb claimed Elberfeld "got up, shot a stream of tobacco juice, and looked me over reflectively. 'Son, that's how it's done—you've got it. More power to you.'" In the other interview, Cobb recalled that Elberfeld was even more intimate, warmly patting Cobb on the back and exclaiming, "That's the way to play, sonny boy."[3]

What actually happened the first few times Cobb met Elberfeld? It seems reasonable to assume that the first encounter occurred roughly as Cobb suggested. In the early decades of the twentieth century, veterans often abused rookies and took advantage of their ignorance. The extremely young and inexperienced Cobb probably received more than his share of abuse by veteran players. No doubt, the wily and irascible Elberfeld had ample opportunity to give Cobb "the teach." But the second encounter? Cobb was the only one to speak of the event and his very different renditions mean he invented at least some of the details. But which ones?

It may not matter. Perhaps what matters most is that Cobb believed something very important happened in the first month of his major league career—that despite his poor showing as a hitter, he had completed a rite of passage, proving himself to be a man capable of going toe-to-toe with one of the game's toughest competitors. Memory has a way of not only embellishing some details and omitting others, but of twisting and distorting events so that they fit a larger life narrative. As Cobb told and retold the critical and formative events of his life, they became part of a larger storyline for Cobb—the tale of how he overcame the vicious opposition of almost everyone to become the era's greatest player. All of this fits neatly into what scholars of memory call "a life review"—a desire to give a full accounting and assessment of one's life as the teller comes to terms with his or her mortality. In this process, the individual does not reminisce randomly, but tries to give order and coherence to the past by accentuating certain events, leaving out others, inventing details, and resolving inconsistencies within the narrative. Obviously, those engaged in such a process reveal a great deal about themselves—their values, their ideals, their personality, and their temperament.[4]

Cobb believed that the Elberfeld encounters were important because of what they revealed about his maturation. "I felt myself a big leaguer," Cobb later recalled about his triumph over Elberfeld. Knocking down the Kid marked his coming of age on the diamond. Why did Cobb believe this moment proved his manhood and not his impressive first game against Chesbro? Because he had proven something beyond his ability to hit big league pitching: he proved that he was man enough to be a big leaguer. Paying back Elberfeld allowed Cobb to display all the attributes of what he believed made a man. He had gotten his revenge by studying the situation and finding an opportunity to act. When presented with that opportunity he had acted decisively, forcefully, and even audaciously. Finally, he had done so in a public place, so that all those who had previously participated in his humiliation now witnessed his triumph. In sum, he had acted in ways consistent with the principles of manhood as taught by his father and his grandfathers and reinforced by his childhood friends and peers. Honor, manly self-assertion, nerve, and mastery had been the watchwords of his culture of origin. Humbling Elberfeld reassured Cobb that these traits would also be essential in his new environment—the world of major league baseball.

Elberfeld had forced him to take stock of himself. Now it was up to Cobb to devise a complete approach to the game that would enable him to survive and possibly to thrive in such a competitive atmosphere. This Cobb did with amazing rapidity. Within two years, he transformed himself from a rookie of questionable skills into one of the most feared players in the game. By the end of his fifth year, nearly everyone connected to major league baseball—fans, his peers, and the press—affirmed Cobb as the greatest player of his or any other generation.

Such are the vicissitudes of baseball that success in one game does not guarantee success in the next any more than one good season foretells a successful career. It was no different in Cobb's day. The league was full of has-beens and wannabes who enjoyed fleeting moments of glory before sinking back into obscurity. Contemporaries eagerly pointed out that the game perfectly mirrored the competitive nature of the new century. Baseball, a leading sportswriter pointed out in 1909, "is a brutal and unsentimental" game, "a survival of the fittest."[5] Cobb thrived in this environment because he embraced the ethic that he must constantly prove his worth to retain his place on the club. Self-assertion, will, honor: in each of his many autobiographies, Cobb paid tribute to these virtues. Clearly, he believed that they were the sources of his success as a player. As far as Cobb was concerned, he had bested all comers over the course of his long career: No pitcher had stopped him—at least not consistently; no hitter had matched his accomplishments with a bat; no manager had been able to out-strategize him. The record books proved this. When he retired, he possessed over eighty individual offensive records, including most hits, most runs scored, most batting titles, most consecutive batting titles, and most stolen bases. "Rivalry," *Baseball Magazine* observed early in Cobb's career, "has made Ty Cobb." He would brook no equal and certainly no superior, the magazine observed; "it galls him to see others even approximate his work." Cobb was less delicate. "I beat those bastards and left them in the ditch," he allegedly told his ghostwriter as they prepared what would be his final autobiography.[6]

"Those bastards" included many of his teammates. Beginning in spring training the next year and carrying through for the rest of the season, they dished out their own version of the "professional teach," but used methods of instruction that were far more ruthless than anything Elberfeld employed. According to Cobb, theirs was a "systematic, carefully schemed campaign." They started by testing his nerve. When that failed, they simply assaulted him—verbally, psychologically, and physically. The resulting confrontations left Cobb and a few of his teammates bruised and bloodied. Cobb always maintained their intent was not simply to test his manhood, but to destroy it and, in doing so, to drive him from the team. In this, they nearly succeeded.[7]

Cobb maintained the abuse he received from his teammates was exceptional. All rookies were "worked over" by older players, he recalled, "but usually it was done more in a joshing spirit than with malevolent intent."[8] Perhaps because he wanted to draw attention to his personal trials, Cobb was not being entirely honest here. Nearly all rookies received "rough treatment" in one form or another. The differences between his experiences and those of other rookies were a difference of degree, not kind. Hans Lobert, who had short stints with the Pirates and Cubs before finally sticking with the Reds, observed the hardest thing he and other rookies faced when they entered the league was overcoming "the abuse and sarcasm" of older players. The mental strain was tremendous, Lobert observed. If the player had "spirit enough" to persevere, he might make good, but "if he becomes disheartened and discouraged, which is more likely the case, he loses his nerve and has no prospect but a speedy return to the minors."[9] Many veterans eagerly tried to hasten a rookie's demise. Fred Snodgrass complained that when he joined the Giants in 1908 as the third-string catcher, veterans treated him like an "outsider" and refused even to let him take batting practice. Infielder Al Bridwell of the Cincinnati Reds also had trouble getting his swings in during batting practice when he first joined the club—until he pointedly told the veterans he would take his swings at them if they didn't give him room. Boston Red Sox veterans completely ignored outfielder Harry Hooper when he joined the team for his first spring training. "Spring *training*. Training for what?" Hooper asked bitterly; veterans refused to let him get anywhere near the practice field. Only when a rash of injuries depleted the outfield ranks did he get a chance to show what he could do. Even Christy Mathewson got the treatment. Although he won twenty games during his first full season, teammates thought him arrogant and refused to socialize with him. When Mathewson faltered during his second year, his teammates persuaded manager Heinie Smith to remove him from the rotation and play him at first base instead. When stationed there, his fellow infielders purposely made poor throws to expose his defensive shortcomings.[10]

Veterans who ignored, teased, and tormented anxious rookies did so for a variety of reasons. Sometimes, it was just callousness born of indifference. If a young player was not expected to make the team, why not have a little fun at the kid's expense? That same rule sometimes applied to utility players whose spot on the team was tenuous at best. Even some players who made the team received the silent treatment. Catcher Luke Sewell spent his first two years sitting alone on the bench. He didn't even get to take batting practice until his third year. "They knew I wasn't going to play, so they didn't want to waste any time with me," he recalled.[11]

Veterans treated young players like Sewell as annoying but generally harmless cankers. They called new recruits "bushers," in reference to the obscure minor league locales from which they came, or "yannigans," a slang term of unclear etymology but which came to imply the disreputability and unimportance of all new recruits (or "rookies"). Veterans used both terms dismissively: until a young player proved his mettle, he deserved no personal recognition. So far as veterans were concerned, a busher could do no good.[12] Even the well-mannered and congenitally polite Christy Mathewson wanted little to do with young players: "The trouble with most of them is that they think they are wonders when they arrive." William Phelon, one of the era's best sportswriters, captured the rookie's dilemma. As Phelon saw it, if a young player tried to blend in by being quiet and unobtrusive, veterans immediately labeled him yellow or "destitute of the cool pluck" needed to play big league ball. If he tried to be overly friendly or familiar, veterans considered him cocky, fresh, and conceited. If he worked hard in practice to prove his ability, he ran the risk of being called a show-off and overly ambitious to displace a veteran. Yet if he went easy at practice to save himself, the same teammates might wonder if he was "a lazy shirk and insubordinate." No matter how the rookie behaved, Phelon concluded, "he is everybody's goat and he simply will not do."[13]

Most typically, veterans treated rookies with disdain because they feared for their jobs. There was no safety net in baseball; the majors would not offer pensions to retired players until the late 1940s. In this ruthless world, players did all they could to retain their spot on the team. Older players were rightly convinced that any "youngster" on the team "was in there after one of their jobs," one old-timer recalled. Hans Lobert observed, "The ranks of big leagues are continually overcrowded." As a result, the competition for jobs was "fierce and constant" and kept "a man keyed up to his maximum endurance" all season. That management often used rookies for their own purposes certainly did not help young players endear themselves to other players. Some managers arbitrarily cut veterans in favor of rookies simply to save money. Others brought rookies in for spring training just to motivate sluggish players to get into shape. Veterans resented rookies as "aliens" at best, management stooges at worst.[14]

Yet hazing was not merely a reactionary impulse; it often played an important role in helping players to shape their team's culture. Veterans might not be able to decide who would be their teammates, but they could at least try to influence how new recruits would act. By teasing, harassing, intimidating, and pranking, veterans enforced a code of behavior upon their potential new teammates. As Ty Cobb learned, rookies faced a tough road if they refused to conform to the veterans' expectations. Just as laboring men tried to retain control over their place of work by socializing new men into the rhythms and patterns of the shop floor so, too, veteran players learned to impose their values upon aspiring teammates. By testing young players, veterans made it clear that when it came to team culture they—not management—were in charge. If a new player wanted to fit in, he would first need to appease his tormentors. What John McGraw called the clubhouse's "very rigid rule of seniority" was reinforced by a number of general practices, common to all teams. Veterans got the first crack at the batting cage. They got to sit on the better seats on the bench, on trains, and at restaurants. On overnight train rides, veterans always got the lower berths on sleepers, leaving rookies to contend with the warmer air and closer proximity to the overhead lights that blazed through the night. Veterans believed such ordeals helped to toughen up younger players so that they would be more prepared for the battles on the ball field. As Cobb himself observed, older players were intent on making each rookie "a man or break his spirit doing it."[15]

As a collective activity, baseball's hazing rituals also fostered team unity. This may have been the practice's most important function. Veterans believed hazing was an indispensible part of team culture. As social groups that needed to function at a high level for an extended period, players established a variety of informal practices and customs that enabled them to integrate new members, establish codes of acceptable behavior, enhance cooperation, and control dissension. Players relied upon managers to help with all these matters, to be sure, but they also believed that the team culture should be an extension of themselves, not just the manager. Thus, ballplayers tried to integrate every new ballplayer into the mix through a variety of means. Most teams were an eclectic, potentially rancorous mix of personalities—divided by regional, class, and ethnic differences. Cobb's teammates, for example, came from the coal mines of Arkansas, city streets of the industrial Northeast, small towns in the Midwest, and the farmlands of the Great Plains. A few had college degrees; most had not even finished high school. The team included sober middle-class Protestants, devout Catholics, and a diverse array of hard-drinking toughs. Players lived, worked, ate, and shared hotel rooms from March through September—and sometimes longer if a team went to the World Series or agreed to play exhibition games immediately after the season. The mix of personalities could be volatile. Hazing was not a cure-all, but it did help alleviate some problems by teaching young players how to behave and by reinforcing general rules of conduct. True, veterans might exacerbate already toxic situations if they became too malicious, but this rarely seemed to happen. Mostly veterans simply wanted to have a few laughs even as they imposed a bit of order on what might have been a very unpleasant environment.

At their most innocent, veterans used hazing to make sure rookies knew how to take a joke and were sociable enough to make their presence bearable for eight months of the year. As players saw it, overly somber players made poor teammates over the long haul. And who better to lift the team's spirits than a naïve busher. To test a rookie's appetite for a good laugh, veterans committed any number of high jinks. The player who could take a joke and dish one out on occasion easily gained the friendship of his peers. Jimmy Dykes had nothing but fond memories of his days with the Philadelphia Athletics in the late 1920s precisely because they learned to laugh together. "It was a hell of a bunch of guys," Dykes recalled. "Anything could happen in that clubhouse"—and apparently did. "Shoes nailed to the floor. Sweat shirts tied into knots. Itching powder in your jockstrap. You're out there in front of thirty thousand people and dying to scratch. Christ. Limburger cheese smeared on your hatband on a hot day." Clearly, Dykes passed the good humor test.[16]

Sometimes veterans decided they had to take drastic action to break in a rookie who seemed reluctant to fit in. Lobert was a teetotaler when he joined the Reds in 1906 in what would become his first full season in the majors. To hard-drinking teammates Cy Seymour, Shad Barry, Larry McLean, and Jimmy Delahanty, this simply would not do. Lobert quickly proved his ability on the ball field, but his peers wanted evidence he could also fit in away from the park. While sitting in a restaurant after a game one day, Seymour and company urged Lobert to join them in a pint. Lobert refused with a curt, "I don't drink beer. I've never tasted it." In a moment, they grabbed him, held him down, and proceeded to pour beer down his throat. Ever obstinate, Lobert kept his mouth closed, forcing the beer to spill until he was drenched. "Finally, I'd had enough," Lobert recalled and agreed to have a beer. Thereafter, Lobert became a regular, though temperate, member of the drinking crowd.[17]

On rare occasions, veterans went even further. If a player proved particularly annoying, conceited, or hardboiled, teammates expressed their disapproval by engaging in petty acts of sabotage. Most often, these were anonymous acts, meant to demonstrate to the victim that the entire team disapproved of his behavior. In a few cases, a veteran might perform the nearly unthinkable: destroy some poor rookie's bats. It did not happen often, but when it did, it was an act loaded with meaning. A bat, obviously, had deep phallic meaning: they were long, hard, and extraordinarily massive—especially in the early twentieth century. As such, they offered the most visible representation of a hitter's power. Today major league bats usually weigh between 31 and 33 ounces and are about 34 inches in length with narrow handles; the bats of the Dead Ball Era usually weighed well over 40 ounces, were an inch or two longer, and far thicker around the handle (in his prime, Cobb used a 44-ounce bat with a thick handle). Sawing such an enormous weapon in half symbolized quite an act of castration. This was a deeply personal act. Most players viewed their bats as extensions of themselves. They often brought them from home where they oversaw the entire construction process, from choosing the wood, determining its size, and selecting the finish. Some even baptized their bats—often using diverse bodily fluids—supposing that whatever unique concoction they came up with would give their bat some mystical power. Many players fussed over their bats as if they were animate objects. To some, they *were* animate objects. Star second baseman and Columbia University graduate Eddie Collins buried his bats in cow manure "to keep them alive." Nearly all named their bats, showing a preference for feminine names (Bessie, Nellie, Betsy), perhaps because engendering the bat as female somehow justified the batter's devotion to his tool. No doubt, female names also helped batters experience a feeling of control over their prized possessions.[18]

Obviously, a bat was a very important piece of equipment. A bat was a tool of the trade, as essential as a baseball glove, but far more conspicuous and fragile. Veterans well understood all this when they set out to destroy some hapless rookie's stick. Perhaps the rookie had proved especially obnoxious for refusing to submit to the usual pranks of hazing in good humor. Perhaps he had raised the ire of veterans simply because management wanted him to replace a popular teammate. Or perhaps he preened too much—as Cobb did when he strode to the plate swinging three bats. Whatever the cause, the message veterans imparted could not have been plainer: the team had the ability to deprive a player of his livelihood, destroy his talisman of power. With no bat, the player became weak, vulnerable, and dependent. Until he had an opportunity to purchase or make a new bat, he would need to ask a teammate for a loaner, a humbling experience to be sure. Beyond the sheer joy of destroying personal property, this may have been the point all along. Veterans who broke a rookie's bat hoped to force the young player into a new relationship with the team—a relationship in which he recognized the team's hold upon him.

Cobb's troubles with his teammates began as soon as he arrived at the Tigers' training camp in Augusta in March 1906. Having hardly distinguished himself the previous fall, he understood it would be difficult to win a spot on the team, much less play regularly. That the Tigers had acquired former Chicago Cub Davy Jones, a good hitting and slick fielding outfielder, during the off-season suggested how little confidence they had in Cobb. The great Sam Crawford was anchored in one outfield position, leaving Cobb, Jones, and Matty McIntyre, a twenty-six-year-old veteran of two seasons, to compete for the other two spots.

As a still-raw nineteen-year-old with only forty-one mostly unremarkable games behind him, Cobb knew he was likely to be the odd man out. Even so, he was not the only one to feel anxious that spring. The light-hitting McIntyre was also worried for his career. Sometime during the winter, McIntyre seems to have decided that the best way to keep his place on the team was to drive Cobb off it. Though McIntyre had completed only his second full season in the major leagues, he possessed enough social capital to enlist the assistance of several principles on the team. Together, these players made Cobb's life unbearable— "the most miserable and humiliating experience I've ever been through," he said later.[19]

McIntyre and his cronies began their assault on Cobb's psyche almost immediately. At first, they resorted to petty insults designed to make his life unbearable. At the batting cage, they shouldered him out of the batter's box, called him "a sand-lotter," and told him the cage was for "men only." At restaurants, they impaled his straw hat on the coat rack and squished rotten fruit into his coat pocket. As he sat eating his meal, they whipped peas at him. On train rides, they targeted the back of his neck with soggy wads of newspaper. When the team made it back to the hotel after a game, players forced Cobb to the rear of the shower line so that he often had to stand in the hallway for hours, dirty and sweat-stained. Such acts were annoying, petty, and spiteful; in time, they became far more malicious. Prior to one spring game, Cobb discovered someone had ripped the stitching of his only good glove and shattered his bats. This truly riled Cobb. Made by a family friend back in Royston, Cobb had chosen the wood for each of his bats personally, fine Georgia black ash, and he obsessed about their care.[20] Though Cobb knew who his enemies were, they rarely had the temerity to confront him face to face. "I could never prove a thing," Cobb complained. Just before the season began, the anti-Cobb faction became bolder. Prior to an exhibition game in Hattiesburg, Mississippi, they told catcher Charlie Schmidt, a former boxer who had once sparred with Jack Johnson, that Cobb bragged that he had licked Schmidt in a fight. Proud of his reputation for pugilism, Schmidt stomped off to prove the boast wrong. Schmidt found Cobb walking toward the field from the dugout. According to Cobb, Schmidt stepped behind him, called his name, and sucker punched him flat in the face, breaking his nose.[21]

Cobb claimed none of this was his fault. All he wanted was to fit in, to be part of the team. One thing about Cobb: he knew how to produce a compelling narrative—the erstwhile young man, fresh from the country, only wanted a chance to play ball. All winter long, he had "dreamed of becoming part of the Detroit organization." Yet when he showed up, he was immediately "greeted with jealousy and persecution." But his enemies, "narrow and uneducated," would not allow him that right. Instead, they forced him into confrontations that ultimately turned violent. In this way, the "hazers" turned the "cheerful young fellow into a lone wolf" and ruthless competitor. The entire episode with the McIntyre clique left him "sick at heart and disillusioned."[22]

That was the way Cobb remembered it. His teammates had a different perspective. They bristled when they heard his rendition of his first year in the majors. Davy Jones expressed complete frustration with Cobb. He claimed he initially tried to befriend Cobb and help him adjust to the major leagues, but gave up early in the season, alienated, he said, by Cobb's "rotten disposition." It was too "damn hard to be his friend," Jones recalled. "He antagonized so many people that hardly anyone would speak to him." Crawford agreed. "We weren't cannibals or heathens," Crawford asserted. "We were all ballplayers together, trying to get along." But Cobb "came up with such an antagonistic attitude," he "turned any little razzing into a life-or-death struggle."[23]

Because of these discrepancies, Cobb's narrative of the confrontation requires far greater scrutiny. One way to approach this is to consider a question that no Cobb biographer has heretofore considered: Why did McIntyre focus on Cobb rather than the newcomer Jones? At the start of spring training, Cobb had little going for him. Manager Armour liked Cobb's speed, but rightly considered him raw and undisciplined. Armour was closer to the veteran players—including McIntyre—and generally gave them a free rein to break curfew, haze rookies (including Cobb), and play the game as they saw fit. He rarely praised Cobb and showed little patience for his rookie blunders and habitual recklessness. At twenty-six, Jones was far more disciplined and mature. Although he had played in the minors the previous year (hitting .346 for the American Association), he had three years of major league experience, mostly with the Chicago Cubs. At the start of spring training, the Detroit press penciled Jones in as a starting outfielder and predicted Cobb would spend most of his time on the bench. If McIntyre was as anxious about his place on the team as Cobb insisted, why target Cobb for abuse and welcome the more accomplished Jones?[24]

Cobb could not have been as naïve or as unknowing regarding the ways of veterans as he claims. If there is a constant to Cobb's career to this point it is that he was always the upstart rookie battling for a job against wily and sometimes desperate veterans. This had been the case when he first played ball for the Royston Roosters as a young teen, when he joined the Augusta Tourists and later the Anniston Steelers as a pretentious seventeen-year-old. Hazing was as endemic to those teams as it was to the Tigers. Indeed, given the marginality of semi-professional and minor-league ball, one might expect that the hazing he received there was far more ruthless and crude than what he initially experienced when he joined the Tigers. Cobb experienced hazing before and apparently knew how to handle it. He was never a particularly popular player among his teammates—he was far too much of a show-off and individualist to be readily accepted by most—but he never attracted the sort of animosity that came his way in Detroit. Therefore, it is reasonable to ask what happened to make Cobb the object of his fellow Tigers' scorn.

The most likely answer is not that some teammates suddenly decided to go after Cobb, but that Cobb himself changed in ways that at first annoyed and ultimately riled his teammates. Off-season events dramatically affected his life, so much so that the Cobb who came to camp in early March 1906 was a very different individual than the young man who joined the team the previous August. Then he was still very much in shock from the tragic and disturbing news of his father's death. He was far away from home, traveling to unfamiliar cities with individuals who were very different from himself. Indeed, many of Cobb's teammates were the descendants of Irish and German immigrants, raised in the big cities and industrial towns of the Northeast. Only a handful came from the countryside like Cobb. Many were Catholics. Some frequented brothels and sporting clubs. Nearly all smoked and drank hard liquor. They swore prodigiously, a habit Cobb had not picked up. As a group, they could hardly have been more different from Cobb in upbringing and personal habits. No wonder Cobb largely kept to himself. For their part, teammates viewed Cobb as something of a shy and painfully polite Southern rube. They could barely understand his thick

Georgian drawl and sometimes teased him about it. They also razzed him when he made the occasional boner. Whatever hazing Ty received that fall he took in good humor, but otherwise kept mostly to himself.[25]

By the spring, Cobb was in a different place. He had developed a more profound understanding of what his father's death would mean to himself and his family. William had raised the Cobbs to a position of social and political prominence in and around Franklin County, but the family was hardly wealthy. William's salary as a teacher, school administrator, and state senator had been high enough to enable him to buy a fine home and own several acres of good farmland to supplement the family income. But the family had probably used up whatever savings they had to save Amanda from prison (and the family from further scandal). The Chitwood family may have helped pay for Amanda's legal defense, but Ty could not expect continued support. Since none of Ty's siblings were old enough to work, the family's financial fate now rested almost solely with him. When he left Detroit in October, he was not even sure he would be able to play ball the following year. Worried, Cobb took a job at the University of Georgia that winter, to coach incoming track and baseball athletes. At nineteen, he was now his family's sole breadwinner.[26]

William's death thrust Ty into a position of family leadership and responsibility that must have seemed overwhelming to the young man. As a youth, he had yearned to set out on his own and make a name for himself. For Ty, leaving home to play ball had marked the beginning of his journey to adulthood. To become a man was one thing, but this was something else entirely. Because William had died, duty compelled Ty to assume his father's role—to not only help support the family financially, but to become the head of the household, the person that the community would now identify with the Cobb name. It was an enormous responsibility given the mark that William had made upon the world. Ty understood what this involved. The privileged status he had enjoyed as a youth—indeed his conviction that he came from a superior blood line—derived largely from his father's labors to lift the family from relative obscurity to a place of local prominence. Although Ty's ancestors were only tangentially related to such southern luminaries as Thomas Cobb and Thomas Reade Rootes Cobb, William had made the connection seem so much more immediate by the strength of his character and his burgeoning career in public life. To Ty, William personified true Southern manhood. He was independent, strong, and intelligent—a man of honor with an iron will. Now William was gone and all that he had worked to achieve for the family was in peril—unless Ty could learn to do as his father had done.

In traditional white Southern culture, young men earned the mantle of manhood by demonstrating moral and emotional maturation. Ty never went through this rite of passage; rather, the responsibility was thrust upon him. Taking the role of patriarch of the Cobb family must have been a drastic turn of events for Ty. Heretofore, he had been something of a man-child—free to indulge his desire to play ball and to enjoy life, responsible to no one. Now with his father gone, the responsibilities must have seemed overwhelming. Assuming the place of one's father was a difficult task for any young man. For Cobb it must have been especially difficult. Heretofore, he had shown little inclination to mature in ways that might help him act the part of the family head. In time, he would prove particularly adept at providing for the material needs and desires of his Georgia kin. That was in the future. For now, his annual baseball salary of $1,500 would have to be stretched to support his mother and siblings.

Cobb must have found it particularly challenging to keep his emotions in check regarding the circumstances of his father's death. He was impetuous, stubborn, and often ill-tempered. Now circumstances demanded he act with grace and reserve. In the face of persistent rumors that his mother had murdered his father, Ty did his best to put family honor above personal grief by publicly showing his continued love and respect for his mother. He sat next to her at all court proceedings and otherwise treated Amanda as if her place in the family was unchanged. If he doubted her story, he never admitted it—either publicly or privately. Although Ty never showed Amanda the sort of reverence he gave his father, he understood his responsibilities to her. She was a frequent guest in Ty's home, often staying for months at a time. In death, Ty buried her next to William's grave in Royston. Later, Ty himself would be buried with them.

Had William's life not ended prematurely, he might have taught Ty that men acted with restraint, wisdom, and grace. But it seems unlikely that at this late date in Ty's maturation the elder Cobb could have had much influence. William had tried to teach these traits to Ty all along, even as he had also taught him to be determined and assertive. Moreover, William was only one of many men who influenced Ty in his formative years. Some of the others, namely Ty's peers and fellow ballplayers, embraced values that undermined William's influence. Finally, Ty seems to have had a personality predisposed to competitiveness and impetuousness. He was a selective learner—picking and choosing from William's words of wisdom as he saw fit. He often invoked his father's dictum—"Beware of entrance to a quarrel, but being in it—let them beware!"—to justify his role in some altercation. That William rarely, if ever, resorted to fisticuffs himself seems to have left no impression on Ty.[27]

The stage was set for one of the most heated and brutal intra-team conflicts in modern professional sports. On the one side were a handful of veterans determined to impose their will upon the team. On the other side stood Cobb, equally determined to prove himself a man in the only way he knew how. By all accounts, Cobb got the worst of it. By the time the season started, Cobb had become a pariah on the team. He ate alone, roomed alone, and sat alone on the long train rides from city to city. For a brief time, rookie pitcher Edgar Willett—a fellow Southerner—shared an apartment with Cobb—but McIntyre and company told Willett that either he move out or he was finished. Thereafter, Cobb rarely socialized with any of his teammates, save a few of the oldest players who offered occasional words of encouragement, but otherwise refused to get involved. Manager Bill Armour offered little help, preferring to stay out of personal disputes. The maltreatment continued and became unrelenting: "When I came off the field, they would hit me with the bad plays I'd made. If I went for the water bucket somebody would kick it over. They cut nicks in my bats, put horse turds in my spare shoes. They were waiting for me every time I turned around."[28]

As the season progressed, the rift between Cobb and his adversaries became an infected sore that seeped onto the playing field. McIntyre told manager Armour that he "hated Cobb and wouldn't play with him." True to his word, while batting in one game, he made "no apparent effort to hit the ball" to score base runner Cobb. When the opposing catcher asked McIntyre about his lack of effort, McIntyre replied, "You don't think I'm going to help that —— to the plate, do you?" and promptly struck out. The incident finally forced Armour to act—albeit tentatively. He suspended McIntyre without pay, but inexplicably reinstated him almost immediately. Thus, the feud continued unabated.[29]

The environment became so hostile that Cobb took to sequestering himself in the groundskeeper's storage shack adjacent to the left-field bleachers before games. While the rest of the team warmed up, Cobb sat alone in the dark, waiting for the game to begin. He became anxious, enraged, and frightened.[30]

McIntyre and company made life hell for Cobb, but in one important respect, their efforts failed miserably—at least at first: try as they might, they could not affect his play. In fact, Cobb proved to be one of the team's best performers that year, showing flashes of the star he would soon become. Although Armour intended to use Cobb primarily as a reserve, Cobb changed the manager's mind by making the most of his opportunities. When Davy Jones went down with a muscle strain in early May, Cobb started in twenty-three straight games, got at least one hit in all but two of them, and raised his average from .281 to a team-leading .330. Meanwhile, McIntyre struggled to find playing time as his average failed to get much above .250. In fact, the entire Tigers' lineup struggled to hit during the first months of the season. During one disastrous eastern road trip, the team batting average plummeted eighteen points to a season low .245. By late June, Cobb led the team with a .355 average, the only Tiger above .300. The press took notice. The *Detroit News* called him "the great little centerfielder" and pronounced him the hit of the league. For two straight weeks in early June, *Sporting News* correspondent B. F. Wright highlighted Cobb's batting exploits while simultaneously chastising veteran sluggers, including McIntyre and Crawford, for their poor showing. When news broke a few weeks later that some established players hated Cobb, Wright blamed it all on the veterans' petty jealousies. Cobb, Wright claimed, was a "batter of rare prowess and promise and a base runner with few peers." Veterans had better get used to playing with the young Georgian, Wright warned, because the young outfielder had proved he belonged on the club.[31] Cobb later claimed that his success during this time stemmed directly from the treatment he received. "The fact is the clique did me a tremendous favor," Cobb boasted. "In driving me off by myself, they gave me time to think"—and Cobb trained himself to think only of baseball. What's more, "the attitude of my teammates gave me the extra incentive of becoming a top player," just so he could "show them up."³²

In fact, Cobb was not as impervious to stress as he later claimed. By late June, it all became too much for the young Georgian. In a matter of a few weeks, his batting average dropped over forty points, from a season high .363, third highest in the league, to .318. But that was not the whole of it. Heretofore playing had served as a distraction and an escape, but now he appeared listless and distracted. Some wondered if he was ill. Close observers noticed that when he batted, his legs and hands shook uncontrollably. He lost speed on the base paths and fielded tentatively. When Manager Armour asked Cobb what was wrong, he answered vaguely that he was just "off his feed." Observers suggested that Cobb looked tired and apathetic. Suddenly, on July 18, during an eastern road trip, Cobb left the team. Armour told the press that Cobb had "stomach trouble" and that he had ordered him to return to Detroit to recover. Nine days later, the *Detroit News* broke the story—Cobb was in a sanitarium and would probably be there for some time.³³

Years later, sportswriter and Cobb's ghostwriter Al Stump claimed Cobb told him he suffered a "nervous breakdown." "My nerves were shot to hell," Stump claimed Cobb told him. "I was like a steel spring with a dangerous flaw in it . . . if wound too tight, the spring will fly apart and then is done for."³⁴ Although Stump was a prodigious liar, the circumstances in which Cobb fell ill, his behavior prior to his disappearance from the team, and the treatment he received—so far as newspapers reported it, suggest Stump may have been telling the truth on this one. If so, doctors probably treated Cobb for "neurasthenia," the almost universal turn-of-the-century diagnosis for men and women who suffered from some sort of nerve trouble. Neurologist George Beard, the leading expert of the day, described neurasthenia as an exhaustion of "nerve force" caused by overstimulation and emotional strain. Most troubling, neurasthenia seemed to paralyze the individual's will, making the patient weak, vacillating, anxious, and timid. The medical community was especially concerned with the disease's impact upon the nation's young men as it robbed them of the virility, stamina, and personal conviction to succeed in life. This certainly seems to have been the case with Cobb: In the weeks before he was hospitalized, McIntyre and his mates seem to have reduced Cobb to the antithesis of the man he wanted and his family needed him to be.[35]

This was a moment of crisis. Cobb's breakdown, whatever its cause, might easily have permanently derailed his career. Other professional ballplayers—older and more experienced than Cobb—had seen their careers ruined by an inability to handle the pressures associated with the game. Most had walked away rather than face the scrutiny and outright ridicule of fans, press, and fellow players. Some had turned to drink. A hapless few—perhaps as many as sixteen during the first two decades of the twentieth century—committed suicide.[36] Cobb rarely discussed his mental state in the wake of his hospitalization. Stump claims Cobb confided to him that he even considered quitting, but decided to stick it out because he believed he was "getting close to making a real reputation" as a player. It was, he said, "a matter of honor." Thus resolved, he "rested up . . . pulled out of it."[37] No matter how sanguine Cobb was in hindsight, we can well imagine that the nineteen-year-old had moments of great anxiety as he contemplated his future as a ballplayer. He had never been away from home for so long, had virtually no support network in Detroit, and was still reeling from the personal family traumas of the previous summer. The typical treatment called for extensive rest and minimal contact with the outside world. Once Cobb was well enough, doctors encouraged him to hike in the woods and fish in nearby streams—all in an effort to help the troubled young man reclaim aspects of his jeopardized manhood. Gradually, doctors reintroduced Cobb to his chosen profession. Once he was up to it, doctors even allowed him to play ball with a team from the Detroit Athletic Club. It proved exceedingly therapeutic. The league was strictly amateur, but included a number of aspiring and former professional players. Most important, Cobb's team accepted him warmly. From there, Cobb made a relatively quick recovery. Medical experts agreed that neurasthenics often took months to recover. According to newspaper accounts, doctors who treated Cobb did not believe he would be able to play again that season. Nevertheless, Cobb returned in a matter of weeks, reentering the lineup on September 2. Although he refused to discuss his whereabouts with the press or teammates, privately he must have reveled in his triumph, proof of his indomitable fortitude. In the meantime, he still had to face down those who had driven him off the team. [38]

Unfortunately, Cobb returned to a team that was even more riddled by dissension and cliques than the one he had left just six weeks earlier. Chief financial officer Frank Navin announced just days before Cobb's return that Armour would be let go at the end of the season and replaced with Hughie Jennings, the former star infielder of the old Baltimore Orioles.[39] Navin's choice proved to be an excellent one almost immediately: Jennings directed the previously underperforming Tigers to three straight World Series appearances in the first three years of his tenure. But the short-term results were disastrous. Players denounced ownership for sacking the popular and easygoing Armour before the season was over. Rather than rally to Armour's defense by playing hard for the remainder of the season, however, most abruptly quit on him. Within days, the *Detroit News* announced in its daily Tigers headline, "No One Seems to Care About Team." According to the accompanying report, only Crawford, third baseman Bill Coughlin, and "the youngsters" played with much "ginger." The rest routinely begged off playing, claiming an assortment of excuses. Just before one game, the manager learned that his scheduled starting pitcher, Ed Siever, was not at the ballpark. In desperation, Armour ran out untested rookie Jack Rowan to start against the second-place Chicago White Sox. Making his major league debut, Rowan gave up thirteen runs, including eight in the first inning; it was the most runs the "hitless wonders" of baseball amassed all year. When reached by the press afterward, Siever shrugged off his unexplained absence, telling the press that he had attended the Michigan State Fair instead, adding incomprehensibly, "What was the use of going to the park? It wasn't my turn to pitch." Cryptically, a reporter asked, "Who is running the team anyway?" Disgusted and discouraged, Armour briefly absented himself, leaving the ever-steady Bill Coughlin in charge. Disgruntled players continued to test the limits of management's control. The situation became so out of hand that league president Ban Johnson felt compelled to stick his head into the mess by publicly criticizing several Tigers' players for not playing up to their abilities.[40]

It was a chaotic situation for Cobb to return to, one that must have exposed him to even more harassment and abuse. Adding to his woes, he was not quite up to par physically. Those close to the team noted that he still appeared weak and frail at times. The *Detroit News* reported that he nearly fainted from the heat toward the end of a mid-September contest. Only a quick shower revived him enough to finish the game. In another instance, Cobb looked so weak late in the game, Armour sent in pitcher George Mullin to bat for him. Still, Cobb believed he had little choice but to play. McIntyre and his clique had driven him from the team once; he could not allow them to do so again. Moreover, he desperately wanted revenge—and that meant he had to stick with the team. Through guts and guile—attributes that would soon become his trademark—he played well down the stretch, batting an impressive .320 for the rest of the season and stealing bases with greater frequency than he had shown before his absence.[41]

McIntyre and company must have been dumbstruck to see Cobb playing so well after all they had forced him to endure. Still, they never relented; instead, they used Cobb's recent confinement to question both his manhood and his mental stability. All the while, they deftly stopped short of provoking an actual fight. Yet a fight is exactly what Cobb wanted. For the entire season he had longed to confront his enemies. His honor depended on it. The McIntyre clique had assaulted his manhood at every turn and shattered his confidence. To redeem his manhood, Cobb believed he had to defeat McIntyre and his cronies at their own game. That is, he had to humiliate them just as they had humiliated him. Now that he was back with the team, payback became his obsession—but on his terms. He was determined to live by the code of honor his father taught him, that is he would not start a fight, but he certainly would finish one. "To force an issue that was thrust upon me, and then follow up, had been part of my training as a boy," he reminded himself.[42]

Cobb finally got his chance for revenge on the night before the last game of the season. Earlier in the day in a game at St. Louis, the Browns' George Stone, the league's top hitter that year, singled sharply past shortstop. Playing center, Cobb started toward the ball only to see that McIntyre in left, whose "responsibility to try for it was as great as mine," had refused to move. Playing tit for tat, Cobb stopped dead in his tracks and yelled at McIntyre to field the ball himself. Of course,

McIntyre remained immobile as the ball came to rest deep in the outfield. Their shared stubbornness enabled Stone to race around the bases for a two-run inside-the-park home run—the hit that decided the game. McIntyre's friend and fellow Cobb-hater Ed Siever just happened to be on the mound while all this transpired. Although both outfielders had been at fault, Siever immediately turned toward Cobb in centerfield and launched into a verbal assault that was loud enough for most everyone in the ballpark to hear. When Cobb returned to the dugout at the end of the inning, Siever started up again, this time denigrating Cobb's ancestry and Southern roots. Cobb was furious. There in front of the Tigers' bench, in full view of the grandstands and with the game still in progress, Cobb challenged Siever to fight. The pitcher demurred. To Cobb, this smacked of cowardice. He could barely contain his rage. "Where I came from, men had been killed for saying what Siever did," he asserted in his final autobiography, still irate a half century later.[43]

That night back in the lobby of the Planters' Hotel, the two went at it again. They almost came to blows when veteran pitcher "Wild" Bill Donovan, a convivial sort who got along with most everyone—including Cobb—stepped between the two would-be combatants and offered a fatherly "Let's not have any trouble, boys." Fighting down his anger, Cobb told Donovan, "I want no trouble," and walked away. That ended things for the moment, although Cobb remained on edge. When he saw Siever talking to McIntyre, he moved closer and hid behind a pillar to catch what they were saying. Siever spied Cobb, called him a "vile name," and swept around the column in hopes of catching Cobb from behind. No chance. As Siever swung wildly at his face, Cobb deftly blocked the blow with one hand and counterpunched with the other. He followed this up with several punches to the face as Siever slumped to the ground. It was the most brutal mauling Cobb had yet administered in the major leagues. When he was done, he calmly stepped over his victim and walked away, satisfied that he was finally able to "let go all my pent-up emotion." Some witnesses claim he returned moments later and administered one last blow—a savage kick to Siever's face. Later Cobb claimed he could not remember kicking Siever, but it would have been in keeping with Cobb's fighting ethic to have done so. Siever had questioned Cobb's honor and denigrated his name. Enraged, he would have wanted to humiliate Siever, not just defeat him. If that wasn't justification enough, Cobb had about six months of rage boiling within him and a convenient opportunity to finally let it out. Clearly, Siever had no idea just what he was getting himself into when he insulted and then physically attacked Cobb. The message Cobb sent the rest of the team could not have been clearer.[44]

Still, Cobb could not relax. He was convinced McIntyre and his cronies would try to retaliate before the season ended and feared they would have the perfect opportunity to do so once the team boarded the train for Chicago for the season's last game. Fearing retaliation, he stayed awake all night in his birth, clutching his pistol and listening to noises in the corridor. "I was armed and ready," he later recalled. "And I remained ready until the day came when I was established as a Detroit regular."[45]

On this tumultuous note, Cobb's first full season in the majors ended. Despite the challenges he faced, he had performed extraordinarily well. He played in just under 100 games, compiling an overall batting average of .316, almost eighty points higher than his average the previous fall. This was good for fifth best in the American League, ahead of such proven hitters as Elmer Flick, Elberfeld, and Wee Willie Keeler. Cobb was the only Tiger to hit above .300 that year and his batting average was seventy-eight points higher than the team's composite average and twenty-five points higher than the next best hitter, Sam Crawford. Team ownership was impressed. When Cleveland approached the Tigers about trading their disgruntled outfielder (and future Hall of Famer) Elmer Flick for one of the Tigers' disgruntled players, team secretary Frank Navin told them that the team would keep Cobb, but might want to move McIntyre. It was a telling statement: Cobb had won the battle for a place on the Tigers. What's more he was rapidly making a name for himself as a star player. Detroit's local correspondent to the *Sporting News*, B. F. Wright, even suggested that Cobb was nearly as popular as the league's best pitcher, George Edward "Rube" Waddell.[46]

Cobb remembered his first full year in the majors with a mixture of satisfaction and regret. On the one hand, he had proven he could play in the major leagues and simultaneously demonstrated to his adversaries on the team that he would not be cowed. When the season ended, he claimed to have "far more confidence" than when he had first been called up fourteen months earlier. On the other hand, the constant run-ins with his teammates left him "sick at heart." He had wanted to be an integral part of the team, but had been met with "jealousy and persecution" instead. "I had an idea," he recalled toward the end of his career, "that (the) big leagues would be anxious to help a young fellow make good: take a fatherly interest. I was soon disillusioned."[47]

"The first disillusionment," as he later called it, was his encounter with Elberfeld. The second was the drama of the McIntyre feud, which culminated when Cobb mauled Siever. The two events bracketed his traumatic fourteen-month initiation into the American League like bookends, offering similar lessons on how to conduct himself in the world of professional baseball. His run-in with Elberfeld convinced him that he needed to take the offensive on the field; his feud with McIntyre and resulting mental breakdown revealed to him that he needed to be equally assertive off the field. That is, he had either to dominate or face the prospect of submitting to the will of those who would dominate him. His father, grandfathers, and adolescent peers had introduced him to this ethic as a child; the events of the past year revealed the true gravity of life and the necessity of following their lead.[48]

NOTES

1. Ty Cobb, with Al Stump, *My Life in Baseball* (1961; repr., Lincoln, NE: Bison Books, 1993), 19–20.

2. Ty Cobb, edited by William R. Cobb, *Memoirs of Twenty Years in Baseball* (Marietta, GA: Self-published, 2002), 42, 6; Ty Cobb, *Inside Baseball with Ty Cobb*, edited by Wesley Fricks (Salt Lake City: Aardvark Publishing, 2007), 134.

3. Cobb, *Memoirs*, 42; Cobb, *My Life*, 19–20; Fricks, ed., *Inside Baseball*, 134; Ty Cobb, "Tricks That Won Me Ball Games," *Life* (March 24, 1952): 63–64.

4. On memory, see Alfred Young, *The Shoemaker and the Tea Party: Memory and the American Revolution* (New York: Beacon Press, 1999), viii–xvi, 11–12; David K. Dunaway and Willa K. Baum, eds., *Oral History: An Interdisciplinary Anthology*, 2nd ed. (Plymouth, UK: AltaMira Press, 1996); Thomas Charlton, Lois E. Myers, and Rebecca Sharpless, eds., *Handbook of Oral History* (Plymouth, UK: AltaMira Press, 2006).

5. "Editorially: The Spirit of the Times," *Baseball Magazine* (October 1909): 1.

6. Al Stump, "Ty Cobb's Wild Ten-Month Fight to Live," 71. Stump fabricated many of the incidents in this article; nevertheless, he was right on this point: Cobb hungered for both vindication and respect. F. C. Lane, "Famous Rivals of the Diamond," *Baseball Magazine* (July 1913): 26.

7. Cobb, *My Life*, 23.

8. Cobb, *My Life*, 23–24.

9. Hans Lobert, "Breaking Into the Major Leagues: The Hard Struggle of Winning Success as a Big League Player," *Baseball Magazine* (May 1912): 29.

10. Tommy Leach, Fred Snodgrass, Al Bridwell, Harry Hooper, Chief Meyers in Lawrence S. Ritter, *The Glory of Their Times: The Story of the Early Days of Baseball Told by the Men Who Played It* (New York: Perennial, 1966), 25, 94, 128, 142, 172–73; *Sporting Life* (February 1, 1913): 5; Frank Deford, *The Old Ball Game: How John McGraw, Christy Mathewson, and the New York Giants Created Modern Baseball* (New York: Atlantic Monthly Press, 2005), 52.

11. Luke Sewell in Donald Honig, *The Man in the Dugout: Fifteen Big League Managers Speak Their Minds* (Lincoln, NE: Bison Books, 1977), 259.

12. Paul Dickson, *The Dickson New Baseball Dictionary*, 3rd ed. (New York: Harcourt Brace and Company, 1999), 951. Dickson offers evidence that the term is Celtic in origin and referred to an item that was easily beaten, like a worn rug or a soft-boiled egg.

13. Christy Mathewson, *Pitching in a Pinch: Baseball from the Inside* (1912. Reprint. Lincoln, NE: Bison Books, 1994), 213; William Phelon, "The Decline and Fall of the Left-Handed Batter," *Baseball Magazine* (July 1913): 62.

14. Lobert, "Breaking Into the Major Leagues," 28; Chief Meyers in Ritter, *Glory of Their Times*, 172; *Sporting Life* (April 17, 1915): 11; Mathewson, *Pitching in a Pinch*, 51–52.

15. John J. McGraw, *My Thirty Years in Baseball* (1923. Reprint. Lincoln: University of Nebraska Press, 1995), 45; Cobb, "They Don't Play Baseball Any More," *Life* (March 17, 1952): 148.

16. Sam Crawford in Ritter, *Glory of Their Times*, 62; Jimmy Dykes in Honig, *Man in the Dugout*, 281.

17. Hans Lobert in Ritter, *Glory of Their Times*, 192.

18. Jonathan Fraser Light, *The Cultural Encyclopedia of Baseball* (Jefferson, NC: McFarland, 1997), 75–80; H. G. Salsinger, *Ty Cobb: Two Biographies*, edited by William R. Cobb (Jefferson, NC: McFarland, 2012), 37–38.

19. Cobb, *My Life*, 20, 23–24; Al Stump, *Cobb* (Chapel Hill, NC: Algonquin Books, 1994), 118.

20. Cobb, *My Life*, 20, 23–24; Stump, *Cobb*, 118, 162, 192; Alexander, *Ty Cobb*, 91–92; Os. W. Brown, "Stories of the Players," *Baseball Magazine* (August 1909): 23–24.

21. Cobb, *My Life*, 25.

22. Cobb, *My Life*, 26, 27; *Atlanta Constitution*, June 1, 1934, 17, quoted in Tim Hornbaker, *War on the Basepaths: The Definitive Biography of Ty Cobb* (New York: Sports Publishing, 2015), 50.

23. Davy Jones in Ritter, *Glory of Their Times*, 41; Sam Crawford in Ritter, *Glory of Their Times*, 62.

24. Charles Leerhsen, *Ty Cobb: A Terrible Beauty* (New York: Simon and Schuster, 2015), 114.

25. Richard Bak, *Peach: Ty Cobb in His Time and Ours* (Ann Arbor: Sports Media Group, 2005), 36–37; Hornbaker, *War on the Basepaths*, 33; Leerhsen, *Ty Cobb*, 108, 115.

26. *Sporting Life* (October 21, 1905): 11; Leerhsen, *Ty Cobb*, 110–11; Hornbaker, *War on the Basepaths*, 29–30.

27. Cobb, *My Life*, 112.

28. Stump, *Cobb*, 119, 128; Cobb, *My Life*, 23–25.

29. Alexander, *Ty Cobb*, 42–43. Leerhsen, *Ty Cobb*, 124–26; Hornbaker, *War on the Basepaths*, 41–43.

30. Cobb, *My Life*, 23–25.

31. *Detroit News* (July 19, 1906): 10; *Sporting News* (June 2, 1906): 2; *Sporting News* (June 9, 1906): 2; *Sporting News* (July 7, 1906): 4.

32. Cobb, *My Life*, 26–27.

33. *Detroit Free Press*, July 19, 1906, 10.

34. Stump, *Cobb*, 128.

35. Gail Bederman, *Manliness and Civilization: A Cultural History of Gender and Race in the United States, 1880–1917* (Chicago: University of Chicago Press, 1995), 84–88; Jackson Lears, *Rebirth of a Nation: The Making of Modern America, 1877–1920* (New York: HarperCollins, 2009), 7–8, 68.

36. Bill James, *The New Bill James Historical Baseball Abstract* (revised edition; New York: Free Press, 2001), 87.

37. Stump, *Cobb*, 129.

38. Bederman, *Manliness and Civilization*, 84–88; Lears, *Rebirth of a Nation*, 7–8, 68.

39. *Detroit News*, September 2, 1906, "Sporting Section," 2.

40. *Detroit News*, September 7, 1906, 12; *Detroit News*, September 9, 1906, 6.

41. *Detroit News*, September 13, 1906, 12.

42. Cobb, *My Life*, 26.

43. Cobb, *My Life*, 26; Stump, *Cobb*, 132–33; *Detroit News*, October 7, 1906, "Sporting Section," 1.

44. Cobb, *My Life*, 26; Stump, *Cobb*, 132–33. On the role of vengeance in the Southern code of honor, see Greenberg, *Honor and Slavery*, 14, 56–59, 62–63, 25–32; Wyatt-Brown, *Southern Honor*, 25–61; Nisbett and Cohen, *Culture of Honor*, 1–12, 41–54.

45. Cobb, *My Life*, 27.

46. *Sporting News* (November 3, 1906): 4; *Sporting News* (November 17, 1906): 6.

47. Cobb, *My Life*, 26, 29, 31; Cobb, *Memoirs of Twenty Years*, 41.

48. Cobb, *Memoirs of Twenty Years*, 41.

4

HONOR

Toward the end of Cobb's difficult first full season in the majors, he made a vow to himself to win the 1907 American League batting championship. The inspiration came one night while walking the streets of St. Louis after having had dinner with the Tigers' utility infielder Bobby Lowe, one of the few players on the team who spoke to Cobb on a regular basis. The veteran Lowe often "took pity on a kid," as Cobb put it, by inviting him to dinner. On this particular night, they strolled past a store window that featured a display of a "gorgeous watch made of three kinds of gold." Under the watch read a banner: "TO BE AWARDED THE BATTING CHAMPION OF THE AMERICAN LEAGUE, 1907." "Bob," Cobb said to Lowe, "if hard work will do it, I'm going to win that watch." Lowe probably found the young man's cockiness amusing. He had been in the majors since 1890. Though he had once been one of the game's best infielders, he was now—at the ripe old age of 41—just a minor role player on a very mediocre team. He could no longer offer the team steady play, but he could offer them a steady presence in the clubhouse and on long road trips—a very valuable commodity on a team rife with dissension and conflict. That was precisely what the veteran decided to offer now—some sobering advice so that the young outfielder would not get too far ahead of himself. "Don't be in a hurry, Tyrus," he gently countered. "It took me ten years to learn to be a ball player. You've only been here for two." Cobb was adamant. "I'm going to win it," he repeated. Thinking back on it years later, Cobb considered the moment a turning point in his career. "Maybe it was then that I chose baseball, forever, irrevocably, as a career," he recalled. "That glittering challenge in the window seemed to me a guiding star."[1]

Cobb loved to tell stories like this. As criticism of him mounted, Cobb responded by portraying himself as a true American success—the young man who made good by pluck and hard work. The story became an integral part of Cobb's success narrative: the moment in which he realized his life's ambition and announced his commitment to achieve it. For good measure, Cobb noted that winning the batting championship proved a constructive way to respond to his adversaries. Now that he had "a goal to reach," he later recalled, he could "take anything the Tigers or the opposition dished out."[2]

Cobb knew how to create a compelling narrative. So what if we have no corroborating evidence to verify the incident? Cobb's primary point remains true—that after 1906 he engaged in a relentless pursuit of absolute greatness, to gain recognition as the best player in baseball—an enterprise in which he was largely successful for an impressive thirteen years. From 1907 through the 1919 season, he was by far the most productive and dynamic offensive force in the game. During that period, he attained a level of success that is almost staggering in its consistency and totality. He won the league batting championship twelve times, including a record nine straight years. During one four-year span, his batting average was just over .400, an almost unthinkable feat. In addition, he led the league in runs batted in four times, runs scored five times, hits eight times, doubles three times, triples four times, home runs once, and stolen bases six times. Cobb's mastery of the game was so complete that by 1909, only his fourth full season in the major leagues, writers from all major sporting journals routinely wondered if he was not just the greatest player in the game, but the greatest of all time. By 1911, when he hit .420, this became the consensus opinion.

How did he do it? Years later, when his status as the game's greatest player was assured, Cobb often implied his rise to preeminence was inevitable. He said this, not because he believed he was the most talented—he readily admitted that there were many other ballplayers with more natural talent—but because he was the most ambitious, most earnest, and most dedicated. He had to be, he said, because he was a Cobb. Family honor compelled him to study harder, play harder, and sacrifice more of himself than any other player. "Years before I saw the light of day," he noted in his final autobiography, "twenty-seven Cobbs had achieved varying degrees of note in the law, military, medical, mercantile, and agricultural fields. This fact I knew all too well." Like those who came before him, he had to bring honor to the family name; he saw no choice in the matter. Late in his career, he accentuated this point in a private letter to Michigan congressman Robert H. Clancy. "The honorable . . . Cobb blood . . . never will be subjected," he asserted. "It bows to no wrong nor to any man. . . . The Cobbs have their ideals and God help anyone who strives to bend a Cobb away from such."³

The ethic of honor permeated every facet of Cobb's life and informed much of his behavior. Indeed, Cobb was so immersed in the culture of honor, he not only accepted its basic tenets as moral facts, he assumed everyone else did, too. As he understood it, the ethic of honor was an uncompromising ethos—one that pushed and pressed him, informing his every act and absorbing his every thought. Honor shaped the way he played the game, the way he approached the media, the way he embraced his celebrity, the way he negotiated with management, the way he conducted himself in public, and the way he crafted his presentation of self. It was the guiding principle of his life.

As a youth in Royston, nearly all Cobb's mentors and friends were devoted to some variant of the ethic of honor—from the stern chivalric ethic espoused by his father and grandfathers to the more visceral ethic embraced by Cobb's childhood friends. When he left the South to make his living in the North, he entered an alien world. In many respects, it was also an inhospitable world—as evidenced by the hostile reception he received from Matty McIntyre and his clique of friends. But in one very important way, early twentieth-century professional baseball offered Cobb a world that was quite familiar to him. Like the playing fields and street corners of rural Royston, professional ballplayers followed an ethic of honor. Theirs was not quite the same ethic as Cobb's (a topic discussed in the next chapter), but it was close enough for Cobb to feel very much at home on the ball field. If it had not been so, he might not have remained in baseball as long as he did. Professional ball stimulated and encouraged many of the same values that had governed his youth. The near exclusive male culture of the ballpark, the physicality of the game, the camaraderie and competition that shaped team culture, the dozens of individual confrontations that made up a baseball game, the role of fans in bestowing and withholding praise—and thus honor—to players, the media's ability to bring fame to some players and infamy to others, the game's growing popularity among the respectable classes—all of these factors gave Cobb ample opportunity to exercise his manhood in ways consistent with his Southern heritage. On the ball field he tested his mettle, defended his status as the game's greatest player against all comers, meted out his individual brand of justice, gained fame, and proved his worth through exhibitions of daring and intrigue.

Cobb believed his successes and failures on the playing field, no matter how small, defined who he was as a person. He abhorred losing. Defeat humiliated a man because it exposed his weaknesses, demonstrated his inability to measure up to his opponents, and made him subject to the will of another. As he saw it, the loser was the antithesis of the true man. Perhaps this explains why Cobb never admitted to losing a duel. In the countless interviews he conducted and his many autobiographical musings, he admitted to setbacks—incidents in which a rival temporarily got the better of him—but in each case he claimed that he always came back to fight another day. When he did return, his recollection of the event was nearly always the same: he established his ultimate superiority by vanquishing the opposition.

Tales of Cobb's obsession to gain that superiority are legion. As a minor leaguer, he once upbraided his roommate, future Brooklyn Dodger George "Nap" Rucker, for beating him to the bathtub after a game. Rucker later told Detroit sportswriter John McCallum, Cobb was nearly unhinged when he confronted him: "You don't understand, Nap," Cobb explained, "I've just got to be first—all the time." Rucker, a fellow Georgian, understood Cobb's compulsion better than most: the two always made a point of getting into the team's dining room first so they could eat their fill without competition from the rest of the team. A dozen or so years later, Cobb was still at it. During spring training, he noticed some of the younger players doing broad jumps into the sliding pit. Although Cobb was now in his mid-thirties, he immediately challenged the players to a contest. Cobb beat everyone, but one—Del Gainor, a former college track star. That might have been the end of it for most people, but not for Cobb. Ten days later, Cobb pulled Gainor aside and asked him for a rematch. They jumped three times; this time, Cobb won all three. How did he accomplish this remarkable comeback? Upon losing the first time, Cobb contracted a local track coach to teach him proper jumping technique. A player who witnessed the event remarked, "Cobb was the kind of guy who just wouldn't finish second." He was also the kind of guy who preferred to finish first by several lengths. Years after they had both retired, former catcher Nig Clarke and Cobb got together with sportswriter Grantland Rice to reminisce about the old days. During the conversation, Clarke admitted to Cobb that he had fooled umpires into believing he had tagged Cobb out at the plate a dozen times or more when in fact he had missed him completely. According to Rice, Cobb was less than pleased by this little revelation. Indeed, he leaped at Clarke's throat and proceeded to strangle him, stopping only when three men pried his hands away from Clarke's neck. Rice and Clarke tried to calm Cobb down, but to no avail. "Twelve runs you cost me that I earned!" he snarled. Cobb already held the record for most runs scored in a career, but it did not matter: he wanted twelve more. As Cobb saw it, those runs were his by right; it was a matter of honor.[4]

Contemporaries were well aware of Cobb's determination to prevail. "Rivalry has made Ty Cobb," *Baseball Magazine* pronounced in 1913, and "has made him the greatest player in the game." He simply "cannot brook a superior; he cannot brook an equal." Ring Lardner quipped that Cobb's drive to win the batting title each year was so intense that if Tris Speaker, Joe Jackson, Sam Crawford, Eddie Collins, and Napoleon Lajoie "went crazy and hit .999, this Cobb would come out on top with 1.000 even." Parroting the voice of a wise old fan, Lardner articulated the prevailing opinion that any team that tried to best Cobb was only asking for trouble. "You're worse off now than you were before you done it because he won't never rest til he shows you up. . . . And after he's did it oncet and got even, he'll do it agin." Branch Rickey, who observed Cobb first as a player and later as manager and baseball executive, stated Cobb was forever "thinking of beating somebody at something—right now and always." Cobb, Rickey believed, possessed an "uncontrollable urge to excel." He diagnosed Cobb's "genius" as a "form of insanity, a do-or-die personal effort to beat someone or something."[5]

Cobb placed enormous pressure upon himself as he fought to remain on top. Trying to stay on top, he said, was a "constant nerve-racking grind." Interviewed in 1914 for the ghostwritten *Busting 'Em*, Cobb candidly described the "batting strain" he faced each season as he fought to hold the batting lead. "Few persons realize the tension that this keeps a man under," he complained. "I am usually 'crabbing' from the beginning to the end of the season. I get worse as the thing goes along." So did the physical pain. Many players came from working-class and farming backgrounds. As such, they had grown up in a work culture that prized a stoic response to the aches and pains of life, corporal stamina, and a commitment to getting the job done, no matter the costs. Rural born and bred, Cobb was certainly familiar with such values. With these, he mixed his distinctly Southern fascination with risk-taking, and physical aggression, traits that he had exercised since his boyhood in Royston. In addition, he also wanted to demonstrate the iron force of his will: as he saw it, playing through injuries was just one more way to demonstrate that he would let nothing get in the way of his quest to be the best. Just as he had determined he must come back after his nervous collapse in 1906 so that his enemies could not claim victory, so too he steeled himself to play despite injuries, fatigue, and illness; he refused to show weakness. He acquired a reputation among his peers as one of the game's toughest players, the sort of man who could take it as well as he could dish it out. By the middle of each season, his body became a maze of welts, bruises, gashes, cuts, and sores from violent encounters with infielders, catchers, and the unyielding hard clay of major league infields. The scars stayed with him and became badges of his manhood. When infielder Fred Haney broke in with the Tigers in 1922, he remembered how repulsed he felt the first time he saw Ty Cobb's thirty-six-year-old legs: "a crisscross of old spikes wounds from instep to hip" mixed with fresh bruises from his most recent encounters with his opponents and the dirt. Cobb approached each game so sore and stiff that "he could hardly get suited up." After games, he would go immediately to his hotel room "and to bed to rest those battle-scarred legs." Even so, he would be at the ballpark the next day, "as fierce a competitor as ever."[6]

Cobb believed honor demanded he adopt an aggressive, attacking style. To wait patiently for an opening—for example, an infielder to make an error or show a lapse in concentration—was no way for a man to behave, Cobb maintained. And to run from danger, as ballplayers routinely did once they hit the ball? This was an anathema. Cobb believed taking the offensive was an expected and natural part of being a man. It was simply part of his social and intellectual inheritance as a child of the South. "Always be on the offensive," he counseled would-be ballplayers late in his career: the aggressor will "win the prizes of life," so "why not train yourself to be a winner?" Or in an even more overt expression of the sort of mastery that Cobb sought, he remarked "The man who holds the initiative in baseball holds the whip hand."

Conversely, Cobb despised what he termed the "negative, defensive player" who was too "timid" and "undetermined" to dictate the action. This aversion revealed an important component of Southerners' understanding of honor and manhood. As they saw it, defensiveness, weakness, and vulnerability were attributes of inferior beings, namely women and African Americans. A man who found himself in a defensive position could not act for himself; he could only react to the actions of others. This meant that he could not determine his own fate. No white man worthy of his status would allow himself to be placed in such a position.[7] How, though, could the player do this in a game in which the lines between offense and defense were so remarkably fluid and ill-defined? A batter is in an obvious defensive position so long as he waits for a ball to hit. Only for the brief moment in which he makes contact is he able to act offensively. Once he is on the base paths, however, he becomes the hunted, not the hunter. Fielders go through a similar reversal of position: they must wait on their heels for the batter to hit the ball; only while the ball is in play do they gain the advantage of taking the offensive. Again, the condition is transitory. Southern white men did not like this about baseball and generally remained disinterested in the sport through much of the nineteenth century—and even into the twentieth. When Cobb joined the Tigers in 1905, he was one of only a handful of ballplayers from the South. Once he began to challenge the offensive-defensive dichotomy of the game, however, it became more popular in the South.[8]

Being caught in a vulnerable position is what irritated Cobb about his first encounter with Elberfeld: he had tried to take the offensive by stealing a base only to make himself exposed to Elberfeld's superior physicality and experience. As Cobb thought about this and other failed encounters, he determined that he had to eradicate all defensiveness in his approach to the game. During his first year, he learned to make the very fluidity of the game work to his advantage by devising ways to take the offensive at every moment. By the standards of the game, Cobb played at a frenetic pace. He was always in motion. "My whole plan on base was to upset batteries and infields," he claimed. How? By "dividing their minds," he made "The Great American Game . . . an unrelenting war of nerves." In that war, Cobb made himself the aggressor. "My idea was to go on the attack and never relax it." Edward Grant Barrow, who spent fifty years in organized baseball as a manager and executive, stated one of the most vivid memories of his career was watching Cobb wreak havoc at the ballpark. It was a thing to marvel at, Barrow claimed, that "vision of him running wild on the bases . . . harassing the pitchers, taunting the catchers, and announcing boldly he was going to steal second on the next pitch, fighting, clawing, and generally throwing the whole other side into confusion." Cobb was "the only person I ever saw who could unnerve a whole club."[9]

Ballplayers uniformly agreed that playing against Cobb was a harrowing experience. After watching Cobb swipe base after base, catcher Ray Schalk of the White Sox—one of the best in the game—remarked in disgust that Cobb "would have stolen my mask if it hadn't been strapped on." Chicago sportswriter Bill Bailey claimed Cobb put so much pressure on infielders they were often unable to make even routine plays. "No question in my mind," wrote Bailey, "that Cobb steals so many bases because the men who are to field that ball get overanxious." Branch Rickey suggested that he had much the same effect on pitchers. Rickey saw Cobb ruin dozens of pitchers' ability to concentrate, reducing them to mere "throwers." Men were not supposed to admit to such things, but the reality was that opposing players were actually afraid of Cobb. Rube Bressler called him the "most feared man in the history of baseball." Hughie Jennings maintained that when Cobb was in his prime, "he had half the league scared stiff."[10]

This was exactly what Cobb wanted—to defend his honor and prove his manhood while simultaneously stripping his opponents of theirs. For Cobb, it was never enough to simply beat the opposition; he wanted to humiliate them and perhaps even force them to do his bidding. He made a habit of showing absolutely no respect for his adversaries once the game began. He exhibited this most clearly in his approach to running the bases. He claimed the right to an unobstructed shot at each base and demanded infielders respect that right. Late in life, he recalled that when he entered the American League, runners acted defensive and vulnerable, acting too much "like a rabbit chased by wolves." Cobb was appalled and vowed to behave differently. He be-

Figure 4.1. New York Highlanders' infielder Jimmy Austin tries to make the tag as Cobb steals third base during a game in July 1910. Charles M. Conlon's photo became one of the most widely distributed during the Dead Ball Era in large part because it captures Cobb's gritty, go-for-broke style of play. *Source:* **Courtesy of Ernie Harwell Collection. Detroit Public Library.**

lieved contests for the bag should reflect the deeper truth that baseball was a survival of the fittest. In that contest, Cobb made sure he would be the aggressor—the wolf, not the rabbit. To make his point, he demanded a "clear shot at the bag," just as the rules promised. To Cobb, it was a matter of mastery and control. He would not allow anyone to impose his will on him for that would entail a loss of manhood. "I . . . fail to see why I shouldn't make the baseman a little respectful of me, rather than have him make me scared," he remarked late in his career. If anyone was going to be scared or imposed upon, Cobb reasoned, it would be the other guy. "An offensive attitude is the key to making any play," he decided, "and if it meant gambling and getting tough, I was willing." To Cobb, "getting tough" nearly always meant punishing those who denied him his due. If an infielder dared to rough him up, he promised to "knock them kicking" as retaliation.[11]

To establish his rights on the base paths, Cobb gave every rookie his own version of the "professional teach." Third baseman Jimmy Austin, who came up with the Highlanders in 1909, got away easier than many. In one of his first games against the Tigers, he kicked Cobb's foot off the base as he swooped down to tag him. Long after the umpire called him out, Cobb lay on the ground, glaring up at the young infielder. Finally, in a slow and measured tone, he spoke: "Mister, don't you ever *dare* do that no more." Rookie Ossie Bluege of Washington got it a bit worse. Bluege was covering third, ball in hand, when Cobb came charging toward him. Bluege estimated Cobb was going to be out by a good ten feet, so Bluege instinctively moved up the line to block the bag and apply the tag. Incensed that Bluege had moved onto his turf, Cobb flew at the young infielder. He "didn't slide. He just took off and came at me in midair spikes first, about four or five feet off the ground, so help me, just like a rocket," Bluege recalled. Cobb hit Bluege in the upper part of the arm, "just grazing the flesh, but tearing open the sleeve." Infuriated, Bluege attempted to "konk" Cobb with the ball, but was stopped by umpire Billy Evans, who promptly ejected Cobb for the vicious slide. The next day, Cobb spotted Bluege at the batting cage. Amicably, Cobb apologized and asked the young infielder if he had hurt him. Bluege affirmed that he was fine. "Good," said Cobb, but added as his eyes narrowed, "Remember—never come up the line for me."[12]

Cobb used all the weapons at his disposal—feet, spikes, elbows, shoulders, legs, arms, and torso—to punish those who failed to comply. In a 1907 game against archrival Cleveland, Cobb tried to stretch a triple into a home run, but the throw to home beat him by a good twenty feet. Undeterred, Cobb "took a flying leap" at Cleveland catcher Harry Bemis. The body blow caught Bemis in the side and knocked him flat. During a game in 1914, third baseman Jim Breton easily retired Cobb by expertly blocking the base as the Georgian tried to advance. Never one to forfeit the base path, Cobb got his revenge in the first inning of the next game, spiking Breton on the arm and leg as he slid into third. That Cobb's sole intent was to punish Breton was made clear by a sportswriter who covered the game. Although Cobb was out by a good fifteen feet, he went into the "bag like a cyclone." When it was over, "Terrible Tyrus" raised himself up, dusted himself off, and sauntered over to the wounded Breton "to gloat over the damage wrought."[13]

Breton and Bemis survived to fight another day; St. Louis Browns' catcher Paul Krichell was not so lucky. Krichell became the object of Cobb's wrath after he flipped Cobb over by hooking an arm around his lead leg as he slid home. Cobb warned the young catcher not to repeat that trick, but Krichell was a brash young man and—by his own admission—refused to heed the warning. The next time Cobb slid home against Krichell, he retaliated with gruesome precision. Leaping at the catcher feet first, he wrapped his legs around one of Krichell's outstretched arms and pulled the catcher down as he landed. Cobb later boasted he came at Krichell with such force he "almost detached (his arm) from his body." Not quite, but he did dislocate Krichell's shoulder so severely that the catcher was forced to retire a year later. Brutal? Cobb did not deny it. Excessive? Not to Cobb. "I'm sorry for it," he explained, "but I warned him." Thirty-five years later, Cobb remained convinced he was right. In an extensive interview with sportswriter Joe Williams "to set the record straight" about his alleged misdeeds, Cobb identified the incident with Krichell as one that needed to be told in its entirety—as if telling the world that being flipped by Krichell justified his deliberate maiming of the young catcher.[14]

Cobb could be equally ruthless toward pitchers. His philosophy was to approach each pitcher as though he was "his master." He began by demonstrating an absolute lack of respect for them. Bluege recalled that whenever Cobb stepped out of the batter's box to grind some dirt into his hands, he "always bent over with his backside to the pitcher," as if he was mooning him. Once in a 1917 game against Eddie Cicotte of the White Sox, Cobb stood at the plate, but with his back to the pitcher, chatting amicably with a teammate. Cicotte had been in the big leagues nearly as long as Cobb and was then at the peak of his career. Even so, Cobb's obvious lack of respect rattled him: he walked Cobb on four straight pitches. It was all part of what Cobb called his "belligerent, take-charge attitude" at the plate. He counseled young hitters to do what he did—"cultivate . . . a 'mad-on' while awaiting your turn at bat, a cold determination to ram the ball down the pitcher's throat." Truly embrace this mentality, he urged, and "it will show up in your walk, in your eyes, in the way you hold your head, the stance you take." The result? "Now the pitcher is fearing *you*."[15]

Woe to the pitcher who tried to intimidate Cobb by brushing him back. Cobb interpreted brushbacks as a challenge to his honor because they placed him in a defensive position and invaded his personal space. Cobb retaliated with vicious aggression. His response to Red Sox hurler Cy Morgan was typical. According to Cobb, Morgan incurred his wrath because he "tried to skull me regularly." Finally, Cobb saw an opportunity to retaliate. He was on second when Morgan uncorked a wild pitch. With that, Cobb streaked for home. He didn't care that he had no chance of scoring. He wanted a chance to assault Morgan. As the catcher gathered the ball and threw to Morgan covering home, Cobb –in his words—came "whipping at him . . . steel showing." Terrified, Morgan received the throw and promptly ran away from the plate, or so Cobb claimed.[16] To pay back Dutch Leonard for the same offense, he devised a more ingenuous approach: he bunted down the first baseline and took out the pitcher as he covered the bag.[17]

So it was with nearly every encounter on the ball field. To maintain the upper hand, Cobb felt compelled to respond to every slight with a more forceful and often more vicious rejoinder. Because his adversaries were just as determined to defend their manhood and their honor, small affronts often escalated into full-scale donnybrooks. What set Cobb apart from his peers was his absolute determination to have the last word—or more common—throw the last punch. Take for example Cobb's confrontation with New York Giants' second baseman Charles "Buck" Herzog. This incident proved to be one of Cobb's bloodiest encounters, but also one of his favorites because—at least the way he told it—he also had opportunity to humiliate one of the game's greatest tacticians and pugilists, the legendary John McGraw. The incident occurred before, during, and after a 1917 spring exhibition game against the Giants in Dallas, Texas. Led by the pugnacious McGraw, the Giants gloried in their ability to torment their opponents, verbally and physically. Though this was a meaningless preseason game, McGraw hoped it would serve notice to the National League that his Giants could push anyone around anywhere—even the great Ty Cobb. Cobb arrived at the ballpark a few minutes before the game, having just completed a round of golf. Herzog and fellow Giant Art Fletcher decided this was opportunity enough to razz Cobb, calling him a "swell-head" and a "show-off" for taking the game so lightly. To rile the Tiger star further, they threw down a challenge—warning him that they would have his number today so he should not try to steal any bases or stretch singles into doubles. Never one to pass on a challenge, Cobb confronted Herzog directly: "Sometime in this game, I expect to get on base," he told the infielder, "and I'll be down to see you, never fear." According to Cobb, Herzog responded with a curt, "I'll be waiting." First time up, Cobb singled. Standing on first, he promptly announced to Herzog that he was coming down. Cobb later admitted he had mayhem, not larceny, on his mind. He purposely took a short lead and ran slower than usual so that Herzog would have time to set himself before he arrived. Herzog responded just as Cobb expected. Upon taking the throw, he moved to block Cobb. Cobb came in hard—"as violent as I could make it"—and slashed at Herzog with his spikes, ripping the infielder's pants from thigh to ankle and creating a small cut on his leg. The two then hit the ground and commenced brawling. Cobb later admitted he might have been the first to throw a punch: "When you get into one of these things, you don't remember all the details." A general brannigan ensued as both benches emptied. Cobb claimed he got in at least one good punch to Herzog's chin before umpire Bill Brennan, a friend of Giants' manager John McGraw, ejected him from the game.[18]

It might have ended there if Cobb's victim had been anyone but Herzog, but the second baseman was one tough player. He had played for McGraw for a number of years and considered himself Little Napoleon's protégé. For his part, McGraw adored Herzog and relied on him to act as his field manager. Both men perceived the incident as a matter of personal honor. That night, Herzog approached Cobb as he ate dinner at the hotel where both teams were staying. Glowering over Cobb, Herzog announced that he wanted to finish what they had started. Cobb was more than willing and suggested the two meet in his room to finish their duel. And duel it was; each chose seconds so that the fight might replicate a true affair of honor. While waiting for his adversary, Cobb cleared his room of all furniture and sprinkled the floor with water so it would be slippery for the sneaker-wearing Herzog. Once Herzog showed, they agreed on "the old rough and tumble . . . anything goes"—as Cobb called it—and started to brawl. Cobb later boasted he pummeled the Giant from start to finish. Witnesses countered that the fight started off fairly close: Herzog even floored Cobb with the first decent punch of the fight. After that, however, it was all Cobb. With a two-inch height and twenty-pound weight advantage—and shoes that did not slip on the floor—Cobb was able to hit Herzog at will. Sure enough, when Herzog appeared in the lobby the next day, he had two black eyes, a split lip, and enough bruises to keep him out of the day's exhibition game.[19]

That was the end of the Cobb-Herzog duel, but not the end of Cobb's test of honor. When McGraw saw what Cobb had done to his player, he exploded. In an obvious effort to shame and humiliate the Tiger star, McGraw accosted Cobb in the hotel lobby, calling him a quitter and a cheat. Once McGraw ran out of steam, Cobb coolly responded, "If you were a younger man, I'd kill you," then cheekily tweaked the manager's rather ample nose. It was a calculated move intended to impose maximum humiliation upon the manager. According to cultural historian Kenneth Greenberg, in the Euro-American culture of honor, the nose represented one of the most important parts of a man's anatomy; after all, the code of honor taught that men expressed their character by how they projected themselves and the nose is the most visible projection of the human body. No, Cobb did not maul McGraw as he did Herzog, but his treatment of McGraw was metaphorically just as violent. By twisting McGraw's nose, Cobb invaded his person in a deliberate and unflattering manner. Essentially, he communicated to McGraw that he was not worthy of respect; he was a man without honor, which is to say no man at all. As if to accentuate the point, Cobb then turned his back on McGraw and walked away, leaving the manager to sputter insults as Cobb disappeared from view. McGraw may not have fully understood the symbolic significance of all of Cobb's actions, but he certainly knew that he had been humiliated. According to Cobb biographer John D. McCallum, McGraw "to his dying day never forgave Cobb" for embarrassing him in public.[20]

Cobb could probably not have cared less about McGraw's feelings. He was more interested in how onlookers responded. After all, shaming requires an audience to be most effective. Though McGraw had gotten the lobby crowd's attention by verbally attacking Cobb, Cobb humiliated Mugsy for doing so. By first invading McGraw's space and then removing himself from that space by walking away, he showed the crowd that McGraw had no power over him and thus his words were meaningless. It was a triumphal twenty-four hours for Cobb: he had faced down the most petulant and intimidating team in baseball by silencing and humiliating its two field leaders. With nothing more to gain from further exchanges with the Giants, Cobb kept himself out of the rest of the series. When New York outfielder Benny Kauff—a tough talker who could smoke a cigar, chew a plug of tobacco, and drink a pint of ale simultaneously—challenged Cobb to a fight for a $1,000 purse, Cobb ignored him. Instead, he promptly left Dallas to train on his own.[21]

Cobb delighted in recalling the specifics of this incident. He understood fully that according to the ethic of Southern honor, he gained status by humiliating his adversaries. Yet Cobb took care in how he retold the story. He portrayed himself as the reluctant warrior who had been forced into battle to defend himself, even telling a correspondent for *Sporting Life* immediately after it happened that he regretted the entire episode. In fact, he portrayed himself as the unwilling combatant after nearly every violent encounter. Invariably, he explained that he had been raised to be a gentleman, not a mauler. His father, he said, had instilled in him a respect for his creed—to conquer his passion so that "the better angel" of his nature might guide him. With this, his scholarly father added a line from Shakespeare's *Hamlet*: "Beware of entrance to a quarrel, but being in it—let them beware." As a dutiful son, Cobb swore to follow his father's wisdom. Cobb made this argument with absolute earnestness whenever someone broached the subject of his violent behavior. Always, he claimed, he followed the dictum of his father. He even took this stance in private letters to complete strangers. When baseball fan Bill Webb wrote Cobb for his autograph, he mentioned he had been at the Dallas game. This was enough to ignite Cobb's passion. "I never initiated a wrong," Cobb asserted; he only responded to his opponents in kind. Referring specifically to his fight with Herzog, Cobb contended that the infielder "blocked me off" and later "challenged me in my own room . . . These are facts."[22]

If repetition is an indication of sincerity, then Cobb certainly was sincere. He claimed over and over again that he had lived an honorable life, that is, that he strove to live up to and enhance his family's noble reputation. At least one of Cobb's most persistent critics seems to have been persuaded by the sincerity of Cobb's argument. A few months after Cobb died, *Sporting News* publisher J. G. Taylor Spink disclosed the contents of his decades-long correspondence with Cobb in an editorial designed to counter charges that Cobb was the game's dirtiest player. "A man bares his soul in his personal correspondence," Spink maintained, and so it was with Cobb. Years of written exchanges with Cobb convinced Spink that the deceased star had been honest when he claimed he never started a fight. During Cobb's playing days, Spink had been one of his sharpest critics, but no longer. Rising to the dead man's defense, he now labeled the vilification of Cobb "an unfair image of a great man and a great athlete."[23]

It was a noble gesture on Spink's part, but somewhat misguided. In making his argument, Spink missed an important aspect of Cobb's personality. In fact, Cobb was extremely sensitive to criticism, sometimes felt slights and insults that were more illusory than real, and often seemed to be smarting for a fight. Again, this was true of Southern men who followed the ethic of honor. The code inspired a heightened sensitivity to insult because they realized any slight could have disastrous consequences for one's reputation. Southern white men had long shown a certain prickliness when it came to being insulted. Solomon Northup, who spent twelve years in the South as a kidnapped slave, claimed Southern white men were often at each other's throats over a perceived "affront." According to Northup, "Every man carries his bowie knife, and when two fall out, they set to work hacking and thrusting at each other, more like savages than civilized and enlightened beings." Such occurrences were so frequent, Northup contended, they passed without notice and almost without comment." Violence continued in the postwar years. Traveling through Georgia at the close of Reconstruction, Northern journalist Edward King observed, "quarrels, as among the lower classes generally throughout the South, grow into feuds, cherished for years, until some day, at the crossroads, or at the country tavern, a pistol or a knife puts a bloody and often fatal end to the difficulty." In the "sparsely agricultural portion of Georgia," King lamented, "there is . . . too much popular vengeance, too much taking the law into one's own hand."[24]

Cobb was the product of this culture. While he usually exercised enough restraint to avoid the worst excesses of his homeland's culture of honor and vengeance, he reveled in this environment of open confrontations and blood rivalries. So did his friends and admirers in the South. Case in point, after Cobb mauled a verbally abusive (and severely handicapped) New York fan in 1912 (examined in the next chapter), Georgia's two senators and ten congressmen telegraphed the beleaguered star to offer their encouragement. "As Georgians we commend your action in resenting an uncalled for insult," they told Cobb. Because he had acted with honor, they anticipated his "complete exoneration." Meanwhile, the mayor of Atlanta told the press, "I glory in the spunk of Ty Cobb in resenting the insults offered him by the spectator in New York. He has lived up to the principles that have always been taught to Southern manhood." The president of the Atlanta Athletic Club agreed, noting that Cobb could soon rid the American League of rowdy fans if allowed to carry on his form of summary judgment. Spoken like true Southern men of honor.[25]

Actually, Cobb went one better than most Southerners. He did not just wait to be insulted; he tried to provoke feuds to ignite his competitive fire. Tiger second baseman Charlie Gehringer said Cobb "taught himself to hate" pitchers so that hitting became "a real vendetta" for him. Teammate Fred Haney claimed he watched Cobb become transformed by the hate he manufactured as he waited on deck: His jaws clenched, his eyes blazed, "his forehead furrowed into an intense frown" as he worked "himself into a fury. . . . By the time he stepped into the batter's box, you could almost see sparks in the air. 'I dare you to pitch to me,' he seemed to be saying. 'I dare you.'" Cobb wanted a fight. To claim that he was a reluctant warrior was disingenuous and misleading.[26]

That little charade also enabled him to assert his personal superiority over his adversaries. The subtext to Cobb's argument was essentially this: his adversaries were rowdies and incorrigibles who could not control themselves; he was their superior, a class apart. He claimed it was simply not in his makeup to act dishonestly or violate the rules of fair play. Once, when asked if he intentionally hurt other players, he responded with an emphatic, "I am not that kind"—a clear assertion of moral superiority. Cobb was convinced that his wealth and fame were a direct result of his noble character and superior morality. "Any good fortune I had is proof that I did not follow wrong," he told one fan. He repeated this statement in his final autobiography: "I do not believe The Maker would have allowed me so much had I violated my father's creed." When he set out on his own, his father had counseled him to align himself with good and to fear no man. Now, at the end of his life, he was convinced that all he possessed—"worldly goods, some ability to help others"—and most importantly his "name," bore witness to the righteousness of his behavior.[27]

Like all men of honor, Cobb believed his superior status entitled him to certain privileges. His was an essentially hierarchical understanding of humankind: some people were superior to others and should be treated accordingly. Cobb learned this in his youth. In Royston, as throughout the South, whites expected African Americans to behave as servile dependents and meted out retribution to any black man or woman who broke from their ascribed role. Even within the white community, customs of deference and privilege flourished. The Cobbs were often beneficiaries of these habits. As noted earlier, Grandfather Cobb's neighbors bestowed on him the title of "Squire" and willingly deferred to his wisdom. In Royston, Ty's father William also enjoyed the advantages of rank: the title of "Professor;" membership in the Masons, the town's most elite male social club; a term in the Georgia state legislature; and a term as mayor of Royston. As Ty ascended the ladder of baseball greatness, he believed it was his turn to enjoy such privileges.

Cobb's expectations dovetailed with changes in commercial entertainment and mass media. In the newly emerging culture of professional sports, fame brought privileges. The best and most exciting players received the greatest attention and publicity. No ballplayer received as much attention as Cobb. In 1908, Cobb's third full season in the majors, *Sporting Life* crowned him "the most sensational young player who ever broke into the national game." By the end of the 1909 season, aficionados declared him the equal—or nearly so—of the game's reigning star, the almost legendary Honus Wagner. When Cobb won his fourth straight batting title in 1910 with a major league best .383 average, most agreed the young star was now Wagner's superior. By then, the only question was whether he was the greatest player ever. Charles Comiskey, owner of the Chicago White Sox and one of the most respected baseball minds in the country, was among the first to proclaim Cobb's ultimate superiority. In a widely circulated interview that appeared first in the *New York Times*, Comiskey pronounced Cobb "the greatest baseball player ever" and then proceeded to offer one superlative after another to describe the young star. Cobb, Comiskey observed, is "strong on all points" with no apparent weaknesses. He was a complete player who "plays with his whole anatomy—his head, his arms, his hands, his legs, his feet," and most especially his head. Cobb was a true student of the game, "willing to learn something new about baseball every day of his life." Two years later, as Cobb completed his second straight season with a batting average above .400, Comiskey's opinion became gospel.[28]

As Cobb's fame as the game's best player spread, his very celebrity became a point of conversation. In the emerging and merging worlds of professional sports and mass media, no sports figure had ever received so much attention—not boxers John L. Sullivan and James Jeffries, not even fellow ballplayers Honus Wagner or Christy Mathewson. Sporting journals scrambled to cash in on Cobb's fame. In just his fourth full season, *Sporting News* gave him a special pull-out section. Two years later, *Baseball Magazine* crowned Cobb the "king of all ball players" and devoted several articles to him. Just nine months after that, the same journal decided this tribute was not enough and devoted the entire issue—"The Ty Cobb Number"—to him. Meanwhile teams throughout the American League enjoyed a spike in attendance of ten percent or more when the Tigers came to town. So great was his impact upon the finances of major league baseball that one sportswriter observed Cobb "is the greatest press agent in the game. There is no one engaged in entertaining the public as widely advertised as he is."[29]

Cobb took it all in stride—a remarkable feat given his youth and backwoods upbringing. Hubris, not modesty, explains the ease in which he accepted his celebrity: he believed he deserved the accolades and attention. Once he became a star, he demonstrated a sense of entitlement no ballplayer had dared exhibit. He began to skip the first few weeks of spring training, arguing—probably correctly—that he did not need that much time to get in shape for the coming season. He also began to find excuses to bow out of morning and off-day practice, unless he believed he needed to make some adjustments in his batting. Many days, he arrived just before the game started; on a few occasions, he actually missed the start of play. He also left a few games before they were completed. Umpire cum author Billy Evans noted, "When Ty doesn't care to play, he usually gets away in some manner," recalling one incident when Cobb had himself ejected during his first at bat because—he claimed—he did not feel well. Sycophantic journalists covered for him, eager to remain in the star's good graces.[30]

Cobb also became downright prickly about a variety of issues. Since his traumatic first full year in the majors, he had learned to go his own way. Now, as his star continued to ascend, he became openly disdainful of teammates who failed to perform to his expectations. At bat and on the bases, he instructed his peers to watch for his signs and to follow his lead. He could be both vicious and petty toward those who refused to obey his orders or made a mistake. He had a particularly well-publicized quarrel with Davy Jones during a game with Boston in 1910. It was summer and the Tigers were on the outskirts of the pennant race, an unhappy reality for the team that had dominated the league for the previous three seasons. Understandably, emotions were raw and tempers were short. With Cobb at bat and Jones at first with two outs, Jones bolted for second. The throw from the plate arrived in plenty of time to end the inning. Cobb was furious; in front of players and fans, he laid into Jones for failing to read his sign. The outspoken Jones refused to take the blame. After the game, he told the press Cobb botched the play, not him. Cobb had called for a hit and run, but had failed to swing. Thus Jones had no chance at second. Moreover, Jones maintained Cobb was lying to save face. That was too much for Cobb. After the game, he announced that he would not play so long as Jones was a member of the Tigers. To show he was serious, he spent the next game in the grandstand, refusing even to make an appearance in the clubhouse. The standoff continued for three days until Cobb finally relented—sort of. Unable to force Jones off the team, he settled for a lesser bit of vengeance. He demanded that shortstop Donie Bush, Jones's friend and a Cobb enemy, be moved from second to the back of the batting order. By this petty gesture, Cobb claimed victory. He had exacted his pound of flesh and demonstrated his authority over the team.[31]

The more Cobb became used to his celebrity and fame, the more critical he became of those he considered his inferiors, a list which seemed to include just about everyone connected to the team. When club trainer Harry Tuthill moved his shower towel from its customary "lucky" peg, Cobb threw a fit. He had another tantrum when the team arrived in Chicago for their second series of the 1912 season. Sick with a bad cold, Cobb hoped to rest up before the first game of the series. Unfortunately, his room was next to the railroad tracks of the Illinois Central. Fearful the passing trains would disturb his sleep, he complained to the hotel night clerk and to manager Hughie Jennings, demanding a different room. When both told him they could do nothing, Cobb demanded that the entire team move to a different hotel. When Jennings responded that this too was impossible, Cobb refused to play the next game—much to the chagrin of the 7,000 fans who came to see him. In a funk, Cobb left the team for Detroit, missing another game in the process. In response, the *Chicago Tribune* mocked Cobb's rarefied view of himself by sarcastically noting, "Ty Cobb is taking advantage of all the high aristocratic amenities. He now has what might be called a bunch of temperaments."[32] Such uninhibited censure revealed just how uncomfortable the public was with the emerging culture of celebrity. Heretofore, star status rarely translated into special treatment. In other forms of entertainment—most notably the nascent film industry—directors and producers were billed above performers. Cobb, by demanding the privileges of honor, helped chart the course of the modern culture of celebrity.[33]

Cobb found it easy to exercise his superiority over almost everyone. The one persistent exception was Tiger president and chief financial officer, Frank Navin. Navin held the purse strings of the Tiger organization. Since Cobb hated to be controlled by anyone, their relationship was extremely acrimonious, especially at contract time. To Cobb, negotiating for salary was an especially demeaning affair—a reminder that his fate was in the hands of another. Predictably, Cobb approached each negotiation as an exercise of honor. Money was certainly a major issue in these negotiations: beginning in 1908, Cobb began to angle to be the highest paid player in the game—a status he was eager to attain on principle alone. Yet finances were never the only issue for Cobb: he also wanted power and control. In his final autobiography, written nearly a decade before Curt Flood challenged the reserve clause, Cobb likened the position of a professional ballplayer to a slave, a startling analogy from someone as proud of his race as Cobb. To salvage his self-image, Cobb approached salary negotiations as a type of duel—one in which his primary goal was to exercise some leverage over Navin. During his contract negotiations in 1908, he demanded a raise from $2,400 to $5,000—far more than any third-year player had ever received. Just as important to Cobb, he demanded that Navin relinquish some of his contractual powers—namely the clause that allowed the club to release Cobb within ten days after giving notice. This became a matter of family honor for Cobb. When Navin criticized Cobb in the press, family members purportedly told him "No Cobb has to take that from anyone"—not that Ty ever needed to be reminded of this. Eventually, Cobb signed a contract with the ten-day clause stricken and for just $200 less than his original demand. It was a principled victory for Cobb. He later told sportswriter John McCallum that he would have been "just another muscle-worker" (shades of his father's warning) had he allowed the clause to remain in his contract. "If Navin hadn't given in, I would have quit baseball and gone to college. Nobody really believed I was serious, but I was."[34]

That Cobb believed Navin was his inferior made negotiations decidedly hostile. Cobb shied away from publicly attacking Navin during his baseball career, but he made his views abundantly clear after he retired. In his autobiography, he referred to Navin by a racial slur—"'The Chinaman' for his cold, implacable expression." He further identified him as a common bookkeeper who had somehow ingratiated himself to team owner Bill Yawkey. Why Yawkey had given Navin a percentage of the team and named him club secretary-treasurer was beyond Cobb. Cobb saw Navin as a conniving and deceitful paper-clip counter who consistently thwarted the team's efforts to improve by refusing to pursue expensive talent. That Navin had once worked as a croupier at a gambling house, frequented race tracks, and had a brother who served time in a Michigan state prison only confirmed to Cobb that Navin was of low birth and not worthy of his respect.[35]

Cobb held out again prior to the 1913 season. This time his asking price was $15,000 a year—an exorbitant salary for a player. Walter Johnson, coming off a thirty-two-win season, only made $7,000. Christy Mathewson, who had won twenty or more for ten straight years, made $9,000. The great Honus Wagner, whose salary had led the majors for years, made an even $10,000. But Cobb had led the league in hitting for the fifth straight year. Moreover, his frenetic, go-for-broke style of play made him the most popular player in the game. Although he modestly told reporters he did not consider himself baseball's greatest player, he clearly expected to be paid as though he was. Navin, however, rejected Cobb's demand outright and counter-offered at $10,500, hoping a salary just slightly above Wagner's would satiate Cobb's ego. It didn't. When spring training started on March 10, Cobb stayed in Augusta and played a series of exhibition games with an all-Georgia team of barnstormers. He was still in Georgia one month later when the season started even though Navin had sweetened his offer by $2,000. He clearly understood his value to the Tigers. As a *Detroit Free Press* editorial lamented in the midst of the impasse, "Hamlet without Hamlet would look better . . . than the Tigers without Ty Cobb."[36]

A week into the season, Navin explained his stance to the *New York Times* via a signed statement. He offered a scathing attack on his star player. "Ty Cobb Must Back Down Or Quit Game" read the headline. While conceding that Cobb was "the best ball player in the world," Navin argued this was not the issue. "To give in to Mr. Cobb now in his present attitude would be to concede that he is greater than the game itself," Navin suggested, "for he has set all its laws at defiance." Navin forecast a bleak future for the game if Cobb got his way. "Where will his 'I-am-above-the law' theory end?" Navin wondered. "We may as well turn the club over to him and eventually the league." Then Navin got personal:

> If Mr. Cobb doesn't like a room a hotel clerk gives him he quits the club for a week. If he doesn't like what a silly man in the grandstand yells at him he punches his face and is again out of the game. He quit the game when were fighting for a pennant and publicly stated that he would not play with his comrade in left field, D. Jones, on account of some misunderstanding with that player. If he doesn't feel like practicing he stays away from the park. He has grown to believe that his greatness precludes his being subject to club discipline. . . . He demands $15,000 for his services and then he goes to the other end of the country to fire ultimatums at me through the public press, proclaiming that no representative of the Detroit Club has "been sent" to talk business with him. Mr. Cobb is an employe *[sic]* of the Detroit Baseball Club; he knows where the office is. In the past I have patiently put up with a great deal from Cobb. It has now reached a point where there must be a showdown.

If Navin hoped to shame Cobb by presenting him as a self-absorbed and spoiled narcissist, it didn't work. Cobb refused to be cowed in matters of honor. Once Navin realized this—and that he needed Cobb to make the Tigers both competitive and marketable, he discreetly asked his star player to meet with him to hammer out a deal. Within a few hours, they came to agreement. Cobb did not get his $15,000, but he came close. His official contract gave him a $12,000 salary, but owner Yawkey sweetened that with a bonus of $2,000. At $14,000 a year, Cobb became the highest paid player in the major leagues. Status did indeed have its rewards.[37]

Status also brought publicity. Ty Cobb may have craved attention even more than he craved the privileges he enjoyed. This may be the least appreciated aspect of an honor-based culture: those who sought honor needed to curry the favor of the public. Honor was relational: those who sought honor depended upon the affirmation and respect of their public, even those they defined as inferior to themselves. This helps to explain why men of honor felt compelled to prove themselves repeatedly: they needed the constant affirmation of a fickle public to affirm their status. From early childhood, Cobb demonstrated he would do almost anything to impress his peers. His daredevil antics were early manifestations of this need as was his need to excel in everything he did. The culture of honor was also a visual culture in that appearances mattered greatly. Those who sought honor offered projections of themselves through dress and mannerisms that they hoped their peers would respect. As a product of this culture, Cobb learned to comport himself with an aggressive self-confidence that made him stand out among players, sportswriters, and fans alike.

On the field, Cobb seemed to choreograph his every act for public consumption. Swinging three bats in the on-deck circle was certainly part of this bid for attention. He gave his uniform unique flourishes; for example, he often turned the collar up and sported long sleeves in the heat of summer, as if to show the crowd he was impervious to the elements (in reality, he burned easily). At bat, on the bases, and in the field, he modeled a frenetic and aggressive style of play that compelled everyone—fans, players, and even the umpires—to watch. Cobb seemed always to be up to something. He ran the umpires ragged in the process. After umpiring his first game with Cobb in the lineup, one exhausted umpire complained to another, "You don't think when he gets on; you just keep running." Cobb routinely gave umpires more close plays to adjudicate than anyone else on the field. Of course, these close plays made Cobb a constant topic of conversation. He would have it no other way.[38]

Off the field, Cobb also lobbied for attention. As a rookie, he opted for a flamboyant image, dressing like a dandy with shiny shoes with spats, a checkered suit, contrasting vest, bright bow tie, and a wide Panama hat. As he matured and began to court businessmen for insider tips, he switched to conservative tailored suits. By all accounts, he struck an impressive pose. A writer for the *St. Louis Post-Dispatch* suggested Cobb "reminded one of a 'Gibson man'" for his grace, poise, and attractive style. The writer observed that the civilian Cobb offered "a shocking contrast to the slouchy-gaited, scrappy-mannered bleacher-defying gentleman who cavorts daily in H. 'Angelface' Jennings' right garden." This became part of Cobb's shtick as well: to change his persona according to environment. Gruff and belligerent at the ballpark, he turned on the charm off the field, presenting himself as polite, accommodating, professional, and even modest—all to dispel the misconception that he was simply just another untutored ruffian of a ballplayer.[39]

In this age before radio and television, most baseball fans first learned about Cobb by reading about him in their local newspaper or through one of the three major sporting journals of the day. Even before he got to the majors, Cobb demonstrated an ability to manipulate the media when he tricked sportswriter Grantland Rice into giving him some free publicity as a beleaguered and underappreciated minor league ballplayer. That was just the start. Over the years, Cobb proved remarkably adept at using the press to help shape his public image. Throughout his career, Cobb generously offered long interviews to nearly any journalist who asked—a practice that made him a favorite among the fourth estate. Sometimes, he even suggested topics for articles. Sportswriters from across the American League praised Cobb for his grace and charm—still rare qualities among the contemporary breed of ballplayers. His kindnesses paid dividends: no matter the controversy, he could always expect a host of influential writers to defend his character. Prominent national columnists like Rice, Fred Lieb, Ring Lardner, Damon Runyon, F. C. Lane, John B. Foster, and John Sheridan all fell under Cobb's spell at one point or another. So did a host of more local sportswriters, including most of the Detroit writers, Ed Wray of the *St. Louis Post-Dispatch*, and Joe Vila of the *New York Sun*. With such an influential army of journalists behind him, Cobb was able to project an image of self that not only highlighted his virtues and minimized his faults, but also embraced his conception of honorable manhood.

F. C. Lane unintentionally helped Cobb nurture his public image when he penned a feature article for *Baseball Magazine* describing a day in the life of the star at his off-season home in Augusta just before the 1916 season. During the visit, Cobb ushered Lane around town in his open-air roadster, a mode of conveyance that enabled Lane to witness the adulation Cobb received as he went about his daily business. Cobb's "progress through town is a continuous review," Lane marveled; "People hail him from the sidewalks, crossing the streets, from other vehicles, everywhere." No doubt Squire Cobb, Professor Cobb, and Captain Chitwood would have been proud—and perhaps even a bit jealous—of the deference Ty received. Along the way, Cobb ruminated on his life's journey, feigning modesty for his many accomplishments even as he expressed a desire to make a lasting contribution to society. When they arrived at Cobb's home—"a typical Southern mansion" according to Lane—Cobb continued his practiced presentation of self by taking the journalist into his inner sanctum, his trophy room and private office, where they chatted amicably. Obviously honored by Cobb's willingness to share his sanctuary, Lane described it in detail: "a mass of accumulated pictures . . . a thousand and one knickknacks . . . scattered in profusion on the bureaus and the bookcases and the floor." Here Cobb kept his most prized possessions—a library devoted to military history, a drawer full of letters from adoring fans, his guns, and his "trophies of the chase." Lane portrayed Cobb as a gracious and accommodating host who, despite a rather frenetic personality, enjoyed his leisure in a style reminiscent of the Southern patriarchs of old. "This is the way I live," Cobb confided. "A good many people come to see me . . . but this is a typical day. Always glad to see my friends, to hunt or lounge around or play golf as the occasion requires." The resulting article presented Cobb as generous, but also decisive, candid, intensely focused on the business of baseball, and rightfully proud of his many accomplishments. Cobb made a point of discussing his contract at length, even showing Lane its contents to verify that he was in fact the highest paid player in the game. Photographs of Cobb, his wife, two infant children, and home accompanied the article to underscore

Cobb's material prosperity and patriarchal contentment. A Southern apologist could not have offered a more appealing presentation of Southern gentility and honor.[40]

Sportswriters liked Cobb because they recognized him as a kindred spirit—an intelligent, educated, and articulate young man who, despite his family's status, had decided to pursue a career in sports. Cobb was extremely curious about the world; he read widely and loved to visit museums, theaters, and other points of interest when he was otherwise engaged in baseball. Although Cobb was an intense loner, he could be a great conversationalist when he was in the mood, as he sometimes was on long train rides or in the evenings as he lounged around the hotel lobby after games. Sportswriters invariably claimed the real Cobb, the one they interviewed off the diamond, was as *Baseball Magazine* remarked, "an extremely likeable person, fair-minded, generous, and altogether a typical American gentleman." At least one Cobb acquaintance, the venerable Branch Rickey, thought it was all part of his grand scheme—to cultivate friendships only with people of influence "for strictly personal benefit to himself."[41]

Cobb was equally gracious when he encountered fans, whether in the grandstands or on the street. Although his wide-open style of play was exciting enough on its own, Cobb strived to create drama and excitement, intuitively understanding the kind of excitement fans desired. He was a natural showman who professed to have the fans' interest at heart. "I have always been ambitious to please the fans and I believe it has helped me wonderfully," he told *Baseball Magazine* in 1912. He could be solicitous, as when he vowed to respond to every fan letter he received—a practice he retained until the last days of his life—or when he insisted on playing all out for exhibition games because he knew fans came to see him. He could also be remarkably endearing, as when he offered a Philadelphia fan $5.00 to replace a straw hat that he inadvertently crushed while chasing a fly ball beyond the outfield ropes, or when he reflexively thanked fans for asking for his autograph.[42]

Yet Cobb was no democrat or populist. He comported himself very differently than the man who eventually replaced him as the fans' favorite—the loveable lunk, George Herman "Babe" Ruth. Cobb believed that the man of honor gained status from the respect the public gave him, but he should do so without surrendering himself to them. Cobb wanted fans to appreciate him, not treat him as some sort of compatriot.

He made sure to retain a line—perhaps even a wall—between himself and his public. He sometimes arrived to the ballpark late just so he could milk his arrival for more applause. Cobb assumed he was superior to all and behaved accordingly; whatever kindness he offered came in response to fan adulation. Conversely, he would not stand criticism from those he considered his inferiors—which is to say almost everyone. The *St. Louis Republic* astutely commented, "Supersensitiveness has been the curse of Ty Cobb's life." While "he thrives on praise, he cannot be patient when the 'panning' begins." Unlike other "big men in public life," Cobb lacked "the ability to stand up silently and gamely under the lashes of adverse criticism." When a newspaper critic and sports editor of the *Birmingham News* panned his theatrical performance in the sports melodrama *The College Widow*, Cobb fired off a public response that clearly revealed his disdain for those who dared to criticize him. "Your criticism is beneath my notice," Cobb wrote, and then proceeded to show he had in fact taken note of just about everything the critic had to say: "I am a better actor than you are, a better sports editor than you are, a better dramatic critic than you are. I make more money than you do, and I know I am a better ball player—so why should inferiors criticize superiors?"[43]

Cobb could make such a statement to the occasional newspaper critic, but a ballpark full of booing fans required a different strategy—and a different perspective. He believed fans' hostility indicated just how much the baseball public respected and perhaps even revered him. Even so, he did not accept their taunts passively. He often sparred verbally with fans, returning invective back at fans who he believed were particularly rude or obnoxious. Most of the time, Cobb took such exchanges in stride; they were simply part of the verbal jousting that erupted whenever strong-willed men congregated. On a few occasions, however, Cobb's famous temper got the best of him. In 1912, he climbed into the grandstand to attack a New York fan who questioned Cobb's whiteness and his mother's virtue (see chapter 7, "The Most Unpopular Popular Man in Baseball," for a full analysis of this incident). After a 1919 game in Boston, an angry fan accosted Cobb outside the clubhouse. To silence the fan, Cobb kneed him in the groin before sauntering into the clubhouse to take his usual postgame shower. When told a crowd had congregated outside demanding justice for the doubled-over belligerent, Cobb dressed hurriedly and rushed out to face them down. Confronting the mob, he asked if anyone cared to argue with him. When no one came forward, he walked directly through the maze of "rowdies" as he made his way back to his hotel, as if to underscore their lack of nerve. Interviewed later that evening, Cobb asserted that while he did not like brawls and avoided them "whenever possible," he believed he was entitled to a "certain amount of respect" and he intended to "insist upon that little measure" as a reward for his success."[44]

Yet Cobb would have considered himself a failure if fans remained eternally hostile or—worse—if he had to gain respect by threats and acts of physical aggression. In his view, fans played a strategic role in his on-field duels. They acted as judge and jury, the ultimate arbiters in his bid for honor. He described his encounters with fans as staged dramas, the content of which followed a similar script. Each time, he faced down a hostile crowd, transforming their jeers to cheers by heroic deeds and displays that revealed the depth of his character. In this, Cobb demonstrated a remarkable ability to influence fans' behavior in ways that ultimately satisfied his need for honor (a topic explored more fully in chapter 7).

The ethic of honor imposed a strict code of ethical conduct, yet men of honor were remarkably ambivalent about one value: honesty. Cobb lied. Often. His lies were sometimes subtle and slight; other times, they were bold, brash, and even Homeric. Indeed, the most fascinating point about Cobb's relationship with the truth is how often he bent it, manipulated it, or simply denied it. While it may seem hypocritical for Cobb to have tried to advance his honor by lying, neither he nor most white men of the South saw it that way. Historically, Southern men of honor had a very different relationship to the truth than Northerners. Southerners valued square dealing and keeping one's word every bit as much as Northerners, but they parted ways with Northerners when it came to matters of self-presentation. Virtuous middle-class Northerners believed appearances reflected the true self—that individuals could never fully hide or disguise their inner or true character. Thus, the North's truly moral person strove to be transparent and sincere. In contrast, Southerners expected men to present crafted images of themselves that might not completely coincide with their true character. But what was character anyway? Northerners obsessed about it, but Southerners were often more interested in appearances than internal realities. So long as the individual had the power to keep others from exposing his true self, or "unmasking" him, he could present himself however he wished.⁴⁵

To challenge another man's presentation of self was a risky endeavor. Southerners called this "giving the lie" and it was about as offensive an insult as one could make. As a product of the late nineteenth-century rural South, Cobb knew all about "giving the lie" and indeed sometimes used the expression.⁴⁶ Like most Southern men, he grew up believing that a statement was not really a lie unless someone else dared to challenge it. His father offered an excellent example of how Southerners might twist the truth for the sake of self-presentation. When he moved from North Carolina to Georgia, he created the false impression that he was part of the prestigious Georgia Cobb clan. Ty not only perpetuated this ruse, he added to it by claiming that his father had followed family tradition by becoming a leader in Georgia state politics, when in fact his immediate family had no such history. Besides that, his father had only served one two-year term in the state House—hardly evidence of state leadership.⁴⁷

Ty created even more elaborate mistruths in regard to himself. Consider, again, the many letters he wrote as a minor leaguer to Grantland Rice; at least then, the content was generally true; only the authors were fictional. Some of Cobb's lies were so blatant he almost seemed to have dared others to call him out. This was especially true when he tried to discredit accusations that he was a dirty player. He confessed several times during his career that he sometimes used his spikes as weapons. What is most notable about these confessions, however, is their inconsistency. The names and number of incidents changed each time he defended himself. At the start of the 1909 season, Cobb answered critics by claiming that he had "cut down" only a "few" players, naming catcher Bill Sullivan and infielder Frank Isbell of the White Sox and third baseman Bill Bradley of the Cleveland Naps as his victims. In his 1925 autobiography, he put the number at four. While it is understandable that the list would have grown since 1909, what is less clear is why none of the people he mentioned in 1909 made his 1925 list; the new list included infielder Hobe Ferris and pitchers Dutch Leonard and Cy Morgan of Boston and St. Louis catcher Lou Criger. In later years, he became somewhat more circumspect when he offered names.

For a *Life* magazine piece he wrote in 1952, he listed just two people, Leonard, who made the 1925 list, and a new name, Cleveland catcher Harry Bemis. Four years later, Cobb gave two answers when John McCallum interviewed him for his biography, *The Tiger Wore Spikes*. In the flyleaf of *The Tiger*, McCallum quotes an emphatic Cobb proclaiming, "I never deliberately spiked a player in my life!" Yet in the body of the biography, he admitted to spiking Bemis and Leonard intentionally. Five years later when he wrote his final autobiography, he tweaked his story one last time: two names again, but this time it was Leonard and Morgan. Noticeably absent from all of his lists were Paul Krichell, Kid Elberfeld, and Buck Herzog, three players Cobb admitted to going after in other contexts. A faulty memory may account for some of the discrepancies, but not all. Clearly Cobb hoped to minimize the damage to his reputation that his confession might create; this seems to have been especially true after he ended his career. At that point, he could no longer demonstrate his honor by playing. Admitting to a limited number of spikings enabled Cobb to demonstrate that he was both man enough to defend himself, but gentleman enough to do so with restraint.[48]

Asserting one's version of events was only half the battle for a Southerner like Cobb. The other half involved defending one's assertions—even to the point of violence. The man of honor could not allow others to question his word. This was an ancient code. A seventeenth-century English writer commented, "It is reputed so great a shame to be accounted a lyer, that any other injury is cancelled by giving the lie. He that receiveth it standeth so charged in his honour and reputation, that he cannot disburden himself of that imputation, but by the striking of him that hath given it, or by challenging him the combat." Like most men of honor, Cobb lived his life by this principle. During a friendly game of golf with famed sportsman P. Hal Sims, both men hit balls into a bunker on the eighth hole. Cobb hit out first. When Sims casually asked Cobb how he did, Cobb reported that he had shot a five on the hole. "A five?" Sims asked incredulously. Cobb exploded. "Listen," he barked as he grabbed Sims's arm, "no one questions my word or score!" Only the quick intervention of the other members of the foursome kept Cobb from attacking Sims.[49]

For Cobb, as for all Southern men, the truth was essentially about power. When men made assertions, they had to be ready and willing to defend their words. They exacted retribution from anyone who doubted their word. They had to: to have one's projection of reality questioned was to be found weak and wanting. Countless times, Cobb tore into others to establish his version of reality, sometimes risking life and limb in the process. This is precisely what motivated Cobb to fight umpire Billy Evans under the grandstand after a game in Washington, D.C., toward the end of the 1921 season. In the fifth inning, Cobb attempted to steal second. He was certain he was safe; Evans thought otherwise. Obviously, Cobb understood he could not challenge the umpire every time a call went against him, but he also believed there were times when he needed to make a statement. This became one of those times. It did not help that the play happened early in the game—the fifth inning—giving both men ample opportunity to jaw back and forth as the contest continued. According to Tiger infielder Sammy Barnes, Cobb finally told Evans he wanted to "give [him] a good whipping," but feared he would be suspended. To this, Evans calmly replied that he was more than happy to give Cobb the opportunity if Cobb were to meet him outside the umpire's dressing room after the game. There, in front of a large crowd which included fans, players from both teams, and Cobb's wide-eyed eleven-year-old son and namesake, the two stripped down to the waist and went at it. Barnes called it "the bloodiest fight I ever saw in baseball." Evans was about the same height and weight as Cobb, just a few years older, and a recreational boxer. He often boasted of his physical prowess and ability to fend for himself, but on this day, he was no match for Cobb. Cobb pummeled Evans, splitting the umpire's left eyebrow and severely cutting his right cheekbone. When Evans collapsed, Cobb jumped on top of him, and proceeded to bang his head against the hard cinder surface. Only the intervention of the ballpark groundskeeper stopped the fight. After Evans showered, he walked over to the Detroit clubhouse with just a towel around his waist. In front of the Detroit players, he shook Cobb's hand and conceded defeat. "Well, Ty, you got the best of it," he said. Later, he told the press much the same thing. Cobb must have been pleased: from his perspective, Evans's concession vindicated his word.[50]

In another legendary incident, Cobb threatened a grocer at gunpoint and assaulted his assistant to defend not his version of the truth, but his wife's. This incident occurred during a dinner party at Cobb's Detroit home in which he was entertaining Washington manager Clark Griffith. Charlie, Cobb's wife, complained to Ty that grocery store owner William Carpenter refused to give her a refund for some spoiled fish he sold her because he believed the fish was perfectly fine. Offended that a mere shop owner questioned his wife's word, Cobb dashed down to the market, .32 automatic revolver in hand, to confront Carpenter. Once there, he ordered Carpenter at gunpoint to call Mrs. Cobb and apologize. At that moment, Carpenter's brother-in-law, butcher Howard Harding, burst into the room. Assuming the armed Cobb was a robber, he came at him with a meat cleaver and ordered him to leave. Instead, the two ended up trading blows on the street outside. Finally, the police arrived and carted Cobb off in a paddy wagon. The following day, the butcher told the press he would file a civil suit against Cobb if the police did not press charges. "I think it my duty to the public to have Cobb suppressed. . . . He's dangerous when he gets mad. I think he's unsafe." In this instance, Cobb paid dearly to defend the veracity of his wife's word and honor. The court ordered him to pay $50 in fines and—far more humbling to Cobb—apologize to Carpenter. Even worse, Cobb broke his thumb during the melee with Harding and was unable to play for two weeks.[51]

Since Southerners believed the truth was mostly an exercise in power, Cobb thought nothing of distorting reality to enhance his stature. After he retired from baseball, he turned this practice into an art. He fabricated an especially fantastic story about the year he stole a batting title from Joe Jackson, the Cleveland slugger who was one of Cobb's closest friends in the game. Once he established himself, Jackson became Cobb's chief rival at the plate, finishing second to Cobb in batting average three times: 1911, 1912, and 1913. Cobb's averages were phenomenal in those years (.420, .409, .390), but so were Jackson's (.408 in his first full year in the majors, followed by .395 and .373). In thirteen seasons, Jackson hit .356, third best on the all-time list and just ten percentage points behind Cobb. Cobb admired excellence and he was especially appreciative of Jackson's natural athleticism. He called Jackson the game's most natural hitter, a "born sticker." Long after both retired, Cobb confessed to Jackson "Whenever I got the idea I was a good hitter, I'd stop and take a good look at you. Then I knew I could stand some improvement. I don't think I ever saw a more perfect swing than yours." Cobb also liked Jackson personally. A common heritage drew them together. Indeed, Jackson may have been the closest person Cobb had to a peer in the major leagues. Both grew up about sixty miles from one another in the Southern Piedmont at about the same time, Cobb being just three years older than Jackson. As two of the game's players from the Deep South, they shared feelings of social and cultural isolation. Like Cobb, Jackson found the transition from rural South to urban North a difficult one. He made the Athletics' roster in both 1908 and 1909, but left the team several times because he missed his home and felt ostracized by players who teased him for his thick accent and rube-like ways. Whereas Cobb had responded to teasing by fighting back, Jackson turned inward, became depressed, and tried to escape by either bolting the team or getting drunk. Exasperated, Connie Mack traded Jackson to Cleveland. Through it all, Jackson found a sympathetic ally in Cobb. Cobb may have acted as Jackson's mentor during these years; he often greeted his shy compatriot as his fellow "cracker," thus turning a pejorative term into an exclusive designation of honor. Jackson quickly became one of Cobb's best friends in the league.[52]

Yet they were never friends on an equal footing. Cobb made sure of that. Cobb's father was an educator and civic leader. He instilled in Ty an ambition for learning, stature, and wealth. Jackson's father was a sharecropper in the impoverished upcountry of South Carolina. When Jackson was just a toddler, his father uprooted the family to find work at one of the region's new textile mills. They ended up at Brandon Mill, a company town outside Greenville. At the age of seven, Joe joined his father in the mill as a "linthead," dusting the floors twelve hours a day, six days a week. With no opportunity for a formal education, he remained functionally illiterate for the rest of his life, even needing his wife to sign his autograph for fans. Both men were products of the New South, but in diametrically different ways. Ever eager for status, Cobb played up his differences with Jackson whenever possible. In his final autobiography, Cobb highlighted Jackson's tortured English when recreating their conversations. During their playing days, Cobb depreciated Jackson's overall batting skills. Yes, he admired Jackson for his physical prowess, but he was also quick to note that Jackson was no student of the game. "I would hate to think how much Jackson could hit if he began to figure on getting the 'percentage,'" Cobb told sportswriter and friend Joe Wheeler. Cobb claimed Jackson had a stubborn streak that hindered his development as a hitter. When in a slump, Jackson "just swings harder at the ball" which made things worse. Because Jackson lacked a scientific approach, he did not know how to place the ball or adjust his hitting to match the situation; for this reason, Cobb claimed he believed Frank "Home Run" Baker—who never hit above Jackson's lifetime average—was a superior hitter.[53]

This was the context in which Cobb lied about a trick he claimed to have pulled on Jackson to win a tight batting race. Cobb first told the story in 1929, the year after he retired. Interviewed by sportswriter Joe Williams, Cobb recalled that the 1913 batting race was a particularly tight one. "Jackson was giving me an unusually tough tussle," Cobb observed. "I couldn't pull away from him . . . and I began to worry." Ever the cunning one, Cobb decided to rile Jackson with a bit of psychology. During a series with Cleveland in early September, Cobb deliberately snubbed Jackson as Jackson waited by the batting cage. "I knew he was waiting for me to come over and join him," Cobb stated, but rather than greet his friend as he usually did, "I walked right past him. He stuck out his hand, and I ignored it." According to Cobb, Jackson was so steamed that his old Southern buddy "publicly scorned him," he "lost all interest in the batting fight" and—good Southerner that he was—became preoccupied with how best to "avenge the insult." Cobb claimed Jackson failed to get a hit during the entire series. After Cobb left town, Jackson finally got wise to the scheme. However, simpleton that he was, he became so angry with Cobb for duping him, he "went another week without a hit."[54]

In later retellings, Cobb embellished the story even more. In a piece he wrote for *Life* magazine in 1952, Cobb now claimed the year was 1911, not 1913, and the teams were to play six games in four days to end the season. Most spectacular of all, he claimed Jackson was nine points ahead in the batting race when the series began. In this rendering, Cobb claimed that he didn't just ignore Jackson; he treated him with abject cruelty. Whenever they met, Cobb looked intently at a point six inches over Jackson's head. He also made a practice of passing near Jackson when the two teams changed sides at the end of each half inning so he could more fully humiliate his adversary by ignoring him. The "simple gullible" Jackson became so preoccupied with trying to figure out why his friend was ignoring him, he could not concentrate and slumped badly. Several years later, Cobb was at it again, this time for his autobiography. In this final rendering, Cobb claimed he not only stared above Jackson's head, he snarled, "Get away from me!" when Jackson persisted in trying to talk to him. Otherwise, the storyline is the same as the *Life* magazine version: Jackson slumped badly in the last days of the season and Cobb won the batting race with a remarkable .420 average to Jackson's .408.[55]

Why did Cobb offer such wildly different versions with each retelling? Perhaps he simply forgot some details as time distanced him from the actual event. This may explain why he misidentified the year, for example. Still, what is truly significant here is the arc of Cobb's thinking. With escalating audaciousness, he recalled the event in such a way as to emphasize his complete mastery over an adversary. Cobb did not believe it was enough to just beat Jackson; he had to humiliate him. How much of the story was true is difficult to determine, but two points are clear: If Cobb did try this ploy, it played no role in his batting race victory. The best guess is that the year was 1913, not 1911. In 1911, both men hit for remarkably high averages, but it was a batting race with little suspense as Cobb led Jackson by ten to twenty points for all but the first month of the season. The 1913 race was much closer as the two traded the lead until the end of the season. But no final six-game series decided the matter: the two teams only met once during the last week of the season and it was inconsequential to the race: Cobb got one hit in four at bats while Jackson went hitless in five official trips to the plate. Moreover, in head-to-head meetings earlier in the month, neither player hit well. In a four-game series, Cobb went four for fifteen while Jackson went two for fifteen. True, Jackson hit worse than Cobb, but he played better than Cobb claimed. By the end of the series, the two were less than two points apart: .3782 for Cobb; .3765 for Jackson. For the remainder of the season, Jackson's average held steady, finishing the season with a very impressive .373, just three points below his average at the end of his showdown with Cobb in early September. Conversely, Cobb went on a tear during the final weeks of the season, lifting his average by over ten points to .390 at season's end. If Cobb did in fact try to get into Jackson's head by ignoring him, the ploy may have given Cobb a lift, but it had little effect on Jackson. As Jackson later stated in a futile effort to set the record straight, "A story you now hear from time to time that Ty bulldozed me by getting my goat in a conceived plan to ignore me in Cleveland in that important final series is just a lot of hooey. Ty was able to beat me out because he got more hits than I did."[56]

Jackson told the truth, but Cobb was not interested in the truth; he wanted to demonstrate that he could humble an adversary at will. Similar motives animated many of the mistruths he created. Lies, whether willfully fashioned or not, enabled Cobb to assert power over others. By telling lies, he forced others to accept his view of reality or to engage in the arduous task of trying to disprove him. He anticipated few challengers. His rhetorical style helped to ensure that. As Branch Rickey observed, "there never were two sides to an argument" for Cobb; he always "knew he was right." Consider his response to Bill Webb, the fan who wrote Cobb to tell him he was at the infamous Herzog game in Dallas. As he often did, Cobb defended his behavior with bald-faced lies. The fight started because "Herzog blocked me off" then later "challenged me in my own room." It was all cut-and-dried according to Cobb. He refused to admit that his behavior contributed to the entire mess. "These are facts," he asserted before signing his name to end the letter. For Ty Cobb, to make an assertion was to make it true, so long as no one disproved his version. Remarkably, few even tried.[57]

Like all Southern whites of the Jim Crow era, race influenced Cobb's understanding of honor and his concept of self. In myriad ways, Southern blacks propped up their white neighbors. The wealth and ease that middle-class families like the Cobbs enjoyed came in large part from the labor of African Americans. Black men, women, and children provided most of the muscle and much of the expertise that enabled Southern farms to flourish and Southern households to function. More abstractly, blacks helped Southern whites' psyches. In this biracial and bifurcated society of white and black, haves and have-nots, whites saw in blacks a constant reminder of what it meant to be without either honor or status—dependent, vulnerable, powerless. Southern whites of all classes and political persuasions assumed African Americans were inferior and demanded they behave as servile beings to demonstrate their endorsement of the racial status quo.[58]

That demand became especially acute during the years that Ty Cobb came of age and established his career. This was an uncertain and volatile era in the history of Southern race relations. Blacks had freedom, but little else. Southern whites believed blacks still needed the protection and discipline of the superior race. Without it, whites contended, blacks would revert to criminality, barbarism, and sloth. Indeed, many whites believed black devolution had already begun. In response, whites employed a variety of legal (segregation, disenfranchisement, chain gangs, and county farms) and illegal (lynching, race riots) means to control and subjugate blacks. Although whites exerted near hegemonic power over blacks, they remained deeply suspicious and even fearful of blacks' behavior. A new generation of African Americans, free of any direct relationship to slavery, was coming of age. Most Southern whites viewed this generation as less submissive, less loyal, less pliable, and thus far more dangerous than those who had grown up under the paternalistic sway of the Peculiar Institution. The year Cobb was born, South Carolina poet Paul H. Hayne remarked, "The accursed negro Race, fickle, unfaithful, half-savage, released from every wholesome restraint, shows itself more intractable and hostile to the Whites every year."[59]

Amid this crisis, whites divided into two distinct camps to solve the so-called "negro problem." The most radical voiced extreme pessimism that African Americans would ever be capable of living in freedom. In 1909, a white college professor in Memphis asked his white students to predict, "What will become of the American Negro." Most in the class concluded that because African Americans were incapable of ruling themselves, they would soon degenerate to a brutish and lascivious barbarism. Uplift for the race was out of the question, his students insisted, as education and political participation only ruined blacks by giving them appetites for things they should not want and could not handle, namely power, freedom, and equality. When the professor reported students' responses in the *South Atlantic Quarterly*, he refused to condemn their negative appraisal of the black potential. "These are not theories that might be, but tendencies that are," the professor explained. "Are not the indications plain"—underlining his words for emphasis—"*that the black man is to be restrained, hampered, brow-beaten, discouraged within the next quarter of a century as never before in all the bitter years of his existence on this continent?*" When in 1904 a

Northern writer toured the South, he reported "men of intelligence" repeatedly told him that "niggers are not wholly human, that they are more akin to beasts and should be dealt with accordingly." A South Carolina farmer explained, "All the men are thieves, and all the women are prostitutes. It's their natur' to be that way, and they never'll be no other way."[60]

Not all whites were as extreme as this. Racial moderates, comprised mostly of the old elite planter class and the newly emerging entrepreneurial class, offered a more hopeful assessment of African Americans. The most progressive possessed a near missionary zeal to improve the conditions of African Americans by integrating them more fully into civilized Christian society. They were especially confident of the reformative powers of education for all members of the lower classes, black and white. They wanted a New South built upon industry and commerce. Moderates were especially critical of the vitriol espoused by racial radicals, believing their incendiary language fueled the ignorant prejudices and violent passions of lower-class whites. As they saw it, race-baiting, race riots, and lynchings threatened to destabilize the business climate and drive off potential Northern investors. Crass racism, moderates contended, should have no place in a modern, progress-oriented South.

Yet moderates were not without racial prejudices. They agreed with radicals on certain fundamentals. Both accepted black inferiority as scientific fact. Both concluded that because blacks were inferior, they should remain in an inferior and dependent social and political status. Finally, both groups endorsed racial segregation laws as necessary to keep the peace and reinforce the racial hierarchy. Moderates sometimes spoke loftily of the two races' ability to work together for the betterment of the South, but they meant this in the abstract, as a kind of spiritual kinship, not unlike the ideas endorsed by Booker T. Washington in his famous Atlanta Exposition Speech. Moderates, no less than radicals, supported disenfranchisement and the physical separation of the races.[61]

Growing up in Royston, Cobb was exposed to both racial radicals and racial moderates. According to the scant records we have of his views on race, Ty's father seems to have been a racial moderate. Although William Cobb was a friend of Georgia's race-baiting governor Hoke Smith, he embraced the Progressives' faith in education as a source of uplift for both races. In a 1901 speech before the Georgia Agricultural Society, William asserted, "The slate and the pencil are more efficient implements of true weal than the hangman's knot and the policeman's club." In soaring language, he proclaimed, "no state ever went on a more heaven sent mission than when she goes down by the cradles of the infants, rich and poor, bond and free, and offers them means of self-preservation, happiness, and success." Although William did not reference blacks in this speech, his subsequent actions as a state senator suggest he wanted blacks to share in the uplift offered by education. When the Georgia legislature considered slashing state funding for black education, Cobb helped defeat the measure, calling the bill "unnecessary and unjust." On the floor of the Senate, he reminded the legislature that African Americans played a vital role in the South's economy, past and present, and appealed to Southern whites' paternal responsibilities to their former slaves. At the same time, he made clear that whatever privileges blacks possessed they did so because of their service to and dependence upon whites. "The negro [has] been loyal to the white man," Cobb asserted; in return, "the white man ought to be grateful." Indeed, "we ought to be generous with the negro and help him to become a useful and helpful member of society." William Cobb's views, though somewhat progressive for the South at this time, fell far short of promoting black equality. He would grant blacks access to public education, not as a right but as a gift for their loyalty to whites. Later, as Franklin County's school commissioner, he oversaw an educational system that was both segregated and discriminatory in its provisions for black children.[62]

William Cobb did his best to teach Ty his moderate views of race relations at home, but he could do little about what Cobb learned on the streets of Royston. Some of his peers and the older boys of town ball surely exposed him to a far coarser understanding of African Americans. Quite possibly, they even showed him the lynching memorabilia that young white men found so fascinating—photographs, postcards, sound recordings, and actual relics like pieces of bone, skin, and even organs. Regardless, lynching was not a vague abstraction to Cobb; white Royston lynched at least two African Americans during his lifetime and murdered two others under circumstances that, according to one historian, "may have been the equivalent of lynching." Three more lynchings occurred in the surrounding countryside of Franklin and Madison counties. Since all occurred in either the spring or summer in the years after Cobb left Royston, he could not have been present for any of them. Even so, this was the milieu in which he lived. He knew, perhaps intimately, many of the men who perpetrated these crimes.[63]

Ty Cobb's understanding of the interplay of race and honor can only be pieced together by his behavior and the scattered statements he made on the subject. In some respects, he acted toward African Americans in ways that would have made his father proud. Late in life, he claimed to have "lived most peaceably with colored folk" and expressed considerable gratitude and affection for those who worked for his family, especially the "Negro 'mammy'" who helped raise him and "Uncle" Ezra, a field hand and general handyman, with whom he worked alongside on occasion. Cobb also credited a black man for patiently teaching him to swim when, as a boy, he was afraid of the water.[64]

Such eulogizing suggests Cobb followed the uniquely Southern pattern of selective intimacy with African Americans—an intimacy orchestrated wholly by whites. Whites, including Cobb, used terms like "Mammy" and "Uncle" with considerable condescension, implying a familial bond of affection that the recipients of these salutations may not have shared. To blacks, these familial titles were poor substitutes for those that reflected actual respect: Mr., Mrs., and Miss. As one older black man told a younger relative, "Son, it's like this in the South. A Negro is a 'boy' until he is a man. Then, he is 'Dad' or an 'Uncle.' Women are 'Aunts' and 'Mammys.'" Whatever relationship Cobb had with the blacks of his household, it existed solely on his terms. Early on, he learned that black people were there to do his bidding. He told biographer John McCallum that when farm work conflicted with an important baseball game, the team captain of the Royston Reds would simply "collar a Negro lad" to labor for him, a practice that met with the approval of William Cobb. Later, Cobb learned to exploit blacks in a far more systematic venture. Together with a couple of his Royston neighbors, he purchased land just northwest of town to rent to black tenant farmers. Cobb called the tract "Booker Washington Heights" in an obvious effort to lampoon the famous black leader's self-help philosophy. He made this clear in an interview with a St. Louis journalist. "We call this nigger property down home, for nothing but Negros live in it," Cobb explained. "There's money in it, I mean in the niggers," he boasted. "You see I get $3 for this, $2.50 for that one, and $2 for this house." Cobb boasted he and his partners doubled their profits within the first few years of ownership.[65]

Unlike the most virulent racists of the Jim Crow era, Cobb at least recognized African Americans had a place in American life, but he believed that place was in the South and under the wise tutelage of the South's benevolent whites. In the midst of Detroit's 1906 spring training, the brash nineteen-year-old boasted to Joe Jackson, a sportswriter for the *Detroit Free Press*, that he knew why black doormen, porters, and the like offered him better service than Northerners like Jackson. Cobb claimed he understood "the negro perfectly" because he was "born and bred in the South." Northerners lacked this sort of insight. As a result, the Northern man "proceeds on the lines that indicate that he believes that the fourteenth amendment means what it says." The Southern white man never makes this mistake and thus receives better service. That is, "the colored man more readily responds to the requests and demands of those of the South who maintains [sic] the old relation of master and man between the races."[66]

Cobb may have thought he understood African Americans, but he did not understand them well enough to empathize with the psychic toll they paid for having to live in a system that expected them to prefer servility to freedom and equality. For that, we need to turn to another Cobb, Ned Cobb, a black sharecropper from Alabama. Born a year before Ty, Ned Cobb knew exactly what whites demanded of him—and what would happen if he failed to conform to their expectations. "I've gotten along in this world by studyin' the race and knowin' that I was one of the underdogs," he said. Survival demanded he "play dumb sometimes . . . humble down and play shut-mouthed." If he followed the rules, he figured he could extract some measure of leniency. "They'd give you a good name if you was obedient to 'em, acted nice when you met 'em and didn't question 'em 'bout what they said they had against you." Yet it was always a precarious existence; one slip and some white man was always ready "to knock me in the head." Dare to "cry about your rights and mistreatin' of you and they'd murder you."[67]

Ty Cobb's relations with African Americans during his playing career confirm the wisdom of Ned Cobb's ethos: blacks who took on a servile persona got along much better with him than those who did not. Cobb was exceedingly indulgent and kind to those who behaved as he demanded. This applied to various African Americans the Tigers employed to help in the clubhouse. During Cobb's career, the Tigers hired—or kept might be a more appropriate term—a number of African American "mascots," individuals who lived and traveled with the team for the good luck they presumably provided. Cobb gave special attention to two who stayed with the Tigers longest, Ulysses Harrison and Alexander Rivers. In 1908, teammate Germany Schaefer allegedly "found" Harrison in Chicago and invited him to travel with the team. The team nicknamed him "Li'l Rastus," a pejorative term for a simpleminded African American youth of questionable moral integrity. Perhaps because Harrison fit the servile stereotype so well, Cobb quickly took a liking to him and became his unofficial steward. Following the 1909 season, Cobb brought Harrison with him to his Georgia home where he worked as Cobb's golf caddy and personal servant.[68]

A few years after Harrison ended his time with the Tigers, the club took on an older black man, Alexander George Washington "King" Rivers of New Orleans, as mascot and clubhouse go-fer. Cobb met Rivers in 1912 during spring training. Prior to joining the Tigers, he had served as a chauffeur to a wealthy New Orleans jeweler. With the Tigers, Rivers became Cobb's personal batboy and servant around the clubhouse—a job he kept for well over a decade. So accustomed to the South's practices of racial deference, Rivers referred to Cobb as "Mistah Cobb" and may have even called him "Marse Ty." Rivers performed the servile role so completely, a correspondent for the *Chicago Tribune* declared Rivers "as much a slave as Uncle Tom was."[69] Rivers was only one of many blacks Cobb brought from the South to serve him. He believed nearly all Northern black servants were too insolent and difficult to manage. Cobb preferred the service of those who knew their place.

To early twentieth-century baseball fans, Cobb's relationships with the Tigers' African American mascots and servants made for a good human-interest story. To Cobb, their presence—and loyalty—meant far more than that. Annoyed by Northern blacks and exhausted by the anti-Southern hazing he sometimes received from other players, Cobb found refuge and reassurance in the devotion of blacks like Harrison, Rivers, and his other servants. They reaffirmed his projection of self and the superiority of his way of life. It was an old story, really. In slavery, masters depended upon the devotion of the enslaved to enhance their reputations as benign patriarchs. After slavery, Southern whites found comfort in celebrating the virtues of the faithful few servants who stayed on to serve their former masters out of sheer loyalty to "their" white families. By the turn of the century, this cult had grown into a culture of nostalgia for a South that never was—an idyllic South of civility, order, deference, and racial hegemony and harmony. In finding two devotees and by nurturing their loyalty, Cobb could live the myth and even give it currency in the North. Because they were not white, African Americans could not bestow honor upon Cobb, but they did help Cobb in other ways. Ultimately, they helped Cobb give the lie to others—and to himself.[70]

Cobb could be downright brutal toward African Americans who refused to conform to his preconceptions of how a black person ought to behave. It did not happen often, but on occasion, he violently assaulted blacks who failed to show him the deference and honor he believed a black man or woman should always show a white man. One of the most violent and—by modern standards—shocking of these incidents was also Cobb's first racial incident that received public attention. During

Figure 4.2. The Tigers pose prior to a World Series game against the Pittsburgh Pirates. Cobb is seated far to the left. Behind him—and separated from the rest of the team—is "Li'l Rastus," a team mascot and Cobb's personal batboy and servant. *Source:* Courtesy of sportingoregon.com.

spring training in 1907, Cobb had an altercation with the Augusta ballpark's black groundskeeper and his wife. Apparently, the groundskeeper, who may have been drunk, recognized Cobb from his earlier stint with the Augusta Tourists. "Presuming an acquaintanceship," as one reporter put it, the man greeted Cobb with an outstretched hand and a very personable, "Hello Ty, Old Boy." Cobb was appalled. As the *Detroit Free Press* reported, Cobb considered it an insult that the groundskeeper put "himself on equal footing of a white man." Rather than extend his hand, Cobb coiled it in a fist and "drove [it] forward, hitting the man with a hard blow." He continued to batter the shaken groundskeeper until the poor man was finally able to make his escape to his shack next to the clubhouse. Cobb gave chase, but was confronted by the distressed groundskeeper's wife who berated Cobb for mistreating her husband. To Cobb, this was an egregious violation of both racial and gender etiquette. Infuriated, he grabbed and choked the woman. He might have hurt her severely had not catcher Charlie Schmidt interceded by pulling Cobb away. When word got to Navin and Jennings of the attack, they immediately discussed the possibility of trading their young star for a lesser talent, just to get rid of him.[71]

Most Southern whites probably wondered what the fuss was about. In their view, Cobb had acted as a white man should act when confronted by African Americans who presumed equality and familiarity with a white man. Cobb's behavior was hardly noteworthy, especially not in Georgia in the spring of 1907. Less than six months earlier, Atlanta had been the sight of a four-day orgy of white-on-black violence, one of the worst race riots in the nation's history. As many as 10,000 whites participated, many of them young men who took to the streets shouting chants like:

> We are rough, we are tough,
> We are rough, we are tough,
> We kills niggers and never get enough.

Others yelled, "Burn him! Kill the nigger! Kill the black devil!" as they pillaged black neighborhoods and violated blacks indiscriminately. When it was over, marauding whites had murdered anywhere from twenty-five to forty African Americans, beaten hundreds of others, and looted and burned nearly all of black Atlanta. The riot was the culmination of months of anti-black agitation played out in the press, political rostrums, and white church pulpits. Throughout the state, Georgia's leading white citizens (including Cobb family friend Hoke Smith) argued for stronger race-based voting restrictions and the aggressive purging of black criminality. Especially in Georgia's major cities, white politicians tried to outdo one another in their denunciations of black bestiality. Many claimed the riot was an act of moral reform, a spontaneous grassroots effort to purify the city by eradicating the black menace.[72]

Cobb was not in Georgia during the riot, but he was there the previous fall and winter as the political climate began to degenerate into violent race-baiting. He was also there immediately after the riot, spending time in both Atlanta and Augusta. Quite likely, his racial consciousness and antipathies had become sharper and more agitated as a result. When the black groundskeeper came at him, Cobb probably interpreted his behavior as evidence of black impudence and degeneracy. He then acted just as the white press had inspired white Georgians to act a few months earlier—with violent moral outrage. None of this justifies Cobb's behavior, but it does set his behavior within the wider context of white Southern racism. Cobb believed he had acted the hero. So immersed in the white South's understanding of race, he could not fathom the response of his fellow Detroit ballplayers. He must have been especially enraged by Schmidt, who pulled Cobb off the groundskeeper's wife. Schmidt, after all, was a Southerner—born in the village of London, Arkansas. How dare he interfere in the affairs of a fellow Southerner? But Schmidt was not of the same Southern cloth as Cobb. A check of the 1880 manuscript census suggests Charlie was most probably the son of John and Mary Schmidt, recent immigrants from Germany.[73] His understanding of race was decidedly different than Cobb's. When asked why he intervened to protect the groundskeeper's wife, he curtly replied, "I have my opinion of anybody who would strike a woman." Cobb—and most white Southerners—would never refer to a female African American as a "woman." Cobb must have viewed Schmidt as a traitor to his race and his home.[74]

Cobb acted with obvious criminal intent. No matter: the law made no effort to arrest, much less punish him. Perhaps the team intervened on Cobb's behalf. More likely, Augusta authorities believed that arresting a white man for the assault on a black man and black woman was not worth their time, especially since both victims had violated the race code. This was the general pattern throughout the South. As an Augusta newspaper reported in 1890, "If a negro kills a white man, he is pretty sure either to be lynched or hung. But if a white man slays a negro, he is in no danger of being lynched, and as to his being hung for the crime, there is not much probability." Following the standards of the white South, Cobb understood he had every right to strike the two with impunity.[75]

A year later, Cobb was at it again. This time his victim was a Detroit street repairman. On a fine June day in 1908, Cobb stepped out of a Detroit hotel and right into some newly laid asphalt. One of the city workers, a black man named Fred Collins, tried to shoo Cobb away so he would not muck up his work. Cobb took umbrage, confronted Collins, punched him in the face, and knocked him down. Collins vowed to swear a warrant for Cobb's arrest. "That white man didn't have any reason for hitting me," he told a reporter. "I didn't tell him anything more than I tell hundreds of people every day." Once he heard Cobb's Southern drawl, Collins even tried to show a bit of the old Southern deference. "I could see that he was a Southerner," Collins said, "and I tried to explain to him, but he kept on insulting me." Collins's white foreman defended Collins and his fellow black employees. All were "good workers and good citizens and never give anybody any trouble," the foreman declared. "There was not the slightest excuse for Cobb hitting Collins." In the subsequent trial, a judge found Cobb guilty of assault, but immediately suspended the sentence. Cobb did not escape completely unscathed, however; under threat of a civil suit, he paid Collins $75. In addition, one of Detroit's dailies, the *Free Press*, chided Cobb for trying to treat blacks in the North as he did "in dear old Georgia." Even more insulting to Cobb, the newspaper also published a cartoon of Cobb and Collins tarred black from rolling in the asphalt. The two are so indistinguishable, a police officer asks, "Which one of youse is Ty Cobb?" as he breaks up the fight. Cobb was truly shaken by the bad publicity the altercation caused—at least for a little while. Two days after his arrest, he told a local journalist that he regretted going to court "about that negro affair." He then tried to explain his perspective. "Up here, they don't understand me, see? Course being from Georgia I think different about Negroes from what they do up here." A few weeks later, however, Cobb sounded much more self-assured. In response to a question about the steep fine he would have to pay for hitting Collins, he denied any wrongdoing. "When insulted, it is worth $75 to get satisfaction," the man of honor asserted.[76]

Remarkably, given Cobb's otherwise volatile temper and propensity to use violence to solve problems, he had only two other (recorded) violent encounters with blacks during his playing career: in 1919, a black Detroit hotel employee named Ada Morris brought suit against Cobb for $10,000, claiming that he kicked her down a flight of stairs and called her "nigger." Cobb was never arrested and Morris mysteriously dropped the suit even though the assault had left her bed-ridden. The *Chicago Defender*, the leading African American newspaper of the day, speculated that "mysterious forces" had "played havoc" with the Detroit justice system. The paper also speculated that Morris may have been bought off, "hypnotized by . . . a few silver dollars." Five years later, this time in Philadelphia, Cobb punched a black groundskeeper at Shibe Park after—according to Cobb—the groundskeeper insulted him.[77] Cobb rarely ruminated publicly on matters of race, so it is difficult to determine why he became less violent toward blacks during the course of his career. Possibly, the decline in altercations was more illusory than real. The *Chicago Defender* alleged in the Morris case that Cobb's representatives persuaded her to drop all charges by doing some serious "mitt greasing." Perhaps Cobb and the Tigers had simply learned to handle such altercations before the press got wind. Or perhaps Cobb's time in the North forced him to temper his views. At the very least, Cobb probably learned to be more circumspect in public as he became more aware of his celebrity. Through bitter experience, he learned that the North was not the South: neither the legal system nor the press were willing to let Cobb get away with mayhem. Instead, the law consistently forced Cobb to do that which he despised—to recognize African Americans' personal autonomy and civil rights. The courts demanded that Cobb pay his victims for damages and—at least on one occasion—to apologize for his poor behavior. No self-respecting Southern white man could do that without feeling that he had lost a good bit of his stature. A man of honor should not apologize to inferiors, for such an act made him both vulnerable and debased. As he struggled to adjust to life in the North, Cobb must have felt angry and humiliated at times.

Cobb never abandoned his distinct understanding of race relations and African Americans—at least not during his playing career. Race was too inextricably tied to his perception of manhood for this. In 1912, he nearly beat a spectator senseless for daring to suggest he was of mixed blood. (Apparently, Cobb could dish it out but he couldn't take it: he routinely called Babe Ruth "Nigger" to needle him.) Unlike most stars of the era, Cobb steadfastly refused to play against Negro League teams in exhibition matches because he believed it beneath his dignity. Even after twenty years in the North, he remained dedicated to the South's code of racial etiquette. Tiger pitcher Bill Moore offered an alarming indication of this in recounting an incident that occurred during spring training in 1925. While dining in the team's hotel, Cobb became almost unhinged when a black waiter failed to use a formal salutation when addressing him. "God almighty, you would've thought a bomb exploded in there," Moore recalled. "Cobb jumped out of his chair and grabbed that waiter by the lapels and told him, 'You so-and-so nigger. It's 'No, sir' and 'Yes, sir' when you to talk to a white man!'" With that Cobb proceeded to launch into "a tirade about the blacks." "Cobb hated a colored person worse than anything," Moore concluded. Moore was wrong, Cobb was not a "black-hater" and said as much in his final autobiography. He maintained a deep and abiding affection for those who behaved with proper deference. He only erupted against those who—in his view—behaved improperly. When this happened, his behavior and attitudes were very hateful indeed.[78]

In January 1960, Ty Cobb was seventy-three years old and fighting cancer, diabetes, high blood pressure, and a weak heart. Infirm and in constant pain, he was nevertheless determined to complete his magnum opus, a final autobiography. He had written autobiographies before, at least three dating back to his playing days, but he vowed this one would be different, not only from his previous efforts but from all sports celebrity autobiographies. He would neither sugarcoat nor romanticize; rather, he would tell his story forthrightly and even tersely, sparing no one's feelings. The result, *My Life in Baseball*, was a fitting climax to his career in public life: just as he had once transformed the game of baseball, he now transformed a genre of sports literature, constructing the first tell-all autobiography. Cobb candidly addressed nearly all the controversies that surrounded his life—his no-holds-barred style of play, his feuds with players, managers, and owners, his managerial career, and the betting scandal that nearly drove him out of baseball. As he strained to make clear, his sole purpose in putting pen to paper was simple: he wanted to "set the record straight"—to confront the lies and dispel the misconceptions about how he played and why he played as he did. Cobb claimed a reluctance to do so. He professed to be at peace with the world and had no desire to pick at old sores that would reopen old wounds. But after years of being accused of everything from vicious play to cheating to thuggery, he had had enough. "For upwards of thirty years," he began, "I've turned away from all offers to speak my piece. I felt no need to justify or defend any act of mine." With "time running short," he had changed his mind. "There comes the moment when a man must speak . . . as a simple duty to himself and those who carry his name. My critics have had their innings. I will have mine now." This—his final public act—was an act of honor to himself and to his family. Ty Cobb died four months before the book's publication. Once released, *My Life in Baseball* received polite, though by no means enthusiastic, reviews. By 1961, few Americans were much interested in Cobb's allegiance to the code of honor. No doubt, those who bothered to read his autobiography probably interpreted his references to honor as the atavistic rants of a tired old man. Sales languished. Ty Cobb's final attempt to salvage his honor came to naught.[79]

NOTES

1. Ty Cobb, with Al Stump, *My Life in Baseball* (1961; repr., Lincoln, NE: Bison Books, 1993), 29–31.
2. Cobb, *My Life*, 31.
3. Cobb, *My Life*, 32; Cobb to Clancy quoted in Al Stump, *Cobb* (Chapel Hill, NC: Algonquin Books, 1994), 386.
4. John McCallum, *The Tiger Wore Spikes: An Informal Biography of Ty Cobb* (New York: A. S. Barnes, 1956), 23, 29; "This Was Ty Cobb: Anecdotes Accent Fierce Competitive Nature," *Baseball Digest* (October–November 1961): 70; Shirley Povich, "Best Player—Not Best Man," *Washington Post*, January 1, 1995, D14. Cobb has vehemently denied the Rucker story in his autobiography. See Cobb, *My Life*, 143.

5. F. C. Lane, "Famous Rivals of the Diamond," *Baseball Magazine* (July 1913): 26; Ring Lardner, "Tyrus: The Greatest of 'Em All," *American Magazine* (June 19, 1915): 20, 21; Branch Rickey, *The American Diamond: A Documentary of the Game of Baseball* (New York: Simon and Schuster, 1965), 27, 28; Stump, *Cobb*, 165–66.

6. Ty Cobb, *Busting 'Em and Other Big League Stories* (1914; repr., Jefferson, NC: McFarland, 2003), 21; Charles C. Alexander, *Ty Cobb* (New York: Oxford University Press, 1984), 58–59; Fred Haney, "My Most Unforgettable Character," *Readers Digest* (June 1964): 99.

7. Ty Cobb, edited by William R. Cobb, *Memoirs of Twenty Years in Baseball* (Marietta, GA: Self-published, 2002), 77–78; "Who Will Win My Batting Crown? An Interview with Ty Cobb," *Baseball Magazine* (September 1920): 473.

8. Kenneth S. Greenberg's *Honor and Slavery: Lies, Duels, Noses, Masks, Dressing as a Woman, Gifts, Strangers, Humanitarianism, Death, Slave Rebellions, the Proslavery Argument, Baseball, Hunting, and Gambling in the Old South* (Princeton: Princeton University Press, 1996), 115–24, offers a provocative explanation concerning baseball's lack of popularity in the nineteenth-century South.

9. Cobb, *My Life*, 175, 171; Edward Grant Barrow with James M. Kahn, *My Fifty Years in Baseball* (New York: Coward-McCann, 1951), 33.

10. McCallum, *Tiger Wore Spikes*, 99; Hughie Jennings, "My Opinion of Ty Cobb: How the Greatest Player in the History of the Game Looks to His Own Manager," *Baseball Magazine* 8, No. 5 (March 1912): 16; Rube Bressler in Lawrence S. Ritter, *The Glory of Their Times: The Early Days of Baseball Told by the Men Who Played It* (New York: Perennial, 1966), 205.

11. Cobb, *My Life*, 172.

12. Jimmy Austin in Ritter, *Glory of Their Times*, 90.

13. *Sporting Life* (July 13, 1907): 2; *Chicago Daily Tribune*, September 9, 1914, 11; *Detroit News*, September 11, 1914, 13; *Sporting News* (June 14, 1950): 16.

14. Cobb, *My Life*, 94; Joe Williams, "Setting the Record Straight, January 27, 1960," in *The Joe Williams Baseball Reader: The Glorious Game, From Ty Cobb and Babe Ruth to the Amazing Mets; 50 Years of Baseball Writing by the Celebrated Newspaper Columnist*, edited by Peter Williams (Chapel Hill: Algonquin Books, 1989), 17; *Sporting News* (April 5, 1950): 4.

15. Cobb, *My Life*, 157.

16. In some retellings of his encounter with Morgan, Cobb claimed he tried to score on a base hit. *Sporting Life* (March 2, 1912): 14; Cobb, *Memoirs of Twenty Years*, 47; Cobb, *My Life*, 125.

17. *Sporting Life* (March 2, 1912): 14; Cobb, *Memoirs of Twenty Years*, 47, 50–51; Cobb, *My Life*, 125; Alexander, *Ty Cobb*, 122.

18. Bill Webb to Wiley Thornton, August 26, 1975, Ty Cobb Materials, Baseball Hall of Fame.

19. Alexander, *Ty Cobb*, 132–33.

20. On the nose as a presentation of self and nose-pulling as a form of insult, see Greenberg, *Honor and Slavery*, 3–21; John D. McCallum, *Ty Cobb* (New York: Praeger Publishers, 1975), 106–107.

21. Alexander, *Ty Cobb*, 132–33; McCallum, *Ty Cobb*, 106–107.

22. Ty Cobb to Bill Webb, May 4, 1955, Ty Cobb Collection, Baseball Hall of Fame.

23. "Diamond Great Revealed Thoughts in Messages to 'Bible' Publisher," *Sporting News* (December 20, 1961): 12, 14.

24. Solomon Northup, *Twelve Years a Slave: The Narrative of Solomon Northup* (Auburn, NY: Derby and Miller, 1853), 204; Edward King, *The Great South: A Record of Journeys in Louisiana, Texas, the Indian Territory, Missouri, Arkansas, Mississippi, Alabama, Georgia, Florida, South Carolina, North Carolina, Kentucky, Tennessee, Virginia, West Virginia, and Maryland* (Hartford, CT: American Publishing Company, 1875), 372. In addition to works already cited on Southerners' penchant for violent retribution, see also Bruce, Jr., *Violence and Culture in the Antebellum South*.

25. *Sporting Life* (April 13, 1907): 11; *Detroit News*, May 19, 1912, 2; *Detroit Free Press*, May 20, 1912, 8.

26. Haney quoted in Alexander, *Ty Cobb*, 120; Fred Haney, "My Most Unforgettable Character," *Readers Digest*, 99; Charlie Gehringer in Donald Honig, *Baseball When the Grass Was Real: Baseball from the Twenties to the Forties Told by the Men Who Played It* (Lincoln, NE: Bison Books, 1975), 42.

27. Cobb, *Memoirs of Twenty Years*, 45–48; Cobb, *My Life*, 280.

28. *New York Times*, April 17, 1910, S2.

29. Special Cobb insert was included in *Sporting News* (August 5, 1909); Allen Sangree, "The Greatest Living Ball Player," *Baseball Magazine* (February 1911): 5–7; *Sporting Life* (October 23, 1909): 8; "The Ty Cobb Number," *Baseball Magazine* (March 1912); "Editorial," *Baseball Magazine* (May 1916): 1; *Sporting Life* (September 21, 1912): 22.

30. Billy Evans, "Fans Look For Star Players in All Games," *New York Times*, March 16, 1913, S4.

31. Alexander, *Ty Cobb*, 93–95; *Sporting Life* (August 13, 1910): 5; *Sporting Life* (August 20, 1910): 7; *Sporting News* (August 11, 1910): 1.

32. Alexander, *Ty Cobb*, 92, 104; *Chicago Tribune*, April 16, 1912, 15; *Chicago Tribune*, April 17, 1912, 14.

33. On the emerging culture of celebrity in entertainment, see Joy S. Kasson, *Buffalo Bill's Wild West: Celebrity, Memory, and Popular History* (New York: Hill and Wang, 2000); Richard de Cordova, *Picture Personalities: The Emergence of the Star System in America* (Urbana: University of Illinois Press, 1990); Charles L. Ponce de Leon, *Self-Exposure: Human-Interest Journalism and the Emergence of Celebrity in America, 1890–1940* (Chapel Hill: University of North Carolina Press, 2002); Gaylyn Studlar, *The Mad Masquerade: Stardom and Masculinity in the Jazz Age* (New York: Columbia University Press, 1996); Jennifer M. Bean, ed., *Flickers of Desire: Movie Stars of the 1910s* (New Brunswick, NJ: Rutgers University Press, 2011); Lary May, *Screening Out the Past: The Birth of Mass Culture and the Motion Picture Industry* (Chicago: University of Chicago Press, 1980), 96–146; Barry Smart, *The Sport Star: Modern Sport and the Cultural Economy of Sporting Celebrity* (London: Sage Publishing, 2005), 1–50.

34. Alexander, *Ty Cobb*, 64–65; McCallum, *Ty Cobb*, 63; Cobb, *My Life*, 76.

35. Cobb, *My Life*, 78–80; Cobb to Mack, February 22, 1955.

36. *Detroit Free Press*, April 14, 1913, 4. Acrimonious negotiations were well-covered by the press. See *Detroit Free Press*, April 9, 1913, 13; *Detroit Free Press*, April 10, 1913, 12; *Detroit Free Press*, April 11, 1913, 12; *Detroit Free Press*, April 17, 1913, 8; *Detroit Free Press*, April 18, 1913, 12.

37. *New York Times*, April 17, 1913, 9; *Detroit Free Press*, April 24, 1913, 10; *New York Times*, April 26, 1913, 12; Stump, *Cobb*, 226.

38. Billy Evans, "According to Billy Evans," *Sporting News* (November 18, 1926): 6.

39. *St. Louis Post-Dispatch*, May 9, 1909, 27.

40. F. C. Lane, "A Day With Ty Cobb," *Baseball Magazine* (April 1916): 47–58.

41. *Baseball Magazine* (March 1912): unnumbered frontispiece; Rickey, *American Diamond*, 27.

42. *Baseball Magazine* (March 1912): 54, 56.

43. *St. Louis Republic*, April 15, 1917, is quoted in Mark Okkonen, *The Ty Cobb Scrapbook: An Illustrated Chronology of Significant Dates in the 24-Year Career of the Fabled Georgia Peach* (New York: Sterling Publishing, 2001), 229; Cobb quoted in Alexander, *Ty Cobb*, 102.

44. *Sporting News* (September 11, 1919): 3.

45. Greenberg, *Honor and Slavery*, 8–9.

46. Greenberg, *Honor and Slavery*, 3–23. For an example of Cobb using the term, see *Detroit Free Press*, June 21, 1914, 1–2.

47. On Northern sensibilities, see Karen Halttunen, *Confidence Men and Painted Women: A Study of Middle-Class Culture in America, 1830–1870* (New Haven: Yale University Press, 1982); John F. Kasson, *Rudeness and Civility: Manners in Nineteenth-Century* America (New York: Noonday Press, 1990). For Southern sensibilities, see Greenberg, *Honor and Slavery*, 3–21.

48. *St. Louis Post-Dispatch*, May 9, 1909, 27; Cobb, *Memoirs of Twenty Years*, 47; Ty Cobb, "Tricks That Won Me Ball Games," *Life* (March 24, 1952): 73; Cobb, *My Life*, 125.

49. Quoted in Greenberg, *Honor and Slavery*, 8, 149, ff. 20; McCallum, *Tiger Wore Spikes*, 126–27.

50. Alexander, *Ty Cobb*, 160–61; "Cobb-Evans Fight Said to Be Bloodiest Ever," *Spartanburg* (South Carolina) *Herald-Journal*, February 25, 1973, B4; *Detroit Free Press*, September 25, 1921, 25; *Washington Herald*, September 25, 1921, 11.

51. *Sporting News* (June 23, 1914): 9. *Detroit News*, June 21, 1914, 1; *Detroit News*, June 22, 1914, 1; *Detroit News*, June 25, 1914, 7.

52. Cobb, *Busting 'Em*, 9; Seymour, *Baseball: The Golden Age*, 86; Macht, *Connie Mack*, 411–13, 431–32; Williams, "Cobb and Shoeless Joe, June 17, 1929," in *Joe Williams Baseball Reader*, 40.

53. Cobb, *Busting 'Em*, 9, 16; Donald Gropman, *Say It Ain't So, Joe: The True Story of Shoeless Joe Jackson* (1979; repr., New York: Citadel Press, 2002).

54. Williams, "Cobb and Shoeless Joe," 40.

55. Cobb, "Tricks that Won Me Ball Games," 64, 66; Cobb, *My Life*, 176–77.

56. *Detroit Free Press*, September 5, 1913, 12–13; *Detroit Free Press*, September 6, 1913, 10; *Detroit Free Press*, September 7, 1913, 17–18; *Detroit Free Press*, September 8, 1913, 8–9; Jackson quoted in Gropman, *Say It Ain't So, Joe*, 114.

57. Rickey, *American Diamond*, 27; Ty Cobb to Bill Webb, May 4, 1955.

58. Early twentieth-century Southern whites' concerns about African Americans are explored by George Fredrickson, *The Black Image in the White Mind: The Debate on Afro-American Character and Destiny, 1817–1914* (Hanover, NH: Wesleyan University Press, 1971), 256–319; Leon Litwack, *Trouble in Mind: Black Southerners in the Age of Jim Crow* (New York: Knopf, 1998), 179–216; Joel Williamson, *The Crucible of Race: Black-White Relations in the American South Since Emancipation* (New York: Oxford University Press, 1984), 111–323.

59. Litwack, *Trouble in Mind*, 197–216; Hayne is quoted on 201–202.

60. Carl Holliday, "The Young Southerner and the Negro," *South Atlantic Quarterly* 8 (1909): 17–31; quoted in Litwack, *Trouble in Mind*, 248; Clifton Johnson, *Highways and Byways of the South* (New York: Macmillan, 1904), 352.

61. Williamson, *Crucible of Race*, 82–87, 254–59; Ayers, *Promise of the New South*, 417–20, 426–37.

62. *Atlanta Journal*, October 16, 1907, 20; *Columbus Enquirer-Sun*, August 16, 1901, 6.

63. Benjamin G. Rader, "'Matters Involving Honor': Region, Race, and Rank in the Violent Life of Tyrus Raymond Cobb," in *Baseball in America and America in Baseball*, edited by Donald G. Kyle and Robert F. Fairbanks (College Station: Texas A&M University Press, 2008), 219, ff. 16. For a listing of lynchings by county in Georgia, see Digital Scholarship Commons, "Georgia Lynchings Project," Emory Libraries. http://dev.emorydisc.org/galyn/lynchings/counties/ (accessed August 31, 2015); each lynching is documented by contemporary newspaper accounts. Also see Ralph Ginzburg, *100 Years of Lynching* (Baltimore: Black Classic Press, 1962); W. Fitzhugh Brundage, *Lynching in the New South: Georgia and Virginia* (Urbana: University of Illinois Press, 1993).

64. Cobb, *My Life*, 94; Charles Leerhsen, *Ty Cobb: A Terrible Beauty* (New York: Simon and Schuster, 2015), 130.

65. Litwack, *Trouble in Mind*, 35; McCallum, *The Tiger Wore Spikes*, 17; Cobb, *My Life*, 17; *St. Louis Post-Dispatch*, May 9, 1909, 1S.

66. *Detroit Free Press*, April 1, 1906, 13.

67. Johnson, *Highways and Byways*, 333, 352; Theodore Rosengarten, *All Gods Dangers: The Life of Nate Shaw* (New York: Alfred A. Knopf, 1974), 545.

68. *Detroit Free Press*, February 6, 1910, 17; Eddie Wells in Richard Bak, *Cobb Would Have Caught It: The Golden Age of Baseball in Detroit* (Detroit: Wayne State University Press, 1991), 154.

69. *Detroit Free Press*, July 5, 1917, 9; *Chicago Tribune*, June 5, 1921, 24; *Chicago Tribune*, September 23, 1928, A1.

70. On Southern whites' expectation that African Americans continue to demonstrate servile devotion and loyalty to them in the decades after slavery, see James L. Roark, *Masters Without Slaves: Southern Planters in the Civil War and Reconstruction* (New York: W. W. Norton, 1977); Litwack, *Trouble in Mind*, 186–97.

71. *Detroit Free Press*, March 17, 1907, 17; *Sporting Life* (March 23, 1907): 5; *Sporting News* (March 30, 1907): 3. At the time, Cobb claimed he only "reproved" the woman and did not choke her. Cobb almost never forgot a lie cast against him and often went to extreme ends to clear himself when he felt unduly maligned; he made no such effort in this case. Regardless, "reproving"

still suggests Cobb believed himself to be the woman's moral superior. Did Cobb beat her? Journalists in attendance did not see the altercation but did see the woman after the altercation occurred; all reported that Cobb beat the woman.

72. On growing concerns of black degeneracy and criminality, see Litwack, *Trouble in Mind*, 246–79, 437–44. On the Atlanta riot, see, Litwack, *Trouble in Mind*, 312–22; Williamson, *Crucible of Race*, 209–23. Cobb named one of his champion Gordon setters "Hoke," possibly in honor of family friend and race-baiter, Hoke Smith. See John D. McCallum, *Ty Cobb* (New York: Praeger, 1975), 100.

73. Heritage Quest Online, United States Manuscript Census for 1880: Inhabitants of London (Village), Pope County, Arkansas, 25. http://persi.heritagequestonline.com.ezproxy.gvsu.edu (accessed August 31, 2015).

74. *Detroit Free Press*, March 17, 1907, 17; *Sporting Life* (April 13, 1907): 11.

75. *Augusta Chronicle*, January 5, 1890, quoted in Litwack, *Trouble in Mind*, 253.

76. *Detroit Free Press*, June 7, 1908, 10; *Detroit Free Press*, June 10, 1908, 4, 16; *Sporting Life* (June 27, 1908): 25.

77. *Chicago Defender*, May 3, 1919, 1; *Chicago Defender*, May 10, 1919, 1; *Chicago Defender*, June 21, 1919, 1; *New York Times*, May 17, 1924, 10; Rader, "Matters Involving Honor," 192.

78. *Detroit Free Press*, October 20, 1923, 9; Bill Moore in Bak, *Cobb Would Have Caught It*, 170.

79. Ty Cobb, *My Life*, 20.

5

THE PLAYERS' ETHIC

Ty Cobb's ethic of honor compelled him to prioritize his and his family's reputation above all else. To defend and demonstrate his honor, he placed a premium on personal autonomy, that is, the freedom to think and act on his own. Most of Cobb's teammates followed an ethic of honor as well. But their conception of honor—fashioned as it was in the factories, shops, bars, and fraternal organizations of the industrial North and West—encouraged them to emphasize very different values—values that emphasized group cohesion above individual glory and reputation. Tiger outfielder Sam Crawford summed up the players' perspective in a single sentence: "We were all ballplayers together, just trying to get along." Therein lay the source of friction that dogged Cobb throughout most of his major league career.[1]

"Getting along" as a professional ballplayer during the early twentieth century was not an easy venture. For at least seven months of the year, grown men from nearly all walks of life and all regions of the country were thrust together to share the forced intimacy of a professional baseball team. Theirs was an itinerant life in a remarkably insular world. That is, professional baseball offered them few opportunities to develop close relationships with anyone but their teammates. Instead, they were forced to socialize with one another, sometimes for fourteen to sixteen hours a day. This phenomenon was captured perfectly, if satirically, by *Baseball Magazine*, in a short piece which purported to provide "the exact records of the life led, each day, by twenty men of a major league club:"

8 A.M.: Arise, dress, mope down into lobby of hotel.
8:30 to 9:30: Mope in lobby, eat breakfast, read morning papers.
9:30 to 12: Mope in lobby.
12 to 1: Lunch.
1 to 2: Mope in lobby
2: Start for ballpark
2:30 to 3 or 3:30: Practice at ballpark.
3: or 3:30 to 5 or 5:30: Play baseball.
5:30 to 6:30: Go back to hotel, mope in lobby.
6:30 to 7:30: Eat supper.
7:30 to 9:30: Mope in lobby.
9:30 to 10: Beat it for bed.

The magazine could have extended this little burlesque even further. Aside from the lobby, players also had time to mope—or wait unremittingly—at train stations and in train cars as they traveled from town to town. "We spent a lot of our lives living out of our grips, on trains and in hotels," Sam Crawford recalled. "In a lot of ways, it wasn't the easiest life in the world." Goose Goslin described his baseball life as if it was one long road trip: "hotel . . . taxi . . . train . . . taxi . . . hotel . . . train . . . and then all over again." Finally, after twenty years, his body had had enough. "The old bones stiffen up and get a little fickle and then it's time to stop," he recalled of his decision to retire. "You can't live out of a grip forever." Pirates' catcher George Gibson came to hate the peripatetic life so much that he built his winter home in far off London, Ontario—"out of earshot of a train whistle. Heard enough of them from April to September."[2] That the tedium was often accompanied by the constant anxiety to keep one's job, perform in front of hostile fans, and ward off the ravages of injury and time only made the waiting that much more difficult. New York Giants' catcher John "Chief" Meyers recalled, "It was tough, don't think it wasn't," Meyers said. "In those days you had to have guts. That's all there was to it."[3]

To make this itinerant life at least tolerable, most players strived to give their teams a functional degree of harmony. Toward that end, they ascribed values like camaraderie, altruism, and mutual support to the concept of team and tried to live accordingly. Cobb may have understood these values only vaguely and imperfectly, but not so his teammates. Most men of the working and lower-middle class—the strata of society from which most ballplayers came—embraced individualism, but they also recognized the necessity of cooperation and mutual support. Many who played ball were sons and grandsons of European immigrants whose devotion to family, neighbors, and community held strong. Some had worked in mines, foundries, and artisanal shops where collaborative work crews served as the foundation for production. Nearly all were familiar with the great social outlet of the turn of the century—the fraternal lodge. Those who could not afford the dues and regalia of such clubs knew another kind of brotherhood—the fellowship of the bar where a code of reciprocity held sway. Even middle-class boys, the sons of clerks, shop owners, and professionals—learned a group ethos through the stories of Baseball Joe, Frank Merriwell, Lefty Locke, and other dime novel heroes whose exploits idealized the importance of duty, fair play, and shared sacrifice. "The team is the biggest thing on Earth to me outside of my home and folks, and it's always a pleasure to give it my best effort," the hero of one novel proclaims excitedly. Perhaps most influential, all ballplayers had been members of teams before, dating back to informal sandlot games. There, they learned the rudiments of sportsmanship by sharing equipment, agreeing on the rules, and calling their own game.[4] Informed by such experiences, ballplayers looked to one another for the same support they had found in the shop, the lodge, the bar, and the sandlot. As men of the early twentieth century, they craved the friendship and respect of their peers. Theirs was a sociable, though almost exclusively male, world: ballplayers craved the attention, companionship, and rancorous accord of other men. Conversely, they distrusted those who refused to be sociable, defining them as disruptive and a threat to the group as a whole.

Even so, diverse forces threatened to undermine the esprit de corps of even the best run teams. Harmony often withered as the season progressed. Teammates on winning teams sometimes turned on one another as pressures mounted during a tight pennant race. Conversely, teammates on losing teams sometimes fought out of frustration and despair. Beyond wins and losses, other factors also caused tensions on teams. Men from all over the country, from all strata of society, and nearly every major ethnic group and religion in America suddenly found themselves living in close quarters with men whose habits, traditions, and morals bewildered and even repulsed them. Early twentieth-century intellectuals and politicians might brag that America was the great melting pot, but such folks rarely knew what it meant to live and work with people different from themselves. Ballplayers knew and most readily admitted that it was not easy. Nearly every club was a volatile mix of personalities many of whom came from the fringes of the American mainstream. "Baseball attracted all sorts of people in those days," Tigers' outfielder Davy Jones recalled. "We had stupid guys, smart guys, tough guys, mild guys, crazy guys, college men, slickers from the city, and hicks from the county. And back then a country kid was likely to *really* be a country kid." At least initially, players were less worldly and thus less tolerant of differences. "We didn't have the mass communication and mass transportation that exist nowadays. We didn't have as much schooling," Jones confided. As a result, "people were more unique then, more unusual, more different from each other." This made players more "colorful," Jones claimed, but also far more set in their distinctive habits and ways.[5]

To temper this volatile mix, players fashioned a work culture that encouraged cooperation, sociability, selflessness, and even humility—all in an effort to smooth over differences. Still, ballplayers were realists. They did not so much try to eradicate conflict, but to channel it in ways so that the team could continue to operate amidst the day-to-day tensions. The process began with hazing, the rite of passage examined in chapter 3 that forced each young player to place himself at the mercy of the team. Once young players proved they possessed the talent and grit to stay the course, veterans gradually accepted them into the fold. Here, too, the socialization process was remarkably similar on most teams. For most rookies, it began with the bestowal of a nickname. During the early twentieth century, nearly every player who spent much time on a major league roster gained a new moniker.[6] Receiving a nickname demonstrated that the other players recognized the new recruit's unique attributes and his distinctive contribution to the team's culture. Granted, some handles were the creations of publicity-conscious sports reporters who wanted to draw attention to star players. This is how Frank Chance gained the nickname "The Peerless Leader" and Walter Johnson received the appellation "The Big Train." *The Detroit Press* was especially eager to give Ty Cobb a moniker when he began to distinguish himself with the bat. Reporters made all sorts of suggestions: Rooster, the Reb, the Dixie Demon. The *Detroit Free Press*'s Joe

Jackson's offering is the only one that stuck—the Georgia Peach (a very young and brash Cobb helped this one along by sometimes referring to himself in the third person as "The Peach").[7]

Mostly though, nicknames came directly from the player's teammates. As such, they reveal a great deal about what players considered important about themselves. Many nicknames reflected the player's ethnicity: Mick, Mugsy, or Black Mike for Irish players; Germany, Hans, Dutch, Dutchman, or even Heinie for German players; Chief for the league's few Native American players; and so on. American-born white players sometimes gained nicknames that highlighted their town or region of origin. This was especially true of ballplayers who came from the farms and small towns of the Midwest. Invariably, teammates denigrated such types for their naivety and lack of urban sophistication: Cy, Hick, Farmer, Country, and—most popular of all—Rube. Likewise, teammates invariably called the handful of Southern-born ballplayers "Rebel," a name that suggested the persistence of sectional animosities.

Most often nicknames emphasized not a player's connection to a distinct group, but his individuality. In this, players proved both creative and resolute in their desire to identify something distinctive about their teammates. A few players who hailed from towns with colorful and unique place names found those names attached to their own, like "Wahoo" (Nebraska) Sam Crawford and "Wheezer" (a bastardization of Weiser, Idaho) Bill Dell. Other times, teammates chose nicknames that highlighted a player's former or supplementary employment: Samuel Leever was called the "Goshen Schoolmaster" because he taught school in that town during the offseason; Frank Corridon gained the name "Fiddler" because he was a concert violinist during the off-season. Occasionally, players highlighted something distinctive about a teammate's physical appearance: Charlie Comiskey gained the name "Old Roman" because he sported a large nose; Edward Mensor was called "Midget" because he was only 5'6"; Christy Mathewson got the name "Big Six" because he was tall (6'1") and angular. Predictably, some players' nicknames were on the salty side. Teammates likened Charlie Herzog's proboscis to a certain male organ and thus dubbed him "Dick Nose;" probably to Herzog's relief, they rarely used the name in polite society, opting for the more genteel "Buck."[8] Sometimes teammates openly mocked a player for a particular handicap. Eugene Hargrave was a stutterer who had a particular problem pronouncing words that included the letter "B"; in a cruel gesture, teammates took to calling him "Bubbles." George Leitner, Luther Taylor, William Hoy, and Herbert Murphy were all called "Dummy" by their teammates because they were deaf. Personality traits inspired other nicknames: Charlie Grimm received the name "Jolly Cholly" because he was an exceedingly jovial chap; Johnny Evers gained the sobriquet "Crab" because of his dour, no-nonsense approach to everything. Sometimes, players tried to be a bit ironic with the names they chose for their teammates. Pitcher Jack Chesbro sometimes went by the name "Algy," a euphemism for a sissy, because players believed he was anything but, especially after he pitched in fifty-five games for New York in 1904. Finally, many players earned nicknames because of some noteworthy aspect of their ballplaying skills, or lack thereof. Speedsters were often given names like Rabbit, Bunny, or Deerfoot; a slow player might gain the nickname Slug; Leon Goslin was one of the game's best hitters during the twenties, but he looked like an awkward bird when he chased after fly balls—thus the nickname "Goose."

Whatever the source of the name, players often found that if the name stuck, it was theirs for life. This sometimes caused more than a bit of ill-feeling. Hargrave challenged all comers who dared call him Bubbles. The same was true for Giants manager John McGraw who absolutely loathed his nickname "Mugsy" because he viewed it as an ethnic slur. When a *New York Times* reporter referred to Mike Donlin as "Turkey Mike," Donlin confronted the reporter and told him not to use it again. Several players with dark complexions were given the nickname "Nig," surely an insult in such a racially conscious era. Some of Babe Ruth's Boston teammates called him "Nigger," "Nigger Lips," and "Big Baboon" because they hated him and hoped to drive him off the team.[9]

Why give teammates nicknames that insulted or pigeonholed them? In part, many of the names revealed how contentious relations could be on a team comprised of young men from nearly all ranks and all regions of the country. At the same time, the use of nicknames also worked to ameliorate hostilities. Like other forms of hazing, nicknames gave established players a chance to test the gameness and collegiality of their new teammates. Although some nicknames were clearly intended to hurt or wound a player's ego, most were relatively harmless and gave players an opportunity to needle and tease one another in a fairly gentle and open manner. In this, nicknames served as a leveler in that nearly everyone had one and was thus subject to the same treatment. A player who protested his nickname appeared humorless, overly sensitive, and even a tad egotistical to his teammates. Moreover, most players understood that the nickname was an indication of acceptance by one's teammates. As anthropologist and former minor league ballplayer George Gmelch has recently explained, "Nicknames imply a degree of intimacy and closeness which are often lacking with given names." Recently retired player Mark Grudzielanek agrees: "If you are worth giving a name to, it means your teammates think you're okay and you're going to be around for awhile." Conversely, despised players were never granted this form of intimacy. Perhaps this explains why Cobb never gained a nickname—at least not a printable one—from his peers; he made it difficult for them to bond with him in this way.[10]

If being christened with a nickname demonstrated acceptance by one's teammates, the name itself also helped the player to stand out as an individual. This was no small feat in a society that was becoming increasingly standardized and bureaucratized. Giants' pitcher Joe McGinnity was just another worker when he labored in a foundry as a youth; no one would have thought to call him "Iron Man" there. But on the ball field, the moniker "Iron Man" gave McGinnity a distinctive and utterly masculine persona. Nicknames also revealed that ballplayers openly defied Victorian conventions. Chances are not many Detroit fans could strut around their place of business with a name like "Wild Bill," but Bill Donovan did as a pitcher for the Tigers. Even nicknames derived by shortening Christian names and surnames—"Jack" for James, "Matty" for Mathewson—demonstrated a casualness that was quite different from both austere Victorianism and the impersonality of modern business. Fans and players loved nicknames because they offered an intimate and provocative glimpse into the utterly masculine world of the ball field—a world that seemed full of bravado, camaraderie, and high jinks.

Gaining a nickname might help a new player break the ice, but if he really wanted to settle into the culture of the team, he needed to demonstrate the right sort of personality and a robust desire to mix with his new teammates. To relieve both stress and boredom, most ballplayers valued teammates who were friendly and outgoing, the quintessential "hell of a fella." In the early history of professional baseball, the quest for sociability and diversion sent many players to the barroom. Before Ban Johnson had his way, professional ballplayers gained a reputation for being rowdies and sporting men. For good reason, the game was full of heavy drinkers—individuals who believed that strong drink enhanced physical prowess. Famous among this ethic's practitioners was slugger Pete Browning who observed, "I can't hit the ball until I hit the bottle." During the early years of the new century, the game still had a fair number of inebriate players. More than one came to a bad end. In 1903, Big Ed Delahanty, one of the game's first great power hitters and a Hall of Famer, became so drunkenly obnoxious on a train headed for New York that conductors stopped the train and had him ejected near the spot where the International Bridge crosses over the Niagara River. Disoriented, Big Ed decided to walk across the train's trestle bridge. He never made it across: he either fell through the open draw or committed suicide by jumping in. Caught in the current, he cascaded down the river and over Niagara Falls; his mangled body was recovered a few days later.[11]

Once Ban Johnson came to power and the game became more popular, players began to sober up. Magnates and players alike realized that there was quite a bit of money to be made through gate receipts and endorsements—so long as they could put forth a consistently good product. But that was the rub: drunken players threatened to jeopardize the entire operation. By the end of the decade, incorrigible inebriates became persona non grata on most teams. Some owners even toyed with the idea of putting abstinence clauses in their players' contracts. Rube Waddell was one of the new severity's casualties. He was the best left-handed pitcher in the game and a fan favorite because of his odd behavior (which may have reflected a personality disorder), but he also had a habit of disappearing on drunken binges. In 1907, he alienated his Athletics teammates when he proved too unstable to depend on during the hotly contested pennant race. Fearing a player mutiny, manager Connie Mack sold Waddell to the hapless St. Louis Browns prior to the 1908 season. He pitched well for a time, but eventually ran afoul of that team as well. By the end of 1910, he was out of baseball, deemed too risky to depend upon despite his superior talent. Waddell's well-publicized troubles became an object lesson for many players. Some of the game's heavier drinkers tapered their habits, including White Sox ace

Eddie Cicotte and Detroit catcher Edward "Tubby" Spencer. Players had long believed they needed to be responsible to one another, but now that ethos of mutual responsibility included proper maintenance of their bodies. "Drinking and carousing cannot be tolerated," Johnny Evers asserted in his insider's guide to baseball. "Players have come to realize that they must care for their bodies if they are to continue in their profession." Although players often divided on just what constituted proper temperate behavior, all understood the importance of being sober come game time. By the time Fred Snodgrass made it to the majors with the Giants in 1908, the era of alcohol-soaked ballplayers was nearly at an end. Snodgrass claimed that notorious drunkard Arthur "Bugs" Raymond was the only teammate he ever saw under the influence of alcohol in a game (and McGraw cut his career short once he determined Bugs would not change). Snodgrass may have been gilding the lily, but the point remains that by the second decade of the century, baseball had become far less tolerant of players whose drinking exploits compromised their on-field performance.[12]

That said, most ballplayers were not about to swear off alcohol—and the sociability it enhanced—completely. Most players wanted moderation, not abstinence. Few drank hard liquor; most were beer drinkers who considered hoisting a few after a game an essential end to their workday. Honus Wagner was an especially devout disciple of the practice. After each game, he stopped at a local bar and drank six beers—no more, no less—before heading home or back to his hotel. No one accused Wagner of being a lush. Players were adamant that team magnates not interfere in such matters. When Chicago Cubs owner Charles Murphy joined the ranks of owners who advocated abstinence, his manager Frank Chance objected. In his view, a glass of beer after a game was harmless at worst and "beneficial" at best. He told the press that Murphy's interference insulted him; he knew how to handle his men and resented Murphy's suggestion that he needed to take a stronger hand. Chance's former shortstop Joe Tinker agreed. Upon taking over the Cincinnati Reds, Tinker promised to rule with a light hand, claiming that he had "no abjections" *[sic]* to a player "taking a glass or two of beer after a game." Just "because a man is placed in charge of a club does not make it necessary for him to be a taskmaster or tyrant," Tinker added. Even Christy Mathewson spoke up on this subject; it was a matter "everyone must decide for himself," the player the press dubbed the Christian Gentleman declared. Many ballplayers were the sons and grandsons of German and Irish immigrants; they believed raising a pint after a hard day's work was more or less a rite of true manhood. Max Carey, the speedy Pirates outfielder, was typical of this group. Though his parents were strict Lutherans, he told *Baseball Magazine* that he had been raised to view alcohol consumption "in a different light than is customary in this country of temperance unions and teetotal societies." So far as he was concerned, "I was never able to see anything harmful in a moderate use of the German's favorite beverage." Others followed the popular dictum that temperate use of alcohol warded off "staleness."[13]

Players who congregated in bars after games exercised their personal autonomy and revealed their disdain for the Victorian code of polite society. Taking a beer with one's teammates also demonstrated an allegiance and commitment to the camaraderie of the team. A saloon was not just a place to take a drink; it was a place ballplayers expressed their manly affection for one another. Mathewson learned soon enough that if he wanted to be accepted by his teammates, he needed to demonstrate that he accepted them. When second baseman "Laughing Larry" Doyle joined the team, he took it upon himself to bring Mathewson into the fold by inviting him out for a drink now and again after a game. Eventually, Mathewson caught on, much to Doyle's delight. "We were a tough lot in those days. All except Matty," recalled the gregarious infielder. "But he was no namby-pamby. He'd gamble, play cards, curse now and then and take a drink now and then."[14]

Ballplayers generally took their beer in sporting saloons located near the ballpark in the society of other men. These saloons were designed as places of respite from the cares and concerns of the commercial world, including the commercial world of baseball. These were not low dives, but often designed to evoke a certain degree of opulence and luxury, complete with brass spittoons, brass foot rails, rich oak or mahogany wood work, colorful—some might say garish—artwork, and cheerful lighting. The culture of the saloon encouraged convivial conversation, good cheer, and robust and utterly masculine socializing. Reciprocity ruled the house as saloonkeepers offered the proverbial free lunch and snacks and customers embraced the time-honored tradition of treating one another. Some saloons also offered entertainment—perhaps a singer and an accompanist—as yet another way to allow customers to take their minds off the day's concerns. At the saloon, ballplayers had the opportunity to socialize with one another in a far less constrained setting than the hotel, the train station, and the Pullman car. As an early sociological study of working-class saloons observed, "that general atmosphere of freedom, that spirit of democracy, which men crave, is here realized."[15] In short, the saloon offered release and escape. In defending his own preference for taking a beer now and then, Cobb explained, "a ball player is only human and cannot be expected to sit around and think of baseball all the time. He must have some recreation and solace. I have said that I did not believe alcoholic liquor helped a ball player, but I think there are some men who can drink a glass of beer occasionally without being harmed. Maybe their system needs the malt."[16]

Or a bit of high jinks. Of all professional athletes, baseball players have gained a reputation for the frequency and hilarity of the pranks they pull on one another. Ballplayers' proclivity for high jinks dates back to at least the early twentieth century. Too much idle time may have been the primary cause. Hugh Fullerton observed, "Take eighteen or twenty strong, vulgarly healthy athletes, with three hours work a day and twenty-one hours for rest and recreation, and something is likely to come off at any minute."[17] Then, as now, players did a lot of sitting during the course of a game, especially reserves. When not constructively occupied, players looked for creative outlets. To alleviate the boredom, they turned on one another—all in good fun, of course. Like beer, practical jokes helped alleviate staleness and tension by giving everyone a good laugh.[18] Those who were especially creative pranksters were highly appreciated by their teammates. Harry Smith, a catcher for the Pirates during the first decade of the twentieth century, was among this group. Although Smith was a poor hitter (a .213 career average) and never started more than seventy games in one season, his peers loved him. "What would you think of a ball player who 'green-appled' every man's clothes in a sleeper by tying pants and legs and coat sleeves in knots?" asked his former manager Fred Clarke. "Or smeared Limburger cheese under the shirt collars on every man's uniform" wondered Honus Wagner. "Or kept you awake in a sleeper all night with tin horns, cowbells, or rackets?" asked George Gibson. Although they called him the "Terror of the club" and "Peck's bad boy for fair," players were fond of Smith, who somehow always managed to keep things interesting.[19]

Unlike hazing, which tried to test a rookie's mettle, a prank could be directed at anyone associated with the team, for no other purpose than to draw a laugh. Most were rather innocuous—short-sheeting a roommates' bed, lighting the corner of a teammate's newspaper on fire while he was reading it, giving someone the hot foot, or spitting tobacco juice on a fellow's freshly polished baseball shoes ("You can just imagine that deal, with everybody on the team chewin' tobacco," Eddie Wells reminisced). Sometimes, however, pranks carried a message. Early in his career, Hans Lobert's Pittsburgh teammates pranked him in an effort to force him to lighten up a bit and relax when he played. During the course of one game, Lobert booted two or three balls in quick succession. When he came to the dugout at the end of the inning, he went directly to the far end to brood and fret about his poor showing. That's when he heard an ethereal voice lambast him: "You big, bloated Dutch stiff! Put molasses on your mitts and learn how to hold the ball." He stood up and surveyed the crowd to see if he could spy the rude fan. Unable to find the culprit, he slumped back into his place on the bench, even angrier than before. Finally, he heard laughing from the other end of the dugout. Curious, he looked over to see Honus Wagner whispering into a large pipe that ran from one end of the dugout to the other. The ghostly voice Lobert had heard was that of his friend and mentor. Lobert could only laugh at himself for his gullibility.[20] Other times, players used pranks to humble an arrogant teammate. The White Sox used an especially elaborate ruse to bring the vain but dim-witted Ping Bodie down a peg. In 1912, teammates sent a telegram to Bodie telling him that he had won a Chalmers auto as the league's Most Valuable Player. Though Cobb's batting average that year was over one hundred points higher than Bodie's (.409 to Bodie's .294) and Bodie did not rank in the top ten in any offensive category, hubris got the better of him as he proceeded to put on quite a spree. Finally, a tender-hearted teammate had to break the news to him—it was all a hoax.[21]

Cruel, but of course, that was the point. Players believed a prank sometimes worked best if it caused some small amount of pain and suffering in the victim. To ballplayers, that's what made the prank funny—and thus worthwhile. In this, pranks served important functions. First, they offered a relatively safe outlet for aggression. Rather than insult another player for his ego or idiosyncrasies, pranks allowed players to poke fun through subterfuge and humor. Second, the somewhat over-the-top cruelty of some pranks allowed players to play out the survival of the fittest mentality that dominated the game by turning it into a comical and comprehensible incident. In this, pranks acted as a form of theater that the participants—pranksters and victims—told about themselves. In this telling, players were able to gain some control—albeit temporarily—over an otherwise capricious environment.[22]

Sometimes a prank went too far. In one incident, veteran catcher Jack Warner of the Tigers told teammate Bill Coughlin to try wrapping his injured knee in a special liniment balm that Warner claimed he used for his trotting horses. In fact, the ingredients were a corrosive solvent that burned Coughlin's leg so badly that he was bedridden for two games and missed nearly a week.[23] The cruelest pranks were born of malice and contempt. Duffy Lewis and Tris Speaker, fellow outfielders on the Red Sox during the early teens, were never particularly fond of one another, but their relationship became especially acrimonious after Speaker humiliated his nemesis by pranking him. During the 1913 season, Speaker decided it would be great fun to sneak up behind Lewis and knock off his cap, thereby exposing his prematurely balding scalp. Embarrassed and angered, Lewis finally told Speaker, "Do that again and I'll kill you." Never one to back down, Speaker did it again. Lewis promptly threw his bat at Speaker, hitting him in the shins so hard that he was unable to play that day and needed assistance to get off the field. Thereafter, the two outfielders stopped speaking to one another, although they played side by side.[24]

Although pranks sometimes created ill will between teammates, the primary intent seems to have been to infuse a bit of democracy into the clubhouse's hierarchical culture. Even the league's premier players got the treatment on occasion. While the Cleveland Naps were training in New Orleans for the 1903 season, someone ran an advertisement in the local newspapers that the team's star Napoleon Nap Lajoie would give away sample hats from his haberdashery to the first thousand fans to arrive at the training field at 3:00 in the afternoon. Over three thousand fans showed up, but found neither hats nor Lajoie, who had long since departed with the rest of the team. Frustrated, some in the crowd decided to track down the missing star. They found him in the lobby of the team's hotel and promptly demanded their hats. A puzzled Lajoie tried to explain that he had no hats to give away. With that, the crowd's anger began to swell—until Lajoie's teammates came clean and admitted it was all a joke to honor April Fool's Day. Honus Wagner was also the brunt of jokes on occasion. During one game, Chicago's Jack Taylor retired Wagner easily three straight times, prompting Wagner's teammate Claude Ritchey to suggest that perhaps Wagner should give up batting right-handed against the pitcher and try left-handed instead. Rather than take Ritchey's remark as an insult, Wagner decided to play along. "Thoroughly disgusted and taking the whole thing as a joke, I walked up there and took the opposite side of the plate. There was a murmur of surprise from the fans. Even the umpire looked as if he thought me crazy." But "doggoned if I didn't hit the ball right on the nose and whipped it down the right foul line for two bases. Everybody, including the players roared with laughter." Everyone that is, except the pitcher: "Taylor, called me a lot of names," Wagner recalled.[25] Sometimes even managers got the treatment. After Bill Armour of the Tigers told his players that he believed cross-eyed people were a bad omen, his players made a practice of inviting every cross-eyed boy they met to come to the park to take on the job of bat boy. It almost drove Armour into hysterics. "He would take one look at him," Sam Crawford recalled, "and get an expression like he was about to die. 'Get rid of him, get rid of him' he'd yell . . . 'get him out of my sight.'"[26]

Just like their journeymen teammates, stars realized they had to take pranks in good humor or be accused of having swelled heads, a reputation most players were loathe to receive. In fact, stars like Lajoie, Wagner, and even the seemingly impeccable Christy Mathewson tried very hard to involve themselves in the high jinks and humor of their teammates. Tommy Leach described Lajoie as "a pleasure to play against . . . always laughing and joking. Even when the son of a gun was blocking you off the base, he was smiling and kidding you. You just *had* to like the guy." Wagner enjoyed much the same reputation—a "friendly good natured guy," according to Sam Crawford. Even as a coach for the Pirates late in life, he remained a "wonderful fellow, so good natured and friendly to everyone," one young player recalled.[27]

At their best, pranksters displayed some of the personality traits that ballplayers defined as ideal. They were generous, other-directed, and giving—what contemporaries sometimes referred to as a "hail fellow well met." When Cobb joined the Tigers, Germany Schaefer filled the role. Decades after his teammates retired, they still reveled in telling stories of his comedic exploits. Davy Jones said Schaefer was "far and away the funniest man I ever saw. He beat Charlie Chaplin any day in the week." In one game, manager Bill Armour asked Schaefer, never a particularly strong hitter, to pinch hit for pitcher "Red" Donahue. Unfortunately, Donahue, who loved to swing a bat, was already well on his way to the plate. When Schaefer called to Donahue to return to the dugout, Donahue slammed his bat down and roared as he stomped back to the bench, "Who the hell are you to hit for me?" Recognizing a comedic moment when he saw one, Schaefer walked to the plate, removed his cap, and turned to address the grandstand. "Ladies and gentleman you are now looking at Herman Schaefer, better known as Herman the Great, acknowledged by one and all to be the greatest pinch hitter in the world. I am now going to hit the ball into the left-field bleachers. Thank you." Although Schaefer had not hit a home run all season and would hit only two that year and nine in twelve full seasons in the majors, he somehow made good on his boast, sending the ball over the left field fence then he really got rolling. He jumped straight in the air, ran to first base, and slid headfirst into the bag. When he righted himself, he yelled, "Schaefer leads at the Quarter!" and started for second. He slid again, popped up, and yelled "Schaefer leads at the half!" He repeated the scene at third. When he slid safely into home, he announced, "Schaefer wins by a nose!" With the crowd cheering wildly, Schaefer again turned to address them: "Ladies and Gentleman," he yelled over their loud cheering, "I thank you for your kind attention," and trotted back to the bench where he was greeted by a dugout full of teammates doubled over in laughter.[28]

It was a hilarious scene, but Schaefer may have topped it a few years later in a game against archrival Cleveland when he "stole" first base— or stole the same base twice, depending upon one's perspective. It happened this way. Late in a tie game during a tense pennant race (the Tigers topped Cleveland by half a game that year), Schaefer was on first and Jones was on third as Crawford settled in at the plate. Needing a run to take the lead, the Tigers decided to pull a delayed double steal, hoping Schaefer would draw the throw to second so Jones could make a break for home. Schaefer did his part, sliding safely into second. But Jones was unable to advance because Cleveland catcher "Nig" Clarke refused to take the bait and just held the ball. That left runners on second and third with the game still tied. Undeterred, Schaefer called to Jones, "Let's try it again!" And with a "blood-curdling shout," he scampered back to first base, diving in headfirst—fearful that Clarke might try to throw him out. Instead, everyone—Crawford, Jones, Clarke, Cleveland first baseman George Stovall, and the two umpires—stared in disbelief. After a brief conference, the two umpires decided that no rule prohibited a runner from circling the bases backwards and allowed play to resume. With the next pitch, Schaefer went again. This time, Clarke inexplicably threw to second. As soon as he did, Jones streaked for home. Both men were safe and the Tigers went on to win the game. It still stands as one of the most memorable capers in baseball history, and Schaefer's signature moment.[29]

The Tigers and their fans understood Schaefer's contributions to the team. As one Detroit newspaper observed, "With all his kidding and fun-making, Schaefer is never offensive, he never gets off anything that hurts, and he is a gentleman at all times. . . . A few men like him on every ball club would do a lot toward keeping down strife and jealousy." Tigers players rarely got along, but they could at least share a laugh together on occasion. In this, Schaefer proved a boon to the team's fortunes. The Tigers won the pennant for three straight years. They traded Schaefer to Washington toward the end of that third year, but almost immediately regretted it. The following year, as the Tigers languished in third place, Jennings tried to reobtain the comedic star. Unfortunately, Washington wasn't selling. Even so, the Tigers thought so highly of Schaefer, they promised him a position as a scout upon retirement.[30]

As much as players appreciated a good laugh, they understood performance on the field mattered most. As professionals, ballplayers understood that they were paid to win ball games and that fans and management evaluated their worth by how much they contributed to the success of the team. Such thinking dovetailed with players' personal understanding of themselves as men. Raised in a production-oriented culture, they similarly evaluated themselves and the worth of their teammates on how much they contributed to the team's success. Here too, the collaborative ethos held sway. Ballplayers wanted to be surrounded by talented teammates, but they also expected teammates to possess certain character traits that contributed to the overall strength of the team. And the trait they admired most was a sort of manly fortitude that expressed itself physically, mentally, and emotionally. Players gave this trait a variety of names. Some simply called it courage. Others described it as possessing "gameness," that is a desire to play no matter what the obstacles. Cobb called it playing "on one's nerve." Christy Mathewson may have offered the most evocative term—the ability to "stand the gaff." Whatever they called it, they all spoke to the same desire. They wanted teammates who would sacrifice for the good of the whole and strive to endure against all obstacles.[31]

Necessity inspired this attitude.

Primitive equipment, lack of protective gear, hazardous playing fields, and grueling schedules forced players to place a premium on physical and emotional toughness. Even their clubhouses lacked amenities. Most did not even offer showers: players had to wear their dirty sweat-soaked wool uniforms from the ballpark back to their rooms where they would then have to wait in line to use the hotel's few bathing facilities. Over the course of a season, players suffered any number of bruises as well as more serious injuries like sprains, jammed joints, broken bones, and torn ligaments—some of which resulted from the pocked and otherwise primitive playing fields. Beginning with the construction of Philadelphia's Shibe Park in 1909, the quality of ballparks began to improve gradually, making playing conditions at least somewhat safer. Then again, the new parks presented problems of their own. Made almost entirely of steel and cement, the unpadded facades could do serious damage to the player who encountered one at full speed. During a 1924 game at Washington's Griffith Stadium, right fielder Babe Ruth chased a fly ball into foul territory, crashed into a concrete abatement and was knocked out cold.[32]

When injured, players had to continue, if possible. Team rosters were smaller (fourteen players until 1906; seventeen players from 1908 through 1912; twenty-one players from 1915 through 1918), making it difficult for teams to substitute for injured players. During a game in 1907, Orvie Overall of the Cubs hit Hans Lobert, then playing for the Reds, square in the temple with a high fastball, knocking him out for ten minutes. Once he revived, Lobert had to remain in the game because Cincinnati had no one else to play shortstop. "Every step I took I felt the ground was coming up to meet my feet, or I was stepping into a hole," he recalled. After a week or two of painful headaches and blurred vision, he finally asked the manager if he could go home to rest. The manager agreed, but only because it was September and the team was buried in the second division and thus out of the prize money. Pitchers had it just as bad. Managers expected starters to finish every game they started, no matter how they felt. Toward the end of the 1926 season, the Indians were still in contention for second place and the bonus of $1,300 it offered. In a critical game against third place Philadelphia, Cleveland's George "The Bull" Uhle started despite a tired arm. When the other team scored five runs off him during the first few innings, he asked manager Tris Speaker to take him out, telling him, "I can't make it any further. I can't raise my arm above my belt." Uhle was a valuable pitcher for the Indians, having led the league in wins, starts, complete games, and innings pitched. Today, a manager would shut the pitcher down rather than risk permanent injury. But this was 1926 and Speaker had no qualms about keeping his star pitcher in. "We'll win or lose second place with you, bad arm and all," he told Uhle. With no other options, Uhle pitched underhanded for the rest of the game; miraculously, he won.[33]

Seriously injured players received little or no compensation from the team. Until the National Commission changed the policy in 1913, teams routinely refused to pay injured players during their period of convalescence.[34] Before 1920 or so, teams offered no real medical care. They carried no doctor, just a trainer, but his primary duty was to take care of the uniforms and the equipment. As Lobert remembered it, the typical trainer "didn't know any more about health or medicine than the man on the moon." On the Tigers, the trainer's sole therapeutic act was to provide rubdowns with a mixture the players called "Go Fast"—a concoction made from Vaseline and Tabasco sauce. It gave players the sweats, but had no real medicinal value.[35] If a player suffered a disabling injury during a game, his teammates' only recourse was to yell into the crowd, 'Is there a doctor in the house?'" In most cases, teams expected players to make their own arrangements for proper medical care. When Smoky Joe Wood broke the thumb on his pitching hand in the spring of 1913, he came back too soon and developed pain in his shoulder. For the next three years, the pain continued to get worse, but it made no difference: the team needed him to pitch. Meanwhile, he visited hundreds of doctors, all on his own dime. Finally, in desperation he visited a chiropractor who worked in an "unmarked office behind locked doors because in those days it wasn't legal for a chiropractor to practice." The chiropractor's rehabilitation program—"to throw as long and as hard as I possibly could"—ended up destroying his arm. "Only twenty-six years old and all washed up. A has-been." Panic-stricken, he tried to cure himself: "I put up a trapeze in the attic and I'd hang on that for hours to stretch my arm out. Maybe that would help—who could say? But it didn't." Smoky Joe was finished as a pitcher. He was at least lucky in one regard: a gifted hitter, he was able to come back as an outfielder. Others were not so fortunate. Many players were forced to retire early for want of proper medical care.[36]

Meanwhile, the hypercompetitive nature of the game also created hazards. What Cobb termed "a battle of muscle and wits" was in fact something akin to an all-out war in which players used every weapon at their disposal—physical, material, and psychological.[37] In the heat of a game, players could be downright brutal toward one another. When interviewed years later, early twentieth-century players asserted the men of their generation were far more ruthless than the players of the modern era. And perhaps they were. Cobb let people believe he filed his spikes, but McGraw may have been the first to pull the stunt. During the 1911 World Series, he ordered his players to do it before each game to scare the Athletics' infielders. Most players were not easily intimidated. Consider the infield play of the Pirates and Tigers during the 1909 World Series. Ill will may have started when Pirates' outfielder Tommy Leach advanced to third on a base hit. No sooner had he gotten there than Tigers' third baseman George Moriarty sauntered over and kicked him in the shins. Leach asked him why he did it, but Moriarty just turned his back and walked away without saying a word. A few seconds later, however, he was back. This time he grabbed Leach's cap and tore it off his head. Leach tried to get his cap back by softening Moriarty with a joke, but the infielder refused to listen. Instead, he took the cap and slapped Leach with it. Infuriated, Leach responded with a swift kick of his own. Luckily, the game resumed before a full-scale donnybrook erupted. Violence escalated as the series continued. In the sixth game, a 5–4 Detroit victory, Tigers' first baseman Tom Jones was knocked unconscious for twenty minutes and had to be carried from the field when Pirates' outfielder John "Chief" Wilson collided with him as he tried to beat out an infield hit. In that same game, catcher Charlie Schmidt received a gash in his right leg while trying to block the plate and Moriarty twisted a knee when Wilson slid hard on an attempted steal. Jones was taken home in an ambulance (he refused to go to the hospital); Schmidt and Moriarty remained in the game. The following day, Moriarty was not so lucky. When Pirates' third baseman Bobby Byrne tried to steal third in the first inning, he stabbed Moriarty with his spikes, causing an ugly gash that required twelve stitches. Moriarty lasted an inning or two before Jennings lifted him. Byrne was also injured on the play—spraining his ankle from the force of impact with Moriarty's leg. A bloody series to be sure, but not atypical.[38]

Ballplayers believed it took a certain kind of man to excel under these conditions—namely the kind who demonstrated toughness and manly forbearance. Players of this era followed a simple rule—men needed to be prepared to take care of themselves no matter the circumstances. When Chicago's Frank Chance spiked Detroit's catcher "Boss" Schmidt in the 1907 World Series, leaving three puncture wounds in Schmidt's leg, the *Chicago Tribune* noted laconically, "No harm done." Players often boasted of their ability to endure no matter what the circumstances. Catcher George Gibson told oral historian Lawrence Ritter, "catching's a pretty rough deal and you better love it or do something else for a living." Gibson then showed Ritter his evidence: a gnarled and twisted right hand, the result of several broken fingers from trapping balls in the dirt, getting nicked by foul balls, and tagging out base runners. When his son, a doctor, x-rayed the hand, "he couldn't believe the number of times each finger had been broken." Gibson rarely—if ever—took time off to let the breaks heal properly. "I used to put on some adhesive tape and keep on playing," he told Ritter. "Just tape two fingers together and make the good one work the bad one." Other catchers were just as tough. When Giants' catcher Roger Bresnahan introduced shin guards during the 1907 season, other major league catchers admitted that only a tough veteran like Bresnahan, whose reputation for grit was widely respected, could dare introduce a new protective item; anyone else might have been suspected of going soft. Bresnahan knew the risk he was taking. "They may holler at me at first," he told the *New York Times* when he announced his plan to wear them in the spring of 1907, "but I can stand that better than being laid up." He predicted, "all the catchers will be using them by the fourth." Not Gibson. He wanted nothing to do with them—even after his manager Fred Clarke ordered a pair for him. Gibson laughed when Clarke approached him, tried them once, and promptly threw them away.[39]

Infielders had to be just as tough. They were "supposed to watch out and take care of themselves," Sam Crawford remarked. "If they got in the way and got nicked, they'd never say anything. They'd just take a chew of tobacco out of their mouth, slap it on the spike wound, wrap a handkerchief around it, and go right on playing. Never thought any more about it." Most tried to give as good as they got. During the 1922 World Series, Reds' third baseman Heinie Groh found himself sprawling on the ground after Babe Ruth of the Yankees steamrolled him. Groh didn't complain because, as he put it, "that's baseball." But as he dusted himself off, Ruth peered down at him and said, "Kid, you know we're both entitled to part of the base path." "OK," Groh responded. "You take your side and I'll take mine. And if I ever find you on my side, you better watch out!" Groh was 5'8" and 160 pounds at most; Ruth was 6'2" and at least 215. Groh understood, "I couldn't have budged that big guy if I'd have hit him with a locomotive, and he knew it, too." Still, "you got to let them know who's boss, right?" That mindset generally discouraged infielders from squawking about even the dirtiest of players. Browns' infielder Jimmy Austin allowed that Cobb could be "real nasty on the field" and that true to his reputation, he "nicked" him more than once. Yet Austin claimed he never complained.[40]

Players believed that all was fair, that violence was an integral part of the game. With some pride, Francis Joseph "Lefty" O'Doul told Lawrence Ritter that he hit nineteen batters one year while pitching for San Francisco of the Pacific Coast League. "On purpose," he added. "No way to say how many I missed." When his arm failed and he became an outfielder, he suddenly found himself on the receiving end of things from pitchers. "Shoe was on the other foot, see?" O'Doul recalled as he recounted the many injuries he sustained when hit by pitches, including a broken elbow and a broken rib. The year O'Doul flirted with .400 (ending up at .398 in 1929) he was knocked down "all day long." Nobody interfered. That was just fine with him; he passed it off as part of the game. "That's all right. Let the ballplayers fight themselves out of it." His solution to being knocked down? "Drag the ball and spike the pitcher."[41] Honus Wagner, perhaps the Dead Ball Era's personification of toughness and manly bearing, provided an even more dramatic way to show up a pitcher. Once, in a game against St. Louis, a young opposing pitcher had the Pirates tied in knots with his hard fastball. The first hitters he faced all walked back to the bench completely discouraged by their inability to connect off the young hurler. Finally, it was Wagner's turn to hit. He let the first two fastballs go by for strikes. On the third pitch—also a fastball—Wagner stuck his hand out and caught it with his bare hand. "Changeup, huh?" he asked calmly. The umpire called Wagner out for interference, but his move so unnerved the pitcher he walked the next five batters.[42]

Wagner's was an impressive show of toughness, but nothing compared to a second baseman Harry Steinfeldt of the Cubs claimed to have met in Dallas in the Texas League around the turn of the century. According to Steinfeldt, the second baseman was guarding the bag when a player from the opposing team tried to steal. Instead of sliding, the runner took a giant leap and landed on the second baseman's feet with his spikes. The "game fellow" took only a minute to shake off the pain and then went right on playing. After the game, he walked back to the clubhouse with Steinfeldt, but stopped short because he felt something in his shoes. Stooping down, he took off his shoe "and shook out two toes."[43] No doubt, Steinfeldt was exaggerating more than a little. Still, his story underscores the sort of toughness that players admired.

Years after he retired as a pitcher, Eddie Wells was asked how modern players compared to players of his generation. Wells was unequivocal: "I'll tell you one thing, slugger," Wells told interviewer Richard Bak, "back then baseball players were dedicated." As evidence, he trotted out the example of Bob Fothergill, an outfielder for the Tigers when Wells first came up. In the bottom of the ninth, with the team behind by a few runs but with a couple runners on base, Cobb—by now manager of the Tigers—needed a pinch hitter. Looking up and down the bench, he asked, "Who here can hit?" Fothergill was nursing a badly sprained ankle and could barely walk, but offered his services. "I'll try," he said. A dead pull hitter to left, he rarely hit the ball the other way. But this time he did, sending the ball on a sharp line just over the first baseman's head. It should have been an easy double, but Fothergill could barely walk; he got about two-thirds of the way to first when he lost his balance. Unable to stand on his leg, he crawled the rest of the way, barely beating the throw in from right field. Wells maintained the players of his generation were unique in the fortitude and courage they displayed. "Can you imagine the ball players doing that this day and age? If you were hurt, it didn't keep you from playing. They don't do that no more, slugger. But that's the way we played ball back there and then."[44]

To players of Wells's generation, such "dedication" or loyalty was a part of manly forbearance. For most players, such loyalty included loyalty to the manager. In fact, some of the toughest managers inspired the greatest expressions of loyalty. The most successful managers of the era ruled their teams like autocrats and expected something akin to servility from their players. Even so, few players openly challenged their managers; most respected—even admired—the men in charge. The game's most strong-willed manager, the pugnacious McGraw, developed something of a cult following from his charges. Mathewson's *Pitching in a Pinch* is essentially an ode to McGraw's ability to command his men. Infielder Al Bridwell remembered his three-and-a-half years with the Giants as the best years of his professional career, thanks to McGraw and his infectious fighting spirit. McGraw, he maintained, was "the kindest, best-hearted fellow you ever saw. I liked him and I liked playing for him." Chief Meyers, who had trouble fitting in on many teams because of contemporary prejudice against Native Americans, found a home with McGraw's Giants. "Once a Giant, always a Giant. That's the truth," Meyers maintained. And it was all "because of Mr. McGraw. Oh, we held him in high esteem. We respected him in every way." "Laughing Larry" Doyle shared Meyers's deep devotion to McGraw and the Giants, memorably proclaiming in 1911, "It's great to be young and a Giant." Another tyrant, George Stallings, received equally high praise from many of his former charges, led by Johnny Evers, who played second base for Stallings during the Braves' historic pennant run. Although Evers had played under "Peerless Leader" Frank Chance, manager of the Cubs, he insisted "without hesitation" that Stallings was "the best manager I ever worked for" and "all things considered, the best manager I ever saw." Chance was good, but apparently not so peerless after all. Jimmy Austin was not quite as effusive as Evers, but praised Stallings as "a fine manager. One of the best."[45]

How to explain such loyalty to managers who could be both tyrannical and vicious? To begin, players recognized and respected the authority of their managers. To most ballplayers, taking orders from a superior was not in itself emasculating. Many came from working-class and ethnic neighborhoods influenced by old world traditions where they had been raised to respect and obey male authority—be it at home, at work, or in church.[46] As much as ballplayers appreciated kind paternal managers like Mack, they may have been more accustomed to assertive, even domineering types like Stallings and McGraw. Rube Marquard, who disliked it when McGraw criticized his play, praised his former manager for running a tight ship: "he wouldn't stand for any nonsense. You had to live up to the rules and regulations of the New York Giants and when he laid down the law, you'd better abide by it." Johnny Evers claimed that he actually preferred a "manager who is harsh on the field." He named McGraw, Chance, Clarke, and Stallings as the best in the National League because they know how to "drive and bully the men and get the last ounce of energy out of them." Players believed tough managers made them tougher.[47]

Even so, theirs was not a blind obedience. It mattered a great deal to players just what sort of authoritarian they took orders from. In this, wins and losses certainly mattered. Pitcher Burleigh Grimes was ecstatic when he was traded to the Giants. "I think most everybody in the league wanted to play for McGraw," he recalled. "Sure he was a strict disciplinarian, but he played the best baseball . . . smartest man I ever played for." Leadership skills also mattered. Players wanted a manager who gained their confidence and respect by demonstrating self-assurance, decisiveness, and the same manly bearing that they hoped to show. Mindful of what was required of them, astute managers found ways to prove themselves to their charges. Although McGraw became more portly as he grew older—earning the epithet "The Little Round Man" from Marquard—late into his career, he made a point of participating in drills and calisthenics during spring training, just to prove he was still physically fit. In addition, McGraw understood the importance of theatrics. When his team played in front of hostile fans, he conspicuously marched onto the field early in the game, just to show his own players that he could not be intimidated. When his team looked lifeless, he moved from the bench to the third base coaching box as if to lead them on the attack.[48]

Probably no manager matched McGraw's sense of the theatrical, but the successful ones also created dramatic personas to inspire their players. For all his blustering, yelling, and cursing, Stallings had one goal in mind—to demonstrate to his men that he was in charge and in control. Hughie Jennings became famous—and a huge drawing card throughout the league—for his antics on the third base coaching box, what with his "Ee-Yah" yells of encouragement, nervous grass pulling, and persistent cheerleading. Cobb called him a "hurrah fellow with everything out in front." Bill Carrigan of the Red Sox was Jennings's opposite. Dubbed the league's "sphinx" by *Sporting Life* because of his quiet and stoic demeanor, he nonetheless understood how to inspire by his comportment. In the heat of the 1916 campaign, the Boston Red Sox lost their star second baseman and team leader, Jack Barry, to injury. To make up for the deficiency, manager Carrigan put himself back on the team as a player, even though he retired the previous year. A catcher by trade, he had gained the nickname "Rough" for his physical and mental toughness. Stepping behind the plate on occasion allowed him to lead by example. Sportswriter Hugh Fullerton credited the move as a pivotal step in winning the pennant that year, writing Carrigan's "presence in the game and leadership in actual play steadied his pitchers and helped them stave off the rush of the White Sox and Detroits."[49]

For sheer martial charisma, however, no one could beat Hugo Bezdek, who managed the Pirates for two seasons to close the 1910s. Charisma was about the only thing Bezdek had going for him on the baseball field because he knew little about the game. When Pittsburgh hired him, Bezdek had been a popular—some might even say legendary—college football coach, most famous for his work at the University of Arkansas and the University of Oregon. As manager of the Pirates, he readily admitted that he knew less than his players. What Bezdek did have was a system based on his love of military discipline. The son of Bohemian immigrants, Bezdek grew up fascinated by the military prowess of the leading European powers. Whether coaching football or baseball, he tried to teach martial discipline and spirit to his players. A baseball team, he opined, was "in many respects . . . a miniature army;" its success depended upon the "same tactics which win out on the field of battle." Just as "the iron discipline of war" molds a military company into a cohesive unit, so too might "training and discipline" transform a baseball team of "untrained recruits" and make them a victorious fighting force, a "well-oiled machine." To prove his point, Bezdek ran spring training much as he ran a football practice—which he in turn modeled after the training practices of the French military. Each emphasized constant drilling to instill discipline. Bezdek believed such practice inspired an esprit de corps that would carry the team to victory, just as loyalty to the regiment inspired soldiers to fight to the death. Bezdek got results: he managed the Pirates to winning seasons in 1918 and 1919 after the team had finished below .500 each of the previous four years.[50]

Conversely, a manager who lacked this sort of manly presence was a source of derision and embarrassment to the club he managed. The legendary Frank Chance passed into this group toward the end of his career when he assumed control of the woeful and very much dysfunctional New York Yankees. Over the years, Chance had been hit by so many pitches that he had become rather pitch-shy. As a precaution, he used a thick leather football helmet when he batted. His teammates thought it hilarious and mocked him unmercifully. Pitcher Chet Hoff recalled in disgust, "He'd go up there and take three cuts and everybody's laughing. He went up there with head gear. The only man in baseball with a head gear." Chance may have believed that the reputation that preceded him when he arrived in New York enabled him to wear the leather helmet, just as Brasnahan did with the shin guards. If so, Chance miscalculated. To his teammates, Chance's precautionary measure reflected weakness, not wisdom.[51]

So players appreciated a manager with a commanding presence. But what about the tirades and personal insults? Connie Mack had the decency to talk to his players privately when he felt they had made a mistake, but hotheads like Stallings and McGraw rarely operated with such restraint. Outfielder Edd Roush said playing for McGraw could be downright traumatizing. "If you made a bad play he'd cuss you out, yell at you, call you all sorts of names," Roush recalled. And what names! Fred Snodgrass claimed McGraw "had the most vicious tongue of any man who ever lived. Absolutely." Jimmy Austin, who played under Stallings, disagreed. "Talk about cussing!" Austin exclaimed. "Golly, (Stallings) had 'em all beat. He cussed something awful." Players who had to contend with such outbursts recognized the manager's diatribes for what they were—salvos in a verbal duel about manhood and honor. When criticized, players understood that they were being called out, challenged to prove their manhood.[52] The question was how best to do this. When pressed, some players interpreted a manager's criticisms as an attack upon their honor and responded in kind. Snodgrass boasted he sometimes yelled back when McGraw railed against him. Infielder

Al Bridwell claimed he went one better. Once after McGraw confronted him over some mistake, Bridwell either socked or pushed McGraw—he could not remember which—so hard that McGraw tumbled down the dugout steps. Red Sox pitcher "Sad Sam" Jones also took on his manager, Ed Barrow, one of the most abrasive in the game. Prior to a game, Barrow ordered Jones to interrupt his game of checkers so the two could have their picture taken for one of the local newspapers. Jones refused, pointing out that since he pitched the day before he was entitled to a day off. "This will cost you $100," Barrow shouted. Jones was not to be cowed; "Make it $200," he responded. "It's $200, all right," Barrow thundered. Jones remained unfazed: "Make it $300 and then go straight to hell." "It's $300," Barrow roared as he stomped out, slamming the door behind him. When Jones finished his game, he calmly walked out to the field and had his photograph taken with Barrow—"arms around each other's shoulders, both smiling, best friends ever," Jones recalled.[53]

For sheer courage—or audacity—in facing down a coarse manager, no one compared with Chief Meyers. After his manager set him up to fail by making him catch a tricky spitball pitcher in his very first game for Harrisburg of the Tri-State League, Meyers decided to confront his boss and "balled him out like a regular veteran." As Meyers told it, "I asked him what the howdy-do he meant by putting me in there to catch a spitball pitcher on a day like that when I had never seen one before—and so on." Surprisingly, his act of nerve paid off. The manager not only apologized, he took the lead to help Meyers become accepted by the rest of the team. Years later, Meyers had an opportunity to face down a manager again—this time McGraw. While catching a game for the Giants against the Chicago Cubs, Meyers ignored McGraw's signal for a certain pitch and ordered the pitcher to throw something else instead. Unfortunately, the hitter, Heinie Youngman, blasted the pitch for a home run. When the inning was over, McGraw was waiting for him. "Meyers! Why did you call the pitch that way?" he stammered impatiently. Remembering that McGraw hated players who thought for themselves, Meyers chose his words carefully. "Well sir," he replied, "it appeared to me—" "APPEARED?" McGraw barked. "Yes sir," Meyers responded, looking McGraw straight in the eye, "It APPEARED." "All right Meyers," McGraw grinned, "You win that one!"[54]

Players understood that defying the manager was a risky proposition. Stallings regularly asked his bosses to trade players who defied his orders. McGraw often did just that, trading such notable players as Frankie Frisch and Buck Herzog (twice) after each expressed disdain for McGraw's constant tongue-lashings. If not traded, players could be benched, sent down, fined, suspended, or released. Of the examples provided above, Jones received a stiff fine; Bridwell was suspended for two weeks without pay; Snodgrass often found himself in McGraw's doghouse. And yet there was also the possibility their tormentor might show them some grudging respect. As Bridwell remembered it, his confrontation with McGraw was settled by an amicable truce. Once his suspension was over, McGraw "forgot about it completely. Never mentioned it again." Bridwell came away from the incident more devoted to McGraw than ever. McGraw knew "how to handle men," Bridwell said. "Some players he rode, and others he didn't." By standing up to the manager, Bridwell made sure he was in the latter group. Jones claimed he reached a similar accord with Barrow. Once things "simmered down, Ed Barrow and I got along just fine." Barrow thought so highly of Jones that when he became general manager of the Yankees in 1921, he traded for him.[55]

Most of the time players had little choice but to follow the orders of their manager, no matter how rudely those orders were delivered. This they did to a remarkable degree. Indeed, some of baseball's most astute and experienced commentators worried that the combination of autocratic managers and acquiescent players threatened the spontaneity and excitement of the game. Sportswriter Hugh Fullerton, who began covering baseball prior to the advent of scientific ball, complained modern ballplayers had become so used to taking orders from the bench, they could no longer think on their own. On the base paths, for example, runners rarely showed the sort of "brain and daring" that used to win championships. Fullerton preferred the era of "Sliding" Billy Hamilton who stole over 100 bases for three straight years, beginning in 1889. That was an age of greater risk-taking and daredeviltry, an age when individuals determined their own fate in the batter's box and on the base paths. Modern players were just as smart as ever, Fullerton contended, but "they have subordinated their intelligence to the brains of the manager, and allow one man, or rather insist upon one man, doing the thinking for the entire team, which is an impossibility." The game "has been reduced to a science, and is in danger of becoming mechanical," Fullerton railed. And if that occurred, then ballplayers would not be players at all; they would be pieces of the machine. Edward Lyell Fox, writing in *Outing*, was even more dismissive, mocking ballplayers as "marionettes" who "never thought" but were ordered around as if in a game of "human chess played on a baseball field between two managers."[56]

The pundits may have seen something emasculating about the modern game, but few players ever made that complaint during their playing careers The game as they experienced it had more than enough challenges, risks, and physicality to make it a manly endeavor. Only in retirement did a few former players reject the notion that they had played the game as mere automatons. Defensively, Burleigh Grimes recalled of his playing days under McGraw, "I did my share of thinking, but I never told McGraw about it."[57]

Most players felt neither weakened nor dehumanized when they took orders from their manager. In searching for language to convey their admiration for strong managers, ballplayers often relied upon military allusions. A good manager, Evers contended, "is a general, gifted with the power to rule men as well as to lead them in battle." He must lead "with a firm hand." Mathewson also relied upon military references to describe McGraw's managerial abilities: he was a great "general," the bench his "tactical headquarters," the players his "privates" in battle.[58] It was one thing to be commanded by a superior, but how much better to be commanded by someone with true military bearing—like "Little Napoleon." Probably few ballplayers read Oliver Wendell Holmes, Jr.'s famous 1895 Memorial Day address to the graduating class of Harvard University in which he eulogized the heroism and courage of Civil War soldiers, but they certainly resonated with the sentiment:

> I do not know what is true. I do not know the meaning of the universe. But in the midst of doubt, in the collapse of creeds, there is one thing I do not doubt, that no man who lives in the same world with most of us can doubt, and that is that the faith is true and adorable which leads a soldier to throw away his life in obedience to a blindly accepted duty, in a cause which he little understands, in a plan of campaign of which he has little notion, under tactics of which he does not see the use.

Like Holmes, ballplayers romanticized the martial spirit and used it as a reference point to articulate an element of their masculine yearnings.[59]

Other players appropriated the language of the machine because—like the military analogy—it dovetailed with their mutualist ethos. Pat Moran, a journeyman catcher for much of his career, understood this perspective as well as any player and used it to good effect when he became a highly successful manager for first the Phillies and then the Reds during the late teens. Moran was thrust into the limelight in 1915 when he took over the hapless Phillies, a team that had never won the pennant and finished in sixth place the year before. He promptly led the club to the league championship. Four years later, he did this feat one better by winning the World Series with the Reds, another team that had never won a pennant. (It was Moran's finest moment, but one that was tragically tainted by revelations that some players for the Reds' opponent, the Chicago White Sox, had thrown the Series.) Moran's approach to managing was informed by his years of sitting on the bench waiting for his chance to play. He was, by all accounts, an extremely humble man who expressed embarrassment when the media christened him the "Miracle Man." "All the credit should be given to the players . . . and not to me," he explained. They did all the work; he "merely directed those efforts because of my experience." Essentially, Moran was a players' manager—though that term was not yet in use. He wanted his players to know that he "is striving for the same thing they are striving for—to win baseball games." He believed the success of the team was a collaborative effort, emphasizing that player and manager must "pay strict attention to business" to be successful. When Moran's Reds won the National League pennant in 1919, he told the press the success of the team could be summed up in two words: "Team work;" it "alone has pulled us up to the fore." He confessed that he would rather manage a team with a "bunch of players who will work together" than the "club that very scintillates with stars but has no team work." One writer observed Moran's approach was strictly blue collar and dubbed him "Moran the toiler, the man in the ranks." This mindset gained him the "true whole-hearted loyalty and good feeling" of his players, the writer concluded. Perhaps so, but Moran only worried about how his team functioned to win ball games. For the team to be successful, "each player must be like a cog in a well-oiled machine. He must fit in and must do his share."[60]

A cog in a machine? To modern sensibilities, using such an analogy might seem rather insulting. Even during the early twentieth century, many American men—especially those in the working and lower middle classes—feared that they were becoming mere automatons, degraded and bottled up as they lost control over their working lives.[61] Had Moran believed his players shared similar concerns, he would have chosen his words more carefully. Of all early twentieth-century managers, the former role player may have been the most sensitive to the feelings and concerns of role players, having been one for most of his ballplaying career. No, Moran did not use the term to demean his players and there is no reason to believe they were insulted. The language invoked an important aspect of players' understanding of team play—the intrinsic worth of all players who worked for the good of the team. Although popular literature of the day often celebrated the gritty and plucky independent spirit of Theodore Roosevelt, Robert Peary, Gilbert Patten's Frank Merriwell and Owen Wister's Virginian as the fullest expressions of true American manhood, the real world suggested that men could not always follow such romanticized ideals. On occasion ballplayers tried to live up to the rugged individualism celebrated so much by various channels of popular culture, but they also understood that the realities of their lives called for something different—a mutualistic ethos that valued altruism and even a certain degree of humility. These men came to baseball before it was invaded by the culture of celebrity; for the most part, they were not driven by egocentric notions of stardom. That ethos was pioneered by their nemesis, Ty Cobb.

Players' allegiance to team play led to a corresponding antagonism toward players who undermined the team's ability to function effectively. Dead Ball Era players were especially critical of two types of teammates who threatened team cohesion: "yellow" players and "swellheads." Yellow players exhibited behavior that was the antithesis of the tough self-assured persona that nearly all ballplayers equated with true manhood. Ballplayers claimed such players harmed the team because they could not be counted on "in the pinches." Umpire Billy Evans, who gained something of a reputation as a sage of the diamond through his side career as a sportswriter, observed "If a player ever shows a sign of yellow, or gets the reputation of being a quitter, he is sure to be the target of all kinds of abuse." Ballplayers, Evans surmised, "detest a quitter." Mathewson claimed that every new player "is put to the most severe test by the other men to see if he is 'yellow,'" and "if he is found wanting, he is hopeless in the Big League, for the news will spread, and he will receive no quarter." To be yellow "is the cardinal sin of a ball player." Cobb contended, "If ever a ball player or an umpire comes into the Big League and displays any lack of nerve, he might just as well pack his grip and pull out again. There is no room for him." For this reason, Mathewson maintained, each player learns to "hide his every flaw," especially "his nerves or temperament," lest he be accused of cowardice. The pugnacious Cobb went a step further: "'Yellow' is a fighting word in the Big Leagues."[62]

Players went to extraordinary lengths to show teammates they possessed the necessary nerve to play well. Around the major leagues, Frank Baker, Philadelphia's star third baseman, gained the reputation as a coward because he was spike shy, that is, he abandoned the base if a runner came at him hard and fast, spikes first. During the 1911 World Series, the Giants tried to take advantage of Baker's phobia by conspicuously sharpening their cleats on the bench before each game. To prove he was not intimidated, Baker risked serious injury, not once but twice. On each occasion, he blocked the bag by kneeling on one knee as Giants' outfielder Fred Snodgrass tried to advance. Each time, Snodgrass had no alternative but to run straight into Baker and try to upset him. That he did, by ripping Baker's pants, bruising his legs, and cutting his arm with his spikes. Even so, the result was a draw. The first time Snodgrass forced Baker to drop the ball; the second time Baker held fast and tagged Snodgrass out. Most important, Baker redeemed himself by standing his ground. Fans and press claimed the second spiking was particularly vicious because Snodgrass seemed to leap at Baker and then added a kick with his spikes once he landed. Yet Baker kept his composure. Even the New York newspapers praised Baker for playing "gamely." Indeed, he seemed to revel in the tension, hitting .375 for the Series and gained the nickname "Home Run" Baker for socking two dramatic home runs off New York aces Rube Marquard and Christy Mathewson.[63]

Players strove to show their fortitude because they wanted to prove themselves as men to their peers. Failing to do so would only leave them open to continued ridicule and scorn. In this, ballplayers demonstrated that they subscribed to an ethic of honor that was in many respects similar to the ethic of honor that Cobb followed so closely. Like Cobb, they believed their worth as ballplayers and as men depended upon how others perceived them. Like Cobb, they believed it essential to respond to any challenge to their reputations. Although few had Cobb's prickly personality or his drive to impress, they certainly recognized the source of his passion and desire to defend himself against all comers. At least to a point. The difference between the two reflects the regional variations in the ethic of honor. Cobb's Southern honor compelled him to separate himself from the pack. He needed to demonstrate not that he belonged, but that he was superior. In this, his actions reflected the highly stratified and socially contentious social world of the turn-of-the-century South. The only collective orientation that Cobb recognized was that of family and—more abstractly—his place of origin, the South. He was not particularly interested in gaining the friendship of peers, only their respect. Most ballplayers felt otherwise. The origins of their understanding of honor developed from the bars, street corners, and shops of Northern cities and towns. For them, honor was another facet of their mutualistic and collaborative ethos. They wanted to be accepted as a vital part of the group, to be recognized for their contribution to something larger than one's status. As they saw it, honor and gameness melded together.[64]

Ballplayers may have loathed "swellheads" even more than cowards. Consider the fate of Dirty Jack Doyle, star infielder for the New York Giants. In 1902, the Giants had problems. Lots of problems. Mired deep in the second division (they would finish dead last with a .353 winning percentage, 53.5 games behind league-leading Pittsburgh), they were a team of weak pitching and exceptionally weak hitting. One bright spot would appear to have been the play of the veteran Doyle, an aggressive, combative player—just the sort of fellow a struggling team might like to have in the clubhouse and on the playing field to help put things right. Earlier in the year, teammates elected him captain in recognition of his experience and leadership. As the team continued to lose, however, Doyle became more a liability than an asset because he refused to play the sort of team ball that might turn the franchise around. True, his .301 batting average was second best on the club, but he often seemed to be more concerned with that than with the team's winning percentage. When the team lost nine straight in late May, Doyle became the scapegoat. His teammates deposed him as team captain, claiming—as one pundit put it—that he was more a "disorganizer" than leader. A few weeks later, they went even further. Because Doyle "refused to play anything but individual ball," they "mutinied" by demanding his release. Management readily complied; Dirty Jack's career in New York was over. Thereafter, he became a journeyman, playing for four teams before leaving the game in 1905.[65]

Players believed egomaniacal players like Doyle hurt the team at least as much as cowards did. After all, the cowardly player did not mean to undermine the team by his actions, but the swellhead knew exactly what he was doing when he placed himself above the team. For this reason, teammates developed a variety of strategies to hold egos in check and encourage team play. Players frowned on teammates who focused too much on their personal statistics, be it batting average, winning percentage, or any other record of personal accomplishments. Players who kept scrapbooks of their newspaper clippings—called "fathead books" or "swellhead books" by disapproving players—did so at the risk of being labeled as overly self-absorbed and conceited. To protect the delicate stability of the clubhouse, teams sometimes gave fawning newspaper writers the cold shoulder, especially if they believed a writer showed favoritism toward one player over the rest. When Fred Snodgrass became a regular for the Giants in 1910, his average skyrocketed over the .400 mark. In response, New York newspapers began to publish his batting average on an almost daily basis. According to Mathewson, Snodgrass quickly grew a head commensurate to his batting average—with less than favorable results. Mathewson interpreted Snodgrass's experience that year as a cautionary tale. According to Matty, Snodgrass soon got the idea that "he was a great batter and that to keep his place in that daily standing he would have to make a hit every time he went to the plate." In time he became so worried about the "printed figures" that he began to press and slumped badly. He ended up with a very good average, .321, but lost the batting race to Sherwood "Sherry" Magee of the Phillies by ten points.[66]

Because ballplayers disliked swellheads, they were extremely ambivalent toward the emerging star system that began to overtake baseball and other forms of mass entertainment during the 1910s and beyond. Though the late nineteenth century had any number of excellent players—Wee Willie Keeler, John McGraw, Cap Anson, Mike "King" Kelly, Hughie Jennings, and Billy Hamilton to name a few—the limited appeal of the game made these players more like cult heroes than national celebrities. That began to change as professional baseball became more popular. The stars of the new century like Mathewson, Cobb, and Johnson benefitted from the increased popularity of the game in numerous ways. They bargained for salaries that were significantly higher than their peers—and sometimes even higher than the star manager. They made endorsements for local and national companies for soft drinks, tobacco, and clothes. From pulpits and podiums, ministers and public orators presented them as examples of virtuous American manhood. National sporting publications sang their praises in feature-length articles. Mathewson and Cobb wrote books (or had them written for them by syndicated columnist and publisher John Wheeler) that purported to give an insider's view of professional baseball. They signed lucrative contracts to write sports columns of their own during the World Series. They used their celebrity to make business and political connections to amass even more wealth. In short, the stars of the new century began to enjoy a quality of life that had eluded stars of an earlier generation and the rank and file players of their own generation.

Average ballplayers were not at all sure how to respond to the burgeoning prosperity of their famous teammates. Although they also benefitted from the game's growing popularity and enjoyed some of the benefits of celebrity, average players were often deeply troubled by the ways in which the emerging star system disturbed traditions of team play and camaraderie. Years later, many chose to remember their era as one of few stars and little of the egotism and rancor that sometimes came with star culture. To make his case that ballplayers in his day were more dedicated to the game, Eddie Wells observed, "There weren't that many salary disputes" because most players were "just tickled to death to be playing in the big leagues."[67]

At the time, they knew otherwise. Most players would have agreed that egotistical players were indeed a problem. The airs certain star players put on and their need to constantly feed their egos by grabbing attention rankled many players. Tris Speaker and Harry Hooper got along fairly well—at least for the first few years they played together. As Speaker's star began to ascend, however, he began to take on certain affectations that annoyed the easy-going and team-oriented Hooper. Although Hooper never aired his complaints publicly, he told family members that he was particularly incensed by Speaker's pompous habit of flipping the ball to him after making a running catch to end an inning—a gesture Hooper believed reduced him to being Speaker's caddy. More seriously, Speaker began to ignore the manager's signs when he was at bat and Hooper was on base. According to Hooper's wife, Speaker intentionally fouled off pitches to frustrate Hooper's efforts to steal a base. Why? He was jealous of Hooper's base-stealing prowess. Finally, Speaker tried to dictate to manager Bill Carrigan where he should bat in the order. To Hooper and other members of the Red Sox, the point could not be plainer—Speaker put himself above the team.[68]

This was a common complaint during the first decades of the twentieth century. Indeed, nearly every player who gained notoriety for his exploits on the field received at least a bit of envious scrutiny from his teammates. The humble and untutored Joe Jackson got the treatment. A year after his stunning debut with the Indians in which he hit over .400, he raised the ire of many of his teammates. According to a contributor to the *Sporting News,* Jackson seemed to have lost his commitment to team play by running "the bases as he sees fit . . . rather than relying on advice from the bench or the coacher." Even the presumed paragon of baseball virtue, Christy Mathewson, was criticized by his fellow Giants on occasion. Giants' teammate Jack Hendricks claimed that Big Six was a "pinhead" and "a conceited fellow" who "didn't care about anybody except himself." According to Hendricks, some players found his holier-than-thou attitude so annoying that they stopped talking to him completely. Mordecai "Three Finger" Brown faced Mathewson in some of the greatest pitchers' duels of the early twentieth century. It irritated the unpretentious Brown to no end the way Mathewson drew attention to himself. Typically, Mathewson waited ten minutes before game time before making an appearance. When he finally showed, he had the entire ballpark on edge. To milk the drama for all its worth, he walked slowly from the clubhouse across the field to the dugout in a long white linen duster—just the thing to accentuate his virtuous persona and statuesque physique. No doubt it was antics like this that led the *Chicago Tribune* to conclude that Mathewson was "so stuck on himself his skin could be used for fly paper."[69]

Nicknames further revealed players' perceptions of "swell-headed" teammates. Early on, Eddie Collins earned the nickname "Cocky" for the self-confidence he demonstrated which often bordered on arrogance (he regularly chastened teammates when they made mistakes). When Babe Ruth was with the Red Sox, teammates dubbed him "Two Head" in reference to both the literal size of his cranium and the figurative size of his ego. For sheer ego, however, few matched outfielder Robert "Braggo" Roth. Although Roth was a talented hitter (.284 career batting average; .367 career on base percentage) and base-stealing threat (he once stole home six times in one season), he alienated everyone he played with because he could not stop talking about himself—hence the nickname Braggo. During an eight-year career, he played for six teams and was forced to retire from the major leagues at the age of twenty-eight despite hitting .283 because no team would take him.[70]

Most players operated from a completely different perspective than the swellheads. They gave more than just lip service to the concept of team play and insisted it encompassed more than mere strategy. By their view, it meant mutual respect and support in action. Teammates believed it especially important to look after one another on the field. When a batter was brushed back or hit by a pitcher, he expected his team's pitcher to retaliate in kind. That was standard operating procedure. So, too, was standing up for a teammate when harassed by players from the opposing team or hostile fans. Even the despised Cobb could count on his teammates coming to his aid when he needed them. During a game in New York in 1912, an obnoxious fan irritated and insulted Cobb so much (an incident that we will examine more fully in chapter 7) that Cobb bolted into the grandstand and mauled him. His teammates did exactly what teammates were supposed to do in such a situation: they grabbed bats and surrounded Cobb so that no one could intervene on the fan's behalf. Shocking by our standards, perhaps, but consistent with the era's team ethos.[71]

Beyond the collective, individual teammates felt compelled to offer assistance to teammates as well. After Harry Hooper talked his manager into playing Babe Ruth in the field on a regular basis, he had a problem. Ruth had the makings of a great hitter, but he was an untrained fielder. Hooper suggested they put Ruth in right field where he could keep an eye on him, coach him, and cover for him as needed from his position in center. It was a harrowing experience at first. With another untutored outfielder in left, Braggo Roth, Hooper had to worry about being trampled by one or the other. "I'd be playing out there in the middle between those two fellows, and I began to fear for my life. Both (Roth and Ruth) were galloping around that outfield without regard for life or limb, hollering all the time, running like maniacs after every ball!" Edd Roush and Jake Daubert of the Reds offered pitcher Rube Bressler a similar kindness. In 1920, Bressler fractured his ankle. When he tried to come back too soon, he had to alter his delivery and ended up ruining his arm. That ended his career as a pitcher. Desperate, he decided to try the outfield. Truth be known, Bressler was a pretty marginal player on the team at the time. In four seasons with the Reds, he had never won more than eight games and never appeared in more than seventeen. Had the injury caused the end of his career, few would have noticed, much less cared. Even so, Roush, an excellent fielder and the Reds' best player, told Bressler that if he could help him, he would be "tickled to death." "Hah! The understatement of the century," Bressler recalled. "The greatest centerfielder in the game saying to me, '*if* I can help you.' Terrific!" So Roush taught Bressler "how to play hitters, how to judge line drives, how to yell for the ball, how to shift on different hitters . . . how to run out after a fly instead of backing up." To enhance his chances of sticking with the club, Bressler also decided to try his hand at first. To do this, he relied upon the generous assistance of the team's veteran first baseman, Jake Daubert. Like Roush, Daubert taught Bressler everything he needed to know to man the position. Together the two players taught Bressler the skills he needed to stay in the majors another twelve years, enjoying far greater success as an outfielder than he did as a pitcher.

Bressler's experience underlines how much average players appreciated the kindnesses of stars; players believed such acts revealed how deeply the values of camaraderie and sociability permeated team culture. Walter Johnson got especially high marks from teammates for his humility, compassion, and good nature. When rookie infielder Ossie Bluege joined the Senators in 1922, he was completely in awe of the living legend, yet soon realized playing behind him was remarkably easy. If a player booted a ball, Johnson would make a point of coming over to say, "That's all right. You'll get the next one." Johnson could be equally generous to friends on other teams. Sam Crawford claimed Johnson grooved him a pitch every now and then. The two were very good friends and according to Crawford, Johnson simply wanted to "'give' me a hit or two, just for old-time's sake." Johnson performed a similar service for Jimmy Austin. Once when Johnson's Senators were beating Austin's Browns by a wide margin, to add a little life to the game, Johnson decided to offer Austin a friendly challenge as he dug in at the plate: "Here's one right in there. Let's see you hit it." Johnson usually over-matched Austin, but this time he decided to be charitable, offering up a so-so fastball, letter high—just where Austin liked it. Austin connected, sending it over the right field fence for a home run. It was all in good fun. "I don't know which one of us was laughing harder as I was going around the bases," Austin recalled. Johnson was also considerate toward young players who were not even in the major leagues. One autumn, the world champion Senators barnstormed through Florida to make a little extra money. In Tampa, they tried to boost ticket sales by letting a few local heroes play with them. Among those chosen was catcher Al Lopez, who was given the rather heart-stopping honor of being Walter Johnson's battery mate. Lopez would eventually go on to a Hall of Fame career in his own right, but in 1925, he was an insecure college player who feared he would be found wanting by the legendary Johnson. Sensing Lopez's anxiety, Johnson made a point of reassuring the young catcher that he would not embarrass him. After the game, Johnson even praised Lopez to the local press.[72]

Once rookies proved themselves worthy, veterans extended the bonds of camaraderie and support to them as well. Hans Lobert received his share of abusive treatment from veterans when he came up with Louisville, but one player who showed him more than a modicum of support was Honus Wagner. Wagner took a liking to Lobert once he learned that the two had much in common—a common heritage, the same first name (Johannes), similar facial features (both men possessed rather large noses), and residence in the same working-class suburb of Pittsburgh. As a gesture of kindness, Wagner nicknamed Lobert "Hans Number Two" and helped him become accepted by the older players. In a similar gesture, Fred Snodgrass found a mentor in William "Spike" Shannon, a veteran outfielder. Shannon took Snodgrass under his wing and showed him the ropes. In retrospect, Snodgrass believed that he "would not have made the club that year if not for Shannon." Jimmy Austin found the unlikeliest of mentors when he joined the Highlanders in 1909, Kid Elberfeld. To make Austin feel welcome, Elberfeld broke with custom by allowing Austin to take his lower berth on overnight train rides—a status usually reserved only for veterans.[73]

Quite often players demonstrated their commitment to the ethic of camaraderie in ways that may have had little to do with the outcome of a particular game but had much to do with the working culture of the team. Two deaf mute players, outfielder William "Dummy" Hoy, of the Cincinnati Reds and Louisville Colonels and Luther "Dummy" Taylor, of the Giants, each prompted their teammates to learn sign language to show they accepted them. Snodgrass claimed that he and his Giant teammates practiced signing constantly. "We'd go by the elevated train from the hotel to the Polo Grounds and all during the ride we'd be spelling out the advertised signs. . . . Even today, when I pass by a billboard I find myself doing it." When Taylor accompanied them to a vaudeville show, teammates signed the jokes to him so that he could share in the fun. Observers noted a similar dynamic when they saw Hoy with his teammates. When dining at restaurants, they often talked exclusively in sign language "to avoid being interrupted by autograph seeking fans." It is tempting to romanticize such behavior—to see such acts as exceptional acts of kindness. But this is off the mark. The true significance of the players' decision to learn sign language is how wholly unexceptional they saw their behavior; they expected teammates to make sacrifices for one another and acted accordingly. Reflecting this ethos, Taylor routinely handed out signing instructions to new players, a clear reminder that he expected them to learn to communicate with him.[74]

Many ballplayers prized sociability and expected each member of the team to show at least a modicum of collegiality. On the Athletics, Mack encouraged players to mix with one another by rooming younger players with veterans, a policy that players readily embraced. Players on some clubs established singing groups and encouraged new members who could carry a tune to join in. On the Cubs, player-manager Frank Chance commented that he did not trust any man who couldn't play cards, believing that poker not only trained men to think under pressure but allowed them to get to know one another better as well. Chance could also be counted on to be the first man to buy a round, a true sign of his commitment to sociability.[75]

Team portraits of the era offer a window into ways ballplayers tried to visually express their gameness, fortitude, and devotion to team play through body language. The photos were almost all staged alike: in the first row, players sit cross-legged on the ground and the rest either sit or stand behind them. Many fold their arms at their chest, a sign of relaxed confidence. Others place their arms at their sides or on their laps. The faces of team members are nearly always serious. Most stare sternly into the camera, chin up, sometimes tilting slightly forward. Their expressions reveal emotional and physical toughness, manly bearing, and self-confidence. The seating is compact in all rows, shoulder to shoulder and sometimes shoulder overlapping shoulder. No players are singled out for special placement. In a 1907 photograph of the Detroit Tigers, for example, Cobb sits slightly to the right of center; Crawford stands farther right still. Manager Jennings is seated in the middle, but his body is partially obscured by a team mascot, a Bull Terrier mix. Overall, the photos make the teammates look formidable, strong, and self-assured. Yet there is also something else. In many photos a few players place their arms around the shoulders of those next to them or place their hands on the shoulders of those in front of them. Occasionally, a player might even rest a hand on the thigh of a player next to him, much like another photographic genre of the era—romantic friendships. Their point is clear: they are united as teammates and demonstrative in their affections for one another.

This is not to argue that every baseball team was an oasis of peace and tranquility. Clearly, cliques and factions were rampant and sometimes ripped clubs apart. When Hughie Jennings took over the Tigers in spring 1907, he inherited a team that was nearly dysfunctional because so many groups of players detested one another. Jennings tried to end the conflicts by infusing the clubhouse with his upbeat and exuberant personality. When that didn't work, he traded off some of the most malevolent members of the team and even toyed with the idea of trading his star player, Cobb. Ethnic tensions were a source of division on many teams. During the 1910s, the Red Sox were so split by ethnoreligious differences that the press took to identifying the two main factions as the "K.C.s," for the Knights of Columbus, and the "Masons," in reference to the anti-Catholic fraternity.[76]

Yet, the commitment to team play forced all of these and other players to make their peace more or less amicably for the good of the team. The Cubs' ability to play so well together was especially noteworthy given how much they hated one another. When the Tigers played Chicago in the 1907 and 1908 World Series, Cobb was struck by how much the players seemed to despise one another. The Tigers were

Figure 5.1. Ty Cobb and the Detroit Tigers pose after winning the American League championship in 1907. While Cobb seems almost enveloped within himself, many of his teammates evince a casual and fraternal masculinity characteristic of Northern working-class culture. *Source:* **Courtesy of Ernie Harwell Collection. Detroit Public Library.**

hardly a den of tranquility, but the enmity Cobb witnessed on the Cubs truly surprised him. They "were always fighting and wrangling among themselves," he observed. He was "certain there would be several fist fights from the names they called each other." Even the manager got into the act: "Chance was beefing and calling names, especially with his pitchers."[77] Even so, Cobb claimed they played more effectively and aggressively than any other team in baseball, even more than the championship Philadelphia Athletics teams, supposedly the model of propriety and good will. Joe Tinker and Johnny Evers exemplified how to work together despite personal animosities. Tinker said, "We used to get along apart." Evers was more effusive: "Tinker and myself hated each other, but we loved the Cubs" and that was enough to enable them to work together.[78] Similarly, Speaker and Lewis of the Boston Red Sox also kept their personal differences in check. "Once a game started we forgot personal feelings," Lewis told a reporter years after the two had retired. "We helped each other as willingly as we helped anybody else in the lineup."[79]

Players found stars like Collins, Speaker, and Mathewson difficult to work with at times, but nothing worse. Conversely, a few became persona non grata because they so blatantly violated the players' ethic of team play. Carl Mays, who pitched for the Red Sox, Yankees, Reds, and Giants during a fifteen-year career, was surely in this class. Though Mays was one of the best right-handed pitchers in the American League, most of his teammates viewed him as a corrosive agent. That perception has lingered long after he retired. One indication of this is his rather glaring omission from Baseball Hall of Fame consideration. Although he won 208 games, had a career ERA of 2.92, and a winning percentage of .623, he has only been included on the Hall of Fame ballot once (1958) and received only 2.3 percent of the vote. Mays seemed to have exactly the wrong combination of personality traits to please teammates. An intense competitor, he bullied and berated anyone who made mistakes when he pitched. Exceedingly religious, he was contemptuous of players who enjoyed a drink after a game or spent their idle hours seeking physical gratification. Equally damning, he was something of a loner who seemed to rub everyone the wrong way in his quest for solitude. When he pitched for the Red Sox, a team full of cliques, Mays achieved the near impossible: he united the team in their hatred for him. As one American League official observed, Mays was simply "one of those unlucky fellows who seem to have a special knack for getting it wrong." Not that it seemed to matter to him. When he joined the Giants late in his career, he told his new teammates to leave him alone. "Don't think I want friends," he said to them. And he meant it.[80]

It wasn't just Mays's personality that troubled his peers. There was another element to his game that was even more disturbing: He gained a reputation around the league as a headhunter, a pitcher who intentionally threw high and tight to intimidate hitters. This was a problematic practice in the annals of baseball etiquette. Most players understood that pitchers had a right to assert their presence in and around the strike zone. But to intentionally try to hit someone in the head and thus endanger his well-being? No pitcher admitted they practiced such brutality, not even the callous Mays. Yet everyone believed that the mean-spirited pitcher was out for blood. Part of hitters' problem with Mays concerned the way he delivered the ball. A submarine artist, he dropped his arm well below a ninety-degree angle as he pitched. As the ball traveled toward the plate, it had a tendency to rise at a trajectory that hitters found hard to gauge. Thus, it was not at all surprising that Mays hit batters on occasion.

Then the unthinkable happened. On August 16, 1920, Mays hit Cleveland shortstop Ray Chapman in the left temple. Chapman sank to the ground, his face knotted in pain, blood oozing from his left ear. He was rushed to a nearby hospital where he died early the next morning. The press, most players, and even some umpires called for Mays's immediate expulsion from major league baseball. It didn't happen, but their willingness to believe the worst about him suggested just how much people truly disliked him. Even his teammates turned against him. Although Mays continued to pitch well for the Yankees—he led the league in wins the following year—he was persona non grata on the team. The following spring, "none of the regular players would mix with him," teammate Bob Shawkey recalled. His peers were especially disturbed that Mays showed no remorse. "Nothing bothered him," Shawkey said in disgust. To Shawkey and others, such callousness indicated just how little Mays appreciated the close bonds of fraternity that were supposed to prevent tragedies like Chapman's death from happening.[81]

New York Highlanders' first baseman Hal Chase became an anathema to his teammates for a very different reason. Crowned "Prince Hal" by an adoring New York press, Chase was the best first baseman of the era and a man of great charm. Longtime New York sportswriter Fred Lieb claimed he was "speed and grace personified." Chase's charismatic personality made him a fan favorite, one of the first marquee players in the American League. But he was also self-centered, horribly corrupt, and possessed, according to Lieb, "a corkscrew brain." At some point, perhaps during the 1908 season, Chase began to throw games for gambler friends. He was such a good fielder that he could commit errors that others could not detect. Teammates suspected Chase was crooked, but had no hard evidence. Besides, there was the matter of team owner Frank Farrell, who liked Chase and was not about to see his most popular player discredited. As a result, Chase remained in the majors for fifteen years. Along the way, he involved at least two other players in his schemes, Henry "Heinie" Zimmerman and Lee Magee. Yet perhaps the most remarkable thing about Chase's long jaded career is that he did not corrupt more players. As Lieb wondered, if Chase could get rich throwing games, why didn't more players follow his lead? In fact, most wanted nothing to do with Chase or his brand of baseball because he constantly put his own welfare over that of his teammates. Former teammate Charles "Gabby" Street even witnessed Chase cheat his teammates at cards. To serious players like Jimmy Austin, Frank LaPorte, Kid Elberfeld, Frank Chance, and Roger Peckinpaugh, playing with Chase was nearly intolerable. Around the league, he gained the reputation as a player to shun. As a Chase associate later recalled, "the man was born with no sense of right or wrong." Or camaraderie for that matter.[82]

Then there was Ty Cobb. Cobb was no rogue like Chase. Teammates understood that Cobb played the game hard and to win; his concern for personal honor would not allow him to do otherwise. Nor was Cobb an angry brooder like Mays. True, especially early in his career, he sometimes came off as a humorless loner, but he could also be a person of unusual charisma; his status-conscious parents had made sure he knew how to charm and how to curry favor from influential people. It was also true that Cobb had a violent streak, but he usually telegraphed his intentions well in advance, just as the "code duello" required; thus players knew when Cobb was out for vengeance and could prepare accordingly. Moreover, even his most ardent critics admitted Cobb usually acted within the unwritten rules of baseball etiquette. So Cobb was no Chase or Mays. No, his major failing, so far as his teammates were concerned, was far more pedestrian than gambling or a predilection for headhunting: he was simply a self-centered bore.

When Jennings took over the Tigers at the start of the 1907 season, he gave Cobb the freedom to run on his own, a great privilege in the age of authoritarian managers and scientific baseball. Obviously, he knew talent when he saw it. In addition, Jennings may have wanted to give Cobb a vote of confidence in hopes this would help the temperamental young player settle down. Or perhaps he realized Cobb would run on his own regardless, so he might as well retain the façade of control by asserting the decision was his, not Cobb's. Whatever the motives, the decision had two immediate consequences. First, the unleashed Tiger became the talk of the baseball world. Although Cobb did not become a master base runner overnight, he demonstrated an ability to disrupt the opposition and electrify the crowd. Second, the still leashed Tigers had one more reason to dislike Cobb. By the end of the season Cobb was doing more than just running on his own; he was ordering his teammates to help him in his various capers. In this, Cobb became a stern taskmaster, treating his peers more like minions than teammates. Whether Jennings actually ceded this power to Cobb is unclear; what is clear is that Cobb presented himself as solely responsible for his daredevil antics. Cobb's ego grew with his fame; the more popular he became, the more reasons he gave his teammates to resent him.

It did not help the players' morale that the press rarely criticized Cobb's antics—as when he bolted the team during the 1908 pennant race to marry Charlotte "Charlie" Marion Lombard in Augusta. Detroit sportswriter Paul Bruske hinted in a national journal that players and management were not pleased with Cobb's actions but noted that the team could do nothing to stop him. "A less tactful man might have told Cobb that absence from this team would mean a fine or other punishment," Bruske observed. But what would be the use? "The Georgian . . . would merely have gone away to the ceremony just the same, and wouldn't have come back until he got good and ready, if at all." Jennings and company realized Cobb was simply too valuable to the team and "a rupture between him and his club is not to be thought of at any price." That was as close as the Detroit press came to telling Cobb off. Most journalists were far more circumspect. Detroit's two leading newspapers, the *Free Press* and the *News*, treated Cobb's decision to leave the team to get married as a routine affair, as if players often absented themselves during a hot pennant race for such reasons. Similarly, newspapers ignored the many times Cobb missed practice and waved aside those instances when he arrived late for games with a joke or an airy excuse. In any controversy, Cobb could nearly always count on a sympathetic item from Detroit writers.[83]

The local and national press lavished Cobb with praise. By 1910, journalists heaped superlatives on Cobb they never offered Lajoie, Mathewson, and Wagner. Consider, for example, *Baseball Magazine*'s 1912 paean to Cobb, "The Ty Cobb Number." The edition offered testimonials from Jennings and Johnny Evers, a word from Cobb himself, and several feature stories on nearly all things Cobb—his childhood, his greatest achievements, his devotion to fans, and his greatest rivals. It was a complete whitewash, carefully avoiding his many controversies and highlighting how much all corners of the baseball world admired him. Nary a word was offered from or about his fellow Tigers. It must have sickened them to read it—probably about as much as reading headlines in various newspapers on the circuit that announced the "Tygers" were in town. If that wasn't enough, local journalists routinely dismissed Cobb's critics on the team as jealous of his superior skills.[84]

Journalists had a variety of reasons for taking Cobb's side. In the case of Detroit's coterie of sportswriters, they were indebted to the team for paying their way on road trips; this had a way of discouraging most reporters from broaching topics that might detract from the team's marketability. In addition, most local journalists liked Cobb personally, despite his idiosyncrasies. As Branch Rickey observed years later, Cobb knew how to turn on the charm when he had to. And he seemed to understand from the start that it was smart to curry favor with reporters. This he did by giving the press what they wanted—namely easy access and presumably candid interviews. Veteran Detroit sportswriter Harry Salsinger marveled at Cobb's ability to handle the press. Salsinger quipped, Cobb "can summon a brand of diplomacy that would make some of our professional diplomats look clumsy." This was especially true "where diplomacy is needed to advance the glory of T. R. Cobb."[85] If nothing else, reporters realized it was hardly in their best interest to alienate the team's marquee player. Better to alienate a Jones or McIntyre or even Crawford than Cobb, they figured. National journalists followed suit. Journals like *Baseball Magazine* and the *Sporting News* raved about Cobb because he was the hottest commodity in the game— the player fans wanted to read about the most. Of the other Tigers, only Crawford and Jennings were considered stars in their own right—but they paled in comparison to Cobb. So far as the press was concerned, they and the rest of the Tigers were mere extras in the drama of Ty Cobb. As a result, the other Tigers were generally denied an outlet in which to air their grievances against the mighty Cobb.

If Cobb's teammates couldn't go to the press, they certainly couldn't go to Cobb. They learned early on that the usual forms of peer pressure that worked so well on other teams to control malcontents and swelled heads would not work with Cobb. They forced him to endure one of the most abusive hazings heaped upon a ballplayer when he first came up, but as Sam Crawford later reported, it did not curb his "freshness."[86] At that point, players realized that the best strategy was to stay clear of Cobb as best they could. No doubt, winning helped the Tigers to endure the misery of having Cobb for a teammate. Beginning in 1907, the Tigers won the American League championship three years in a row— and that resulted in sizeable paychecks at the end of each season. Having Cobb on the team wasn't all bad.

Relations between Cobb and the team reached their nadir during the ill-fated 1910 season. Although many pundits had picked the Tigers to win the championship again, they struggled to stay in contention. A hot start put them out in front during the first week of May. Then they slumped back into third and then fourth place. The Tigers rallied in early June, enough to share the lead with Philadelphia and New York. But that was it. They slumped again just as the Athletics took off on a torrid win streak. In the span of three weeks, they lost twelve games in the standings to Mack's streaking team. It got worse. Detroit ended the season in third place, eighteen games out of first. Without a World Series to look forward to, the Tigers began to point fingers—mostly at Cobb.

Crawford, perhaps the one Tiger whose status was high enough to allow him to take on Cobb, vented to the local press that the reason the Tigers lost the pennant was that the team had "too much Cobb." By this Crawford meant that Cobb had acted selfishly down the stretch and had shown himself to be more interested in winning the batting championship than winning ball games. He was especially incensed that Cobb had stated publicly that he would be better served if someone besides Crawford batted behind him because Wahoo could not hit as he once did. Crawford called the accusation groundless and complained that it was further evidence that Cobb could not see beyond his selfish ambitions. Crawford claimed there was plenty of blame to go around for Cobb's poor work down the stretch. Crawford was particularly angry with Jennings and Navin, observing that both coddled the star, allowing him to do "as he pleased." This, Crawford contended, "made harmony in the ranks impossible." In addition, Crawford was none too pleased with the Chalmers Motor Car Company, maker of luxury automobiles, because they promised a new car to the winner of the batting race. The possibility of winning that car, Crawford claimed, "made Cobb forget team play and look only for base hits."[87]

At first blush, Crawford's outburst sounds petty and perhaps even desperate. After all, Cobb hit .383 in 1910, despite suffering from a mysterious eye ailment that forced him to miss two weeks down the stretch. But Crawford did not criticize Cobb's individual performance; he criticized Cobb's behavior as a teammate. Imbedded in Crawford's remarks were the sensibilities of a player who claimed to follow the players' ethic. He revealed no sympathy for Cobb's eye problems, implying that Cobb should have toughed it out. Even if Cobb was incapable of batting to his fullest potential, he could have helped the team in other ways, especially given his unmatched skills as a base runner and offensive strategist. Crawford's central complaints—that Cobb received preferential treatment and became too obsessed with winning a luxury automobile—were related. Both revealed how uncomfortable ballplayers were with the treatment some elite performers were beginning to receive. The award for the batting title particularly rankled Crawford. By his view, players should be rewarded for their contribution to the team, not for individual records. No doubt, Crawford was particularly offended by Cobb's habit of computing his average with every at bat. It smacked of ego.[88] In this, Crawford represented the sensibilities of most players and the public at large. Indeed, players and baseball's brass decided that the race for the auto had become such a distraction that they pressed the Chalmers Company to change the nature of their award. Henceforth, the company would give an auto to one player from each league who proved "himself as the most important and useful to his club and to the league at large in point of deportment and value of services rendered."[89] This was a clear victory for the advocates of team play.

Crawford may have been the only Tiger to go public, but many on the team agreed with his sentiments. It was at this time Cobb blew up at Davy Jones and Donie Bush for missing his signs. Jones and Bush countered that Cobb cared more about his batting average than playing winning ball or protecting the honor of his teammates. By the end of the year, both had come to resent the control Cobb exercised over them. Meanwhile, teammates whispered that Cobb's eyes were not bothering him at all, that he had made the whole thing up to protect his batting average. In essence, they believed Cobb had turned yellow. Although Cobb had to wear smoked glasses for a spell and even showed up at the park a time or two with a patch over one eye, players suspected the worst about him. It was a sad indication of how low he had sunk in their estimation. Writing in the *Sporting News*, Detroit sportswriter F. A. Beasley observed Cobb had become very unpopular with his teammates "and it is all brought about by his great love for Ty Cobb himself."[90]

How, though, could players vent their frustrations and offer Cobb a bit of payback? The heated competition for the batting title offered the perfect opportunity. The race went down to the closing days of the season. Cobb went on a tear during the last games of September and the first games of October, lifting his average to .383, several points above Lajoie. With just two games in Chicago left, Cobb decided to leave the team and drive to Philadelphia where he had been hired to play the league champion Athletics in a series of tune-up games while they waited for the National League season to end. After that, Cobb planned to cover the World Series as a journalist for the *Wheeler Syndicate*. The rest of the Tigers clearly resented Cobb for leaving, not just because they had to play out the string, but because Cobb's two gigs were more evidence of the privileges granted to celebrity players at the expense of the rest of the team. But what did Cobb care? He had done the math: he knew Lajoie trailed him by eight percentage points and would need two nearly perfect games to catch him. Only one problem: the fix was on. In a season-ending doubleheader in St. Louis, Lajoie made eight hits in nine at bats. Of Lajoie's hits, only one was legitimate—a long triple over the head of the Browns' centerfielder. One other hit resulted from lackadaisical fielding by the Browns' shortstop on a slow roller. The other six were bunt singles courtesy of manager Jack O'Connor, who instructed rookie third baseman John "Red" Corriden to play deep so as to invite Lajoie to bunt. This Lajoie was very happy to do—six times in fact. Five were ruled hits; the sixth was ruled a fielder's choice. Eight for nine: it looked to all observers as if Lajoie had his batting title.[91]

It was a horrible moment for baseball—and everyone knew it. The St. Louis dailies immediately castigated O'Connor for throwing the batting title. Umpire Billy Evans promised an investigation. Ban Johnson denounced the entire affair and promised that no more batting champions would receive automobiles. Cobb's teammates didn't care. They were overjoyed to see someone besides their prima donna win the car. In a rare moment of team solidarity, several Detroit players—perhaps as many as half the roster—made their feelings clear: they sent Lajoie a short telegram congratulating him for his triumph: "Glad you won" the message said. These players knew what had happened in St. Louis. They had probably heard the rumors that hurlers throughout the league were grooving pitches to Lajoie. Why? For the same reason the Tigers wanted Cobb to lose: they detested the way he presented himself as a ballplayer and as a man. Conversely, they saw Lajoie as the anti-Cobb. He was the classic hell of a fellow—generous, kind, welcoming, and considerate. As a Detroit columnist observed, Lajoie "was directly the opposite from Cobb in disposition"—"a big, jovial, good-natured one; is gentlemanly and modest and should a popularity contest be on, (Lajoie) would undoubtedly cop the prize offered." In essence, he personified the players' ethos.[92] The Detroit ballplayers addressed the telegram to Lajoie, but they hoped Cobb would get the message as well: they detested his approach to the game. Essentially, they hoped this bit of subterfuge might help deflate one very swelled head. As a *Detroit Free Press* editorial commented, many followers of the game believed Cobb "needed a warning against excessive self-esteem."[93]

Cobb recognized at once the motives behind his teammates' action and was mortified. At least that's what he told the press. Although he subscribed to a more individualistic ethos than they did, he recognized the importance of team play. Equally important, he understood that he needed to possess the reputation of a team player. For this reason, he publicly denounced the accusation that he was driven by ego. "I dread being called swell-headed worse than any other thing," he told the press; "many a time have I walked out to the outfield stoop-shouldered so as to keep the fans from thinking I was cocky or swelled up." It was all a gross misunderstanding, he maintained. "I tried to be a good fellow with the other players," he lamented, but "instead of having the desired effect, the players thought I was fresh." Perhaps, he should have just kept to himself "and not tried to be a mixer." "I guess I got too familiar too soon," a contrite Cobb surmised.[94]

Unfortunately for the Tigers, whatever humiliation Cobb experienced from the episode was short-lived. When Ban Johnson released the final batting statistics showing that Cobb had maintained his lead by mere thousandths of a percentage point, he was delighted and—at least publicly—magnanimous, telling reporters that he was "tickled" that he had won. "I have no one to criticize, I know the games were on the square," he claimed—apparently with a straight face. When told that Lajoie would also be awarded a car by the Chalmers Company, he added, "I am glad that I won an automobile and am especially pleased that Lajoie also gets one." It was a gracious statement and apparently a heartfelt one.[95]

Yet if baseball people hoped the sordid episode might prompt Cobb to change his behavior, they would be disappointed. Players and pundits continued to accuse Cobb of placing self above team. During spring training in 1911, the *Charlotte Observer* (North Carolina) noted that all the Tiger players had "allied against Cobb" and brazenly shunned him. Not even Cobb's "best plays . . . draw any attention from his teammates," the newspaper reported. Even American League president Ban Johnson felt compelled to condemn Cobb's lack of esprit de corps. When writers from across the country named Cobb the first recipient of the Chalmers Company's Most Valuable Player in the American League award for 1911, President Johnson injected he was not at all sure Cobb was deserving of the honor since he still "caused dissension in the Detroit team." The accusations continued. "Cobb is for Cobb," J. G. Taylor Spink stated just days after Cobb ended a contract holdout at the beginning of the 1913 season. "That is the way he plays the game, whether it is on the field or negotiating a contract." Spink's words proved especially prophetic that year. With the Tigers mired in sixth place as the season came to a close, a Detroit sportswriter observed that Cobb was again "playing for batting averages more than ball games." His teammates were disgusted. Once the season ended, Tigers' second baseman Oscar Vitt confided to a San Francisco newspaper that he and his teammates "had very little use for Cobb because of his desire to play for an individual record."[96] So it went, at least for the next few years. When the 1917 season ended, Detroit sportswriter H. G. Salsinger noted that reports of dissent and animosity surrounding Cobb, "the prima donna of the club," had become an annual event. This time, players were upset because Jennings favored Cobb, at the expense of everyone else. The team's other three outfielders—Crawford, second-year outfielder Harry Heilmann, and Bobby Veach—were especially resentful of the influence Cobb seemed to have over Jennings. As usual, Crawford—who by now had become a bit of a crank—was the most vocal of Cobb's critics. Cobb pretty much ran the team, Crawford complained, and did so "to suit himself." When Wahoo Sam was released at the end of the season, he blamed Cobb. "While I was with Detroit, I saw a number of men sent from the team because of Cobb's dislike for them," he stated, but "I never thought he would be able to get me." The final snub came during Crawford's testimonial at Navin Field late in the season. As the rest of the team gathered round the veteran to congratulate him for his years of service, Cobb and Jennings stayed in the dugout. That sort of behavior, Crawford concluded, made Cobb "a disorganizing influence" on the team.[97]

An ethos of mutual support, camaraderie, good humor, and fortitude sustained and enhanced the lives of most early twentieth-century ballplayers. This ethos had little appeal to Cobb. His conception of manhood was more individualized, informed as it was by the rural South's traditions of personal honor and personal autonomy. Late in life, Cobb sometimes confided to friends that he wished he had embraced the players' ethos more fully and thus made more friends. At the time, however, Cobb expressed no such remorse. He wanted—and needed—to be the best player in the game and marshaled all his resources to do so. That his teammates disliked him affected him not at all. He interpreted the enmity as evidence of their emotional, mental, and physical inferiority and professional pettiness. His "vying nature," as he succinctly described his personality in his final autobiography, did not allow him to view the game as anything but "a struggle for supremacy, a survival of the fittest." For Ty Cobb, much of the players' ethos was an anathema, a negation of all that he believed.[98]

The irony in all this is that while Ty Cobb alienated most players of his day, he won over millions of fans. The very behavior that inspired his peers to hate him contributed to his popularity among fans. So far as they were concerned, Cobb was the most compelling and the most popular player of his era. Understanding why this was so—that is, why fans resonated so fervently with Cobb even as he alienated his peers—helps to explain Cobb's historical significance as well as the broader cultural significance of the male sporting culture in which he thrived.

NOTES

1. Sam Crawford in Lawrence S. Ritter, *The Glory of Their Times: The Story of the Early Days of Baseball Told by the Men Who Played It* (New York: Perennial, 1966), 62.

2. "Between Innings," *Baseball Magazine* (August 1919): 230; Sam Crawford in Ritter, *Glory of Their Times*, 65; George Gibson in Ritter, *Glory of Their Times*; 75, Goose Goslin in Ritter, *Glory of Their Times*, 279–80.

3. Jeffrey P. Powers-Beck, *The American Indian Integration of Baseball* (Lincoln: University of Nebraska Press, 2004), 78–79.

4. Mark C. Carnes, *Secret Ritual and Manhood in Victorian America* (New Haven, CT: Yale University Press, 1989), 2; Amy Koehlinger, "'Let Us Live for Those Who Love Us': Faith, Family, and the Contours of Manhood Among the Knights of Columbus in Late Nineteenth-Century Connecticut," *Journal of Social History* 38 (2004): 455–69; David Beito, "To Advance the 'Practice of Thrift and Economy': Fraternal Societies and Social Capital, 1890–1920," *Journal of Interdisciplinary History* 29 (1999): 585–612; Jason Kaufman, "The Rise and Fall of Joiners: The Knights of Labor Revisited," *Journal of Interdisciplinary History* 31 (2001): 553–79; Madelon Powers, "'Poor Man's Friend': Saloonkeepers, Workers, and the Code of Reciprocity in U.S. Bars, 1870–1920," *International Labor and Working-Class History* 45 (1994): 10; Harold Seymour, *Baseball: The People's Game* (New York: Oxford University Press, 1990), 26–38; quotation is on 35.

5. Davy Jones in Ritter, *Glory of Their Times*, 34–35.

6. Bill James, *The New Bill James Historical Baseball Abstract* (revised edition; New York: Free Press, 2001), 83; James K. Skipper, *Baseball Nicknames: A Dictionary of Origins and Meanings* (Jefferson, NC: McFarland, 1992), xx–xxiii. A table provided in a February 1911 edition of the *Sporting News* titled "'Dope' on Detroit Team for 1911" gives the nickname of *every* player on the team. Although many nicknames were just shortened versions of Christian names (Ty for Tyrus, for example), the chart still demonstrates that nicknaming was indeed a ubiquitous practice, even on a team as divided as the Tigers. *Sporting News* (February 11, 1911): 6.

7. *Detroit Free Press*, March 10, 1906, 10.

8. Frank Deford, *The Old Ball Game: How John McGraw, Christy Mathewson, and the New York Giants Created Modern Baseball* (New York: Atlantic Monthly Press, 2005), 135.

9. Leigh Montville, *The Big Bam: The Life and Times of Babe Ruth* (New York: Anchor Books, 2006), 21, 43–44, 54.

10. George Gmelch, *Inside Pitch: Life in Professional Baseball* (2001; repr., Lincoln, NE: Bison Books, 2006), 61.

11. Harold Seymour, *Baseball: The Golden Age* (New York: Oxford University Press, 1971), 104; Mike Sowell, *August 2, 1903: The Mysterious Death of Hall-of-Famer Big Ed Delahanty* (New York: Macmillan, 1992).

12. John J. Evers, *Touching Second: The Science of Baseball* (1910; repr., Danvers, MA: General Books, 2009), 10, 38; Norman L. Macht, *Connie Mack and the Early Years of Baseball* (Lincoln: University of Nebraska Press, 2007), 403–405; *Sporting Life* (October 5, 1912): 4; F. C. Lane, "Joseph Tinker the Shortstop Manager and His Remarkable Career," *Baseball Magazine* (July 1913): 53; Christy Mathewson, "My Life So Far," *Baseball Magazine* (December 1914): 57; "Max Carey, The Minister-Ball-Player," *Baseball Magazine* (September 1914): 3; Fred Snodgrass in Ritter, *Glory of Their Times*, 96–98.

13. "Max Carey, the Minister-Ball Player," 63; *Sporting Life* (September 25, 1915): 7.

14. Deford, *Old Ball Game*, 125.

15. Madelon Powers, "'Poor Man's Friend,'" 1–15; Royal Melendy, "The Saloon in Chicago," *American Journal of Sociology* 6, no. 3 (November 1900): 289–306.

16. Ty Cobb, *Inside Baseball with Ty Cobb*, edited by Wesley Fricks (Salt Lake City: Aardvark Publishing, 2007), 148.

17. Hugh Fullerton, "Odd Pranks of Baseball Players," *Chicago Daily Tribune*, September 2, 1906.

18. Eddie Wells in Richard Bak, *Cobb Would Have Caught It: The Golden Age of Baseball in Detroit* (Detroit: Wayne State University Press, 1991), 161–162; Gmelch, *Inside Pitch*, 64–65.

19. *Sporting Life* (March 28, 1914): 13.

20. Wells in Bak, *Cobb Would Have Caught It*, 162; J. C. Kofoed, "The Star of the Phillies' Infield," *Baseball Magazine* (September 1914): 42.

21. Kofoed, "The Star of the Phillies' Infield," 42; *Sporting Life* (February 6, 1915): 5.

22. On the meanings and significance of pranks, see: Alan Dundes, "April Fool and April Fish: Towards a Theory of Ritual Pranks," *Etnofoor Jaarg* 1, Nr. 1 (1988): 4–14; Susan J. Rasmussen, "Joking in Researcher-Resident Dialogue: The Ethnography of Hierarchy among the Tuareg," *Anthropological Quarterly* 66, no. 4 (October 1993): 211–20.

23. *Sporting Life* (March 24, 1906): 7.

24. Paul J. Zingg, *Harry Hooper: An American Baseball Life* (Urbana: University of Illinois Press, 1993), 114; Timothy M. Gay, *Tris Speaker: The Rough-and-Tumble Life of a Baseball Legend* (Guilford, CT: Lyons Press, 2007), 90.

25. *Sporting Life* (April 11, 1903): 15; Arthur Hittner, *Honus Wagner: The Life of Baseball's "Flying Dutchman"* (Jefferson, NC: McFarland, 1996), 115.

26. Sam Crawford in Ritter, *Glory of Their Times*, 64–65.

27. Tommy Leach in Ritter, *Glory of Their Times*; Sam Crawford in Ritter, *Glory of Their Times*, 33, 61; Paul Waner in Ritter, *Glory of Their Times*, 339.

28. Tommy Leach in Ritter, *Glory of Their Times*, 35–36.

29. Ty Cobb, with Al Stump, *My Life in Baseball* (1961; repr., Lincoln, NE: Bison Books, 1993), 87; Davy Jones in Ritter, *Glory of Their Times*, 43, 45.

30. *Detroit Free Press*, May 9, 1908, 8; *Sporting Life* (February 18, 1911): 2; *Sporting Life* (November 18, 1911): 15.

31. Christy Mathewson, *Pitching in a Pinch: Baseball from the Inside* (1912; repr., Lincoln, NE: Bison Books, 1994), 35–36.

32. Lawrence Ritter, *Lost Ballparks: A Celebration of Baseball's Legendary Fields* (New York: Viking Studio Books, 1992), 86.

33. Hans Lobert in Ritter, *Glory of Their Times*, 191–192; George Uhle in Bak, *Cobb Would Have Caught It*, 175.

34. Jonathan Fraser Light, *The Cultural Encyclopedia of Baseball* (Jefferson, NC: McFarland, 1997), 203, 625.

35. Sam Crawford in Ritter, *Glory of Their Times*, 60; Hans Lobert in Ritter, *Glory of Their Times*, 191.

36. Joe Wood in Ritter, *Glory of Their Times*, 166–167. On health and safety issues in early twentieth-century baseball, see Robert F. Burk, *Never Just a Game: Players, Owners, and American Baseball to 1920* (Chapel Hill: University of North Carolina Press, 1994), 129–30, 161–62, 182–83; Seymour, *Baseball: The Golden Age*, 192–94.

37. Cobb, *My Life*, 13.

38. Tommy Leach in Ritter, *Glory of Their Times*, 28; *New York Times*, October 15, 1909, 12; *Chicago Tribune*, October 15, 1909, 8; *Detroit Free Press*, October 17, 1909, 17.

39. *Chicago Tribune*, October 11, 1907, 2; George Gibson in Ritter, *Glory of Their Times*, 72–73; *Chicago Tribune*, February 27, 1907, A2.

40. Sam Crawford in Ritter, *Glory of Their Times*, 60; Jimmy Austin in Ritter, *Glory of Their Times*, 89–90; Heinie Groh in Ritter, *Glory of Their Times*, 303.

41. Lefty O'Doul in Ritter, *Glory of Their Times*, 274.

42. Louis P. Masur, *Autumn Glory: Baseball's First World Series* (New York: Hill and Wang, 2003), 24.

43. *Chicago Tribune*, October 29, 1905, A4.

44. Wells in Bak, *Cobb Would Have Caught It*, 165.

45. Rube Marquard in Ritter, *Glory of Their Times*, 14–15; Jimmy Austin in Ritter, *Glory of Their Times*, 83; Al Bridwell in Ritter, *Glory of Their Times*, 131; Chief Meyers in Ritter, *Glory of Their Times*, 174; John J. Evers, "Stallings's Genius Proved," *New York Times*, October 14, 1914, 9; C. P. Stack, "A Day with John Evers," *Baseball Magazine* (February 1915): 74.

46. Robert L. Griswold, *Fatherhood in America: A History* (New York: Basic Books, 1993), 42–43, 71. These values endured into post–World War II America. See Joshua Zeitz, *White Ethnic New York: Jews, Catholics, and the Shaping of Postwar Politics* (Chapel Hill: University of North Carolina Press, 2007), 79; John J. McGraw, *My Thirty Years in Baseball* (1923; repr., Lincoln: University of Nebraska Press, 1995), 1, 2.

47. Rube Marquard in Ritter, *Glory of Their Times*, 14; Stack, "A Day with John Evers," 74.

48. Burleigh Grimes in Honig, *The Man in the Dugout: Fifteen Big League Managers Speak Their Minds* (Lincoln, NE: Bison Books, 1977), 41; Mathewson, *Pitching in a Pinch*, 98, 101, 110, 122–23.

49. Ty Cobb, *Busting 'Em and Other Big League Stories* (1914. Reprint. Jefferson, NC: McFarland, 2003), 65; Hugh Fullerton, "Role of Managers in World's Series," *New York Times*, October 5, 1916; "World Champion Manager a Sphinx," *Sporting Life* (February 5, 1916); Gay, *Tris Speaker*, 67–69.

50. Hugo Bezdek, "A New System of Big League Management," *Baseball Magazine* (August 1918): 331–32.

51. James A. Riley and Renwick W. Speer, *The Hundred Years of Chet Hoff* (Cocoa, FL: TK Publishers, 1991), 12.

52. Bob Shawkey in Honig, *Man in the Dugout*, 172; Jimmy Austin in Ritter, *Glory of Their Times*, 83; Fred Snodgrass in Ritter, *Glory of Their Times*, 91.

53. Al Bridwell in Ritter, *Glory of Their Times*, 131; Sam Jones in Ritter, *Glory of Their Times*, 243–44; Mathewson, *Pitching in a Pinch*, 130.

54. Powers-Beck, *American Indian Integration of Baseball*, 80–81, 85–86.

55. Al Bridwell in Ritter, *Glory of Their Times*, 131; Sam Jones in Ritter, *Glory of Their Times*, 243–44.

56. Hugh Fullerton, "Why Doesn't He Steal?" *Baseball Magazine* (March 1910): 1–7; Edward Lyell Fox, "What is 'Inside Baseball?'" *Outing Magazine* 58 (July 1911): 489.

57. Burleigh Grimes in Honig, *Man in the Dugout*, 43.

58. Evers, *Touching Second*, 33; Mathewson, *Pitching in a Pinch*, 93, 129.

59. Oliver Wendell Holmes, Jr., "An Address Delivered on Memorial Day, May 30, 1895, Called by the Graduating Class of Harvard University," *The Essential Holmes: Selections from the Letters, Speeches, Judicial Opinions, and Other Writings of Oliver Wendell Holmes, Jr.*, ed. Richard A. Posner (Chicago: University of Chicago Press, 1992), 88–89. For full analyses of the masculine martial spirit of the era, see Gerald Linderman, *Embattled Courage: The Experience of Combat in the American Civil War* (New York: Free Press, 1987), 266–97; Kristin L. Hoganson, *Fighting For American Manhood: How Gender Politics Provoked the Spanish-American and Philippine-American Wars* (New Haven: Yale University Press, 1998).

60. "Moran Tells His Method," *New York Times*, September 14, 1919, 100; John J. Ward, "Manager Pat Moran," *Baseball Magazine* (November 1915): 37, 40; "'Team Work' Says Moran," *New York Times*, August 24, 1919, 21.

61. Numerous historians have examined the "crisis of manhood" many men experienced in the early twentieth century. See Gail Bederman, *Manliness and Civilization: A Cultural History of Gender and Race in the United States* (Chicago: University of Illinois Press, 1995), 1–44; John F. Kasson, *Houdini, Tarzan, and the Perfect Man: The White Male Body and the Challenge of Modernity in America* (New York: Oxford University Press, 2001), 3–19; Michael Kimmel, *Manhood in America*, 57–79; John Pettegrew, *Brutes in Suits: Male Sensibility in America, 1890–1920* (Baltimore: Johns Hopkins University Press, 2007), 48–61.

62. *New York Times*, December 10, 1911, C7; Mathewson, *Pitching in a Pinch*, 36, 42, 53, 98; Cobb, *Busting 'Em*, 55, 84.

63. Fred Snodgrass in Ritter, *Glory of Their Times*, 113–114; *Philadelphia Inquirer*, October 18, 1911, 10; *New York American* quoted in the *Philadelphia Inquirer*, October 19, 1911, 10.

64. Few historians have examined the Northern variant of honor. Two who have are Elliott Gorn, *The Manly Art: Bare-Knuckle Prize Fighting in America* (Ithaca, NY: Cornell University Press, 1986), 142–44, 253–54; and Lorien Foote, *The Gentlemen and the Roughs: Violence, Honor, and Manhood in the Union Army* (New York: New York University Press, 2010).

65. *New York Evening World*, June 2, 1902, 1; *Detroit Free Press*, June 3, 1902, 8; *New York Evening World*, June 19, 1902, 8; *Sporting Life* (July 19, 1902): 6.

66. Marv Owen in Bak, *Cobb Would Have Caught It*, 223; Gmelch, *Inside Pitch*, 54–56; Mathewson, *Pitching in a Pinch*, 40–41.

67. Wells in Bak, *Cobb Would Have Caught It*, 164; Roger Peckinpaugh in Honig, *Man in the Dugout*, 223.

68. Gay, *Tris Speaker*, 149.

69. *Sporting News* (July 6, 1911): 5; Cindy Thomson and Scott Brown, *Three Finger: The Mordecai Brown Story* (Lincoln: University of Nebraska Press, 2006), 55, 65; *Chicago Tribune*, October 4, 1908, B2; Geoffrey Ward and Ken Burns, *Baseball: An Illustrated History* (New York: Alfred A. Knopf, 1994), 71.

70. Rick Huhn, *Eddie Collins: A Baseball Biography* (Jefferson, NC: McFarland, 2008), 60, 96; Eliot Asinof, *Eight Men Out: The Black Sox and the 1919 World Series* (1963; repr., New York: Owl Books, 1987), 62–63; Montville, *The Big Bam*, 54; Skipper, *Baseball Nicknames*, 237; James D. Szalontai, *Small Ball in the Big Leagues: A History of Stealing, Bunting, Walking and Otherwise Scratching for Runs* (Jefferson, NC: McFarland, 2010), 73–74.

71. Charles C. Alexander, *Ty Cobb* (New York: Oxford University Press, 1984), 105–107.

72. Sam Crawford in Ritter, *Glory of Their Times,* 56–57; Jimmy Austin in Ritter, *Glory of Their Times*, 87; Al Lopez in Honig, *Man in the Dugout*, 180–81.

73. Fred Snodgrass in Ritter, *Glory of Their Times*, 93–94; Hans Lobert in Ritter, *Glory of Their Times*, 188–89.

74. Fred Snodgrass in Ritter, *Glory of Their Times*, 101; R. A. R. Edwards, "No Dummies: Deafness, Baseball, and American Culture," in *The Cooperstown Symposium on Baseball and American Culture, 2007–2008*, edited by William M. Simons (Jefferson, NC: MacFarland, 2009), 120–31.

75. Rube Bressler in Ritter, *Glory of Their Times*, 201–202; Cait Murphy, *Crazy '08: How a Cast of Cranks, Rogues, Boneheads, and Magnates Created the Greatest Year in Baseball History* (New York: Smithsonian Books, 2007), 47; Bob Shawkey in Honig, *Man in the Dugout*, 178.

76. Gay, *Tris Speaker*, 67; *Detroit Free Press*, May 9, 1908, 8; *Sporting Life* (February 18, 1911): 2; *Sporting Life* (November 18, 1911): 15.

77. Cobb, *Busting 'Em*, 72.

78. Quoted in Murphy, *Crazy '08*, 145.

79. Quoted in Zingg, *Harry Hooper*, 114.

80. Mike Sowell, *The Pitch That Killed: The Story of Carl Mays, Ray Chapman, and the Pennant Race of 1920* (Chicago: Ivan R. Dee, 1989), 302–304; James T. Farrell, *My Baseball Diary* (1957; repr., Carbondale: Southern Illinois University Press, 1998), 265–66.

81. Sowell, *The Pitch That Killed*, 170–76, 193–95, 206–211; Bob Shawkey in Honig, *Man in the Dugout*, 169.

82. Fred Lieb, *Baseball As I Have Known It* (1977; repr., Lincoln, NE: Bison Books, 1996), 97–103; Quoted in Murphy, *Crazy '08*, 158.

83. *Sporting Life* (August 15, 1908): 6. Some biographers have suggested that Cobb did not receive permission to leave the team to marry Charlotte (Charlie) Lombard, but the *Detroit Free Press* announced Cobb's intention a week before he left, adding that management gave Cobb approval. See *Detroit Free Press*, July 23, 1908, 9; *Detroit Free Press*, July 26, 1908, 17.

84. *Baseball Magazine* (March 1912).

85. Branch Rickey, *The American Diamond: A Documentary of the Game of Baseball* (New York: Simon and Schuster, 1965): 27; *Sporting News* (December 30, 1920): 3

86. *Sporting Life* (October 18, 1910): 18.

87. *Sporting News* (October 13, 1910): 5; *Sporting Life* (October 18, 1910): 18.

88. Gmelch, *Inside Pitch*, 54–55, observes players reprove teammates who fret or boast about their personal statistics.

89. Paul Dickson, *The New Dickson Baseball Dictionary*, 3rd edition (New York: Harcourt Brace and Company, 1999), 107. Ironically, Cobb was the first recipient of the award. See *Sporting Life* (October 21, 1911): 2.

90. Alexander, *Ty Cobb*, 93–94; *Sporting News* (October 20, 1910): 7.

91. Alexander, *Ty Cobb*, 95–96.

92. *Sporting News* (October 20, 1910): 7; *Detroit Free Press*, October 11, 1910, 9.

93. *Detroit Free Press*, October 11, 1910, 10.

94. *New York Evening World*, August 12, 1911, 7, quoted in Tim Hornbaker, *War on the Basepaths: The Definitive Biography of Ty Cobb* (New York: Sports Publishing, 2014), 112–113.

95. *Sporting News* (October 20, 1910): 5.

96. *Charlotte Observer*, March 14, 1911, 8; *Sporting Life* (October 28, 1911): 5; *Sporting Life* (May 6, 1911): 1; *Sporting News* (May 1, 1913): 4; *Sporting News* (October 2, 1913): 2; *Sporting Life* (November 8, 1913): 7.

97. *Sporting News* (November 22, 1917): 6; *Sporting News* (January 24, 1918): 6; *New York Times*, February 16, 1918, 13.

98. Cobb, *My Life*, 280.

6

FANS

In 1911, a humor magazine decided to have a little fun satirizing America's fascination with the national game by ridiculing its most devoted adherent, the "baseball bug."

> The Baseball Bug, when he's at home,
> Has Baseballitis in his dome;
> He reads the dope, he keeps the score,
> At office, restaurant, and store;
> He talks the Game with wisdom deep,
> He dreams and talks it in his sleep;
> You may well smile with comfort smug
> If you are not a Baseball Bug![1]

In fact, very few smiled "with comfort smug," for nearly every American seemed to have fallen victim to the infectious disease of baseball. The evidence of its popularity was everywhere. From 1903 through 1909, overall attendance in the two major leagues climbed from 4.75 million to 7.2 million. Writing at the conclusion of the 1910 season, the dean of sportswriters, Albert Spalding, observed that for the last ten years "each Base Ball season has seemed to be a climax of prosperity, only to find the succeeding season further advanced in every way than its predecessors." Although attendance stagnated for the next several years, attendance generally remained well around six million through World War I. Predictably, the winningest teams experienced the most significant gains in attendance. The New York Giants, the most valuable franchise in either league, averaged over 8,000 fans per game throughout the era. Other successful franchises, like the Chicago White Sox, Boston Red Sox, and Philadelphia Athletics, generally averaged over 7,000. Special occasions—the opening game of the season, a series against a heated rival in the midst of a pennant race, or a World Series game—sometimes attracted crowds that simply astounded contemporary observers. By the end of the decade, crowds of 20,000 or more became commonplace for important games, even though most ballparks rarely had seating for more than 15,000. In August 1909, 55,000 Bostonians came to watch the Red Sox host the Tigers in a pair of doubleheaders—a major league record for a two-day series. A month later, the Tigers played in front of another record crowd—120,000 for a critical four-game set in Philadelphia. Three years later, a quarter of a million fans witnessed the World Series between the Boston Red Sox and the New York Giants. A crucial end-of-the-season game between the Chicago Cubs and the New York Giants in 1908 drew as many as 100,000 fans (40,000 in the park and another 60,000 on the bluff behind the ballpark, straddling the tracks of the elevated train, or perched on rooftops, billboard signs, and even train signal posts). A reporter for the *New York Times* struggled to explain the scene: "There is no record of a sporting event that stirred New York as did the game yesterday. No crowd so big ever was moved to a field of contest as was moved yesterday. Perhaps never in the history of a great city, since the days of Rome and arena contests, has a people been pitched to such a key of excitement as was New York 'fandom' yesterday."[2]

As the demand to see professional baseball grew, magnates began to build larger and more permanent ballparks. The Philadelphia Athletics made the first move, opening the magnificent Shibe Park for the 1909 season. Built of steel-reinforced concrete, the edifice featured Renaissance-inspired ornamentation, arches, gabled dormers, a copper-trimmed slated mansard (or French) roof, Ionic pilasters, and decorative friezes with baseball motifs. The main entrance was capped by an octangular tower with a domed roof that reminded some of a church spire. Its 28,000 seating capacity was nearly three times as big as the Athletics' former ballpark. Over the next six years, every team in the league except the Cubs, Phillies, and Cardinals either built a new park, rented from a team that did, or completely refurbished their old park. Constructed of steel, brick, and concrete, these new structures not only seated more fans—typically around 30,000—but did so with a greater concern for safety and comfort. In tandem with the construction of skyscrapers, railway terminals, museums, schools, and courthouses, these new ballparks heralded a new age of progress. Massive and imposing, these structures announced to the public that major league baseball planned to be a permanent part of urban leisure culture and could easily accommodate all fans.[3]

Social commentators attempting to explain America's newfound enthusiasm for baseball often found themselves grasping for words. One journalist quipped that "baseball is sleep, meat, and drink." When watching or talking baseball, the typical fan "frequently achieves a Nirvana that enables him to express untold passion by a mere eye-glint" though he "may elect to roar." For such fans, "baseball has become synonymous with life and freedom." Another claimed simply "baseball is the beginning and end of everything."[4] The intensity of fan interest was such that observers were reduced to using psychological terms to explain public interest in the game. Some called it a "mania"; others termed it a "craze"; one claimed it was like a form of "delirium"; another referred to it as "madness"; still another called it a "fetish." Whimsically, a reporter for the *St. Louis Post-Dispatch* warned that perhaps one-tenth of the population of the United States was now in the first throes of this condition: "a more or less violent . . . visitation" which psychiatrists "are beginning to diagnose as neurological in nature, and which is growing in intensity yearly." Most commonly, the illness was characterized by "a strange emotional versatility, those stricken plunging instantly from transports of joy to rages of despair, either of which hysterical extremes may induce fainting spells, apoplexy or heart trouble." The *Post-Dispatch* warned the condition was contagious: "the fever of excitement which seizes the shallowest persons" in the crowd "quickly infects the more staid and grave, and soon the whole grandstand is in an uproar." One wag even referred to it as the true form of "Dementia Americana," a term popularized by the lawyers of Harry K. Thaw in 1907 who used it to convince a jury that Thaw was insane when he murdered architect Stanford White.[5]

Had Americans gone too far in their fascination with a mere game? Leftist political commentator Ellis O. Jones thought so. He cynically observed that art, letters, religion, and politics had all subordinated themselves to baseball. It was no longer a matter of "art for art's sake," but "baseball for baseball's sake." According to Jones, Americans' obsession was such that "now, nightly, in every neck, nook, and niche of the nation, the world nervously pauses until the ticker ticks this tale which is fraught with so much that is vitally important to the starving hordes of this great United States." That is—who won the game?[6] He may not have been exaggerating by much. Mania for baseball transcended the ballpark as fans did not just want to watch baseball, they wanted to read it about and argue about it through every medium available. On days when their team was playing but they could not go to the game, fans sought the almost immediate gratification of knowing what was happening play by play. To satiate fans' desires, newspapers printed extra editions, erected massive scoreboards on the facades of their buildings, and finally—in a fit of American ingenuity—created electronic game reproduction boards. The displays of these boards were often quite elaborate, offering the image of a baseball field outlined in electric lights which flickered on and off to show the movement of the ball, the placement of hits, and the progress of base runners. During important games, hundreds—and sometimes thousands—congregated in front of these devices, spilled onto the street, choked off traffic, and brought business to a halt. In the heat of the 1908 pennant race, a Detroit sportswriter commented, "trying to get near a scoreboard is much like trying to reach the counter in a department store when there is a bargain sale on." During the 1912 World Series, the *New York Times* reported, newsboys, construction workers, and office employees all suspended work to watch their 7x14-foot board at Times Square. Only "a big squad of policemen" kept the main arteries open. The next year the *Times* outdid itself, constructing what it boasted was the "last word in automatic baseball contrivances"—an 18x24-foot board. The vast board attracted some 15,000 earnest and quite vocal fans, most of whom staked their place well before the first pitch. Standing 46 feet above the ground, the *Times* boasted that spectators could watch the imaginary action from 100 yards away. The *Times* estimated another 30,000 watched the game at inside venues, with Madison Square Garden drawing the largest crowd, "Fully 8,000 of the faithful." Baseball was never more popular.[7]

Frank B. Elser, a contributor to *Outlook*, claimed no other "activity of man is as thoroughly reported" as baseball. "Baseball is 'must' news," he observed. "It must go promptly and go ahead of everything except markets." He was particularly struck by nearly every newspaper's commitment to printing daily box scores of all sixteen major league teams as well as local minor league and college league box scores. As Elser pointed out, a box score "is a pretty intricate sort of thing to be sent by telegraph and copied by typewriter. A good telegraph operator takes about seven minutes to type one box score. If all major league teams are playing—making a total of eight games—that meant fifty-six minutes of wire time. And if locals wanted details of minor league and college games, the amount of wire time might double or even triple. That fifty-six minutes equaled about three thousand words of straight news. "It's a mighty good story that gets that much space in the average newspaper," Elser added cryptically. By comparison, Elser noted, the Associated Press reported the Triangle Shirtwaist Factory fire, the deadliest disaster in New York prior to 9/11, in about 4,000 words and sent its report over the wires in about half the time it commonly took New York City newspapers to send box scores. To Elser, it was a telling indication that "baseball mania has upset all standards of news proportion."[8]

What propelled the baseball craze? Observers noted that the unabashed enthusiasm of middle- and upper-class men for the game was the biggest factor in the spike in attendance figures. In 1912 *Baseball Magazine* reported that the game was "no longer confined to the masses, but has taken hold upon the serious classes—men who a few years ago would not have dreamed of spending an afternoon in the open air to watch a game." Now "the great throngs who watch the local teams comprise men of standing in ever increasing numbers." Commentators gave American League president Ban Johnson much of the credit for this. By curbing disorder, he made it possible for respectable men and women to enjoy the game, no small feat for a sport that previously had been associated with rowdyism and idleness. "Years ago," the straight-laced Connie Mack recalled, "the fan was more or less of a thug" who would not hesitate to "hurl a pop bottle at an umpire . . . or indulge in loud-mouth profanity." All that changed in the first decade of the twentieth century. "Practically all the leading men in the country are baseball fans," Mack claimed. This was the conclusion of the *St. Louis Republic* regarding its fans as well. From a "decidedly impolite assemblage, the spectators at baseball games in St. Louis have become the best-bred, best dressed, political people . . . in baseball"—all because baseball officials cleaned up the game.[9]

Of course, this is only a partial answer. More orderly ballparks were as much a consequence as a cause of baseball's broad appeal, a reflection that the game had begun to attract the more respectable classes to the ball park. Why did these more orderly types—that is to say upper-, working-, and middle-class men—find the game attractive? How and why did baseball resonate with their sporting tastes? What inspired them to attend a game, stand in front of an electronic scoreboard for hours, check the box score in the morning paper first, memorize batting statistics, won-lost records, and team rosters, and make heroes out of athletes? What made the game so compelling? To answer these questions we need to look more fully at the context in which these more respectable men discovered the game.

Baseball became the National Game during a period of profound social, political, and economic transformation for urban men, especially urban middle-class men. They were, in fact, a new breed of urban men. Throughout the nineteenth century, most men in the middle ranks were independent producers—farmers, shopkeepers, business owners, and the like. Fitting the economic environment of the time, they defined success as the realization of personal autonomy and extolled virtues that best facilitated this goal: self-reliance, hard work, forbearance, and physical prowess. The men who came of age in the first decades of the twentieth century had to operate by a very different formula. The rapid economic transformation of the industrial era had much to do with this. The unremitting expansion of business enterprise dramatically changed the way middle-class men made a living. Greater concentrations of wealth and the explosion of corporate power made it increasingly difficult for individuals to find success by striking out on their own. Contemporaries were well aware of the economic transformation of the workplace. In 1903, *The Independent* warned, "the middle class is becoming a salaried class, and rapidly losing the economic and moral independence of former days." A decade later economist Simon Patten, chair of the Wharton School, observed without a hint of remorse, "The individual has been lost; the group is now everything. No one can succeed today who does not attach himself to some well-defined group."[10] He might have added that the individual needed to be as well-defined as the group—or corporation—that employed him. After all, the new business environment of the large corporation required a new type of white-collar employee: the specialist. The modern corporation operated efficiently and profitably because salaried supervisors, accountants, statisticians, industrial engineers, financial officers, quality control inspectors, and marketing agents meticulously managed its inner workings. Below them was a veritable army of clerks who kept the books, copied correspondences, prepared reports, and managed records. By 1930, salaried employees comprised 60 percent of the middle-class workforce, an eightfold increase from 1880.[11]

The salaried white-collar employees of this new order possessed very different skills than those exhibited by the old middle class of independent proprietors. Successful proprietors of the previous century were celebrated as men of independence, conviction, and spirit. Even those men of business who worked for someone else typically enjoyed considerable personal autonomy at work. At Aetna Life Insurance, for example, work was task-oriented. A clerk who wished to take off early to catch a ballgame or go fishing had only "to get his work done as far as he could and then ask his desk companion if he would take over if anything unexpected came in," one former worker recalled.[12] Such informal arrangements worked less well in the highly bureaucratized world of the modern corporation. By the 1910s, a managerial consensus began to take hold as upper and midlevel supervisors adopted the philosophy, if not the actual practices of Frederick Taylor and other industrial engineers; they wanted efficiency, standardization, obedience, and order.[13]

The young men who joined the ranks of this new corporatized world did so with some ambivalence. On the one hand, most did not necessarily see themselves as victims of the new order; rather, they identified themselves as its beneficiaries and even its creators. Trained and educated as specialists and expert technicians, they understood that the intricate bureaucracy of the modern corporation offered them both a livelihood and a professional standing. They believed in the rational order and scientific efficiency that characterized their work. In this respect, they saw themselves as apostles of modernity. On the other hand, they also had some affinities to the Victorian ideals of their fathers' generation. Growing up, they had been schooled by *McGuffey Readers* and Horatio Alger novels and been raised to worship the courage and vitality of the founding fathers, trail-blazing frontiersmen, and great inventors.

Throughout the early 1900s, popular culture still idealized the aggressive and determined self-made man through popular novels like Owen Wister's *The Virginian,* Thomas Dixon's *The Clansman,* Edgar Rice Burroughs's *Tarzan of the Apes,* and Jack London's *Call of the Wild* and *White Fang.* Even contemporary politics offered a potent reminder of the heroism of the rugged individualist: the president of the United States from 1901–1909, Theodore Roosevelt.[14]

Essentially, the men of this new middle class wanted the best of both worlds. They wanted to embrace the present and the future through their careers but they also wanted to retain at least a semblance—and hopefully more than that—of the virility and dynamism of an earlier age. They did not see this as inconsistent and did not believe these two desires were incompatible. Perhaps as an indication of just how truly modern they were, they saw their manhood as complex and multifaceted, capable of metamorphosis from civilized to brutish. Depending upon time and place, they could be rugged, rough-edged, and impassioned or sedate, rational, and restrained. As parents and lovers, they could even be doting, romantic, and passionate.[15]

The clothing these apostles of modernity wore—the modern business suit—reflected their desire to both fit in to the new order and stand out as men. During the 1910s, the business suit became so popular that some ready-to-wear manufacturers produced no other style for men. Some companies, most notably Brooks Brothers, built national reputations on the cut and quality of their business attire. Conservative, functional, and even a tad austere in design and color, this new suit contrasted sharply with the heavy frock coats and ornate waistcoats that were popular in the late Victorian era. In that era, successful businessmen opted for clothing that helped them to look substantial, formal, and aristocratic. This new suit was quite different. The jacket featured broad shoulders with a slightly narrower waist and a skirt that ended just below the hip. Men typically fastened all three or four of the buttons of the single-breasted suit to present a lean silhouette. The straight tailored leg of the pants enhanced the wearer's athletic profile. To complete the ensemble, businessmen typically wore "American style" dress shoes. Featuring rounded toes, these shoes were more comfortable for walking than the narrower European shoes while the raised heel further accentuated the lean cut of the suit. Historian Thomas Schlereth has observed the suit enabled the modern man to present himself as a member of the corporate world, a "thinker, expert, and manager." At the same time, the suit also offered hints of the more dynamic and athletic man beneath it all. Clothing advertisements of the day fully embraced this multifaceted modern man. No matter the publication, he was invariably presented as young, poised, and agile with facial features that suggested dignity, purpose, and confidence. In donning the new uniform of the corporate man, a man of the new middle class hinted by his attire that despite the veneer of civilization he was no less a vigorous and active man than his frontier forebearers.[16]

Away from work, middle-class men searched for ways to demonstrate their masculine yearnings. In the early twentieth century, the search for manly experiences led the new middle-class men down many paths. Some lost themselves in the uber-masculine popular literature of the day: adventure tales, western lore, and military history. Some embraced newly defined masculine hobbies like home repairs, arts and crafts, motoring, bodybuilding, physical fitness, and camping. Many turned to sports as participants and especially as spectators. For the new middle class, baseball became an especially popular form of leisure diversion because its blend of physicality, sophisticated strategy, and high tension resonated most completely with their multifaceted conception of themselves as men. So great was the new middle class's interest in professional baseball, nearly all clubs established start times to accommodate their work schedules. Both Chicago teams started games at 3:00, an hour-and-a-half after the close of the Board of Trade and an hour after the close of the Stock Exchange. In New York, teams did not start games until 4:00 because the Stock Exchange there did not close until 3:00. As a further convenience to the city's financial sector, public transit ran a special train from Wall Street to the Polo Grounds at the close of the business day.[17]

The coronation of baseball as America's game was not a foregone conclusion. Wealthier Americans, including many of the country's leading figures, wanted sport that invoked what Theodore Roosevelt termed "the strenuous life." They were especially drawn to football and prizefighting, sports that required stamina, strength, tolerance for pain, a martial spirit, and raw cunning. Following the lead of prominent men like President Roosevelt, tycoon William Vanderbilt, editor Charles A. Dana, and psychologist G. Stanley Hall, the emerging middle class of the new century developed an affinity for these sports, too. Nevertheless, nothing appealed to middle-class men as much as baseball. They claimed their game inspired manly virtues every bit as much as prizefighting and football. True, baseball could not match these other sports for its unrelenting physicality, but to baseball fans, that was not necessarily a bad thing. Although prizefighting and football remained popular even as baseball's popularity ascended, many believed these sports encouraged excessive violence and should be either fundamentally reformed or banned entirely. By contrast, baseball seemed to offer manly physicality with a proper level of restraint. Yes, ballplayers sometimes acted aggressively and sometimes even violently—as when runner and infielder collided, a pitcher sent a purpose pitch toward the cranium of the batter, or a fielder hurtled his body onto the grass or into the stands to stop a ball. These constituted some of the most exciting and memorable plays in the game and no true fan wanted to diminish the aggressive manner in which players approached such moments. At the same time, baseball fans were quick to point out the aggression of the diamond was unlike that found in more violent sports like football and prizefighting. Those sports encouraged brutality for its own sake whereas violence in baseball resulted from acts of skill, daring, and strategy and occurred in a mere instant. Writing for *Baseball Magazine*, F. C. Lane observed baseball appealed to Americans above all other sports "because we expect to witness a hard, fast, scientific and above all clean contest between rival teams trained to the minute and in the pink of condition."[18]

This is what set baseball apart from all other sports, baseball's pundits contended: it offered far richer and more complete exhibitions of manhood by calling upon all forms of masculine character—physical, intellectual, and emotional. "Baseball is war," the reigning patriarch of the game Albert Spalding proclaimed—a war that "required every faculty of brain and body," a war that "arouses no brutal instincts" because its combatants relied more on "skill than strength." "I know of no other medium," Spalding continued, that so "joins the physical, mental, emotional, and moral sides of a man's composite being into a complete and homogeneous whole." This made baseball "a man maker," Spalding concluded. Hugh Fullerton was equally effusive, describing baseball as "the most highly developed, scientific and logical form of athletic pastime evolved by man, and the ultimate evolution of the one universal game."[19]

This potent combination of brains, brawn, and bravado appealed to the new middle classes. Modernity, they claimed, required new standards of manhood, standards that baseball expressed with greater clarity than any other sport. Yes, they wanted to be assertive, self-reliant, and physically intimidating when need demanded it. But these apostles of modernity also believed the speed and complexities of modern society required men to exhibit a new set of masculine attributes—intellectual agility, resolve, and emotional control. Baseball, its fans realized, balanced old and new conceptions of manhood, and thus created the ideal training ground for modernity.

As baseball attendance soared, a diverse array of journalists—many of whom were themselves closely tied to the new middle class as self-defined professionals working within large corporate bureaucracies—explored the game's appeal to the growing middle-class fan base. Baseball, they claimed, dramatized the pressures of modernity and demonstrated how to endure and even flourish within it. In pieces that graced both business and sporting publications, these writers interpreted baseball's edifying meanings for those striving to succeed in the new economic order. A correspondent for *National Magazine* observed that the "short, sharp, but nonetheless decisive conflict of the ball field" closely resembled the "hustling business methods of today." Small wonder, Thomas T. Hoyne, a business writer for the *Chicago Tribune*, observed, "Baseball furnishes a man as fine a business training as anything could." Writing in *Outlook*, popular journalist H. Addington Bruce, employing his wide knowledge of sociology and psychology, amplified the point: baseball was popular because young boys "instinctively" and "unconsciously" favor "those games which . . . tend most strongly to form and establish the characteristics that will be most serviceable to them in later years." Bruce allowed that "all outdoor games played by groups of competitors" instilled these values, but he contended "no other game—not even excepting football—develops them so much as baseball."[20]

Remarkably, one facet of the game that received surprisingly little attention from the pundits was baseball's ability to encourage teamwork. Bruce was an exception to this trend. Playing baseball, he observed, left an "indelible impression of the importance in all affairs of life of unselfish cooperation" and the "subordination of self for the common good."[21] More typically, commentators interested in showing parallels between baseball and American life emphasized altruism's opposite: baseball, like the modern business world, forced individuals to compete against one another in a no-holds barred battle for supremacy. In an early editorial clearly designed to appeal to the self-defined go-getters of the business world, *Baseball Magazine* harped, "The spirit of the age is one of hustle and bustle" in which "each man of position knows that he can improve himself, and strives to do so." Indeed, modern man "gives his very blood that it may be." In this combative world, "there is . . . no such thing as sitting back, resting on laurels, and being satisfied with results achieved." Rather, "every moment is tense with anxiety, lest something already gained be lost." The most successful is "the daring one," the one "who will risk his all on some unexpected chance, or . . . who is ever watchful of the weakness of others and turns them to his own vantage." "Today," the magazine proclaimed, "we witness the survival of the fittest, the mighty—in mind and ambition—killing the weak." It was a world devoid of sentiment: "altruistic principle and higher thought enter not into it." It is just the same in baseball. Here, too, the leaders are "essentially men of brains and daring" who "take the chances and run the risks that their less able fellows fear to attempt . . . Like the man in business, they never let up, never for a moment sleep." In both worlds, "a man must fight his way to the top, and his little world, though fighting against him, admires his unyielding spirit and respects him." "Life is a game of ball," a popular lecturer observed, "with few of us playing out the nine innings or getting through without an error." The competition to find a place was intense. To survive, "a man has to be an all-round player because there is an army of candidates for every position." Even then, the game of life, like the game of baseball, "calls for all a man has got in him."[22]

How to survive in this cutthroat environment? The interpreters of baseball's didactic meanings agreed that men needed to possess two key attributes. Not surprisingly, both spoke to popular obsessions in American culture that went well beyond the ball field. The first was speed of thought, sometimes defined as "quick thinking" or alertness. Contemporaries marveled at the hastening pace of American life. The age of steam and steel, they noted, had given way to "The Age of Speed." With surprising rapidity, new technologies created faster trains, faster ships, faster streetcars, and even faster elevators. By the second decade of the century, "aeroplanes" and automobiles added to the escalating tempo of modern life. Meanwhile, advances in the telegraph, ticker tape, and telephone obliterated distance—and thus time—as an obstacle in communication. Meanwhile, industry's love affair with scientific management and corporations' commitment to greater efficiencies pressured individuals to act quickly so that they might keep up with the accelerated pace of the economy. A writer for the *Chicago Tribune* suggested "the world has gone speed mad."[23]

Small wonder many contemporaries began to refer to life as a "race" for status, place, and wealth. Commentators presented this race as a grueling competition with few winners. "The race of life," a magazine editorial remarked, "goes to those who can stand its pace, who measure up to its standards, who maintain themselves under its test." "Arouse yourself. Get a consciousness of your forces. Begin to drive yourself until you will arouse all your sources of ability," the Reverend Madison C. Peters, a leading minister of the era, urged young men in his nationally syndicated newspaper column. "Without earnestness in your work you have lost before you start." Modernity was no place for laggards and loafers. Rather, young men were encouraged to be ever diligent and resourceful so they could take advantage of even the slightest opportunity. After all, "it is only the few in each generation, men of capacity and alertness, who make use of the opportunities which that generation presents." In response, leading psychologists and education reformers encouraged schools to adopt pedagogies that taught children to think quickly and act decisively.[24]

Many sports experts claimed that this form of mental training was best conducted on the baseball diamond. After all, the game required lightning fast reflexes and near instantaneous decision-making skills. "A ball player has approximately two-fifths of a second between the time that ball hits the bat and he sees it coming toward him in which he must decide how to make a play," Hugh Fullerton observed authoritatively. And "often he must think quicker than that, for an accident, an unexpected turn of a play, may force him to abandon his plan and adopt a new one. A fifth of a second is a long time at the finish of a steal." Sportswriters like Fullerton nearly always identified "quick thinking" as an essential attribute of good players. Ballplayers agreed. In an oft-repeated piece, Connie Mack told *McClure's Magazine* that his Athletics owed their success to two things: moral living and mental agility. Eddie Collins, star second baseman for the Athletics and White Sox, called mental alertness "the watchword of baseball."[25]

A broad spectrum of American men believed the skills ballplayers developed on the field gave them real advantages off it. In this, baseball seemed uniquely in step with the needs and desires of ambitious modern American men. The Young Men's Christian Association's official journal, *Association Men*, claimed, "there is little doubt that this game has done more than all other agencies to make the youth of America physically fit, quick-thinking, and self-reliant." L. E. Sanborn, sportswriter for the *Detroit Free Press*, noted "the necessity for physical activity breeds mental alertness naturally and the brain which gets the habit of producing quick action of muscles retains that characteristic as a rule and results in an alertness of speech as well as movement." Moral reformers, ministers, and politicians claimed baseball helped breed a superior race of men: "a race of hardy, quick-thinking men . . . the best that is in a man . . . the backbone of any nation," a correspondent for *Sporting Life* put it. General Charles H. Taylor, publisher of the *Boston Globe*, claimed baseball taught young men distinctly American traits, defined by Taylor as "alertness, resourcefulness, self-control, and self-confidence." For this reason, baseball "reflects all the manhood and vigor of this splendid nation." Added H. Addington Bruce, "it is . . . a splendid mind-builder" because it taught players to "think and to think quickly." Even Bernarr Macfadden, chief architect of the physical culture fad, offered support for baseball. The game's dual emphasis upon both "extraordinary activity of the body" and "mental quickness and alertness," Macfadden argued, offered men excellent preparation "for the strenuous game of life."[26]

Along with mental and physical agility, the experts believed that the successful ballplayer had to possess a certain emotional reserve that most contemporaries referred to simply as "nerve." Though harder to identify than either mental or physical attributes, the experts insisted that this emotional strength was no less important. Indeed, those close to the game obsessed more about the importance of nerve than they did quick thinking. Here, too, ardent fans of the game reflected the nuances of broader cultural trends. Americans in the early twentieth century were fixated on nerve. They were convinced that the modern era placed unprecedented emotional strain on humankind. Less than a generation earlier, medical experts—genuine and charlatans alike—observed that many Americans were teetering on the verge of nervous collapse. Ironically, they blamed the same economic and social developments that had produced Americans' obsession with speed and the need for mental alertness—the dynamism of American capitalism. In 1880, neurologist George Miller Beard gave the condition a name—*neurasthenia* or "lack of nerve force." Beard posited that each person possessed only a limited quantity of this essential element. Once depleted, the afflicted were left prone and vulnerable. Their only recourse was complete rest—preferably in a rural sanitarium where they could shut themselves off from the various stimulations that had caused the collapse. According to Beard, modernity was the great enemy of nerve force. Those afflicted with neurasthenia had become over-stimulated and emotionally exhausted by the pace and complexity of contemporary life.[27] Subsequent literature suggested that businessmen were especially vulnerable. The medical community identified such men as the victims of "over-civilization," the sacrificial lambs of rapid and unrelenting progress. Placed in sedentary occupations, these men became reactive rather than active. Incapable of processing the diverse stimuli of modernity they complained of feeling overwhelmed and assaulted by their environment—the extreme competition of the marketplace, the sensory overload of urban street life, the ever-quickening pace of technological change, the inability to shut one's self off from—anything. Women and the poor suffered too, but the sight of afflicted middle- and upper-class men seemed especially poignant and tragic because they were the ones tasked with leading the world into modernity. The new professional class may have suffered most of all, the doctors claimed. Such men "get up in a hurry, eat breakfast with their eye on the morning paper, rush to their offices and through the day's work with ceaseless energy," taking little time for relaxation. "The age of specialization," two Philadelphia doctors warned, "tire out one group of nerve cells while not bringing others into play at all." So-called modern conveniences like the elevator and telephone, staples of the modern business office, only added to their troubles—the former by speeding up the pace of life, the latter by creating a "nerve-inducing annoyance."[28]

By the turn of the century Freud's theories of the subconscious rejected Beard's formulation of nerve scarcity; as this happened, professional diagnoses of neurasthenia declined.[29] In less academic circles, however, aspects of the old theory lived on. Most Americans continued to give nerve and nervousness considerable attention. They believed if nervousness indicated an inability to cope with modern urban life, then it made sense that its opposite, "nerve," reflected its reverse—an ability to cope, to triumph over the adversities and challenges of life. From there, it was only a small step to claim that "nerve" was a vital attribute of modern manhood.

Professional baseball confirmed this reasoning. In feature articles and daily accounts, sportswriters and players alike counted nerve as an essential component of a professional ballplayer's makeup. Indeed, the consensus was such that it became de rigueur to list nerve as an essential attribute for success. Star Cleveland pitcher Addie Joss counted nerve alongside control and luck as the three things "every slab artist finds that he must have" to be a consistent winner in the big leagues. *Baseball Magazine* made a similar argument. "Mechanical gifts are not alone the requirements of the successful pitcher," the magazine counseled; the best also exhibit "extraordinary nerve." Players who evinced steady nerve were prized by their fellows. "Let a man fight," *Baseball Magazine* asserted, "and the world, though fighting against him, admires him, and gives him his due."[30]

Baseball's obsession with nerve was such that some very prominent individuals in the game claimed it was the defining characteristic of the superior player. Charles Comiskey, a true patriarch of the game, having spent over thirty years as a player, manager, and owner, identified nerve as "one of the most important assets" of all great players. In *How to Play Baseball*, Timothy Hayes Murnane, the dean of early twentieth-century sportswriters, told boys the "baseball fraternity" viewed nerve as "one of the essential ingredients to a winning player's makeup," valued more perhaps than all other "brilliant qualities." Without nerve, Murnane cautioned, "a ball player has little chance of winning a place among the stars of the profession." A Detroit sports columnist offered, "Nothing is so valuable to a young player breaking in as good old-fashioned, nonshrinkable nerve."[31]

As a matter of course, writers made a connection between the nerve needed in baseball with that needed in the business world. One of the most persistent and well-respected voices of business values, the Rotary Club's monthly magazine *The Rotarian* often turned to baseball analogies to illustrate the values that led to success. In a typical article, the magazine urged readers to be persistent, even when enduring on raw and frayed nerves. "Do not die on third!" like a hesitant and forlorn runner who has lost his nerve, the magazine warned. "Bring to third every bit of your honest strength; study conditions, dig your spikes into the soil and get ready to run." In another piece, the magazine drew business lessons from the heroism of Jimmy Lavender, a young pitcher for the Chicago Cubs who was given the unenviable assignment of facing the great Ed Walsh of the Chicago White Sox in the annual postseason battle for the supremacy of Chicago. Though Lavender appeared shaky at times, as if his "nerve was broken, his strength gone," he rallied at the end, striking out the final batter with the winning run in scoring position. By game's end, Lavender proved that he was more than just a "wonderful pitcher"; he was a true disciple of the "Never Quit" doctrine. All could learn from Lavender's effort *The Rotarian* offered. "It takes nerve to overcome obstacles. . . . Without it, a man is doomed to defeat, be he an athlete, merchant, manufacturer or clerk." And lest anyone miss the point, the journal made the message personal: "Perhaps you are pitching to-day in a crucial game. Perhaps every muscle of your salary arm is aching, your head is throbbing, your heart is heavy. Perhaps your nerve is shaken and your confidence in yourself is broken. Don't quit. Lavender didn't. With the jeers of twenty thousand ringing in his ears, with doubting teammates behind him, with excruciating pains shooting through his tired body, he kept on and won for himself the admiration of his foes. Mr. Business Man, be a Lavender!"[32]

Nerve, agility, quick thinking, speed, strength, concentration, and self-reliance. These attributes made baseball "the recreative embodiment" of American manhood according to *Baseball Magazine* publisher F. C. Lane. "This is why baseball is the typical American sport" and its most popular. The fan saw in baseball "a revelation of what is in himself, a display of what he most admires."[33] Ultimately, such admiration riveted attention upon the athletes, raising them up as idealizations of true manhood. This fascination with the stars of the game was an intensely homosocial experience, one that bonded young and old in a mutual admiration of manly pursuits. As a child growing up on the South Side of Chicago, writer James T. Farrell recalled his initiation into this world by his two uncles who lived nearby. At home, they spoke of "players and games in an almost legendary way." Farrell remembered these conversations as "part of an oral tradition of baseball" that they consciously passed on to him. Once he was old enough, they took him to ball games and beamed with joy when he joined his cheers and shouts with their own. They were especially "proud of his rapidly developing and precocious knowledge of players, line-ups, teams, and averages" and gently instructed him on the proper decorum to show as a fan. From them he learned to revere players, especially the stars of his beloved White Sox, as exemplars of ideal manhood. Not surprisingly, Farrell remembered nearly all the stars of his youth as confident, generous, strong, and determined. Only later did Farrell realize that his uncles' efforts to teach him about baseball were part of a larger socialization process by which they eased his entrance into adult male society. "It corresponded with a natural period of development," Farrell later reflected, a process that "probably has . . . been true for many Americans" and "for this reason it retains a hold upon us through our long years of maturity and adulthood." As essayist Rollin Lynde Hartt quipped, "the child is father of the 'fan.'"[34]

Raised in Brooklyn at about the same time, future baseball historian Harold Seymour had an almost identical experience as Farrell. Nearly every male, from child to old man, embraced the game by either watching or playing. Dubbed the "city of baseball clubs," its many fields were in constant use afternoons, evenings, and weekends from April through October. All males, from young boys to old men, participated as either players, fans, or both. "Contact with baseball was therefore well-nigh inescapable for Brooklyn boys," Seymour recalled. "They grew up in an environment pervaded by the game." Consequently, baseball offered the boys and men of Brooklyn a common experience and common grammar that connected males horizontally across ethnic lines and vertically across generations. These connections were further enforced by all males' mutual love of the local heroes, the members of the long-suffering Brooklyn Dodgers.[35]

At times, contemplation of star athletes became subtly homoerotic. After an important series against the Pirates, a Cincinnati journalist paid tribute to Pittsburgh's star shortstop, Honus Wagner. Claiming that he "stood head and shoulders above all living players," the author marveled at his physique—"a stupendous combination of bone, muscle and sinew." Though he gave the impression of awkwardness, he was "as fast as a colt that has slipped the tether" and is "unchained lightning on the bases." A writer for *Baseball Magazine* admired Cleveland's Joe Jackson with equal gusto: "Tall, lithe, easy-moving, graceful in every unconscious pose"; he gave "evidence of speed in his whole frame." Yet even "though built for speed rather than strength," he possessed "tremendous power in his long, sinuous muscles . . . and so admirably geared that he can command the last ounce of strength in his whole system easily, without effort, wherever the occasion demands." Indeed, "a sculptor would choose him from the field as the model of what an outfielder should be." Perhaps in no other forum but the sporting page could one man dwell unabashedly and unashamedly upon the physical attributes of another man.[36]

The relationship between fans and players was often informal and intimate, especially by the standards of today. Fans enjoyed remarkable access to players. Ballplayers often lived in the neighborhoods of the ballparks and walked with them to and from the game. They frequented the same bars, the same restaurants, and the same barbershops. The ballpark further enhanced this intimacy. Even after teams converted to steel and concrete structures, ballparks remained cozy environs. Grandstands remained close to the field. Players had few secrets in this environment: fans could hear almost everything, from the grunts of physical exertion to expletives players expressed during the course of the game. The reverse was also true: players heard nearly every compliment and criticism directed at them. Certain ballpark traditions further enhanced the physical intimacy of fans and players. For important games, overflow crowds were allowed to stand along the foul lines and deep on the outfield grass. When young Smoky Joe Wood, having won thirteen games in succession, pitched against the mighty Walter Johnson, so many people jammed the area between the grandstand and the foul lines that the two pitchers hardly had room to warm up. In addition, fans often rushed the field after each game so they could walk the same ground as their idols and gather round them as they exited the field. Sometimes fans offered praise; sometimes they offered criticisms. Either way, players had to be thick-skinned and patient. At old Hilltop Park in New York, Highlander fans set up a "human alley," near the lone clubhouse door in the centerfield fence. As players ran through the makeshift gauntlet fans indulged their desire to be intimate with the players by giving each a "well-meant thumping" on the back. As one elderly reporter remembered it, most players and managers bore the experience in good humor, but not Kid Elberfeld: he "stalked through and no boy dared lay a hand on him."[37]

Fans sought a form of intimacy with ballplayers that was as much cerebral as it was spatial. They saw themselves as true aficionados who strived to be as knowledgeable of the game as the players and sports journalists. These devoted fans attended games regularly, studied box scores, read the sporting pages, and talked over the finer points of each game with their peers. They hoped their assiduous study of the game would draw them closer to the players they so admired, perhaps even put them on an equal footing. For this reason, they believed they were worthy judges of all things concerned with the game. They contended their dedication, knowledge, and patronage gave them every right to voice their opinions at the ballpark; after all, they were experts. As experts, they self-consciously rose above parochial loyalties to applaud players from the opposing team. As a St. Louis sportswriter observed after a hostile Browns crowd applauded Cobb for a "beaut of a running foul-fly catch" during a 1909 series, "merit wins its reward whether you are on a home team or on the visitors' cohorts." This same appreciation for excellence apparently motivated a Senators' fan to stand up just before Cobb took his last at bat in Washington that year to announce, "Ladies and Gentlemen. This is positively the last appearance this season on Washington grounds of the Great and Only. Here's hoping he makes a hit." Two weeks later when Cobb made his final appearance in Boston, fans again "cheered heartily" for him in honor of his fine year.[38]

Journalist Allen Sangree paid tribute to these ardent fans in a discerning analysis of fandom for *Everybody's Magazine*. According to Sangree, baseball crowds comprised three kinds of enthusiasts—bugs, rooters, and fans. The first two were neophytes, immature fans. The bug was a petty little man, according to Sangree, too "absorbed in details" to fully appreciate—much less enjoy—the artistry of the game.

The "rooter" was the bug's opposite, but equally lacking—an "irresponsible and uncritical" bag of wind who "howled at anything and everything." But the fan? "He is far above the others as a mahatma [is] above a coolie," Sangree declared. Having "passed through the stages of rooter and bug," the fan offered the best of both without evincing their annoying weaknesses. He understood the game with a wisdom born of experience. He could be extremely passionate, but he never acted irrationally. Rather, his behavior—whether passionate or restrained—was informed by a keen awareness of what his team needed at any given moment in the game. "He may elect a roar," Sangree observed, but he could just as easily reveal "untold passion by a mere eye-glint." Not surprisingly, bugs and rooters revered the fan and aspired to be just like him.[39]

Sangree had tongue planted in cheek when making these classifications; even so, his observations revealed two important points about baseball fans. First, fans craved respect from one another and performed accordingly. Second, they hoped to present an image that revealed the best of what it meant to be a man of the modern era: an informed expert of sound, rational judgment who was nonetheless capable of behaving with passion and even aggression when necessary. Clearly, this was what Farrell's uncles had in mind when they mentored him on the ways of the game. Likewise, newspaper sports pages and the three baseball journals appealed precisely to this type of individual when constructing their presentations of professional baseball. By presenting detailed statistical analysis, team profiles, and critical appraisals of the game's leading stars, sports media appealed to fans' desire for even greater expertise.

These middle-class fans may have been grounded in the business mindset of the modern city, but they also reveled in the emotion they could display at the ballpark. Even as they rejected the violent rowdyism that made attending games so unpleasant a generation earlier, they still hoped to retain some elements of the ballpark's former raucous culture—namely the right to cheer and boo lustily. In this, they defied the wishes of their social superiors. By the turn of the century, upper-class experts of good taste and proper decorum had largely succeeded in imposing rigid rules of behavior at a variety of public forums attended by middle-class men and women. Theaters, concert halls, and lecture halls all demanded that spectators behave with restraint and rigid civility. Audiences were instructed to remain quiet throughout much of the performance and to demonstrate only polite appreciation at designated moments in the performance. Booing and other forms of derisive behavior were strictly forbidden.[40] The ballpark was also part of this reform effort, but only to a point. League officials prohibited the worst forms of fan rowdyism (physical violence, extreme forms of verbal abuse, and public drunkenness), but they had neither the desire nor means to enforce the same rules of decorum as, say, the opera house or symphony hall. As a result, ardent fans still had considerable opportunity to express their passions. By their behavior, middle-class men demonstrated they wanted it this way. Although they had largely embraced audience reform in other entertainment venues, they helped keep the ballpark a haven for rawer forms of audience behavior. Here, at last, was a place respectable men could explore a full range of masculine behavior.

Indeed, working- and middle-class men gravitated to the ballpark because it was an unabashedly male arena. At a time when other public and private spaces were coming under increased feminine influence—including the home, political meetings, downtown retail districts, theaters, and even the office thanks to the growing use of female secretaries—the ballpark remained an essentially masculine reserve. Photographs of baseball crowds support this: despite magnates' efforts to attract women to the game, nearly all those in attendance were male. Thus, the ballpark retained a traditionally masculine atmosphere, complete with advertisements for men's consumer goods—beer and liquor, men's furnishings, tobacco products, and political candidates.

In many respects, it was a world of male bravado. Here men still cocked their straw hats rakishly to the side to reveal a bit of conceit, still slapped one another on the back in aggressive familiarity, and still thrust their fists in the air and cursed the sky when a local hero struck out or made an error. They still vied for the honor of voicing the best insult and they still puffed from fat cigars and sipped whisky from hip flasks in fraternal communion.

Liberated from both feminine and upper-class standards of propriety, baseball fans expressed themselves freely and vociferously. Managers and players expected fans to be a constant source of moral support, offering, as one sportswriter termed it, "encouragement of a clean and legitimate nature." Fans believed unquestioning loyalty belied their

Figure 6.1. Fans sit crowded together in makeshift stands just beyond the outfield fence at Bennett Park. Advertisements for cigars, rye, clothing, and political candidates identify the ballpark as a masculine space. Nary a woman can be seen in the photograph. *Source:* Courtesy of Ernie Harwell Collection. Detroit Public Library.

status as aficionados. Yes, when their team was winning, they showered the manager and players with praise. When the Tigers were most competitive, 1907 through 1909, Detroiters rooted for their team with impressive intensity. When the team left for important road trips, they often staged elaborate send-offs and acknowledged their return with equally elaborate welcomes. On the eve of important home games, they lit bonfires near the ballpark as a sort of ritualistic vigil in anticipation of the excitement to come. When the team won the American League each of these years, fans swelled downtown streets in spontaneous demonstrations that one writer called "orderly disorder." More formally, booster clubs and civic leaders feted the team with banquets, public testimonials, and personal gifts. When the team's fortunes waned, however, many fans turned on the team. Just a year-and-a-half after the

Tigers won their last flag, several players complained to the press that fans did not support them as they should. Although the Tigers were in first place, a bad stretch had reduced their lead from nine games to two. Apparently, this was enough to bring the boo birds out. Players were "incensed" by the "unfair treatment" of the fans. "If the majority of the Tigers had their way, all of the remaining games on the schedule would be played away from home," the *Free Press* reported. Fans even went after Cobb. After striking out and misplaying a base hit, fans turned on him, the *Free Press* reported, "as if he had never done anything but fall down in his life."[41]

In their exuberance, fans flirted with—and sometimes succumbed to—the same forms of rowdy behavior league officials wanted to prohibit. Relations between the players and a team's booster clubs were often especially tenuous when a team faltered. Although magnates often gave booster clubs front row seats (sometimes even on the field in front of the grandstands) as a reward for their support, these stalwart fans refused to be swayed by such generosity. The Cincinnati Reds' boosters, situated along "Rooters' Row" were especially vicious towards the home nine when the team lost. Hans Lobert, a veteran third baseman, became so unnerved by the acid-tongued boosters, Griffith was forced to trade him away following the 1910 season. When Rooters' Row turned their full wrath on Griffith the following year, he ordered that the seats be dismantled. *Baseball Magazine* applauded the decision, predicting the demise of "the crowd of raving lunatics" would usher in a "brighter day in Cincinnati."[42]

As such experiences reveal, fans could be extremely volatile in their treatment of the home team, expressing emotions that ran from pure adulation to utter outrage. Players attributed such reactions to mere fickleness. As Davy Jones offered philosophically, "That's baseball. A hero one day and a bum the next. But always a lot of laughs."[43] In fact, the reasons for fans' emotional responses to the action on the field had many causes. As some observers pointed out, cheering and booing offered men in an increasingly atomized society an opportunity to bond with one another—albeit briefly—in a common male culture. Sangree remarked that the bonding that occurred at the ballpark made baseball "second only to Death as a leveler." A journalist for the *Philadelphia Inquirer* came to a similar conclusion as he observed a huge crowd enjoy a late season game between the Athletics and the Tigers. "Brokers, bankers, physicians, lawyers, politicians, and merchants mingled with the working classes on the best of terms, exchanging opinions with each other as to the respective merits of this or that sphere tosser or joining in a mighty outburst of joyous noise" when something dramatic occurred during the game. It was, he concluded a "typical American crowd." Typical and perhaps a bit rowdy as men enjoyed the late season high jinks of crushing one another's straw hats. "If there are any straw hats left in this burg," the writer observed, "it is no fault of those who packed the big bleachers" and grandstand as every man "was soon relieved of his head covering and forced to sit hatless" through the game. A city united in manly capers: what could be more reassuring? For it was all in good fun the journalist reported—a "wonderful spectacle," "a bully good time," and the "most remarkable convention of fans ever held in this or any other burg."[44]

Some of the game's most thoughtful commentators went a step further, arguing that attending a baseball game offered catharsis for the overworked and overstressed minions of the new economic order. H. Addington Bruce, ever intrigued by the therapeutic value of sport, claimed watching a ball game gave fans "a method of gaining momentary relief from the strain of an intolerable burden" and provided a "harmless outlet for pent-up emotions which, unless thus gaining expression, might discharge themselves in a dangerous way."[45] The argument is compelling with one significant caveat: fans did not blow off steam by avoiding tension and stress; on the contrary, they acted in ways to increase the tensions of the ballgame. By booing, bullying, chanting, challenging, and cheering, fans tested ballplayers, those models of manhood, to see if they had what it took. Were they indeed men of nerve? For male fans, baseball was more than a game: it was a drama that presented the athletes' emotional makeup in all its complexities and explored the tensions and anxieties that they themselves felt. This was release, but it was also a form of intense engagement. According to *Baseball Magazine*'s F. C. Lane, men loved baseball because the emotions they experienced at the ball game were "typical of (their) own endeavors and ambitions." Indeed, the two were so close as to be analogous: "every fan who watches a game has really played it himself and his blood has tingled to the thud of willow against leather, just as if he himself had made the drive and raced madly down the stretch to the initial bag." This close identification, Lane contended, made baseball "the physical and mental tonic" a man "likes to take . . . because it is a revelation of what is in himself, a display of what he most admires."[46]

Leave it to introspective Johnny Evers to articulate the downside to such admiration. Most players considered it unmanly to admit, much less discuss, the impact fans had upon their confidence. But Evers was baseball's most sensitive soul. In a disturbingly candid piece for *Baseball Magazine*, he described the pressures that ballplayers experienced on a near daily basis. "The nervous strain is terrible," Evers confessed, similar to what "a soldier feels before a big battle. Is it any wonder that he is a little shaky or slightly off color?" According to Evers the stresses grew with the popularity of the game: more fans meant more media attention and thus greater scrutiny. Evers felt the anxieties keenly. Some in the press wondered openly if he was not wound too tight to play, though most believed his intensity made him—and the game—far better. At one point, it nearly became too much for him; he nearly quit because of "nervous prostration." But his competitive fire was too strong. About all he could do to lessen the stress was to make an awkward plea: "The ball player is only human," he observed. "Be gentle, then, in your criticism of the man who may make a trifling misplay. It's all in the game."[47]

Evers offered a cautionary tale of the price of fame. By his call for greater compassion at the ballpark he revealed himself to be sensitive, empathic, honest, and caring. Fans did not want any of this. They did not want to offer compassion. They wanted to witness real men stand the gaff. They wanted to cheer and boo. They wanted excitement. They wanted melodrama. And they wanted players who fed these desires. Above all, they wanted Ty Cobb.

NOTES

1. "The Baseball Bug," *Puck* (May 3, 1911), 19.
2. For baseball's growing popularity, see John P. Rossi, *The National Game: Baseball and American* Culture (Chicago: Ivan R. Dee, 2000), 75–77; Charles C. Alexander, *Our Game: An American Baseball History* (New York: MJF Books, 1991), 91–92; Harold Seymour, *Baseball: The Golden Age* (New York: Oxford University Press, 1971), 38–48; Benjamin G. Rader, *Baseball: A*

History of America's Game (Urbana: University of Illinois Press, 1992), 82–87; *Sporting News* (August 12, 1909): 1; *New York Times*, October 9, 1908, 1; H. Addington Bruce, "Baseball and the National Life," *Outlook* 104 (May 17, 1913): 104–107.

3. Albert Spalding, *America's National Game: Historical Facts Concerning the Beginning, Evolution, Development, and Popularity of Base Ball, with Personal Reminiscences of Its Vicissitudes, Its Victories, and Its Votaries* (1911; repr., San Francisco: Halo Books, 1991),, 329, 300; Rader, *Baseball*, 82–87; Alexander, *Our Game*, 93–96; Seymour, *Baseball: The Golden Age*, 38–48.

4. Allen Sangree, "Fans and Their Frenzies," *Everybody's Magazine* 17 (September 1907): 378, 380; Dick Luckman, "Notes of a Sportsman," *Town and Country* (September 2, 1911): 32.

5. *Detroit Free Press*, October 1, 1907, 4; "Marvelous Growth of Baseball," *Baseball Magazine* (January 1912): 102, 104; Lillian Russell, "The Rejuvenation of a Fan," *Baseball Magazine* (September 1911): 53; Sangree, "Fans and Their Frenzies," 378; *St. Louis Post-Dispatch: Sunday Magazine*, May 16, 1909, 2; *Salt Lake Herald*, April 21, 1907, 9.

6. Ellis O. Jones, "Baseball," *Lippincott's Monthly Magazine* 82 (September 1908): 814.

7. Frank B. Elser, "The Baseball Fan and the Box-Score," *Outlook* (April 19, 1913): 856, 857; *Chicago Tribune*, October 18, 1910, 24; P. F. Stratton, "The Baseball Scoreboard," *Baseball Magazine* (April 1914): 73–77; *Sporting News* (July 23, 1908): 3; Eric Dewberry, "Imagining the Action: Audiovisual Baseball Game Reproductions in Richmond, Virginia, 1895–1935," in *The Cooperstown Symposium on Baseball and American Culture, 2003–2004*, edited by William M. S. Simons (Jefferson, NC: McFarland, 2005), 141–55; *New York Times*, October 9, 1912, 4; *New York Times*, October 8, 1913, 5.

8. Elser, "Baseball Fan and the Box-Score," 856, 857.

9. Connie Mack, "The Evolution of Baseball," *Baseball Magazine* (July 1910): 7; *St. Louis Republic*, April 25, 1909, 11.

10. Quoted in John F. Kasson, *Houdini, Tarzan, and the Perfect Man: The White Male Body and the Challenge of Modernity in America* (New York: Oxford University Press, 2001), 11; quoted in William Leach, *Land of Desire: Merchants, Power, and the Rise of a New American Culture* (New York: Vintage Books, 1993), 236.

11. On the emergence of the new middle class, see Kasson, *Houdini, Tarzan, and the Perfect Man*, 3–20; Robert Wiebe, *The Search for Order, 1877–1920* (New York: Hill and Wang, 1967); Alan Trachtenberg, *The Incorporation of America: Culture and Society in the Gilded Age* (New York: Hill and Wang, 1982), 70–88; Jackson Lears, *Rebirth of a Nation: The Making of Modern America, 1877–1920* (New York: HarperCollins, 2009), 87–90,

222–23, 258–65, 282–84, 296–98; Olivier Zunz, *Making America Corporate, 1870–1920* (Chicago: University of Chicago Press, 1990). Within this salaried class, certain occupations grew in number and professionalized concomitantly. The 1850 census listed only 2,000 engineers in the United States. Nearly all were trained informally on the job. By 1920, the number of engineers swelled to 136,000, most of whom were educated formally at a college or university. A similar transformation occurred in accounting. In 1900, only twelve colleges offered courses in accounting; by 1916, the number rose to 116.

12. Quoted in Lears, *Rebirth of a Nation*, 57–63, 156–57; Aetna quote is on 263–64.

13. Thomas J. Schlereth, *Victorian America: Transformations in Everyday Life, 1876–1915* (New York: Harper Perennial, 1991), 69–71.

14. Kasson, *Houdini, Tarzan, and the Perfect Man*, 179–83, 203–215; Gail Bederman, *Manliness and Civilization: A Cultural History of Gender and Race in the United States, 1880–1917* (Chicago: University of Chicago Press, 1995), 170–216; John Pettegrew, *Brutes in Suits: Male Sensibility in America, 1890–1920* (Baltimore: Johns Hopkins University Press, 2007), 77–127.

15. E. Anthony Rotundo, *American Manhood: Transformations in Masculinity from the Revolution to the Modern Era* (New York: Basic Books, 1993), 222–46.

16. Schlereth, *Victorian America*, 64: Maria Costantino, *Men's Fashion in the Twentieth Century: From Frock Coats to Intelligent Fibers* (New York: Costume and Fashion Press, 1997), 21–24; Claudia Brush Kidwell, "Gender Symbols or Fashionable Details?" in *Men and Women: Dressing the Part*, edited by Claudia Brush Kidwell and Valerie Steele (Washington: Smithsonian Institution Press, 1989), 124–43.

17. On the overwhelmingly middle-class nature of baseball crowds, see Steven A. Riess, *Touching Base: Professional Baseball and American Culture in the Progressive Era* (Urbana: University of Illinois Press, 1983), 32–38; "Famous Baseball Fans Who Haunt the Polo Grounds," *New York Times*, October 5, 1913, SM3.

18. "Editorial: The Spirit of Sportsmanship," *Baseball Magazine* (February 1910): 1.

19. Spalding, *America's National Game*, 533; *New York Times*, November 13, 1910, SM13.

20. Nicholas J. Flatley, "Baseball—The Play of the Nation," *National Magazine* 35 (November 1911): 502; Thomas T. Hoyne, "Baseball as Business Training: Old Players Who've 'Made Good,'" *Chicago Tribune*, January 15, 1911, B4; "The Psychology of Baseball: The Game Elevates and Fits the American Character," *New York Times*, November 13, 1910, SM13; Bruce, "Baseball and the National Life," 105.

21. Bruce, "Baseball and the National Life," 105.

22. "Editorially: The Spirit of the Times," *Baseball Magazine* (October 1909): 3; Martin Green, "Life is a Ball Game," *Baseball Magazine* (June 1908): 50–52.

23. "More Speed Is the Cry," *Detroit Free Press*, February 10, 1907, C11; "The High Speed Mania," *Saginaw Evening News*, February 28, 1905, 2; "Has the World Gone Speed Mad?" *Chicago Tribune*, October 18, 1908, F4.

24. Junius Henri Browne, "The Bread-and-Butter Question," *Harper's New Monthly Magazine* 88 (December 1893–May 1894): 273, 274; "The Passion for Speed," *Chicago Tribune*, September 12, 1900, 12; "Editorial: Enduring the Tests of Life," *New York Observer and Chronicle*, February 10, 1910, 167; Madison C. Peters, "Talks with Young Men: The Man in Earnest," *Detroit Free Press*, October 22, 1911, D5; R. G. Clarke, "Seizing of Opportunity Leads on to Fortunes," *Chicago Daily Tribune*, June 11, 1905, E3; George T. Canfield, "Competition: The Safeguard and Promoter of General Welfare," *Annals of the American Academy of Political and Social Science* 42 (July 1912): 91. On the need to teach "alertness" in schools, see Dudley A. Sargent, "Physical Training as a Compulsory Subject," *School Review* 16 (January 1908): 42–55.

25. Hugh S. Fullerton, "Quick Thinking in Baseball," *Chicago Tribune*, September 9, 1906, A2; Connie Mack, "Clean Living and Quick Thinking," *McClure's Magazine* 43 (May 1914): 53; Eddie Collins, "Alertness, the Watchword of the Major Leaguer," *Baseball Magazine* (March 1915): 23.

26. Edwin A. Goewey, "Youth Holds the Spotlight in Sport," *Association Men* 45 (February 1920): 349; J. C. Kofoed, "Why Base Ball Is Our National Game," *Sporting Life* (November 27, 1915): 2; General Charles H. Taylor, "Is Baseball on the Level?" *Baseball Magazine* (November 1908): 10–12; Bruce, "Baseball and the National Life," 106; Bernarr Mcfadden, "Editor's Viewpoint," *Physical Culture* 23 (June 1910): 517.

27. Bederman, *Manliness and Civilization*, 84–92; Tom Lutz, *American Nervousness* (1903; repr., Ithaca, NY: Cornell University Press, 1991); Lears, *Rebirth of a Nation*, 45–46, 68–69, 239–41.

28. *Philadelphia Evening Bulletin*, August 25, 1909, 10.

29. Lears, *Rebirth of a Nation*, 239–48.

30. "Spirit of the Times," *Baseball Magazine*, 2; "Thirty Days of Baseball History," *Baseball Magazine* (March 1913): 17; *St. Louis Post-Dispatch*, September 7, 1909; J. Ed. Grillo, "As to 'Quitting,'" *Sporting Life* (May 30, 1908): 16.

31. Bruce, "Baseball and the National Life," 103–107; Henry Curtis, "Baseball," *Journal of Education* 83 (January 1916): 466–67; "Spirit of the Times," 2; "Editorials," *Baseball Magazine*, (May 1916): 32; *New York Times*, April 17, 1910, S2; Timothy H. Murnane, *How to Play Baseball* (New York: American Sports Publishing, 1914), 52; *Detroit Free Press*, December 14, 1910, 12.

32. "Editorial: Tyrus Cobb, Who Gets Home From Third," *Rotarian* 5 (July 1913): 36; "Business Lessons from the Fields of Sport: Jimmy Lavender Who Was Supreme in Crisis," *Rotarian* (April 1913): 21–24, 38.

33. F. C. Lane, "Need a Tonic: Try Baseball," *Baseball Magazine* (August 1909): 1.

34. James T. Farrell, *My Baseball Diary* (1957; repr., Carbondale: Southern Illinois University Press, 1998), 29–32, 35; Rollin Lynde Hartt, "The National Game," *Atlantic Monthly* 102 (August 1908): 221.

35. Seymour, *Baseball: The Golden Age*, 457–58.

36. *Sporting Life* (August 28, 1909): 25; F. C. Lane, "The Man Who Might Have Been the Greatest Player in the Game," *Baseball Magazine* (March 1916): 66.

37. Joe Wood in Lawrence S. Ritter, *The Glory of Their Times: The Story of the Early Days of Baseball Told by the Men Who Played It* (New York: Perennial, 1966), 159; John Kieran, "Sports of the Times," *New York Times*, October 3, 1937, D2.

38. *St. Louis Star*, May 7, 1909, 9; *Detroit News*, September 24, 1909, 8; *Sporting News* (October 7, 1909): 6.

39. Sangree, "Fans and Their Frenzies," 378–80.

40. John F. Kasson, *Rudeness and Civility: Manners in Nineteenth-Century Urban America* (New York: Noonday Press, 1990), 215–56.

41. *Detroit Free Press*, October 3, 1909, 1; *Detroit Free Press*, July 26, 1911, 12.

42. Seymour, *Baseball: The Golden Age*, 154–55; M. Van Buren Lyons, "The Power of the Bleachers," *Baseball Magazine* (June 1912): 37–38; *Sporting Life* (July 15, 1911): 2.

43. Davy Jones in Ritter, *Glory of Their Times*, 36; "Editorial: Baseball Rowdyism," *Baseball Magazine* (October 1911): 1.

44. Hartt, "The National Game," 226; Sangree, "Fans and Their Frenzies," 387; *Philadelphia Inquirer*, September 18, 1909, 10.

45. Bruce, "Baseball and the National Life," 107; Sangree, "Fans and Their Frenzies," 385.

46. "Need a Tonic: Try Baseball," *Baseball Magazine* (August 1909): front matter. This analysis is informed by anthropologist Clifford Geertz's analysis of "deep play," a concept constructed by philosopher Jeremy Bentham. Bentham termed deep play as engagement in a game in which the stakes are so high that

from a practical standpoint, no rational person would engage in it. See Geertz, "Deep Play: Notes on the Balinese Cockfight," in *The Interpretation of Cultures*, edited by Clifford Geertz (New York: Basic Books, 1973), 412–53. I have also learned a great deal from reading the work of anthropologist Victor Turner, especially Turner, *Dramas, Fields, and Metaphors: Symbolic Action in Human Society* (Ithaca, NY: Cornell University Press, 1974); and Turner, *From Ritual to Theatre: The Human Seriousness of Play* (New York: PAJ Publications, 1982). I can't claim I understand either completely.

47. F. C. Lane, "The Gamest Player in Baseball," *Baseball Magazine* (September 1913): 51–61; John J. Evers, "Do Players Lose Their Nerve?" *Baseball Magazine* (April 1909): 41–42.

7

"THE MOST UNPOPULAR POPULAR MAN IN BASEBALL"

With two weeks remaining in the 1915 season, the second place Detroit Tigers arrived in Boston for a crucial four-game series against the first place Red Sox. As the Red Sox led by only two games, Boston fans were wild with excitement, hoping that their beloved Sox would take the series and thus increase their lead heading into the last fourteen games of the season. They filled the ballpark for the first game, eager to cheer for their Red Sox and boo the hated Tigers. And boo they did, directing much of their vitriol at Ty Cobb. Throughout the contest, fans razzed Cobb, hoping to disrupt his concentration, if not break his nerve completely.[1]

They should have known better. A popular target of scorn during his first decade in baseball, Cobb was used to the fans' wrath and often boasted that a loud and hostile crowd motivated him to play better. True to form, the passion of the Boston fans seemed to energize him. In the first game, Cobb drove in the first run and scored the second as the Tigers won easily, 6 to 1. In typical Cobb fashion, he even displayed his infamous temper, defiantly throwing his bat at a Boston reliever in the eighth inning after the pitcher hurled two balls near his head. This really set the fans off. After the game, several hundred swarmed onto the field and surrounded Cobb as he walked from the outfield to the clubhouse. Those who got close enough shouldered and taunted him. The rest contented themselves by shouting obscenities and throwing wads of paper into the middle of the mob that encircled him. They finally dispersed after police arrived to escort Cobb to the clubhouse. The *Detroit Free Press* identified the fans as "rioters" and called the entire scene "disgraceful." Throughout the tumult, Cobb walked steadily on, occasionally returning shoves with a stiff shoulder of his own. He had experienced this sort of thing before and behaved as if this was just another day at the ballpark. Cobb homered the next day—as if to accentuate how unruffled he was by the previous day's events.[2]

Fans loved to try to bait Cobb. Cobb's reception at another game in Boston, this one in 1911, was typical. Early in the game, Cobb took a long lead at first base after receiving a base on balls from Boston pitcher Larry Pape. Cobb made a few breaks to second, only to be rushed back by Pape's quick pick-off throws. As the drama unfolded, fans along the first base line began to chide Cobb, daring him to make a run for second while simultaneously encouraging the Boston pitcher to keep trying to pick Cobb off. After a dozen attempts, the pitcher finally caught Cobb leaning the wrong way. With a quick snap throw, Pape nailed Cobb "like a rat in a trap," according to one sportswriter. Once the umpire yelled, "He's out!" the crowd "broke loose" in a chorus of "jeers and sneers" for Cobb as he jogged back to the dugout. Later he tried to steal second base again, only to be cut down by a near perfect throw from Boston catcher Bill Carrigan. Although the Tigers eventually won the game, the journalist noted, "the fans went home happy" for "Ty Cobb, the most feared base runner in Major League baseball, had been twice caught attempting to steal second. That was enough for the fans, what matter if the Tigers did win." In fact, they may have felt satisfied in contributing to Cobb's bad day by daring him to take so many risks.[3]

Nevertheless, Cobb was more than just a favorite target for derision and scorn, a player fans loved to hate—though this was certainly part of his public persona. He was, in fact, a sports celebrity. Posterity remembers Cobb as the best player of the first two decades of the twentieth century. What time has forgotten is that he was also the game's most popular player. At the height of his career, the *Sporting News* observed Cobb "has attracted considerable attention in. . . . every hamlet in the country as a player extraordinary." In this, he had become the personification of a celebrity: so well known, that "he needs no introduction." *Baseball Magazine* was even more effusive. In a 1916 piece, the journal christened Cobb "the national Hero of the diamond, as well-known throughout the United States as the president himself." *Sporting Life* called Cobb "the greatest press agent in the game. There is no one engaged in entertaining the public as widely advertised as he is." People who "care little for baseball and many who have no particular interest in any team go to the park when Detroit plays for no other reason than to see Tyrus perform." He was the greatest draw of his age, increasing attendance by as much as ten to twenty percent for an average league game. Cobb's fame was such that throughout the 1910s, the Tigers—also-rans most years—regularly outdrew such pennant contenders as Philadelphia and Boston on the road. The *Detroit News* opined, "only the peerless Tyrus knows when, where, and how to set America agog."[4]

Cobb became a media sensation. He dominated the sports headlines more than any athlete of his generation. He graced the cover of all the leading sports magazines, including a special edition of *Baseball Magazine* that was devoted almost entirely to him. In time, his fame transcended the game itself. To cash in on his fame, promoters from a variety of venues positioned the star to take advantage of his celebrity. He was invited to do vaudeville, once toured in a theatrical production, starred in a feature film, and wrote (or had written for him) one of the first "insider" baseball memoirs. Even his progeny got in on the act. In 1918, his three children even made it into *Woman's Home Companion* for a photo spread entitled "Small People with Great Names." His was the lone athlete's family in a feature that also included the children and grandchildren of statesmen Theodore Roosevelt, Woodrow Wilson, Charles Evans Hughes, industrialists Cyrus McCormick and John Rockefeller, impresario Florenz Ziegfeld and concert violinist Efrem Zimbalist. So great was public demand to read about Cobb that the leading journals strained to find a new angle. Thus, when *Baseball Magazine* learned that Cobb had recently attended the New York Metropolitan Opera with famed prima donna Frieda Hempel, it dutifully broadcast the news under the headline "A New Ty Cobb Story." Public obsession continued unabated. *Sporting Life* observed that it could not be otherwise: "Ty Cobb simply forces his name into the sporting pages by some sensational feat in batting, fielding, or base-running almost daily."[5]

Ever the master strategist, Cobb learned how to play to the press to increase his fame. In an era before players employed press agents, Cobb understood how to court journalists. He was smart, articulate, glib, and polite. And astute: He satisfied beat writers' constant need for fresh storylines by feeding them entertaining anecdotes about his exploits. Although he might tell the same story in seven different cities, each writer crowed that he possessed an exclusive from the great Cobb. Cobb's hold on the press was such that a Detroit journalist kiddingly offered this vignette to explain Cobb's ability to garner attention: "Early in life, some great genius rested his hand upon T. R's curly head and said, 'My boy, it pays to advertise.' And Tyrus looked up into the face of the genius with his bright eyes brighter and answered, 'I gotcha.'" When word spread at the end of the 1926 season that Cobb had been fired by Detroit management, sportswriters across the country mourned his anticipated retirement. A Cleveland sportswriter explained why: "He was always good copy," the journalist observed; he had "a news sense that few baseball men possess . . . Whenever there was a scarcity of news Ty always could be depended upon to make a story. He was the greatest rainy day help a baseball writer could have."[6]

Luminaries from all walks of life lobbied to be seen with Cobb. His list of famous fans, friends, and acquaintances reads like a "Who's Who" of the early twentieth century. Cobb played golf with Presidents Taft and Wilson and poker with President Harding and his White House cronies. All three presidents invited him for dinner at the White House. Taft became especially enamored with Cobb; he never missed an opportunity to see him play and invited him to the White House whenever the Tigers were in town. Cobb was so close to Harding that when the president died suddenly during a speaking tour in the Far West, his aides telephoned Cobb to break the news to him. Lesser political lights also understood it was good politics to be seen with Cobb. During the 1916 season, presidential hopeful Henry Cabot Lodge made an (unsuccessful) effort to get Cobb's endorsement. While the Tigers were training in the Deep South one spring, the state legislature of Mississippi invited Cobb to speak before a joint assembly. In celebration of his twentieth year in Major League Baseball, leading members of Congress threw a banquet for him and presented him with an extensive collection of biographies. Cobb also hobnobbed with the elites of entertainment and business. George M. Cohan called him a friend. So did comedian and vaudeville star Joe E. Brown, race car driver Barney Oldfield, and golfer Bobby Jones. Baroness Irmgard von Rothenthal, a Croatian dancer and choreographer, came to watch Cobb play and created a scene in her *Temptation of Eve* based upon Cobb's graceful sliding techniques.[7] Like many other stars of his day, Cobb parlayed his baseball fame into other ventures. Vaudeville wooed Cobb for years; he finally took the stage in a melodrama that toured the East and South and received mostly good reviews, for a ballplayer that is. A few years later, he branched into film, starring in another melodrama. He also made a splash as an after-dinner speaker at conventions and conferences. His fame also enabled him to get in on the ground floor of some of the nation's fledgling business enterprises, most notably Chevrolet and Coca-Cola. His early investments in these businesses enabled him to become the first millionaire ballplayer.[8]

It helped Cobb's fame immeasurably that he was quite handsome, especially early in his career: blonde, fair-skinned, tall and angular, a square jaw, and piercing eyes that bespoke his utter determination to win. To early twentieth-century America, he was the image of vigorous youth and invincible white manhood. In prose bordering on homoerotic, *Baseball Magazine* anointed Cobb the ideal player: "Speak of a baseball player and visions of Ty Cobb, lithe, sinuous, eager, swinging his restless bat, rises [sic] into the field of view." A features writer for the *Detroit Free Press* remarked. "His face has a smoothness and a firmness of fiber that makes you think of a carefully cut sculpture." A Louisville paper was even more laudatory, calling Cobb "closer to the athletic ideal" than any other ballplayer:

> Built like a greyhound, his wonderful lithe body is always a study. His slight waist, his magnificently formed shoulders, his wiry limbs, lithe, slight ankles, and wrists, and his well-poised head make one think of the idealized Grecian youth who lives now only in the marble of the museums and art schools.

Small wonder Cobb was among the first athletes to cash in on endorsements: Tuxedo Tobacco, Coca-Cola, Ide Collars, Royal Tailor suits, and Nuxated Iron all used Cobb's name and face to sell products. Tin Pan Alley penned a song for him, aptly titled "They All Know Cobb." Long before the Curtiss Candy Company honored Babe Ruth with his own candy bar, the Baby Ruth, the Benjamin Candy Company of Detroit favored Cobb with his own confectionary treat—a milk caramel nut bar, that was "a sure hit"—or so claimed the wrapper.[9]

Given all the attention the media favored Cobb with, it is not surprising that fans sometimes mobbed him in a manner usually reserved for theater and film matinee idols. On one such occasion, his presence at the National Treasury caused a near riot as a "mob" of "fanettes," young women who worked at the Treasury as bill counters, recognized

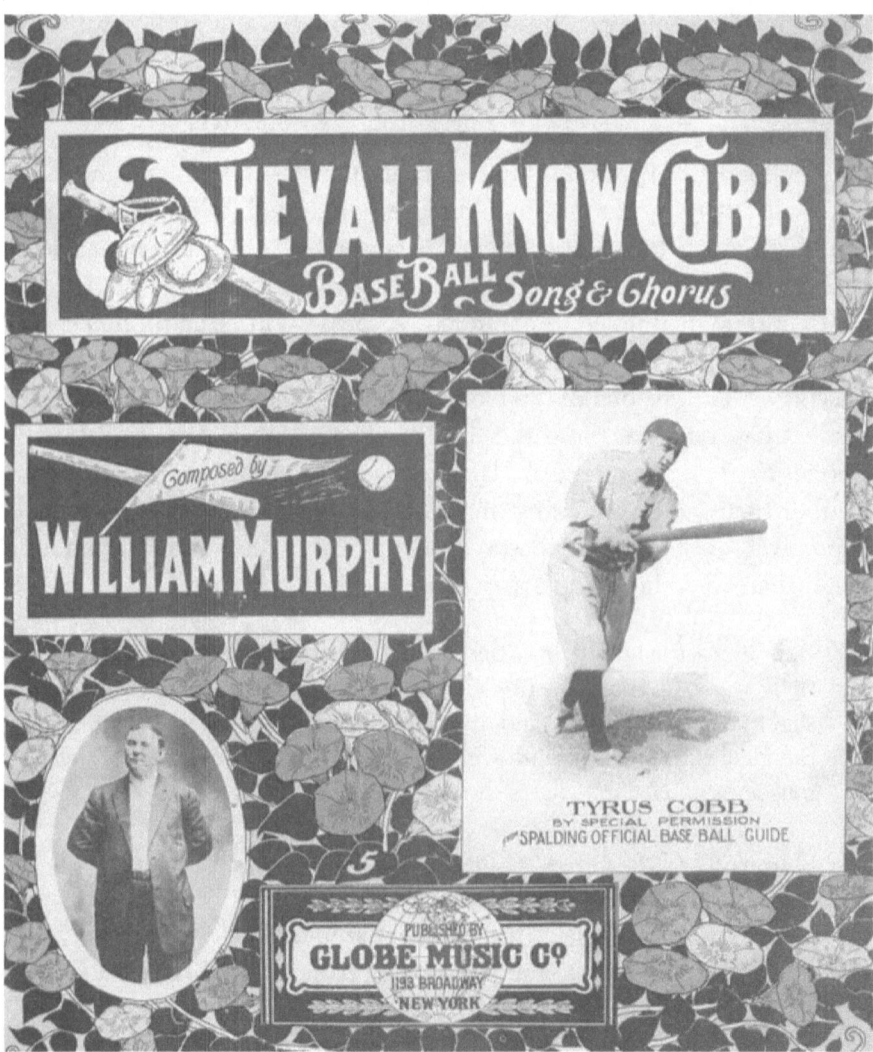

Figure 7.1. In 1913 Cobb got his own song. The title, "They All Know Cobb," suggests the universality of his celebrity in early twentieth-century American popular culture. *Source*: Library of Congress.

Cobb and rushed toward him. In response, the Treasury changed its policy regarding celebrity visits: guests would no longer be allowed to tour the building's bank vaults.[10] After the 1909 World Series, Cobb set off on an auto tour from New York to Atlanta to promote better roads. Although over one hundred people in sixty plus cars participated in the caravan, the event quickly became a mobile tribute to Cobb. Race car driver F. Ed Spooner could not believe the adulation the young outfielder received along the way. "We had no sooner left New York than the ovation to Cobb started. In Philadelphia they paid him homage. In Gettysburg he was toasted, wined, and dined." The farther South the tour went, "the more they cried for Cobb." Even in sparsely settled rural areas, fans stood along the road waiting for Cobb, carrying signs like "Hurray for Good Roads and Ty Cobb" and "How Do You Like Our Roads Ty Cobb?" Future Red Sox pitcher Ernie Shore was among the throng. A freshman at Guilford College in Greensboro, North Carolina, Shore walked six miles in the dark of night just to get a glimpse of the great Cobb as he passed by at dawn. Some were so interested in Cobb that they camped all night just to spy his little blue Chalmers as he raced past.[11]

Although historical memory often portrays Cobb as a brooding malcontent, most fans of his day had a far different perception of him. Serious to the point of obsession while playing, he was often quite approachable before and after games. Estranged from many of his teammates, he found solace by spending a good portion of his pregame warm-up chatting casually with fans. Sometimes he was even a bit playful. Prior to a game in Washington, he crouched behind the plate to play catcher for the Senators to help their pitchers warm up—much to the delight of the local crowd who gave him a "tremendous hand" for his first at bat. He even found time to joke and tease fans before a World Series game in Pittsburgh. As he warmed up in the outfield, he pantomimed throwing balls into the bleachers, entertaining hundreds of fans who came early to watch him practice.[12] Off the field, he was especially generous with his time. The *Sporting News* reported that it was almost impossible for Cobb to make his way through hotel lobbies without being approached by scores of fans eager to talk to him. At home in Augusta, he proved especially magnanimous, taking time to visit with anyone who approached him. He also made a point of responding to fans who wrote him, though he confessed that he was often overwhelmed by the sheer volume of letters he received. According to *Baseball Magazine's* F. C. Lane, Cobb was "as democratic and easy to meet as anyone could wish."[13]

Cobb could also be extremely disarming. He often presented a genteel persona when talking to the press, keeping to himself the vile things he said to other players in the heat of battle. Indeed, he often went out of his way to praise his peers. There were exceptions, of course, most notably when he was quarreling with teammates. But when he had control of his temper, he usually came off as considerate and thoughtful. In addition, Cobb was also quite candid about his own foibles. With the exception of Johnny Evers, no player discussed the pressures of major league baseball as forthrightly as Ty Cobb. No, he never disclosed his nervous breakdown and subsequent stay in a sanitarium. Nor did he discuss the trauma of his father's murder. He buried those tragedies deep within himself. In other ways, however, he was very honest about the difficulties of being a professional ballplayer. In his insider's monograph, magazine interviews, and newspaper columns, Cobb explained the emotional cost of striving to maintain his reputation as the game's best player. The wear and tear of a six-month season, near continuous travel, and the unrelenting pressure to play up to his own exacting standards often left him emotionally exhausted. "Those long seasons of batting wear on the nerves," he confessed. His annual drive to win the batting title was especially stressful. "Few persons realize the tension that this keeps a man under," he remarked; I am usually 'crabbing' from the beginning to the end of the season." Yet what could he do? In baseball, he observed, "a man has to deliver all the time and the more he is paid the more he has to deliver." Quite likely, fans found Cobb's admissions rather endearing. Unlike Evers, Cobb did not ask for sympathy or compassion; rather, his tone was matter-of-fact, neither weak nor vacillating. He understood fans' expectations and accepted them. In this way, he presented himself as someone who was very much like his fans saw themselves—a serious professional who faced the stresses and strains of life as best he could.[14]

Journalists and public figures held Cobb up as an example to live by. A popular minister of the day, George McPherson Hunter, presented Cobb as the ideal Christian athlete. Norval Abiel Hawkins, the sales wizard of the Ford Motor Company, profiled Cobb as a model for business success. So did the *Rotarian* and something called the

American Gas Engineering Journal, Boys' Life, The Youth's Companion, and the YMCA's journal *Association Men* frequently held Cobb up as an inspiration for adolescents and young men. Meanwhile, the leading celebrity sports journalists of the era—Ring Lardner, Grantland Rice, Hugh Fullerton, Billy Evans, Fred Lieb—extolled Cobb's virtues in popular magazines like *Collier's Everybody's Magazine, Literary Digest, American Magazine*, and *Outing Magazine*. John Sheridan, who wrote a regular column in *Sporting News* for several years, nimbly reconstructed Cobb's turbulent first years with the Tigers into a tale of virtue's triumph over evil. Forced to battle against hostile veterans to make the team, Cobb defeated his enemies by the force of his iron will. While most boys "want the road smoothed for them" and expect "help from everyone," Cobb relied solely upon himself, thus demonstrating that "the only person who can help any man is himself." His unlikely rise to stardom, Sheridan concluded, makes "good reading for youngsters who desire to make good in baseball or in any other occupation."[15]

Why did baseball fans, that is to say the modern men of the early twentieth century, become so enamored with Cobb? An obvious, though incomplete, answer is that Cobb was simply the best player in the game. At his peak, he achieved an extraordinarily consistent record of excellence: twelve batting championships in thirteen years, including a record nine in a row. Through 1919, he was nearly always at or near the top of almost every major offensive category including batting average, runs scored, runs batted in, stolen bases, and extra base hits; he even led the league in home runs one year. None of the game's other great stars of the era—Napoleon Lajoie, Eddie Collins, Tris Speaker, Joe Jackson, George Sisler, Honus Wagner, Rogers Hornsby—matched Cobb's exploits.

Yet Cobb offered more than just statistical superiority. His appeal was also emblematic. Cobb embodied both the ideals and strivings of the new modern professional man. For one thing, in this dynamic era of specialization and expertise, Cobb presented himself as the game's most thoughtful and successful authority on the game. He shared his knowledge freely: he wrote (or had written for him by friendly sportswriters) countless newspaper and magazine articles on the nuances of the game. He also penned (with ghostwriter John Wheeler) one of the first insider's guides to baseball strategy. When interviewed, he often offered expansive and detailed explanations of his tactics and approach to the game. Indeed, he presented himself as the most intelligent and intentional of ballplayers, plotting out plays and imagining scenarios sometimes weeks in advance. When feature columnist Prosper Buranelli interviewed Cobb for the *Detroit Free Press* at the end of the 1921 season, he marveled at the level of Cobb's technical expertise. Cobb, Buranelli noted, "devoted considerable ratiocination" to the tactics of baseball. He spoke thoughtfully, employing "such phraseology of science as is in current use. His ideas run the course of recent psychological and sociological reasonings. One fancied that he had been spending his off-season weeks in the company of intellectuals." That was Cobb— the quintessential specialist hard at work.[16]

Equally impressive to the newly emerging professional class, Cobb embodied their relentless striving to improve and advance. While trade journals and popular men's magazines like *Bankers' Magazine*, *American Magazine*, *Collier's*, and *New Success* lectured men to go the extra mile ("Remember, no matter how well you do a thing, it can be done better" and "Never say it can't be done"), stick to business ("Any legitimate business well managed will pay"), and persevere through failure ("The successful man rarely, if ever, acknowledges defeat"), Cobb showed men how to act on such advice.[17] Using language that would have pleased Charles Schwab, Henry Ford, and other apostles of the new age, *Sporting Life* observed, Cobb never "stopped studying his line of business, even after he had been recognized as the best player in the game." *Baseball Magazine* editor Lane declared Cobb was "the type of man who would be big no matter in what walk of life he would be found" and had the stuff to make it in any business venture. Why? Because "he is the most restless, untiring young man in public life today. Everything interests him; nothing seems to escape him. He is on the go, morning, noon, and night." He was the quintessential young man on the make, eager to advance by making the most of his opportunities. It also helped that Cobb identified himself as a professional man. Baseball was his business, he told reporters, and "like any other business, it was a matter of push and fight every instant. I must get ahead of the others and keep ahead of the others." Writing in *Baseball Magazine*, he told his readers that this unrelenting spirit would work in every profession. "The man who gets ahead is the chap who tries, and if he falls down comes up smiling and tries again, undaunted," he explained.[18]

Watching Cobb—as opposed to just reading about him—offered further encouragement to the new professional class. Cobb's play on the field proved something of a revelation because he demonstrated man's potential in the competitive and stress-inducing environment of modern business. For the previous two decades, the medical community expressed concern that most men lacked the nerve to survive this new age. Cobb demonstrated that man could not only survive in a highly competitive environment; he could thrive. Fans in the stands and in the press box were convinced that Cobb possessed more nerve than any player in the game, perhaps more than any man alive. Perhaps even more remarkable, Cobb's nerve seemed unlike anything they had seen before in a ballplayer. In the common parlance of the day, to possess nerve meant to be able to withstand pressure, to think and act coolly and calmly in the face of crisis. Cobb certainly did this. Indeed, he boasted he played his best when the pressure was most intense. But Cobb went even further. He not only had the stamina to endure stress, he had the strength and the guile to put stress on others. That is, he used his nerve as an offensive weapon to unnerve and emasculate his opponents. In these ways, Cobb refuted Beard's thesis that nerve was a limited commodity that needed to be conserved. After all, the challenges of the game did not sap his strength; rather, they energized him. For Cobb, nerve was like a muscle—ready to expand and develop when exercised properly. Cobb had "proved a valuable point," Grantland Rice observed in the *New York Herald Tribune*, late in the star's career: He had "shown that few persons actually wear themselves out by working too hard." Indeed, Cobb claimed he played best when he was most stressed, what he termed being "on his nerve." He even maintained that he would rather endure a batting slump at home than on the road "because I like the opposition." Nothing enlivened him more than "the crowd hooting at me for failing to hit." Here then was a new formulation of nerve. For the resolute man of action, nerve could be a renewable resource, produced by the challenges of modern life.[19]

For many fans, this was a primary source of Cobb's appeal: to watch Cobb test the human potentials of nerve. "Fans crowd the bleachers to watch Cobb play," manager Hughie Jennings explained. They expect "something startling, something unusual . . . and Cobb seldom disappoints them."[20] His every move seemed to promise the possibility of high drama. This is what struck Gilbert C. Brook, an ardent baseball fan from western Pennsylvania. Though Brook had seen the great Honus Wagner play as many as forty times, watching Cobb in two games during a business trip to Chicago convinced him that Cobb was far the superior player because of his "nerve and ability." Enthralled by Cobb, he shared his experience in a lengthy letter to *Baseball Magazine*. In a matter of minutes, he witnessed Cobb stretch a single into a double, take third on a sacrifice, and steal home. The events unfolded so quickly, Brook scarcely had time to absorb it all. Indeed, he was still deciding whether he thought Cobb safe or out at second when a "great shout" induced him to turn his head just in time to see Cobb streak toward the plate. "In five minutes," Brook gushed, Cobb had treated him to "more real baseball" than he had seen in fifteen years of watching Wagner and the Pirates. It was a common refrain—Cobb created excitement because he took chances that no other player would take, much less accomplish. He made the game exciting and unpredictable.

The *New York Times* tried to capture Cobb's appeal with a detailed description of how he almost singlehandedly defeated the Yankees by committing one act of daring after another:

> Ty Cobb's Daring Upsets Yankees
> Steals Bases, Home Plate, and Shuts Out New York, 3 to 0
> Look; there he goes!!
>
> Ty Cobb is loose again on a base galloping spree. He romps to first on a single. Slim Caldwell pitches to Nunamaker, and the ball settles in his big mitt. Cobb, a few feet off first, suddenly bolts into action and races to second. Nunamaker, amazed at the Georgian's daring, stands dumbfounded.
>
> He throws the ball to Dan Boone just as the Southern Flyer jumps into second base. . . . Nunamaker's nervous toss rolls into center field and the Georgia Gem bounds to his feet and tears to third. . . . Cobb's sarcastic smile angers his hoodwinked opponents.
>
> Now the speed-crazed comet dashes up and down the third-base line, trying to rattle Caldwell. Will Cobb have the nerve to try to steal home? You said it; he will. Caldwell doesn't think so. No one thinks so, but Cobb. The Yanks' lanky pitcher hurls the ball at the batsman like a rifle ball. As the ball left his hand, Cobb bounded over the ground like a startled deer.

> At the plate crouched Nunamaker. He was so surprised that he didn't know his own name. Cobb dashed through the air toward the scoring pan. His lithe body swerved away from Nunamaker's reach and clouds of dirt kicked up by his spikes blinded the eyes of Nunamaker, Caldwell, and [umpire] Silk O'Loughlin.
>
> The umpire ruled that the catcher didn't touch Cobb. He also ruled that Cobb hadn't touched the plate. While the Yankee players were protesting, Cobb sneaked around the bunch and touched the plate.
>
> A smart young feller, this same Cobb. The bold piracy of Captain Kidd was like taking ice-cream cones from children compared with that. . . . Cobb pulled the wool over their eyes like a "sharper" unloading mining stock on a Rube.[21]

As the writer suggests, it was almost impossible for spectators to keep up with Cobb, much less predict what he might do next. For this reason, he demanded fans' constant attention. A writer for *Outing Magazine* observed, "Somehow you forget to look at anyone else when Cobb comes to bat." To take one's eyes off Cobb was to risk missing the play of the game, the year, or perhaps even a lifetime. He even drew attention to himself when he failed. Because of his "willingness to take any kind of chance," umpire Billy Evans observed, "nine-tenths of the plays on Cobb are close." So close that no matter how the umpire called it, he was sure to rile some fans and please others—and thus make Cobb the center of attention. Cobb loved these close plays because they forced everyone to watch him—and to reconsider again his tactical genius, his base-running prowess, and his indomitable will.[22]

Many fans sought more visceral thrills than just watching Cobb. Most came to the ballpark because they wanted an opportunity to cheer, boo, and bait him. They yearned to be active participants in the contests of manhood that played out before them on the baseball diamond. Cobb proved a master at this as well. He seemed to find special enjoyment in riling fans. His actions showed that he loved to play the villain that fans loved to hate. Although Cobb did not like to tip his hat after a great play in front of an appreciative crowd, he delighted in doing so if the crowd was against him. He reveled in the role of antagonist. As one stalwart fan observed, Cobb liked to interpret jeers "in the nature of dares" and "usually accepted [the fans'] challenge."[23] Indeed he did: when booed,

Cobb strutted, waved his cap, yelled back, and gestured obscenely. During a game in Philadelphia, bleacherites pelted him with lemons. Cobb responded by tossing the lemons back at them, stopping only when one of the umpires implored him to quit lest he incite a riot. He claimed he resorted to such theatrics to "to show them (the fans) I did not care what they thought." He lied; he cared deeply, but probably not in the way most players did. He wanted fans' respect, not their affection, and hoped to gain it by countering their hostility by winning them over with his talent and nerve. He was eager to trade challenges and insults with fans. For this reason, he relished those sellout games in which fans lined the outer limits of the outfield and stood along the foul lines. Standing near one another gave each numerous opportunities to confront and bait the other. Cobb even claimed that he enjoyed wading into the crowd to track down balls—the closer the contact the better. The congested ball field proved to be the perfect stage for baseball's man of honor and for the fans who came to see him.[24]

Fans loved it. In an irony reflective of early twentieth-century fan culture, Cobb's very belligerence gave fans reason to enjoy watching him; he satisfied their desire to let loose, to reveal their own manly bearing and to affect the game. Eddie Collins, the great second baseman for the Athletics and White Sox, astutely explained how Cobb energized baseball crowds to make the game more entertaining and meaningful for all. Interviewed in 1925 when the Age of Babe Ruth threatened to overwhelm public memory of Cobb, Collins confessed nostalgia for the earlier age. Yes "Ruth is a great showman" and "we have *concrete stadiums* [with] bigger crowds today," Collins conceded, "but somehow there is something missing." That something, Collins believed, was the passion Ty Cobb generated in fans. They "flocked to the ballpark to razz Cobb," Collins recalled. Indeed, the intensity of the "hoots and jeers that greeted Cobb as he trotted to the outfield" left Collins with an indelible memory. Collins understood that fans' reaction to Cobb stemmed from his approach to the game. "He has the fire, the dash, and love of the game that will always make him a great figure." Such traits also meant that he inspired very strong emotions: the rare player who was "hated and loved in the same breath," Collins astutely observed. Equally significant, the passion Cobb generated was contagious. When Collins's Athletics visited Detroit, they received much the same treatment that Cobb and the Tigers received in Philadelphia.

"More than once, we were pelted with vegetables as we entered the ballpark. More than once we had to have police escort us to our hotel." All the players "liked the spirit," Collins contended. "And personally I enjoyed every minute of it. It made the winning of ball games a big thing in our lives." Collins understood that Cobb was more than just a foul-mouthed, ill-tempered, and overly aggressive target of fan contempt. He was a showman—an expert showman who understood the importance of cultivating a dynamic rapport with his audience.[25]

It was in this context—on the ball field with all eyes upon him—that Cobb gave up the façade of modesty and demonstrated his tremendous ego. At the height of his fame he often milked his entrance onto the field by waiting until shortly before the game began to warm up. That way, he was sure to get a bigger hand from fans who were waiting anxiously to get a look at the game's greatest player. After watching Cobb pull this stunt at Comiskey Park, a Chicago journalist quipped, "Cobb despises the limelight like a fish hates water."[26] Some observers accused Cobb of acting downright haughty at the ballpark. The *Chicago Tribune* curtly noted, Cobb "always swaggers on the ball field." A writer for *Outing Magazine* observed, "His whole attitude is braggadocio. Every move seems to say, 'Quail, thou craven pitcher! I am the great Cobb! Any ball you pitch I will knock a mile!'" It was, the writer conceded, all part of Cobb's "game."[27]

Yet for all his bravado and apparent vanity, Cobb never acted aloof from fans. Instead, he tried to cultivate an open and honest, though sometimes hostile, relationship with the men and boys who crowded the grandstands and bleachers to watch him perform. In his insider's monograph, *Busting 'Em*, he remarked that "probably no Big League ball player has as much experience with crowds as I have." It was a boast based on fact. Cobb was the biggest draw in the game and he welcomed the challenge of meeting fans' expectations. If nothing else, he understood who paid his bills. When asked to offer an opinion of fan behavior, he replied diplomatically, "The crowd makes the ball game" and then continued "How much pepper, how much enthusiasm, and how much baseball do you suppose a player would show if games were played to empty seats?" And for himself? "I have always been ambitious to please the fans, and I believe it has helped me wonderfully," Cobb claimed with perhaps more than a bit of smugness.[28]

Cobb's feel for the dramatic coupled with his sensitivity to criticism and his need for attention sometimes created dangerously volatile moments. The *Sporting News* told of one such incident during the 1919 season. A fan spent the better part of the game telling Cobb that he was "yellow." Several neighboring fans warned the rowdy that Cobb was anything but yellow and that he should be careful not to rile him. Foolishly, the fan interpreted their cautionary advice as a dare; emboldened he decided to tell Cobb he was yellow "to his face." After the game, he marched onto the field and confronted Cobb. Words were exchanged, a "mix up" ensued, and Cobb ended up "bunt(ing) the fellow in the groin with his knee." The man staggered and fell to the ground, attracting a sizeable crowd as he did so. Several of this group decided to wait for Cobb outside the clubhouse. Cobb was in the shower when he heard about the gathering mob. Rather than finish, he grabbed his clothes, dressed without drying off, and marched outside. Playing the role of aggrieved man of honor to the hilt, he faced the crowd, asking if anyone cared to argue with him. When no fans came forward, he returned to the clubhouse to finish dressing. Still, the mob refused to disperse. When it was time to leave, Jennings tried to protect his star by ordering a cab to the door so that Cobb would not have to work his way through the crowd. Cobb refused the ride and walked back to the hotel. Still bristling from the charge that he was yellow, he stopped to ask anyone who looked even a bit aggressive if they wanted a piece of him. Of course no one did. So Cobb retired to his hotel room, content that he had once again proved his manly superiority. Meanwhile, the obnoxious fan was probably in a bar somewhere boasting that he had provoked the great Ty Cobb into one of his legendary tiffs.[29]

If gender is a kind of performance as some cultural anthropologists have argued, Cobb offered fans a great deal to think about both on and off the field.[30] Quite often, he presented himself as a man who followed the standards of modern etiquette. Especially when interviewed and away from the ballpark, he was considerate, polite, humble, agreeable, and even deferential to management, be it his manager, the team owners, or the league president. When he behaved in this way, one might have easily confused him for a midlevel manager, bureaucratic functionary, or corporate officer. On the field, however, Cobb was anything but self-effacing, predictable, and cautious. Here, Cobb defied the predictability and systematization that scientific management and bureaucratic rationalization required of human behavior; as a ballplayer he mastered the art of the unexpected and thrived on risk-taking. His personality was often surly, combative, and prone to mercurial mood swings. Far from presenting a corporate identity, Cobb often chose to act alone and in open defiance of managers, owners, and his teammates. It is not too much to say that Cobb sometimes inverted the very values that were becoming identified with the urban middle class. Perhaps then, fans found in Cobb the embodiment of their stifled frustrations and unspoken desires.[31]

Yet Cobb performed these feats in the world of commercialized sports—a world that was entwined with the same modernizing processes as the workplaces of many baseball fans. Like them, Cobb often confronted an impersonal and often unwieldy hierarchical power structure, intense scrutiny by superiors and customers alike, and daily statistical assessments of his productivity. Through his many deeds and his confident and bold demeanor, Cobb demonstrated that contemporary males could live in the modern world and still be men. That Cobb performed some of his most daring deeds—stealing home, running from first to third on an infield out or from second to home on a pop fly—against the combined efforts of the opposing team (a metaphor for the modern corporation?) added to this persona.

One incident, in particular, reveals how fans used their dynamic relationship with Cobb to explore their concerns about manhood in the modern world—his infamous spiking of Philadelphia Athletics' third baseman Frank Baker. The incident unfolded within the context of a heated championship race between Philadelphia and Detroit late in the 1909 season. In the last week of August, the Athletics visited Detroit for a crucial series. Although the American League was less than a decade old, the two teams had already become bitter rivals. And Cobb was at the center of the rivalry. His aggressive base stealing and bullying and blustering demeanor irked the Athletics, who tended to follow the more conservative manners of their manager, Connie Mack. Since the beginning of the season, teams had accused Cobb of intentionally hurting opposing players as he ran the bases. Now, just before the first game of this important series, the Athletics claimed that they had overheard Cobb boast that he intended to take out each of the Athletics infielders with his sharp spikes and hard slides.[32] Coincidentally or not, in the first inning of the first game Cobb spiked Frank Baker's left arm as he tried to steal third. Though the resulting wound was not serious enough for Baker to leave the game, the Athletics claimed Cobb had deliberately tried to disable the third baseman. Even the normally reticent Mack said it was "just Cobb's nature to act mean on the ball field." Mack promised to make a formal complaint to the league and suggested that Cobb should be arrested for assault.[33]

Meanwhile in Philadelphia, the city's dailies tried to outdo one another in their denunciations of Cobb. The day after the incident, the *Philadelphia Inquirer* condemned Cobb's action on its editorial page. A few days later, the paper's sports columnist, "The Old Sport," wrote the first of a series of editorials condemning Cobb's "brutality." According to "Old Sport," Cobb possessed "homicidal instincts" which he selectively unleashed against those players who were most likely to give Detroit trouble in their fight for the pennant. Other journalists were not as scathing as those employed by the *Inquirer*, but each still found opportunity to denounce Cobb. The Philadelphia correspondent to the *Sporting News* suggested that if justice were served, the pennant race would be between Philadelphia and Boston. A Detroit pennant would be bad for baseball, the writer suggested, because the Tigers "resort to foul means to win games." With a rematch scheduled in Philadelphia for mid-September, the writer even offered a veiled threat, predicting that if Cobb and the Tigers did not behave "mighty well," fans would exact revenge. The *Evening Bulletin* noted that fans were "very much wrought up over the Cobb incident" as "all kinds of stories are being flooded . . . some of which would appear to make Cobb the lowest kind of murderer." Only the more staid *Philadelphia Press* tried to quell animosity between the two teams, suggesting that true fans would forget the Cobb incident and concentrate on the game itself. "Games are never won by showing animosity towards a player, no matter what his character," the newspaper counseled.[34]

The provocative language of Philadelphia's newspapers encouraged some fans to take matters into their own hands. As the rematch approached, Cobb received over a dozen "Black Hand" letters threatening him with bodily harm if he played in the series. One assured Cobb that he would "get shot in Philadelphia"; another warned him that he would be mobbed if he ventured onto the streets alone.[35] Anti-Cobb sentiment intensified as the series began. From the moment the Tigers arrived in the City of Brotherly Love on September 16, fans hounded and harassed Cobb. Fearing for Cobb's safety, Philadelphia's police commissioner arranged a special police escort to protect Cobb as he traveled to and from the ballpark. Attendance at each game broke league records, a testament—at least in part—to how eager fans were to annoy Cobb. Vengeful fans came to the park early to claim a spot near Cobb's right-field position so they could have unobstructed access to him. To protect Cobb at the park, Athletics' officials employed nearly three hundred off-duty policemen to patrol the stands and suspended the sale of bottled beverages at the park lest fans be tempted to use them as missiles.[36] The extra security helped, but only to a point. During the first game, no one launched anything dangerous at Cobb, but many tossed straw hats and seat cushions at him as he patrolled the outfield. After the game, a wave of fans overwhelmed security and rushed toward Cobb, briefly obstructing his path to the clubhouse. Later that evening, a large crowd—perhaps several hundred strong—gathered outside Cobb's hotel in yet another act of intimidation. According to one Cobb biographer, the crowd "looked about ready to lynch him."[37]

Cobb was not lynched, but he was intimidated—at least initially. He played poorly the first game and newspaper reports agreed he looked agitated and scared. Even those most sympathetic to Cobb, the Detroit sportswriters, noted Cobb was off his game. The *Free Press* observed Cobb "was at high nervous tension and . . . in no shape to do himself justice." He went hitless, flailing at pitches that he normally let pass. While playing the outfield, he mistook a car's backfire for a gun's report and jumped "about eight feet," or so he remembered it. He was so upset, centerfielder Sam Crawford, a player who was barely speaking to Cobb at the time, shouted over a few words of encouragement to help Cobb regain his composure.[38]

After that first game, it looked to all as though Philadelphia fans had done what no one else could—intimidate Cobb. Then something remarkable happened. Cobb gathered his courage and as he did, Philadelphia fans relented, gradually but surely. As the second game ended, fans once again surrounded him as he walked off the field, but this time, a reporter observed, "not a man of the lot seemed desirous to annoy" him. Instead, several stopped to shake his hand, while others patted him on the back and offered words of praise and encouragement. *The*

Detroit News boasted that Cobb had "gone from being an object of contempt and hatred" to a "hero in the eyes of the Quaker fans in just one day." The *Detroit Free Press* crowed Philadelphia fans were "rapidly becoming friends of Cobb." By the third game, the newspaper noted that the "anti-Cobb crusade seems to have spent itself." Now, the "good-humored" fans "warmly applauded" Cobb for his aggressive play. Philadelphia dailies also noted the fans' changed response. In a self-congratulatory piece, the *Philadelphia Press* praised the local fans for acting the part of true aficionados. The *Press* noted that many recognized Cobb's "brilliant work" by greeting him with cheers each time he went to bat or made a good play. Although some booing continued, the local press noted that cheers now drowned out the jeers. Even after Cobb spiked shortstop Jack Barry in the final game—effectively ending Barry's season and possibly the Athletics' chances at the pennant—Philadelphia's dailies reported that fans refrained from booing and otherwise gave Cobb a warm reception.[39]

The Barry spiking underlines two important points regarding fan behavior during this era. First, the incident reveals—once again—that fans did not boo as a reflexive action to a designated enemy, but followed a distinctive ethos of spectatorship. In making a distinction between the Baker and Barry spikings, Philadelphia fans demonstrated an appreciation for context and intent. In their view, Cobb had not tried to hurt Barry, so he was not deserving of blame. Second, the incident reveals how eager fans were to witness dramatic exhibitions of nerve—so much so that they accepted the sacrifice of one of their own. Rather than condemn Cobb, fans showed respect for his aggressive play. They understood that men needed to take risks and that sometimes risk-taking resulted in defeat and injury. This was the cost of being a man of nerve. They refused to condemn the outcome.

In this, Cobb performed his role to perfection. By playing on, despite his obvious anxieties, he proved he was a man of courage and fortitude. In fact, Cobb made a point of confronting the home crowd head-on. After each game, he took his usual evening constitutional—even though it meant he had to walk through the large crowds that assembled outside his hotel to scare him. On the playing field, he exhibited the kind of aggressiveness and daring that had made him the talk of the game—hitting, bunting, stealing, taking the offensive to place added pressure on the opposition. He seemed to make a special point of showing Philadelphia fans that they had not gotten his goat. On more than one occasion he waded into the hostile outfield crowd to catch fly balls. When fans threw straw hats at him after he struck out, he used his bat to mutilate a few of them, as if to enfeeble their attempts to humiliate him. After the first game, he even resumed his habit of jawing with fans who hurled insults at him. Although Cobb did not have a particularly memorable series at the plate, he showed enough moxie to convince all that he had not let the fans unnerve him. Fans had come to challenge him and he stood up to them. His hard slide into Barry was the final example of this: he showed Philadelphia fans that he would not allow them to make him change his game.[40]

Ultimately, this is what Philadelphia fans wanted to see during that 1909 series. And this is why they paid to see Cobb—not merely to boo him, but to challenge him, to see him struggle, and to witness either his triumph or his failure. Midway through the series, the *Philadelphia Inquirer* said as much when it tried to explain fans' changed response to Cobb. After Cobb made an excellent play in the field on a long fly, the *Inquirer* remarked, "Cobb was right on the job, demonstrating none of the lack of nerve" that caused his "sorry showing" in the first game. Now, Cobb "was primed with ginger from the instant he trotted on the field" so much so that "even the most rabid ones warmed up to him." Equally important, fans appreciated Cobb because he appreciated them. Rather than complain about his hostile reception before and during the first game, he correctly interpreted the fans' response for what it was—a challenge to his manhood and an attempt to affect the game. He accepted the challenge by giving them what they paid for—his all-out effort to prove them wrong. In this way, he modeled the modern attributes of manliness even as he acknowledged fans' right to be active participants in the game. Thereafter, Cobb singled out Philadelphia fans as being the most abusive—although he also claimed their behavior inspired him to play "his best ball against the Athletics."[41]

Baseball fans and Cobb developed an interdependent relationship with one another: fans needed fiery players like Cobb to test raw definitions of manhood; Cobb needed the active engagement of fans to goad him to further exploits of nerve and masculinity. Theirs was a dynamic association. Each recognized that manhood was something that needed to be continuously reestablished. Whatever goodwill Philadelphia fans bestowed upon Cobb during that dramatic 1909 series was abruptly withdrawn the following summer when the two sides met again. In the midst of another pennant race, Philadelphia fans again jeered and taunted Cobb, spurred on perhaps by the city's dailies which revived their attacks on Cobb's playing style.[42] Such oscillating emotions may help to explain why one sportswriter labeled Cobb the "most unpopular popular man in baseball." After all, a good dose of his appeal came from his unpopularity. As the same writer observed, "no matter whether he comes to cheer or to jeer him, the cash customer still pays tribute for the privilege of seeing Cobb in action."[43] Neither Cobb nor the fans seemed to want it any other way.

Just how eager fans were to see Cobb at his tumultuous best is illustrated by their generally favorable response to Cobb's behavior during another infamous event in his career—his mauling of New York Highlanders' fan Claude Lucker (sometimes spelled Lueker in the press of the day). The incident occurred on May 15, 1912, the last game of a four-game series between the hometown Highlanders, as the future Yankees were then called, and the visiting Tigers. For the previous three games, Lucker and a few others sat in the grandstand, just down the line from the Detroit dugout, hurling insults at the Tigers, especially Cobb. Although Cobb had heard invective before, he found the comments of Lucker and friends especially obnoxious.[44] At the top of the fourth inning, things came to a head. As Cobb jogged to the dugout, Lucker mocked him for a blunder he had made earlier in the game. In response, Cobb made a disparaging remark about Lucker's sister. Lucker retaliated by shouting a slur that implied Cobb was of mixed blood, the product of an affair between his mother and a black man. When Cobb sat down, teammates told Cobb he would be "a gutless no-good" if he let the insult pass. This seems to have been enough to ignite the outfielder. He bolted from the dugout, leaped the fence that separated fans from the field, scaled through the crowd—twelve rows deep according to one account—and confronted Lucker. "Even then," Cobb recalled, "he insulted me again." With that, Cobb hit Lucker in the face, knocked him down, and kicked him with his spiked shoes. Though Lucker could not fully defend himself, having lost parts of both hands in an industrial accident less than a year earlier, Cobb continued the assault. When fans pleaded for mercy, shouting "Don't kick him! He is a cripple. He has no hands!" Cobb roared back, "I don't care if the ——

has no feet!"—or words to that effect—and pummeled him some more. He stopped only when several of his teammates and the umpires pulled him away. He was immediately ejected from the game.[45]

From the first, most fans showed support for Cobb. According to the *New York American*, "When Cobb walked off the field, the few boos that greeted him were drowned in vigorous applause." After Cobb left, several fans protested to security guards that Lucker should at least be expelled from the park, too (which he summarily was). Later, fans defended Cobb, telling reporters that he had given "the fan ample warning of the impending assault, but [Lucker] refused to give heed."[46] Public support continued in the days that followed. In his final autobiography, Cobb boasted that he received hundreds of letters from New York fans, many of whom claimed to have been at the game, in support of his actions. Even the nationally syndicated comic strip *Mutt and Jeff* expressed support for Cobb. A strip published a few weeks after the incident featured Mutt scheming "to be a hero like Ty Cobb." While playing the outfield for the local team, he instructs Jeff to harass him from his place in the stands. "Call me a big stiff," he tells Jeff, "and I'll come up after you like Ty Cobb did. I won't hurt you. I'll only make a bluff."

Perhaps the most revealing example of the public's general support for Cobb came in a poll conducted by the *New York American* a few days after the incident. Using secret ballots, the newspaper asked fans entering Highland Park whether Cobb "was right or wrong in attacking a fan." Although every major newspaper in town denounced Cobb, the poll revealed that nearly three-fourths of those who voted (3,013 to 1,167) backed Cobb. Several weeks later when Cobb returned to New York, the *Detroit Free Press* reported that fans greeted him with a "great ovation . . . before and during the game on every instance he presented himself."[47]

Fans' support for Cobb after the Lucker incident reflected an abiding appreciation for Cobb's prerogatives as a man. Yes, Cobb had allowed a fan's comments to get to him, but most believed that his behavior was entirely warranted given the nature of the insult. Most early twentieth-century white Americans were extremely sensitive to issues of race. White men equated their skin color with manliness, civilization, and authority. When Lucker questioned Cobb's racial purity, he did more than simply insult Cobb's mother's morality; he questioned

Figure 7.2. Bud Fisher gives his take on Ty Cobb's altercation with New York Highlander fan Claude Lucker in his syndicated cartoon strip, *Mutt and Jeff*. As Mutt explains, Cobb was a "hero" worthy of emulation for pulverizing Lucker. *Source*: Illustration appeared in the *Cleveland Plain Dealer*, May 22, 1912, 11.

Cobb's claims to the very essence of his self-identity and racial superiority. Although some, like Christy Mathewson, suggested a true man ignored such epithets, many felt otherwise. They feared that over-civilization and the luxuries of modernity had left the white race unable to assert its authority over others. Unless white men acted decisively, they would be overrun by the hordes of African Americans, Asians, and Southern Europeans who threatened to overtake their "White Man's Country." Cobb's willingness to take matters into his own hands demonstrated that he knew how to defend himself and his identity. As Red Hoff, then a twenty-one-year-old Highlanders' pitcher, remembered it, Cobb "went into his stands and did his duty."[48]

Class considerations may have also factored into some fans' support for Cobb. Accounts friendly to Cobb colored their descriptions of Lucker to emphasize his lower-class roots, calling him a "rowdy," a "low life," and a "Bowery type." Conversely, these same sources referred to the fans who refused to follow Lucker's lead as "the better type of people," "the better class in the grandstand and bleachers," and "decent men and women." Some journalists also made special mention of Lucker's clothing to define his social status, noting that he wore an alpaca sweater, the outerwear of choice for working-class men at the time. Some accounts noted that Cobb identified Lucker by his sweater, a hint that the working-class Lucker stood out in the sea of middle-class men who typically sat in the grandstands. One account even noted that Cobb yelled, "Go back to your waiter's job!" to Lucker.[49] Finally, news accounts noted Lucker's affiliation with Tammany Hall, a political organization long associated with lower-class ethnic demagoguery in the eyes of nativist middle-class Americans. Some reports made this case explicit.[50] Perhaps Cobb's behavior resonated with white middle-class spectators who felt similarly besieged by the seemingly intractable assertiveness of lower-class groups—not only at the ballpark but in all forms of social exchange. For a generation of middle- and upper-class men who were eager to reestablish a stronger hand in municipal affairs and defeat what they considered to be illegitimate sources of power, Cobb's actions matched their desire to act decisively and forcefully in the face of challenges from below. No, they could not physically thrash their adversaries, but they probably enjoyed the vicarious thrill of watching Cobb do it. Men who were obsessed with the loss of vitality and nerve force may have seen Cobb's actions as a quick and sure tonic.

This is speculative to be sure, but the point remains that most New York baseball fans—like baseball fans across the country—supported Cobb despite knowing of his penchant for physical aggression. At least tacitly, such fans aligned themselves with a larger cultural movement that preached the productive powers of violence for a just cause. No doubt, many Americans believed that when Cobb mauled Lucker he simply put into action ideas that had been percolating in various forums for the previous decade or so. That Cobb acted spontaneously only heightened the dramatic heroism of his act. Yet baseball fans often wanted it both ways: displays of manly self-assertion and nerve coupled with an appreciation for order, self-control, and decorum. The Lucker-Cobb incident created an opportunity to express this. Yes, most patrons wanted to boo and to cheer, but they also wanted clear limits as to how far one could go. Hurling insults at players was one thing, but Lucker crossed a line when he used racial slurs.

Was the public troubled by the viciousness of Cobb's response? Certainly, some fans—a quarter of those polled—disapproved of his actions. Many of these probably agreed with the position laid out in an editorial in the *New York Times*. The "sole underlying cause" of the entire episode, the *Times* warned, reflected "the growing resentment of all authority and discipline throughout the world" and warned that support for Cobb might lead to a breakdown in public order.[51] Many of those who sided with Cobb may have had similar concerns, but were reassured by the limited scope of the assault and the subsequent actions of league officials. Both Lucker and Cobb were eventually forced to leave the ballpark and American League president Ban Johnson immediately suspended Cobb. The next day, Cobb issued an apology through the press. Appearing chastened and contrite, he stated that he only acted when the Hilltop Park police refused to protect him. In other words, the rule of law and Cobb's subsequent contrition may have assured many fans that the conventional standards of ballpark decorum were not in danger.[52]

Perhaps most fans agreed with the opinion *Baseball Magazine* offered a month after the incident. In its summary assessment, the editors suggested that Cobb only did what was "natural" and "only such as might have been expected from any man of hot blooded tendencies." True, Cobb needed to be punished for taking matters into his own hands. That is why baseball needed Ban Johnson—to enforce "law and organization" by suspending Cobb for ten games. Yet far from censuring Cobb, the magazine praised him, claiming that his behavior "was on the whole creditable to the most brilliant player the game has ever known." Above all, he had proved himself to be the "the champion of individual rights," a necessary counterpoint to Johnson's passion for order and discipline. According to the magazine, society needed rebels like Cobb to goad established institutions. To spectators who experienced overly managed and depersonalized work experiences, this interpretation must have had a certain appeal. Cobb acted for himself and braved the consequences. To these fans, Cobb was as exciting and unpredictable as the heroes of popular literature, but had the advantage of being an authentic person whom they could watch and even test for the price of a ball game ticket.[53]

Finally, Cobb's Southern origins may have also played into fans' acceptance of his aggressive behavior. Perhaps more than any other player in either league, Cobb was identified with his place of birth. The nicknames he received from the press reflect this. Although most commonly called the Georgia Peach—or Peach, for short—the press also referred to him as the Georgian, the Southerner, the Royston Flash, the Dixie Demon, the Dixie Hero, the Jewel of Georgia, and countless other nicknames that drew attention to his birthplace. Their attention to Cobb's origins was constant and pervasive. Even the most common of sports articles—game summaries, for example—used Cobb's various monikers interchangeably with his name and did so far more frequently than for any other player on the field. No doubt, the press believed they honored Cobb by offering these sobriquets. But the constant references to his Southern roots also marked Cobb as different and unique, as if there was no other Georgian or Southerner in the league. Southern ballplayers were rare, but not that rare.

In fact, Americans' interest in Cobb's Southern roots was part of a broader cultural trend. Beginning in the late nineteenth century, Northerners became enthralled with the South as a region. To many Northerners, the South conjured up exotic images that contrasted sharply with their modern world of factories, skyscrapers, and congested city streets. Bestselling novels by Thomas Dixon and Thomas Nelson Page presented the American South as a land of chivalry, Old World grace and honor, frontier gallantry, and heroic individualism. In contrast to the North, but much like that other region of popular fantasy, the American West, the South seemed like the sort of place where a man could still be a man. Concomitantly, these authors, along with Owen Wister in his wildly popular *The Virginian*, offered a new type of hero: the Southerner. This new archetype was nearly always aristocratic by nature if not by birth, fiercely independent, courageous, proud, tempestuous, and determined to mete out justice in even the most dangerous of circumstances.

Coincidently, the same year that Cobb began his major league career, Dixon offered the most evocative rendering of this new hero in his best-selling novel, *The Clansman: An Historical Romance of the Ku Klux Klan*. In the story, Colonel Ben Cameron, a dashing Confederate veteran and scion of a great Southern family, nearly single-handedly redeems the white population of South Carolina from the perils and follies of Negro Rule by leading the Ku Klux Klan in revolt. As Grand Dragon of the Realm, Cameron oversaw the lynching of an African American rapist, the summary execution of three of his accomplices, the disarming of the entire local Union regiment, the brutal whipping and forced eviction of all Republican leaders in the state, and the forced disenfranchisement of all African Americans. Dixon presented Cameron as a gallant figure—the "Hero of Piedmont"—for he was brave, loving, and utterly devoted to his race and region. The novel quickly became a best-seller. Almost immediately, Dixon revised the novel into a play and it toured the nation in various forms for several years. In 1915, the film version, *The Birth of a Nation*, became the first modern blockbuster, earning $10 million in its initial release and another $40 million over the next thirty-five years. This made it the highest grossing film prior to the release of *Gone With The Wind*, another film that romanticized the South and its swashbuckling and independent heroes. Obviously, Dixon's *Clansman* resonated with many Americans.[54]

So far as we know, Cobb was not a member of the Klan, but his resemblance to the fictional Cameron is striking. One might even argue that Cobb was baseball's version of the valiant Cameron. This seems to be how many journalists saw it. Though journalists did not compare Cobb to Cameron, they often portrayed Cobb much as Dixon portrayed Cameron: impetuous, impassioned, vengeful, and daring. Those who offered biographical information on Cobb invariably attributed much of Cobb's character to the culture in which he was born. Cobb, these accounts claimed, ran wild as a youth. According to one of the most elaborate—and romanticized—profiles of Cobb's Southern roots, Cobb was "a constant continual scrapper" who "possessed an insatiable desire to play ball" and fight nearly anyone in sight. Happily, the account claimed, fighting and baseball were wedded in the rural South. Because the Southerner could not tolerate losing, a "battle royal . . . red with hot blood" of vengeance followed nearly every game. Although Cobb was born with "animal spirits" which often rose to a "concert pitch," he was no barbarian. He was much "too thoughtful of the Caucasian race to pummel the countenance of a white boy"; he thus made do by "venting his spleen on the ebony 'pickaninnies' of the surrounding plantations."[55]

Sportswriters invariably claimed that the adult Ty was deeply wedded to the South of his youth. Writing for *Baseball Magazine*, F. C. Lane visited Cobb at his Augusta home prior to the 1916 season. He presented Cobb as a man of remarkable independence. He kept no regular hours and filled his day with a mix of both leisure activities (hunting, golf, and raising dogs were favorite pastimes) and tending to his various business ventures. During his short visit, Lane followed as Cobb breezed through town. The excursion had the feel of a grand procession as Cobb stopped every few minutes to chat with friends, neighbors, and people he barely knew. Later, Lane and Cobb sat down in Cobb's trophy room for a wide-ranging conversation. Cobb told Lane he was "particularly anxious" that his son Ty Junior not "become a mollycoddle." Cobb explained that after he witnessed Junior fail to stand his ground in a dispute with an older boy, he took his son aside and warned him, "Now that boy may be older than you but he is no bigger. He has insulted you and if you don't go out and lick him, I will lick you."[56] Such were the concerns of a Southern man of honor. Through this vignette, Lane made clear that true primal manhood still held sway in the South. For the same reason, journalists, players, and fans often linked Cobb's violent propensities to his Southern roots. Nearly every sportswriter who spent any time with Cobb linked his mercurial temperament to his roots and used phrases like "hot Southern blood," "fiery Southern blood," "hot-tempered Georgia boy," "fighting Georgian," "Georgia firebrand," and so forth. Many Northerners found this identification fascinating, exotic, and alluring.[57]

The public persona that the media crafted for Cobb—with Cobb's cooperation—was both complex and contradictory. On the one hand, Cobb seemed the ideal of modern manhood—cool, intellectually agile, calculating, a devotee of scientific and systematic analysis. On the other, he often acted as modernity's antithesis—prone to violent rages, incapable of following orders or conforming to other people's rules. Conveniently for Cobb, the early twentieth century was an age that was unusually receptive to worshipping a man who evinced this sort of duality. G. Stanley Hall, the father of American psychology had long encouraged civilized men to nurture their savage natures to ward off the feminizing influences of over-civilization. The heroes of popular fiction—Wister's Virginian, Dixon's Ben Cameron, Burroughs's Tarzan, London's canine protagonists in *White Fang* and *Call of the Wild*—also balance elements of savagery and nobility. In politics, Teddy Roosevelt offered the living embodiment of such a man. At various points in his life, Roosevelt played the role of Harvard pugilist, Western frontiersman, Rough Rider, political and social reformer, doting father, statesman, African big game hunter, and Amazon explorer. In these various incarnations, Roosevelt offered Americans a new model of manhood that infused the civilized with the primitive in ways that could only have given anxious men new hope for the future.

Cobb did not replace Roosevelt as the face of hypermasculinity. Probably no one could do that. But Cobb did give American men a slight variation of the theme, a presentation of manhood that was rawer, more visceral, and less scripted. Perhaps even more important, Cobb was more accessible than Roosevelt. Roosevelt's manly demonstrations occurred in remote locales—the West, the Amazon, Africa, the White House. Cobb used the very public medium of the ballpark. Moreover, by engaging the crowd, Cobb gave fans an opportunity to play an active role in his masculine performances. They became part of the great battle of wits and nerve. This meant, of course, that fans did more than experience Cobb's manhood vicariously; by their active encouragement and engagement, they performed their manhood as much as their idol. That is why Cobb was the most popular player of his day.

Cobb retained his hold upon the public well into his baseball career. In some respects, the apex occurred toward the end of the 1918 season when he very publicly enlisted in the military to fight in World War I. During the first months of the season, league officials and the magnates had tried desperately to protect professional baseball from military mobilization. Their objectives were completely economic—they wanted the profits from a full season of play. Their efforts came to naught, however, when Secretary of War Newton D. Baker ruled in late July that because professional baseball was not essential to the morale of the country, baseball players could be drafted. After Baker's announcement, ballplayers began to enlist by the dozens. Many of these hoped to find safe and easy positions in shipyards and factories where they hoped to ride out the war playing ball for industrial teams, under the pretense of boosting morale.[58]

Meanwhile, all eyes riveted on Cobb. He was the game's biggest draw and best player—well on his way to his second straight batting title and eleventh in twelve years. A news report prior to the 1918 season suggested he was worth $150,000 to major league baseball, more than seven times his actual salary.[59] From the start, Cobb's response to the war set him apart from many of his peers. A supporter of President Wilson and an enthusiast for military history, Cobb supported the war from the start, but was not sure whether or not he should enlist. Because of his age (he was then thirty-one years old) and family responsibilities (a wife and three children), he originally requested—and received—a deferment. The decision did not sit well with him. Weeks before Secretary Baker's decision, Cobb told Wilson's private secretary Joseph Tumulty during a visit to the White House that he felt "mean every time he looks over the American casualty list." For this reason, he announced that he would quit baseball at the end of the season for the duration of the war so that he could "do my duty to my country in the best way possible." By the time the Tigers returned to Washington a month later, Cobb had decided what that duty would be. In mid-August he visited the War Department to take his army physical and apply for a commission in the Chemical Warfare Service (CWS). A week-and-a-half later, word came that the army had accepted his request and ordered him to report for service as a captain in the CWS on October 1.[60]

Cobb's announcement further solidified him as the game's preeminent symbol of manhood. Americans well knew that the CWS was among the most dangerous—and most glamorous—branches of military service, traits that fit perfectly with their impression of Cobb. In the days that followed Cobb's announcement he ably lived up to Americans' expectations of heroic manhood. During a Savings Stamps Drive between games of a doubleheader at the Polo Grounds, Cobb was asked to say a few words. From the roof of the visitor's clubhouse,

Cobb formally announced that he had been called to service and that he did not expect to return to baseball once the war was over. He then made what the *New York Times* called a "simple, impressive plea for the stamp drive." He told the crowd that he had just purchased $250 of war stamps himself and urged everyone to "buy and buy and buy." During the next week, he finished the war-induced abbreviated season with a flourish. In the first game of the New York doubleheader, he drove in four of Detroit's five runs with two hits, one a home run. A few days later in St. Louis, he made nine hits in three games and even pitched a couple innings as a stunt. He ended the season going three for five in both games of a doubleheader against Chicago. The media was wholly enraptured. For Cobb's final game at the Polo Grounds, the *New York Times* announced in its headline "Cobb Exit is Made in Blaze of Glory: Georgia Peach Plays Final Games at Polo Grounds—Is Bound for France." A few days later, the *Chicago Tribune* offered a headline, "Salute!" in bold block capital letters, followed by the subheading "Ty Cobb Commissioned Captain in Chemical Warfare Service." A later report from the *Tribune* praised Cobb for taking a position that involved "real" work and was not a "bombproof" job. A spokesman for the military noted that Cobb and other baseball men (including Branch Rickey and Christy Mathewson) were chosen for the CWS because they were "strong robust fellows" who "have good average common sense" and were eager to serve. The *Pawtucket* (Rhode Island) *Times* showed a silhouette of Cobb at bat with the bold heading "Cobb Goes to Bat For the Starry Flag." When Major League Baseball verified at the end of August that Cobb had won the batting title, some newspapers referred to the star outfielder as "Captain Cobb" in reference to his military rank. For once, the media identified Cobb for something other than his Southernness.[61] Subsequent news reports in most major urban dailies followed Cobb's travels carefully, offering updates on when he arrived for duty, where he trained, when he traveled to Europe, and when he arrived in Europe. Word even arrived that Cobb's advice on conditioning had been enthusiastically endorsed and adopted by the Air Service. Along the way, sportswriters reminded the reading public that Cobb was eager to see action, had opted for a branch of the military that promised to send him to the frontlines fastest and to which there was "actual risk of life." Moreover, Cobb risked losing his great speed by serving in a ground war, and might not return to the United States for several years—far past his prime as a ballplayer. In sum, he was risking his life, his livelihood, and his star appeal for the country—a true patriot.[62]

Alas, Cobb never experienced the thrill—or carnage—of battle that he had been "promised." "Through no fault of his own," the *Detroit Free Press* merrily reported, the "war fell flat before the diamond star could be attacked." If only the war had lasted another month, the newspaper mused, Cobb might have become part of a "unit in the vast army that left this country to fight for democracy." Even so, he returned a "bigger hero than ever" for volunteering his services for so dangerous a mission.[63] In fact, Cobb would never be more popular, never held in such near universal high esteem. As fate would have it, this idol of American manhood was done in not by the "Hun," but by the Babe.

NOTES

1. *Boston Herald*, September 17, 1915, 1, 6; *Boston Gazette*, September 17, 1915, 8; *Washington Post*, September 17, 1915, 8.

2. *Detroit Free Press*, September 17, 1915, 12; *Detroit Free Press*, September 18, 1915, 8; *Detroit Free Press*, September 19, 1915, 22.

3. Harry Casey, "The Pivot of the Baseball Diamond: Thrilling Plays Which Center About First Base," *Baseball Magazine* (October 1911): 33–34.

4. *The Sporting News* (December 26, 1912): 8; "Editorial," *Baseball Magazine* (May 1916): 29; *Sporting Life* (September 21, 1912): 22; *Detroit News*, May 19, 1912, S2.

5. "Small People with Great Names," *Woman's Home Companion* 45 (December 1918): 43–46; "A New Ty Cobb Story," *Baseball Magazine* (August 1916): 114; *Sporting Life* (May 13, 1911): 11.

6. *Detroit Free Press*, May 19, 1912, 2; *Sporting News* (November 11, 1926): 2.

7. J. Ed. Grillo, "World Famous Fans," *Baseball Magazine* (September 1911): 8; *New York Times*, August 27, 1916, SM13; *Sporting News* (August 9, 1923): 1; *Sporting News* (May 15, 1924): 3; *New York Times*, May 15, 1914, 24; "Ty Cobb as Model for a Dancer," *Washington Post*, September 26, 1915, ES2.

8. Charles C. Alexander, *Ty Cobb* (New York: Oxford University Press, 1984), 125, 129–30, 136, 227; Charles Leerhsen, *Ty Cobb: A Terrible Beauty* (New York: Simon and Schuster, 2015), 183, 253, 268, 320.

9. John Evers, "'The Rowdy Ball Players' Side of the Argument," *Baseball Magazine* (November 1916): 33; Louisville newspaper reprinted in *Detroit Free Press*, November 21, 1909, 19; *Detroit Free Press*, September 25, 1921, E1.

10. *Detroit Free Press*, September 22, 1913, 8; see also *Chicago Defender*, May 27, 1911, 6; *Detroit Free Press*, September 22, 1913, 8; *Detroit Free Press*, September 24, 1913, 13.

11. "Our Letter Box," *Baseball Magazine* (November 1916): 92; "The New York-Atlanta Good Roads Tour," *Horseless Age: The Automobile Trade Magazine* 24 (October 27, 1909): 473–77; *Washington Post*, November 28, 1909, 2–3; *Sporting News* (December 16, 1909): 5; *New York Times*, October 28, 1909, 10; R. F. Potts, "A Baseball Outing," *Baseball Magazine* (January 1916): 108.

12. *Sporting Life* (October 16, 1909): 7; *Detroit Free Press*, October 9, 1909, 8; *Washington Post*, July 19, 1914, 9; *Detroit Free Press*, June 20, 1915, 15B.

13. "Sidelights on Ty Cobb," *Baseball Magazine* (March 1912): 54; *Sporting News* (September 26, 1912): 5; F. C. Lane, "A Day with Ty Cobb," *Baseball Magazine* (April 1916): 47–58.

14. Ty Cobb, *Busting 'Em and Other Big League Stories* (1914; repr., Jefferson, NC: McFarland, 2003), 19, 21; Lane, "A Day with Ty Cobb," 53.

15. John Sheridan, "Back of Home Plate," *Sporting News* (January 21, 1926). Literature that identified Cobb as a role model for adults includes: "Editorial: Playing the Game," *Rotarian* 7 (October 1915): 327–28; "Editorial: The Game of Baseball," *Rotarian* 8 (June 1916): 439–40; George McPherson Hunter, *Morning Faces* (New York: George H. Doran Company, 1918), 184; J. D. Dillon, "Two Queens in the Kitchen: Milady and a Gas Range," *American Gas Engineering Journal* 116 (March 4, 1922): 209; Norval Abiel Hawkins, *Certain Success*, 3rd ed. (Detroit: Self-published, 1920), 109, 164. Examples of juvenile periodicals that presented Cobb as a role model include: "The Georgia Peach," *Youth's Companion* 49 (December 9, 1926): 100; Frank Weaver, "He Takes Care Of Himself," *Young Men* 47 (1921): 344; Walter Camp, "Batter Up," *Boy's Life* (July 1924): 7. For an intriguing analysis of Cobb in contemporary juvenile literature, see Ted Hathaway, "Cobb as Role Model: Ty Cobb in Juvenile Periodical Literature: 1907–1929," *Nine: A Journal of Baseball History and* Culture 11 (Spring 2003): 64–72.

16. Prosper Buranelli, "Ty Cobb Talks About Baseball," *Detroit Free Press*, September 25, 1921, E1; Cobb, *Busting 'Em*. Cobb, with the aid of various ghostwriters, shared his baseball wisdom in a number of magazines and newspapers; I have cited many of his pieces elsewhere in this monograph.

17. For a survey of success literature in the early twentieth century, see Tom Pendergast, *Creating the Modern Man: American Magazines and Consumer Culture* (Columbia: University of Missouri Press, 2000), 111–66. Examples of published success maxims include: "Business Maxims of A. T. Stewart," *Chicago Tribune*, September 12, 1909, E8; Edward H. Doyle, "Business Maxims and Suggestions Worthwhile," *Bankers' Magazine* 98 (March 1919): 329; "Editorial: Playing the Game," *American Architect* 117 (June 23, 1920): 791.

18. "Why Cobb Remains at the Top," *Sporting Life* (July 24, 1915): 2; F. C. Lane, "Ty Cobb, The King of Ball Players," *Baseball Magazine* (July 1911): 3; Tyrus Raymond Cobb, "Is There Any Luck in Baseball?" *Baseball Magazine* (July 1911): 11.

19. Cobb, *Busting 'Em*, 17, 26; "Sidelights on Ty Cobb," 56; Grantland Rice cited in *Sporting News* (June 12, 1924): 4; Ty Cobb, "Introduction," in M. G. Bonner, *The Big Baseball Book for Boys* (Springfield, MA: McLouglin Bros., 1931), unpaginated. For discussions of the medical understanding of nerve in the early twentieth century, see Gail Bederman, *Manliness and Civilization: A Cultural History of Gender and Race in the United States* (Chicago: University of Chicago Press, 1995), 77–79, 92–101; Jackson Lears, *Rebirth of a Nation: The Making of Modern America, 1877–1920* (New York: HarperCollins, 2009), 7–8, 45–46; Tom Lutz, *American Nervousness* (1903; repr., Ithaca, NY: Cornell University Press, 1991), passim.

20. Hughie Jennings, "My Opinion of Ty Cobb: How the Greatest Player in the History of the Game Looks to His Own Manager," *Baseball Magazine* (March 1912): 16.

21. *New York Times*, June 5, 1915, 10.

22. Edward Lyell Fox, "The Hard Job of a Baseball Star," *Outing Magazine* 60 (1912): 359–69; Billy Evans, "Fans Look for Star Players in All Games," *New York Times*, March 16, 1913, S4. See also C. E. Van Loan, "Baseball as the Bleachers Like It," *Outing Magazine* 54 (September 1909): 650; Grantland Rice, "The Grand Old Batting Eye," *McClure's Magazine* 45 (June 1915): 19.

23. Sverre O. Braathen, *Ty Cobb: The Idol of Baseball Fandom* (New York: Avondale Press, 1928), 138.

24. Cobb, *Busting 'Em*, 31; *Washington Post*, June 9, 1911, 8.

25. *New York Times*, December 18, 1925, 27.

26. *Washington Post*, September 12, 1915, S2.

27. *Chicago Daily Tribune*, August 25, 1912, J10; Fox, "Hard Job of a Baseball Star," 361.

28. Cobb, *Busting 'Em*, 23–24; *Pittsburgh Press*, December 4, 1911, S1.

29. *Sporting News* (September 11, 1919): 3.

30. For gender as performance, see Judith Butler, *Gender Trouble: Feminism and the Subversion of Identity* (revised edition; New York: Routledge, 1999), 163–80.

31. Sociologists have identified the desire for stimulation as a primary motive for sport spectatorship, particularly in modern, industrial societies. See Daniel Wann, Merrill J. Melnick, Gordon W. Russell, and Dale G. Pease, *Sports Fans: The Psychology and Social Impact of Spectators* (New York: Routledge, 2001), 38–40, 207–208; Norbert Elias and Eric Dunning, *The Quest for Excitement: Sport and Leisure in the Civilizing Process* (Oxford: Basil Blackwell, 1986). For an explanation of symbolic inversion, see Barbara A. Babcock, ed., *The Reversible World: Symbolic Inversion in Art and Society* (Ithaca, NY: Cornell University Press, 1978). Elliott J. Gorn, *The Manly Art: Bare-Knuckle Prize Fighting in America* (Ithaca, NY: Cornell University Press, 1986), 136–44; and Ted Ownby, *Subduing Satan: Religion, Recreation, and Manhood in the Rural South, 1865–1920* (Chapel Hill: University of North Carolina Press, 1990), 3, 90, 95–99 find evidence of inversion rituals in male leisure culture at about the same time Cobb dominated baseball.

32. *St. Louis Post-Dispatch*, April 22, 1909, 36; *St. Louis Post-Dispatch*, May 1, 1909, 6; *St. Louis Republican*, May 30, 1909, 6; *Sporting News* (August 26, 1909): 3; Alexander, *Ty Cobb*, 77, 79. Connie Mack made the accusation that Cobb threatened to spike the Athletics' second baseman, shortstop, and third baseman. See *Philadelphia Evening Bulletin*, August 27, 1909.

33. Alexander, *Ty Cobb*, 81; *Philadelphia Evening Bulletin*, August 27, 1909; *Philadelphia Inquirer*, August 27, 1909.

34. *Philadelphia Inquirer*, August 26, 1909; *Philadelphia Inquirer*, August 30, 1909; *Philadelphia Inquirer*, September 5, 1909; *Philadelphia Evening Bulletin*, August 29, 1909; *Sporting News* (September 9, 1909); *Philadelphia Evening Bulletin*, August 27, 1909; *Philadelphia Press*, August 30, 1909.

35. *Detroit Free Press*, September 17, 1909, 8; *Philadelphia Evening Bulletin*, September 16, 1909.

36. Alexander, *Ty Cobb*, 81; Ty Cobb, with Al Stump, *My Life in Baseball* (1961; repr., Lincoln, NE: Bison Books, 1993), 116–18; *Detroit Free Press*, September 16, 1909, September 21, 1909, 1, 8; *Detroit News*, September 15, 1909, 10; *Detroit News*, September 21, 1909, 10; *Philadelphia Evening Bulletin*, September 16, 1909.

37. *Detroit Free Press*, September 17, 1909, 1, 8; *Philadelphia Press*, September 17, 1909; *Philadelphia Inquirer*, September 17, 1909; Alexander, *Ty Cobb*, 81.

38. *Detroit Free Press*, September 17, 1909, 1, 8; *Detroit News*, September 17, 1909, 1; Cobb, *Busting 'Em*, 26.

39. *Philadelphia Press*, September 18, 1909; *Philadelphia Press*, September 19, 1909; *Philadelphia Press*, September 21, 1909; *Philadelphia Evening Bulletin*, September 18, 1909; *Philadelphia Evening Bulletin*, September 21, 1909; *Philadelphia Inquirer*, September 18, 1909; *Philadelphia Inquirer*, September 21, 1909; *Detroit Free Press*, September 18, 1909, 1, 8; *Detroit Free Press*, September 21, 1909, 8; *Detroit News*, September 18, 1909, 10; September 21, 1909, 8.

40. *Detroit Free Press*, September 17, 1909, 1, 8; Alexander, *Ty Cobb*, 82.

41. *Philadelphia Inquirer*, September 18, 1909; Cobb, *Busting 'Em*, 26, 30–31.

42. *Philadelphia Inquirer*, July 29, 1910, 10; *Philadelphia Inquirer*, August 1, 1910, 10.

43. "In the Press Box with Baxter," *Washington Post*, July 10, 1924, s3.

44. Alexander, *Ty Cobb*, 105; Fred Lieb, *Baseball As I Have Known It* (1977; repr., Lincoln, NE: Bison Books), 59.

45. Ty Cobb, edited by William R. Cobb, *Memoirs of Twenty Years in Baseball* (Marietta, GA: Self-published, 2002), 93; Cobb, *My Life*, 131–32; Leerhsen, *Ty Cobb*, 259.

46. *New York American*, May 16, 1912; *New York American*, May 16, 1912; *Detroit Free Press*, May 16, 1912, 10, 11, estimated that about 80 percent of the fans in attendance cheered Cobb as he walked off the field three innings after he was ejected.

47. *Detroit Free Press*, May 16, 1912, 10; *Detroit Free Press*, May 27, 1912, 10; *Detroit Free Press*, July 10, 1912, 10; *Cleveland Plain Dealer*, May 22, 1912, 11; *New York American*, May 21, 1912.

48. Bederman, *Manliness and Civilization*, 1–5, 10–15; Kimmel, *Manhood in America*, 57–62, 80–84; Gorn, *The Manly Art*, 192–94; John F. Kasson, *Houdini, Tarzan, and the Perfect Man: The White Male Body and the Challenge of Modernity in America* (New York: Oxford University Press, 2001), 11–12, 46–50; Donald J. Mrozek, *Sport and American Mentality, 1880–1910* (Knoxville: University of Tennessee Press, 1983), 24–26; Clifford Putney, *Muscular Christianity: Manhood and Sports in Protestant America, 1880–1920* (Cambridge, MA: Harvard University Press, 2003), 25–33; John Higham, *Strangers in the Land: Patterns of American Nativism, 1860–1925* (revised edition; New York: Atheneum Press, 1967), 142–44; Red Hoff quoted in Richard Bak, *Peach: Ty Cobb in His Time and Ours* (Ann Arbor: Sports Media Group, 2005), 93–94. Three years earlier, a writer for the *Philadelphia Inquirer* made the point explicit, though sardonically. He suggested that Cobb meet heavyweight boxing champion Jack Johnson in the ring, but be allowed to keep

his spikes on. "This ought to settle things for a bit," the writer suggested. "The unrest among Anglo-Saxons is getting serious." *Philadelphia Inquirer*, October 21, 1909, 8.

49. *New York Times*, May 19, 1912, 1; *Philadelphia Inquirer*, May 18, 1912, 10; *Sporting News* (May 30, 1912): 4; *Detroit Free Press*, May 19, 1912, 10; "Ty Cobb vs. Ban Johnson," *Baseball Magazine* (July 1912): 12.

50. *Sporting News* (May 30, 1912): 4; *Detroit News*, May 18, 1912, 8.

51. *New York Times*, May 19, 1912, 12; *Sporting News* (May 30, 1912): 4.

52. *New York American*, May 21, 1912, 1; *Detroit Free Press*, May 21, 1912, 10.

53. *New York Times*, May 19, 1912, 12; *Sporting News* (May 30, 1912): 4.

54. Thomas Dixon, *The Clansman: An Historical Romance of the Ku Klux Klan* (New York: A Wessels Co., 1907); Joel Williamson, *The Crucible of Race: Black-White Relations in the American South Since Emancipation* (New York: Oxford University Press, 1984), 172–76.

55. Howell Foreman, "When Ty Cobb Was A Boy," *Baseball Magazine* (March 1912): 1–3.

56. F. C. Lane, "A Day with Ty Cobb," *Baseball Magazine* (April 1916): 56.

57. *Sporting Life* (May 25, 1912): 1; C. E. Van Loan, "Baseball as the Bleachers Like It," *Outing Magazine* 54 (September 1909): 650; *Detroit Free Press*, August 17, 1922, 12; Edward Lyell Fox, "Finding the Stars of Baseball," *Outing Magazine* 62 (August 1913): 536; *Sporting Life* (August 8, 1908): 7; John Kieran, "Sports of the Times," *New York Times*, February 10, 1927, 19; *New York Times*, May 15, 1922, 20.

58. Harold Seymour, *Baseball: The Golden Age* (New York: Oxford University Press, 1971), 247, 255.

59. *Detroit Free Press*, February 12, 1918, 10; Alexander, *Ty Cobb*, 139–41.

60. *Detroit Free Press*, July 14, 1918, 15; *Detroit Free Press*, August 28, 1918, 9.

61. *New York Times*, August 25, 1918, 25; *Chicago Tribune*, August 28, 1918, 7; *Chicago Tribune*, September 10, 1918, 11; *Pawtucket Times*, August 29, 1918, 4.

62. *Detroit Free Press*, October 19, 1918, 10; *Sporting News* (November 14, 1918): 2; *Detroit Free Press*, December 17, 1918, 13.

63. *Detroit Free Press*, November 18, 1018, 11; *Detroit Free Press*, December 17, 1918, 13.

8

COBB IN THE AGE OF RUTH

The military transport that brought Captain Ty Cobb home arrived in Hoboken, New Jersey, on December 16, 1918. Although most of the transport's 10,000 plus passengers were battle-hardened soldiers and sailors, the dozen or so journalists in attendance focused attention on Cobb. "Ty Cobb came home on the biggest boat afloat and still was able to hog all the notices," a reporter for the *New York Tribune* marveled. That made him "the undisputed champion of the publicity league, quite as much as in baseball." The reporter had it wrong. For once, Cobb tried to diminish his celebrity, not advertise it. As the ship's most famous passenger, Cobb might have milked the event by deftly grafting his fame to his shipmates' heroics. During the voyage, Cobb had given a stirring speech in which he promised to treat all his fellow passengers to a game at the Polo Grounds and to visit the wounded at Walter Reed Hospital the next time he was in Washington. Surely, he could have made mention of these gestures if he hungered for notoriety. Or he might have explained how eager he was to return to the grand game of baseball. Rather than seize the moment, however, Cobb demurred. Even though his arrival was front-page news, he barely spoke to the press. What he did say was not what his audience wanted to hear. He waved off inquiries about the coming season, claiming he was "tired" of the game. He even hinted at retirement. "I've had fifteen years of it, and I want to quit while I'm still good," he explained.[1] Even here—in this highly visible moment, brimming with patriotic possibilities—Cobb preferred to go his own way, even if it meant forfeiting some of his hard-earned popularity. No doubt, Cobb realized he could be cavalier; he was the game's greatest player, after all. His hold upon the baseball public was such that fans and reporters alike had to accept his moods and idiosyncrasies no matter how coyly, capriciously, and even hurtfully he sometimes behaved. But Cobb was not simply being whimsical when he spoke of retirement. From about the time he turned thirty, he had begun to tell reporters that he had accomplished just about everything he wanted to and was thus almost ready to call it quits. For Cobb, such statements were an important exercise in personal autonomy: he wanted to show the baseball world that he was his own man and would not be seduced by fame and fortune, no matter how much his actions said otherwise. Only Detroit sportswriters were unruffled by Cobb's latest threat to retire. The *Detroit Free Press* calmly predicted, "Navin won't worry or lose any sleep . . . Frank knows Ty better than anybody else in baseball and how he feels toward the game." To wit: "It would kill Cobb were he compelled to retire . . . and none is aware of the fact any more than the Peach himself."[2]

True enough, Cobb changed his mind by the early spring. He hemmed and hawed all of March so that he could skip the first weeks of spring training, but he was with the Tigers when they made their way North in mid-April. Nineteen nineteen proved to be a particularly rewarding year for the Georgian. Although he could no longer count on his speed to generate infield hits and suffered through various minor injuries, he still led the league in hitting for the third straight year and the twelfth time in thirteen. Equally gratifying to Cobb, the Tigers remained in contention for much of the season, finishing in fourth place, twenty games above .500, eight games out of first. The pennant race alone was enough to awaken Cobb's competitive spirit. In late August, the Detroit correspondent for the *Sporting News* reported Cobb had "struck the top of his stride." What's more, he had assumed a valued leadership position on a team in which he was now the oldest regular. With most of the old guard gone, Cobb found it easier to influence the direction of the team. "Cobb is the busiest man on the Tigers team and any time he is not on the field, doing defensive work, or at bat, or on the bases, he is spending his time coaching."[3]

That winter, Cobb made no mention of retirement. The 1919 season had buoyed his hopes that the Tigers might be relevant again. But that was not all of it. The 1919 season had also ushered in dramatic changes that threatened to transform the baseball world in ways that troubled Cobb deeply. A new star of the game had arrived—George Herman "Babe" Ruth. Ruth did things to the ball that folks believed were just not humanly possible. He hit home runs—long, majestic, gargantuan home runs—and he did so with freakish frequency. Intuitively, Cobb interpreted the Ruth phenomenon as a threat, not only to his celebrity but to his person and his manhood. Given how much Cobb carried his concept of self onto the field, he could not have reacted otherwise. Cobb feared—rightly, as it turned out—that Ruth's style of play would diminish his status and that this in turn would diminish his manhood. Babe Ruth was Cobb's ultimate challenge. And Ty Cobb never backed down from a challenge to his manhood.

Babe Ruth was an unlikely candidate to take on the mantle of sports hero. He was not handsome, physically impressive, agile, clever, or articulate. He did not impress anyone as being particularly charismatic when he arrived in Boston halfway through the 1914 season to pitch for the Red Sox. Rather, he seemed both dreadfully simple and grotesquely uncouth. "Only lightly brushed by the social veneer we call civilization," is how outfielder Harry Hooper put it. Ruth was a 195-pound manchild, possessing the physique of a longshoreman coupled with the intemperance of a willful brat. He belched freely, farted loudly, and swore prodigiously. His favorite topic may have been male genitalia; he referred to it constantly, as in "I can knock the prick off any ball that was ever pitched." His appetites were enormous. When he first came up, he astounded his teammates by the amount he could eat at one time. Almost immediately, his appetites became far more wide-ranging—for gambling, for alcohol, and for women. Although he married at the end of his first season with the Red Sox, he refused to let his new bride bridle his libido or keep him from having a good time. By the end of his first full year in the majors, he had visited nearly every whorehouse in the American League circuit—probably more than once. He was less a miscreant than impetuous and perhaps even naïve. Although he had spent a good portion of his childhood under the strict care of Catholic priests at St. Mary's Industrial School for Boys in Baltimore, they failed to tame him. He often ate without aid of utensils, rarely wore underwear (when he did, it was hardly ever clean), neglected to flush the toilet, and used his roommate's toothbrush.[4]

Teammates divided on what to make of the young pitcher. The righteous and conservative Protestant clique, led by Tris Speaker, decided almost immediately that Ruth was a discredit to the team and to baseball; they gave him a rookie hazing that rivaled Ty Cobb's, sawing his prized bats in two and calling him "Baboon," "Big Monkey," and—most insulting of all—"Nigger Lips." But Ruth had friends, too. A German Catholic, he found ready allies among the team's rowdy Irish Catholic clique who appreciated his libidinous and bacchanal desires—although they must have realized early on that they could not keep up with him. They valued his companionship. After all, with a wastrel like Ruth on the club, a rollicking good time was always close at hand. A typical night for Ruth rarely ended much before dawn and usually included plenty of booze, women, and high jinks. According to sportswriter Roger Kahn, Ruth was a man of "measureless lust, selfishness, and appetites." To the raucous members of the Red Sox, Ruth exhibited swaggering manhood in epic proportions.[5]

Remarkably, Ruth's voracious appetites did not impede his maturation as a pitcher. In his first full year, he won a spot as a starting pitcher on the best staff in the major leagues, contributing eighteen wins as the Red Sox won the World Series. During the next few years, he emerged as the best left-hander in the game and arguably the best pitcher in the league, winning over twenty games twice. 1916 may have been his best year. He led in the league in ERA and games started and set an American League record for most shutouts by a left-hander in one season (nine; the record still stands). During this time, he gained a reputation as an intense competitor who came up big in important games. He beat Walter Johnson six straight times, including two 1–0 nail-biters, and set a World Series record for consecutive scoreless innings (29 2/3).

Even more impressive, Ruth also developed as a hitter. Although many of the team's position players—led by Speaker—refused to share the batting cage with the youngster and campaigned against him being anything but a pitcher, circumstances gave Ruth an opportunity to bat more frequently. In 1918, Red Sox owner and theatrical producer Harry Frazee began to trade and sell off some of his best players to fund his various Broadway ventures. Then the war in Europe siphoned off even more players. As a result, the Red Sox needed position players. Team captain Harry Hooper persuaded manager Ed Barrow that Ruth could help fill the offensive void. In a war-shortened season, he appeared in ninety-five games and hit eleven home runs to lead the league. He also finished first in slugging percentage, second in doubles, third in triples, eighth in total bases, and third in runs batted in. Eleven home runs. By the records that Ruth was about to set it wasn't much, but in the context of the still very Dead Ball Era, it was enough for umpire and sports columnist Billy Evans to claim that Ruth's arrival as a hitter was the story of the year. True, Ruth's home run mark was nowhere near Ned Williamson's major league record (set in 1884) of twenty-seven. He was not even all that close to Socks Seybold's American League record of sixteen. But given the limited number of games he played, his was still an impressive accomplishment. By comparison, the rest of the Red Sox hit a grand total of four that year. Even more extraordinarily, Ruth hit his home runs in binges of power, including four in as many games—a feat that no player had yet accomplished. In addition, many of Ruth's homers were mammoth blasts. Heretofore, "heavy hitters" as they were called—like Ruth's idol Joe Jackson—hit hard drives into the gap for doubles, triples, and the occasional inside-the-park job. When they cleared the fence, they barely did so. Ruth's home runs were majestic, dramatic, awe-inspiring, potent—shots that left little doubt as to their destination from the moment he made contact. Even when Ruth missed—and he did so with great frequency—the results were entertaining. The momentum of his go-for-broke swings forced him to twist into a corkscrew. He swung with such uninhibited force that he developed a permanent red mark across his chest that looked like stretch marks. Ruth was sui generis—so extraordinary he began to attract folks to the ballpark—men *and women*—who previously had shown no real interest in the game. When the season was over, Ruth was the new idol of baseball.[6]

Nineteen eighteen was only the start. The next year, Ruth appeared in nearly every game (130 as effects of the war continued to impose on professional baseball). Playing either first or the outfield nearly every game, he began to show greater consistency with that awesome power of his. The results were startling. He hit a record twenty-nine home runs, nineteen more than National League leader Gavvy Cravath and his closest American League competitor George Sisler. Fans took notice, of course, but so did people who heretofore had taken only a passing interest in the game. The Red Sox were a horrible team in 1919, but large crowds came to see them anyway. Folks wanted to see this "Colossus" for themselves. Attendance numbers increased as the season progressed and Ruth neared and then surpassed every known home run record in the books. He was particularly popular in New York where weekend games drew 30,000 plus and weekday games drew as many as 12,000—phenomenal numbers in 1919. He even drew well at Cobb's home turf: 25,000 came to see him for each of two weekend dates when the Red Sox visited the Motor City in late August. Ruth's fame grew exponentially with each home run. By season's end, he was receiving so many fan letters, a New York reporter remarked, "even if he should devote the full twenty-four hours to opening letters every day he would not reach the bottom of the heap." The reporter helpfully suggested Ruth hire a secretary. Instead, he hired a business manager who promptly scheduled a series of exhibition performances throughout New England and California for the off-season. Now it was obvious: Ruth was well on his way to supplanting Cobb as the nation's most popular ballplayer. The *Sporting News* got it right: "As an attraction, Ty Cobb runs a poor second nowadays to this . . . Ruth." All Cobb did that year was lead the league in hitting for the umpteenth time. Then again, Cobb only hit one home run. People wanted to see home runs—Ruth home runs.[7]

The next year, Ruth gave them even more of what they wanted. And at a pace that defied comparison—except with himself. In 140 games, he hit fifty-four home runs: more than any American League *team* hit that season; thirty-five more than George Sisler, the runner-up in the American League; thirty-nine more than National League champ Cy Williams. His hitting prowess alone was only half of what made Ruth special now. The other half concerned location. Prior to the 1920 season, Boston sold Ruth to the New York Yankees. Henceforth, Ruth would perform his wonders in the nation's largest city and the epicenter of a powerful new force in American life—mass media. It was a fortuitous turn of events for the Babe. By moving to New York, he gained a level of national exposure and adulation that he would not have received had he stayed in Boston.

In 1920, New York was home to eighteen daily newspapers. Competition for readership was intense. To boost circulation, most offered extensive sports coverage: baseball coverage alone often took a third of the front page of most metropolitan newspapers. To encourage the sports mania, New York's dailies hired the best sportswriters from around the country. In the years following World War I, New York became home to Ring Lardner, Damon Runyon, Grantland Rice, Paul Gallico, W. O. McGeehan, Marshall Hunt, Fred Lieb, Heywood Broun, John Kieran, Westbrook Pegler, Dan Daniel, Richards Vidmer, and Ford Frick. They were a talented and competitive group, eager to outdo one another by getting the best lead, telling the most sensational story, and offering the most intimate portrayal of the leading personalities of the sports world. Most were unabashed rooters. In feature columns for their home newspapers as well as contracted pieces in the leading magazines of the day, they promoted star athletes as the new heroes of modernity. Some went even further—shamelessly pinning their fortunes to the coattails of these golden boys by acting as their de facto press agents. In this, they helped fashion a distinctive form of journalism—"ballyhoo." That is, they promoted, exaggerated, and even lied about their subjects to lure readers. Ballyhoo journalists hyperbolized and sensationalized every event, fixated on the personal and the exotic, presented gossip as real news, and leaped from one fad to the next to entice and excite readers. The chosen style was "bouncy . . . very biff, bang, boom stuff," according to one journalist.[8] Ruth's various hitting accomplishments often sent reporters into a frenzy of hyperbolic verbiage. When he hit three home runs in a game against the Senators during the 1920 season, the *New York Times* reported it thusly:

> The fruitful bat of the unmatchable Babe Ruth carried him still higher into the realm of greatness up on Coogan's bluff yesterday, the swaggering swat king blistering the ball for three home runs in the doubleheader with Washington as a crowd of 28,000 people fumed and fussed in the midsummer heat and sang the praises of the fencebuster in as thunderous a community chorus of cheers as ever jarred the eardrums of the gay populace.
>
> A modern Goliath of the bludgeon is Ruth. He is hitting them harder and sending them further every day. He has become a national curiosity, and the sight-seeing pilgrims who daily flock into Manhattan are as anxious to rest eyes upon him as they are to peek at the Woolworth Building or the bungalows of the impressively rich on Fifth Avenue.[9]

Babe Ruth's inimitable accomplishments, bigger than life persona, gargantuan appetites, scandalous affairs, and juvenile zeal for excitement made him an ideal subject for this form of journalism. Intent on riding Ruth's personality and accomplishments to greater circulation, New York's sportswriters constructed an image of the "Bambino" that exaggerated his best qualities and hid his worst. Essentially, they transformed the loutish miscreant into a fun-loving and generous overgrown adolescent. The Ruth who came to life in the pages of the New York dailies was playful, dedicated, endearing, heroic—a far cry from the crude, self-absorbed, intemperate beast that Ruth sometimes revealed himself to be.

No newspaper did a better job of mythologizing Ruth than the *New York Daily News*, a photo-filled tabloid that specialized in human-interest stories, celebrity gossip, muckraking, and nearly anything sensational. When the Babe moved to New York, the *Daily News*'s young sports editor, Marshall Hunt, talked publisher Joseph Medill Patterson into assigning him to cover Ruth 24-7-365. Hunt did not want to miss a thing. And he didn't. "We recognized the Babe as a guy we could really do business with," Hunt recalled years later. "So the Babe became sort of a *Daily News* man because we covered him more—more pictures, more stories. We covered him twelve months of the year . . . We got along fine." Did they ever. Hunt followed Ruth everywhere—to fancy restaurants, on vaudeville tours, to spas to "boil out," and to the best cathouses in the country. Hunt cozied up to Ruth as best he could. When Ruth developed a taste for a home-cooked chicken dinner and a farmer's daughter while taking the cure near Hot Springs, Arkansas, Hunt hired a car every night and drove Ruth around looking for farmhouses; Ruth satiated both desires "more often than you would think." During spring training in Florida, Hunt helped Ruth break training by hiring a boat so the two could sneak out at night to fish and drink. Hunt was closer to Ruth than any other writer and it showed in the stories he provided. He offered readers a steady stream of colorful vignettes about New York's favorite citizen. Nothing was too trivial—or too stupid—for Hunt. Hunt was there when Ruth fired a shotgun out of his Massachusetts farmhouse just to watch his cat leap several feet in the air after the blast. He was there when Ruth inexplicably visited an art gallery, just so he could record the Babe's reaction to high art ("Goddamn it! How do those bastards do it?" Ruth wanted to know). Hunt wrote about only the fun-loving unscripted Ruth. He was so enamored with his subject he refused to cover the occasional scandals that embroiled Ruth, demanding that the *Daily News* send another reporter to do the dirty work. Hunt recalled, "I don't think he was ever aware of his role as a circulation builder."[10] Or maybe he was. When someone pointed out to Ruth that he received twice the daily publicity as President Calvin Coolidge, Ruth responded, "I deserve it." Modesty was not a Ruth virtue.[11]

Neither was meekness. From the moment Ruth arrived in New York, he played an active role in shaping his public persona. It would be too much of a stretch to claim that Ruth possessed an intuitive grasp of public relations, but he was smart enough to exhibit his affable, playful demeanor most every time newsmen and cameras were nearby. Equally important, he was wise enough to connect with people who understood the art. The most influential of these was Christy Walsh, a lawyer-turned-newspaper-cartoonist-turned-advertising-executive. Walsh cultivated an intimacy with Ruth, calculating he could make a tidy sum acting as his ghostwriter. Eventually, he became much more than that, essentially operating as Ruth's business manager and booking agent. He also protected Ruth from con artists, lecherous friends, and bamboozling pitchmen. Along the way, he massaged Ruth's public image, becoming the first public relations rep in sports. Walsh arranged for Ruth to visit orphanages and hospital wards, pose for publicity shots with film, theater, and sports stars, and speak to august assemblies, like a national convention of Presbyterians.

When Ruth's carousing and volatile demeanor earned him five separate suspensions and plenty of bad publicity during the 1922 season, Walsh orchestrated one of the first public apologies by a professional athlete. That this has become a staple of erring athletes ever since is testimony to Walsh's artistry. Walsh decided to use two recent revelations to good effect: Ruth's purchase of a farm in Sudbury, Massachusetts and the Ruths' decision to adopt a sixteen-month-old girl (in fact the child was the product of a Ruth affair). To commemorate these events, Walsh planned a testimonial for Ruth at New York's Elks Club with the theme "Back to the Farm." Walsh billed the event as a goodbye celebration for Ruth before he left to winter in Sudbury. This was pretense; Walsh actually hoped to use the event to rehabilitate Ruth's tarnished image. For this, he enlisted state senator and New York socialite James J. Walker. The dapper "Beau James," whose appetite for chorus girls and liquor rivaled Ruth's, acted—ironically enough—as Ruth's conscience. Before an assemblage of sportswriters and Broadway celebrities, Walker gently prodded Ruth, calling him a "great fool" for wasting his God-given talents on liquor "faster than . . . . brew masters can make it." Everyone in the room, Walker observed, was "sad and dejected" because Ruth had "let them down." Then Walker really let him have it: "Worst of all . . . you have let down the kids of America . . . they look up to you, worship you. And then what happens? You carouse and abuse your great body. . . . It is exactly as though Santa Claus himself suddenly were to take off his beard to reveal the features of a villain. The kids have seen their idol shattered and their dreams broken."

Over the top? Maybe, but the man-child responded just as Walsh had anticipated: he wept. When Walker turned to the mighty slugger and pleaded, "Will you not give back to those kids their great idol?" Ruth was reduced to tears. "So help me, Jim, I will," he promised. "I'll go back to my farm in Sudbury and get in shape." All the journalists present dutifully reported that the Babe had seen the error of his ways and was eager to rededicate himself to America's game.[12]

Was Ruth sincere in his pledge to reform? Hard to say. Newsreels and newspaper photos taken at the farm—all orchestrated by Walsh—show a robust Ruth eagerly chopping wood, doing farm chores, and doting over his wife and daughter. Even so, it's doubtful whether Ruth controlled his voracious appetites for women and booze when he returned to the team that spring. At best, he learned to moderate his behavior just enough so that his dissipations did not hinder his playing, as he led the league in home runs in 1923 and in home runs and batting average in 1924. This was all New York writers needed to continue the fiction that Ruth was a model citizen. Along the way, they consciously suppressed stories about Ruth's more sordid goings on. New York sportswriter Richards Vidmer boasted he could have "written a story every day on the Babe" if he had wanted to write about his personal life. There was plenty to tell, Vidmer said. "Babe couldn't say no to certain things. Hot dogs was the least of 'em. There were other things that were worse. Hell, sometimes I thought it was one long line, a procession."[13]

Other writers also pitched in to help the Ruth brand. Ford Frick, Westbrook Pegler, and William Slocum all worked as Ruth's ghostwriter at various times—penning as many as three stories a week for his syndicated byline. Ruth was not much interested in what they wrote, but he loved what they earned for him—as much as $15,000 a year at the height of his popularity.[14] Writers did all they could to keep their cash cow on the diamond. More than once, a writer intervened in Ruth's contract talks by helping bring the slugger to terms so that he would not face public criticism. At the start of the Great Depression, Dan Daniel of the *New York Telegraph* saved Ruth from a public relations nightmare when he persuaded the slugger to sign for $70,000 rather than hold out for more. "What's the matter with you?" Daniel demanded when he found Ruth relaxing by a pool at a swanky Florida hotel. "Did you know that this afternoon in Union Square in New York there was a riot? A lot of people were rioting for bread. . . . They're broke. . . . And you're holding out for eighty-five thousand a year while they're starving. It's making a very bad impression and hurting baseball." A dumbstruck Ruth replied he knew nothing about the Depression and asked Daniel what he should do. Daniel told him to end his holdout immediately.[15]

Ruth arrived at precisely that moment when Americans were most able to appreciate both his breathtaking talents and his impulsive personality. For more than a quarter century, urban American culture had been in the process of a dramatic transformation. A new middle-class eager for excitement and thrills had slowly abandoned the rigid Victorian morality of their parents and grandparents. Immersed in an economy that promised unprecedented prosperity, older values of self-discipline and personal asceticism slowly gave way. In their place, Americans adopted a consumer ethic that promised personal fulfillment and instant gratification through the purchase of goods. Almost any goods—cosmetics, clothing, electric appliances, automobiles, amusements, athletic equipment. Cobb had been an early beneficiary of this new age, having made his livelihood as a professional athlete who offered fans vicarious thrills. But Cobb lacked Ruth's dynamic personality and had the nasty habit of pontificating on the virtues of hard work and self-restraint. To these new arbiters of modernity—the ballyhoo journalists—Cobb seemed awkwardly out of step with the new age. Ruth was something else entirely. Through the very bigness of his personality, he personified the glamour of consumption, the pursuit of pleasure, and the liberation of play. Americans thrilled at watching Ruth because he audaciously lived the life that they craved. He made gluttony attractive.[16]

Fans—millions of them—swarmed to the ballpark precisely so they could see Ruth or some other slugger smash the ball as hard as he could. These news fans were not the aficionados of old; they cared little about strategy and nuance. Baseball was a fad for them. They thrilled at high scoring games and the majestic arc of the long ball. "I love to see the ball go flying through the air. It's so exciting," a Chicago woman explained to a Chicago reporter when asked why she liked baseball. Another Chicagoan agreed. "When I go to a ball game, I like to see a lot of hitting. It is so exciting when you can go up there and yell for your favorite team." When a Brooklyn Dodger fan was asked why he had become more interested in the game, his answer was succinct: "They've jazzed the old game up," he said. The jazz helped drive attendance up. In 1917, just over 5.2 million fans attended major league baseball games; only the New York Giants drew more than 500,000 fans. In 1920, that number rose to over 9 million, with Ruth's New York Yankees drawing a staggering million fans, a threshold no team had yet crossed. Attendance averaged over 8.5 million for the rest of the decade. In 1922, two teams drew over a million fans, seven teams drew over 500,000, and four more drew over 400,000.[17]

Ty Cobb watched it all and it exasperated him to no end. Ruth challenged Cobb's stature in nearly every way that mattered to Cobb—as the best player in the game, as the target of media attention and adulation, as an idol of fandom, and perhaps most fundamentally as the embodiment of how baseball ought to be played. From the time Cobb returned from military service until his retirement from the game in 1928, he did everything he could to demean Ruth and undermine his star status. Even after the two reached a sort of rapprochement in 1924, Cobb remained adamant that Ruth's style of play was not only inferior to his own but damaging to the welfare of the game. His was a battle for the soul of the game—and preservation of his stature as the game's greatest player.

Cobb had fought off any number of rivals for the title of the game's greatest player—Joe Jackson, Honus Wagner, Nap Lajoie, Tris Speaker, Eddie Collins. The competition had been severe and unremitting.

Yet he had always prevailed. Even through the late teens as his skills declined, he pushed himself forward, incapable—it seemed—of failing. His case for preeminence was encapsulated in the honor that mattered to the players and fans of his generation: the batting championship. Now this began to elude him. 1919 was the last year he finished on top. 1920 was especially depressing for the Georgian. Those scribes who were friendly with Cobb had done their best to crash the Ruth bandwagon by suggesting his twenty-nine home runs in 1919 were a freakish aberration; Ruth, they said, would have to put several such years together before he could supplant Cobb as the game's greatest player. All Ruth did in 1920, of course, was almost double his home run total. Adding injury to insult, Cobb was hampered by a variety of ailments—most troubling torn ligaments in his left knee. He ended up hitting .334, only tenth best in the league, and more than seventy points behind league leader George Sisler, whose .407 average made him the first player to break .400 since Cobb did it in 1911. In every way, the year was a painful reminder to Cobb that he was no longer the game's best player. Indeed, with the arrival of Sisler, he could not even lay claim to being the second best. Cobb proved in subsequent years that he was still an excellent player, but he was not the player he once was—at least not consistently.

Had any other player usurped his place as the idol of fandom, it might not have hurt so much. Cobb genuinely respected most of his fiercest rivals. Indeed, he routinely credited them for making him a better player. Late in life, he told Joe Jackson, "Whenever I got the idea I was a good hitter, I'd stop and take a good look at you. Then I knew I could stand some improvement. I don't think I ever saw a more perfect swing than yours." He especially admired players whose devotion to the game and competitive fire and aggressive play matched his own. "The great stars of the game," Cobb observed in 1914, "are all thinking men." He gave special credit to Eddie Collins, calling him "the most dangerous man . . . on any . . . team in either league."[18] Cobb was on friendly terms with many of the game's greatest players. He enjoyed visiting with Jackson. He counted Tris Speaker as one of his closest friends. He liked to talk shop with brainy players like Collins, Ray Schalk, Nap Lajoie, and base-stealing phenom Clyde Milan. In his youth, he revered Honus Wagner and even invited him down to Georgia for a week of hunting following their clash in the 1909 World Series.

Had Ruth been like any of these—men who were sober and dedicated students of the game—Cobb might have relinquished his status as the game's best player more amicably. No, he would not have gone quietly into that good night. The *Detroit Free Press* had been right about that: Cobb loved to compete too much to quit. Still, he might have accepted Ruth's ascendance as a transcendent moment in which an older player gives way to a youth and in the process proudly dares the new star to match his record of accomplishment. That Cobb could have done. In fact, he did do that with another young challenger to his legacy, George Sisler of the St. Louis Browns. During the late teens, many baseball observers dubbed Sisler the next Cobb. By the early twenties, many of those same observers argued Sisler had surpassed Cobb as the game's best all around hitter, especially after his stellar 1922 season in which he led the league with a .420 average. Cobb's reaction? As the season ended, he told the young first baseman via telegram that he was "delighted" for him. For his part, "Gentleman George" often deferred to Cobb, frequently telling journalists that Cobb was his "model" and inspiration. Cobb believed that was how a young player ought to behave—solicitous and respectful. For this, Cobb called Sisler "a rare credit to the game."[19]

But Ruth? Cobb could not abide the man-child and refused to extend to him the respect, good fellowship, and generous praise he offered his other rivals. Cobb hated everything associated with Babe Ruth: his appearance; his appetites; the undisciplined way in which he approached the game; the way reporters fawned over him; the imbecilic fans who followed him to the ballpark just to watch him swing for the fences. Cobb loved baseball because he relished the sweat and blood challenge of working his way around the bases. For him, every run was a testament of guile, speed, nerve, and courage. He perceived baseball as a series of pitched battles—against the pitcher, the catcher, the infielders, outfielders, managers, and even the fans. Cobb took them all on. Scoring a single run offered visceral thrills he could find nowhere else in life. Now Ruth—aided it seems by a livelier ball first introduced in 1920—wanted to undermine all this. To Cobb, the burgeoning home run mania that Ruth introduced threatened to destroy what was best about baseball—the remorseless war of nerves. Ruth bastardized the game. No surprise there, Cobb believed: to Cobb, Ruth was a bastard.

Cobb didn't need to go through his usual machinations of building up his hate when it came to Ruth: his contempt for him was sincere and enduring. It began with Ruth's origins. After fifteen years in the majors, Cobb had become used to working with players from diverse backgrounds and origins, but that didn't mean he had abandoned his prejudices. He remained deeply suspicious of lower-class urbanites, immigrant Catholics, and rowdies. Ruth, of course, was all these things—the son of a saloon keeper in Baltimore's worst slum, the aptly named "Pigtown." Reflecting the prevailing class and ethnic biases of the age, Cobb believed Ruth to be weak, degenerate, primitive. As Cobb saw it, Ruth lacked the necessary character to assume the mantle of stardom.

Cobb believed Ruth's physical attributes reflected his biological and moral degeneracy. His overlarge head, unruly curly hair, large nose with flared nostrils, swarthy complexion, and plump lips reminded some of a caricature from a minstrel show. Cobb was not the first to call Ruth "nigger," but he was one of the few who suspected—at least at first—that the epithet might be true. One winter, Cobb, Ruth, and several other players gathered at Dover Hall, a hunting lodge near Brunswick, Georgia. When it came time to divvy up cabins, Cobb refused to room with Ruth. "I've never bedded down with a nigger and I'm not going to start now," Cobb was reported to have told the other players. Perhaps it was true that Ruth did not actually have any negro blood in him, Cobb admitted, but his appearance certainly suggested something about the big man's constitution was amiss. The taint damned Ruth in Cobb's eyes.[20]

To Cobb, these were all important reasons to demonize Ruth. But they were all just pretense. Cobb's contempt for Ruth stemmed from causes that were far more personal. For one, Cobb felt threatened. He understood that if Ruth's star continued to ascend, the game would change so that he, Cobb, would be little more than an anachronism, an aging and irrelevant reminder of the game as it had once been. Cobb was not so much jealous of Ruth as he was fearful of how Ruth's accomplishments and growing celebrity might impact this. As he grew older, Cobb became increasingly concerned about his legacy. He wanted to leave the game as its greatest player. By his way of thinking—steeped as it was in the Southern code of honor—the praise others lavished upon him confirmed his superiority as both a ballplayer and as a man. Now the Ruth phenomenon threatened to undo everything he had achieved. He had to stop him.

More fundamentally, Cobb's critique of Ruth and the home run craze rested upon his generation's distinctive understanding of manhood. He considered it axiomatic that men—true men, anyway—hungered for more visceral drama than the long ball could provide. After all, men were warriors at heart. Those who played ball had the opportunity to live out their primordial desires on the ball field. Others, the fans in the stands, could only enjoy such experiences vicariously, by watching their favorite players do battle against one another. As Cobb understood the game, home runs lacked the necessary drama to satisfy men's basic needs for both confrontation and excitement. The home run ball, in Cobb's view, was a cheap thrill. As a dramatic confrontation, it engaged only the batter and pitcher and it lasted for the briefest of moments—the time it took for a batter to hit the ball and send it over the outfield fence. Cobb earnestly believed the excitement his style of play brought to the game was more satisfying. The Cobbian player pitted himself against the opposing team—first by placing his hit and then by circling the bases, one base at a time. And he did so using all his faculties—brains, power, speed, coordination, and will. Each moment—literally—was filled with endless possibilities, theatrical moments of life or death. "And," Cobb observed, "all the maneuvers were in the open, where each fan might see."[21] That point was crucial: Cobb's style of play offered the visceral intimacy of confrontation that true men desired. How could watching Ruth lumber around the bases on those skinny piano legs compete with a series of violent and dramatic clashes? It couldn't. Ergo, the home run craze would soon fade. At base, Cobb doubted whether the home run hitter was a true ballplayer. The slugger could only do one thing well—hit the ball hard and far. Big deal.

For all Cobb's maliciousness, he preferred to relegate his disputes to the field of battle. He believed this was the manly and honorable thing to do. This is how he conducted himself with Ruth as well. Though he may have been tempted to expose Ruth as the gluttonous rake he knew him to be, he generally refused to talk to the press about his private feelings about Ruth. In this, he followed the same pattern of behavior he had always used when confronted by a player or players who meant to do him ill: he refused to be drawn into a war of words. Only once in his near decade-long rivalry with Ruth did Cobb slip up. And that occurred early on. In the winter of 1919, after Ruth set the baseball home run record at twenty-nine, he told the Red Sox he wanted a new contract commensurate with the game's best hitters. Ruth's stance made headlines, not only because his hitting had become the talk of baseball, but because of the extraordinary nature of his demands: he was in the middle of a three-year contract that paid just over $30,000 per year; now he wanted to triple or even quadruple that salary. Some believed Ruth was worth nearly that and much more; others wondered about the ethics of it all since Ruth was demanding the Red Sox tear up his current contract. Cobb found himself drawn into the dispute. No doubt, reporters goaded him on: they wanted to know what the game's biggest star had to say about the young phenom whose approach to the game was different from his own. Perhaps, too, Cobb may have been eager to unload on the young slugger. He probably assumed once the country met the real Babe Ruth, they would abandon him. He also believed Ruth, unsophisticated boor that he was, would melt under the intense public scrutiny of the sporting press. One way or another, hubris and gluttony would ruin Ruth; why not do his part to hasten Ruth's inevitable demise along? While playing winter ball in California, Cobb told a reporter Ruth would "convict himself of being a contract breaker" if he made good on his promise to hold out. "I'm for a ball player getting all he's worth," Cobb maintained, "but I am opposed to his breaking a contract to do it." It was an odd show of high-mindedness by the player who made holding out a near annual event. Ruth interpreted Cobb's comments for what they were—an insult to his integrity. "I will take a poke at Ty Cobb the first minute I lay eyes on him . . . impugning my reputation just because he's jealous of me," he told reporters.[22] Ruth never made good on his threat; he didn't need to. By holding out, he priced himself out of Boston and got himself sold to the Yankees, who quickly acceded to his demands. What's more, New York's adoring press corps embraced him immediately as baseball's next best thing. "Babe Ruth, you've certainly outbatted Ty Cobb in the headline league," one sportswriter quipped. "We feel we know you pretty well. Every sports page we pick up—from tank town to metropolis—has you prominently headlined . . . Keep it up." The moral was clear: In this modern era of sports media, nearly all publicity was good publicity.[23]

Cobb learned his lesson. On the playing field, he continued to show nothing but scorn for his great rival; to the press, he tried to avoid mention of Ruth, but when this proved impossible, he prudently gave Ruth his due. In the middle of the 1920 season, *Baseball Magazine* asked Cobb to pen an article on possible American League batting champions for the current season. Although Cobb suggested Sisler, Jackson, and Speaker were the most likely candidates, he gave the most attention to Ruth, "the man who overshadows all of them right now ... the biggest drawing card in baseball." Cobb waxed on: Ruth was "undoubtedly the greatest slugger who ever lived." Perhaps the best nature could create: "He has the build. He has the eye. He has everything." Even so, Cobb claimed he was neither jealous nor intimidated. After all, they were very different types of hitter. Ruth was a "slugger" while he was a scientific hitter. Taking on a paternal tone, he remarked, "I don't begrudge him his fame. He is having his day." Only time would tell whether Ruth's success would match his own, he seemed to suggest. "Some other day he will also grow old and watch a younger player usurp the limelight in his place. It comes to all of us."[24]

In fact, Cobb was in no way ready to concede the stage to Ruth. As always, he reveled in the rivalry. Cobb viewed his competition with Ruth as a duel for supremacy, as yet another affair of honor. Like every other such affair, he embraced the confrontation with every resource at his disposal. He insulted, threatened, and strutted as if to suggest to Ruth he was unimpressed by the power he wielded with his stick. After Ruth died, Cobb liked to brag that he bested Ruth just as he had defeated every other adversary—with superior talent and guile. In his final autobiography, he boasted "over the years—and Babe was well aware of it—I'd discovered his one vulnerable point." Ruth, Cobb claimed, did not like to be teased about his personal appearance: Tell him "that he looked like an egg on stilts or a beer keg balanced on two straws," Cobb gloated, and "he'd turn purple." He also liked to ridicule Ruth for his often foul body odor. What Cobb failed to disclose is that he often punctured his insults with racial slurs. Ruth's brawn, Cobb suggested, was not matched by his brain. "You could play Ruth like a zither," Cobb boasted. "At least when I heckled him, he always answered the call."[25]

Once again, Cobb falsified the historical record. Ruth proved to be a formidable adversary. Despite Cobb's low opinion of him, Ruth was talented, intelligent, and as proud and combative as Cobb. In head-to-head confrontations, Ruth more than held his own: he hit more doubles (89) and home runs (123), drove in more runs (342), and scored more runs (338) against Detroit than any other team. His .338 average against Detroit pitchers was slightly lower than his career average (.342), but more than respectable. In all, Ruth's performance against the Tigers gives the lie to Cobb's contention that he knew how to rattle the Bambino. In fact, the opposite seems to have been closer to the truth.[26] Cobb resorted to this tactic in one notable 1921 series, his first in New York as manager of the Tigers. Cobb hoped to use the four games to demonstrate his superior skills as both player and tactician. From the start, he heckled and harassed Ruth, so much so that the two nearly came to blows at least half a dozen times. But stop Ruth? Hardly. Ruth channeled his anger into hitting and put on an impressive demonstration of power, belting two doubles and six home runs in four days. As an added bit of revenge, he even convinced manager Miller Huggins to let him pitch the third game. He lasted nearly five innings and struck Cobb out the final time he faced him. For the series, Ruth nearly doubled Cobb's average, hitting .750 (9 for 12) to Cobb's .388 (7 for 18).

It was an awful four days for Cobb. Rather than bridle Ruth, he had embarrassed himself. The New York press ridiculed Cobb for his inability to keep up with the magnificent Ruth, while New York fans jeered and hissed Cobb incessantly. Detroit's sportswriters blamed Cobb for the debacle. H. G. Salsinger, the *Detroit News*'s beat writer and one of Cobb's best friends, admitted that the Peach was no match for the Sultan of Swat, at least not this time. "No other club has lost seven out of eight games to New York, simply because no other club would show the same policy in pitching to Ruth," Salsinger lamented. Of course, Cobb enjoyed streaks in which he proved the more dynamic player, but he never got Ruth's goat.[27]

For the next few years, Ruth and Cobb continued to bring out both the best and the worst in one another. The culmination of their mutual animosity occurred on Friday, June 13, 1924 during the third game in a four-game set in Detroit. It was a crucial series for the rejuvenated Tigers who were only a game behind the first-place Yankees. How the Tigers played might reveal whether the team could stay with the vaunted New Yorkers for the season. The Tigers started things off right, winning 6–2. Cobb led the offense, knocking out two triples and a single in three official at bats. He also walked once, scored three times, and executed—in the words of the *New York Times*—"two dust-raising slides." It was vintage Cobb.[28]

Then things went bad for the Tigers. In the next game, the Yankees pummeled them 10–4—thanks in part, to Ruth's fifteenth home run of the season. Cobb hated Babe Ruth home runs and apparently decided to let Ruth know it: the next time Ruth came to bat, Detroit pitcher Syd Johnson drilled a fastball into Ruth's ribs. A bit later, New York second baseman Ernie Johnson, who had tripled in an earlier at bat, got the same treatment. A coincidence? The Yankees didn't think so. The ill will continued into the next game. Players from both teams traded barbs—and sometimes worse. On a close play at first, Ruth straight-armed Detroit starter Bert Cole. Cole retaliated in the top of the ninth by aiming two straight fastballs at Ruth's head before getting him to foul out. As Ruth walked past the on-deck circle, he warned teammate Bob Meusel that he saw Cobb signal Cole to throw at him as well. With his very first pitch, Cole did exactly that, catching the outfielder in the ribs. Meusel stormed the mound. So did most everyone else: every Yankee, every Tiger, both umpires, several hundred Detroit fans, and dozens of uniformed police officers who were desperately trying to keep order. Ruth rushed through the crowd looking for Cobb. He found him just beyond the pitcher's mound. With elbows bent and fists clenched, he accused Cobb of ordering his pitchers to throw at him and his teammates. When Cobb yelled back that he had done no such thing, Ruth challenged him to a fight. The moment the baseball world had anticipated for so long had finally come: the violent faceoff of the game's two biggest stars. It was not to be. Several New York players rushed toward Ruth and held him back, thwarting what might have turned out to be the bloodiest blood feud in baseball history. Alas, Ruth and Cobb would never come this close to a fight again.

As for the game itself, the umpires tried to restore order by tossing Ruth and Meusel out of the game. As they exited, however, they mixed it up with some Detroit players (other reports identified Meusel and "Bullet Joe" Bush as the culprits) near the home dugout. The commotion incited even more fans to rush onto the field. A melee soon erupted with fans fighting the police, fans fighting each other, and fans attempting to storm the Yankee clubhouse. Once umpire Billy Evans realized the police could not restore order, he ordered the game forfeited to the Yankees.[29] American League president Ban Johnson called the riot "one of the most disgraceful incidents in all baseball history." Probably not, although all sides were shocked by how quickly matters had escalated. In response, Johnson laid down the law, fining Meusel $100, Cole $50, and suspending both for ten days. For his "frenzied effort to participate in the trouble," Ruth was fined $50. And rightly so claimed the *Sporting News*. He had "no place in the shindy, except as he sought the limelight," the journal concluded. Hubris. Cobb escaped the entire affair without further blemish to his already rutty reputation.[30]

The brawl was the last serious confrontation involving Ruth and Cobb. Though the two teams met fourteen more times that season, neither star was able to incite the other to do anything newsworthy. At the end of the season, the two met at the World Series between the Senators and Giants as paid correspondents for one of the newspaper syndicates. While there, Ruth's wily agent Christy Walsh decided to orchestrate a rapprochement between the two stars, no doubt figuring that Ruth's part in the June riot did nothing for his client's marketability. Somehow, he got the two to sit together and play nice. It must have been an uncomfortable meeting. Days earlier, Cobb had told a journalist how delighted he was that the Senators, not the Yankees, had won the American League flag; clearly, he had no great love for Ruth and his teammates. The meeting occurred on October 5, just before the first game of the Series. A photograph of Ruth, George Sisler, and Ty Cobb was taken to commemorate the moment. Two days later, however, the two reverted to strained silence when they happened upon one another. A half-hour before game time, fans swarmed upon Ruth as he sat in a press box near the Senators' dugout. Then Cobb showed up. When the throng of fans asked him to sign autographs alongside Ruth, he graciously complied. The only seat available for Cobb was directly across from Ruth's, not three feet away. According to a sportswriter who witnessed the event, what followed was exceedingly awkward: "Ty looked at the Babe, then the chair, and without further ceremonies, took possession." There they sat "within three feet of each other, but during the ten minutes they were in such close contact not a word passed between them." Still, stony silence was better than insults and threatening gestures. It wasn't much, but it was a start. Thereafter, the relationship softened considerably and the two rivals acted with greater civility. In time, they would even develop something akin to a friendship.[31]

Ruth's reasoning for making peace is easier to understand than Cobb's. He disliked Cobb personally, but he was less inclined to hold grudges and he was not bound to the South's culture of honor. Besides all that, Cobb had nearly always been the instigator; if Cobb now decided to behave himself, Ruth would, too. So why did Cobb suddenly decide it was time to forego the Babe-baiting? After all, Cobb was never one to give up the fight, not if he believed it a matter of personal honor. The most likely explanation is that Cobb realized this was a battle he could not win, at least not by open confrontation. For twenty years, he had taken on all comers and won nearly every time. He had outwitted them, outfought them, outperformed them, or outlasted them. Now in his late thirties, he could not mount the same offensive he had used in his youth. He had to concede. Walsh's offer to play peacemaker came at an opportune time for Cobb. He had become increasingly frustrated by his inability to stop Ruth. Weeks earlier, he as much as admitted defeat to one of his confidants, Grantland Rice. While watching Babe Ruth launch pitch after pitch into the bleachers during batting practice, Cobb confided to Rice, "Well, the old game is gone. Babe Ruth has changed baseball. I guess more people would rather see Babe hit one over the fence than see me steal second." The realization saddened Cobb. "I feel bad about it for it isn't the game I like to see or play," he said. "The old game was one of skill and speed. And quick thinking. This game is all power."[32] By season's end, Cobb was exhausted. Though thirty-seven, he played in 155 games, more than he had in nearly a decade. His 727 plate appearances and 625 official at bats were his most ever. His 211 hits gave him eight years with 200 or more hits, a new record. But a .338 batting average placed him well below his career average and far behind the league's best hitters. For the first time in his long career, Cobb failed to make the top ten batters. The leader that year? Babe Ruth with a .378 average. Cobb had to accept reality: the Babe had become more than just a slugger; he had become a hitter whose skills by 1924 were vastly superior to those of the aging Cobb.

By mid-decade, Ruth had the advantages of youth, charisma, New York's ballyhoo journalists, and the legions of baseball fans. Cobb could at least take consolation in the adulation he still received, especially from older members of the press and more tradition-minded fans. Leading sports journalists of the day now lauded Cobb with a kind of reverence reserved for a living legend. Many writers took to calling Cobb "The Peerless Georgian" and left it at that. Others like Damon Runyon, Bide Dudley, and Fred Lieb believed it only proper etiquette to include a phrase like "the greatest ball player who ever lived" or "world's greatest ball player" whenever they profiled Cobb. Some were even more effusive. *Sporting News* columnist John B. Sheridan was particularly unceasing in his praise for Cobb during the 1920s. "As for the greatest player of all time," Sheridan proclaimed, "there can be no disagreement among free, unbiased, competent judges. He was, and is, Tyrus Raymond Cobb, in a class by himself."[33] To F. C. Lane, editor of *Baseball Magazine* and perhaps Cobb's most ardent fan, Cobb was simply the game's "most brilliant star." Even J. G. Taylor Spink, editor of the *Sporting News*, came around. When Cobb's former critic heard the rumor that Cobb planned to retire following the 1924 season, Spink was devastated, predicting that it would be "approximately impossible" to replace him. Two years later, when word came out again that Cobb planned to retire, he was unequivocal in his praise. "The majors have lost the greatest human asset they ever possessed," he asserted. Ruth might have built Yankee Stadium, Spink observed, but "Cobb built the American League . . . Where Cobb played, the fans went. That is financial fact."[34]

Such praise was genuine, but also reflected ulterior motives. Those who praised Cobb most lavishly tended to share his concerns about Ruth's impact on the game. Baseball fans may be the most conservative fans of any American sport. This has been particularly true of sportswriters, who tend to define themselves as guardians of baseball's sacred traditions. Something about the game's culture evokes nostalgia and tradition. It is, after all, "the Grand Old Game" and has been called such since at least the turn of the last century—when it was only a few decades old. Predictably then, many writers responded negatively when Ruth began to launch home run after home run and inspired an entire generation of youngsters to aspire to do the same. Sounding very similar to Cobb, they presented the Babe as more aberration than hero. Even as writers expressed wonder for his accomplishments, they often described him as brutishly abnormal—"a monster," "a freak," "a bear," "a brute," "a behemoth slugger," "a gorilla," or some form of primordial ancestor of man.[35] In a few instances, the attacks against Ruth became quite personal. "To students of baseball Ruth is simply a freak . . . a cave man slugger," Cobb partisan Salsinger proclaimed. Sheridan was even more demeaning. To him, Ruth's "pre-Adamic appearance, his great shaggy head, his immense shoulders and arms, the manner in which his legs are fitted into his feet . . . the primeval paddle of his gait, the tales of his fearful feats of eating, drinking, love-making, etc." were all "suggestive of the Tree Dwellers."[36]

Though vicious, these writers believed they were protecting the game. As baseball purists, they reveled in the strategies and drama of inside baseball—the hit and run, place hitting, sacrifice hits, stolen bases, and taut defense. Prior to Ruth, most baseball strategists viewed the home run with a certain amount of disdain. These experts asserted the player who went to bat looking for the home run hurt the team orientation of the game. Albert Spalding, author of the *Official Base Ball Guide*, denounced the home run hitter as coming from "that rutting class of slugging batsmen who think of nothing else when they go to bat but that of gaining the applause of the 'groundlings.'" "The homer," he continued, "is one of the least difficult hits known to batting in baseball, as it needs only muscle and not brains to make it." Almost four decades later, many of those closest to the game accepted Spalding's opinion as gospel. All aspiring hitters were taught to take short compact swings or even chop at the ball rather than swing from the heels. The Ruthian revolution did not sit well with many. Giants' manager John McGraw, who once fined a player $25 for hitting a game-winning home run after he had ordered him to bunt, reflected the frustration of many when he observed, "Scientific baseball, which the public thoroughly enjoyed for the past forty years, apparently has given way to a go-as-you-please game." Or as umpire and baseball columnist Billy Evans soberly commented, "the 'home run epidemic' had put the game out of whack; it was time to return to "normalcy."[37] Many purists hoped the aging Cobb might still be the antidote to Ruth and the public's newfound obsession with the long ball. Early on sportswriter Ernest Lanigan predicted the baseball world would tire of Ruth soon enough and once again make Cobb their favorite. "We know that the Easterner

[Ruth] is likely to drive the ball out of the lot," he remarked, but so what? Cobb offered more excitement by doing "the unexpected." Surely, he believed, the public preferred "brain to brawn."[38]

Although Cobb's supporters sometimes sounded wistfully nostalgic, they were not pure atavists. They believed Cobb's approach to the game offered important lessons that were profoundly relevant to contemporary life. Collectively, they suggested modernity could use a touch of Victorian morality and used Cobb's years of success to show how the past could inform the present. For example, take the pundits' efforts to explain Cobb's remarkable longevity as a ballplayer. The longer Cobb played—and the more records he set while doing so—the more he impressed sports journalists and fans alike for his remarkable staying power. Writing in 1922, longtime booster Lane remarked that Cobb's career was nothing less than "one long masterpiece, surpassing anything hitherto achieved, worthy to serve as a model for generations of ball players to come." Lane termed Cobb's efforts "superhuman" and wondered how long he could keep it up. So did Spink. "Records!" the *Sporting News* editor exclaimed, midway through the decade. "If Ty Cobb and his truculent bat can keep it up he will soon have hoarded all of them." He was not far off. By the time Cobb retired, he had set some ninety records—not every record, but close. By the time he retired, another writer recalled, Cobb had become "a museum piece of legend and achievement."[39]

Cobb's supporters claimed he was able to excel for so long because he approached the game like a professional. That is, he treated the game as a business and demonstrated the same commitment to success as the era's great leaders of finance, industry, and commerce. In this, the writers consciously tried to tap into the spirit of the age. Yes, Americans were fascinated by the hedonistic excesses of celebrities like Ruth, F. Scott and Zelda Fitzgerald, William Randolph Hearst, and Louise Brooks, but they also lionized the great business leaders of the age. Industrialists like Henry Ford, Charles Schwab, and John D. Rockefeller, and financial wizards like Andrew Mellon, William C. Durant, and John J. Raskob gained stature as modernity's true heroes. Through magazine profiles, biographies, news accounts, and even advertisements, the purveyors of popular culture glorified the businessman as the primary agent of material progress, promoter of the public good, and protector of democracy and free enterprise. This was no exaggeration, not to the leaders of 1920s America. President Calvin Coolidge famously proclaimed, "The man who builds a factory builds a temple. The man who works there, worships there." Advertising executive Earnest Elmo Calkins was even bolder, writing in 1928 that the "eternal job of administering the planet must be turned over to the business man. The work that religion and government have failed in must be done by business." After all, "business is today *the* profession. It offers something of the glory that in the past was given to the crusader, the soldier, the courtier, the explorer . . . the test of wits, of brain, or quick thinking, the spirit of adventure, and especially the glory of personal achievement." Equally hyperbolic, a writer for *The Independent* proclaimed, "Through business, properly conceived, managed and conducted, the human race is finally to be redeemed." Rhapsodically, he observed, "What is the finest game? Business. The soundest science? Business. The truest art? Business. The fullest education? Business. The fairest opportunity? Business. The cleanest philanthropy? Business. The sanest religion? Business."[40]

With business in ascendance, men on the make searched for the edge that would enable them to find success in the bustling world of modern capitalism. A host of mediums catered to them—self-help books, advice columns, specialty products—all promising that success was in reach for the man astute enough to heed their advice. Chroniclers of sports were eager to tap into the business mania if only to show the continued relevance of sport in a world obsessed with pecuniary gain. Cobb became a favorite subject because he seemed to model the business ethos so perfectly. "Playing ball is Cobb's business," *The Rotarian* observed in 1915, "and the same rules that he uses with such great success can be applied by every other man to his business."[41] By the 1920s, chroniclers of Cobb routinely connected the Peach to business, suggesting that he not only embodied the success ethic of the business world but that every man could profit from Cobb's advice and example. A contributor to *Young Men* suggested, "Cobb has reached his present position because of this fact—he began with the definite aim of becoming a success. . . . He regarded the game as his profession." That is, Cobb's mind was always on the job. His "thoughts about his work did not end with the last inning of the day's game, but he continued to study, to review the plays which had been made to think what might be done to win tomorrow's game." In this, Cobb "applied the same rules to his playing that other men apply to achieve supremacy in 'higher' professions."[42]

Writers of juvenile literature also admonished their readers to heed the example of Cobb as they started out in life. The most widely read male youth magazines—including *Youth's Companion, St. Nicholas, Boys' Life*, and *American Boy*—all raved about Cobb. In fact, they ran more features on Cobb than on any other athlete. The message of these pieces was nearly always the same: Cobb was an ideal role model because he demonstrated the rewards of clean living, ambition, and devotion to hard work. "Only a professional ball player, you say?" *The Youth's Companion* asked near the close of Cobb's career. "That is true but the possessor nevertheless of qualities that made him in that occupation a by no means unworthy object of boyish admiration, and a figure of national reputation." After all, Cobb "played hard and eagerly," but also "cleanly, honestly, fairly . . . A man to be respected because success and admiration did not at any time turn his head or set him on fire with conceit. Boyhood may easily find many less admirable heroes than Ty Cobb."[43]

Some sportswriters were so eager to demonstrate Cobb's relevance to the business world they nearly bludgeoned the reader with didactic interpretations of Cobb's life. Sheridan sounded almost shrill when he encouraged young men to follow Cobb's model of self-reliance. "One of the great weaknesses in American life is the disposition of father, 'big brothers,' and others to give too much help to young men," Sheridan complained. This, Sheridan warned, had a tendency to "disable a boy" for "when a man needs help he is beaten." Far better to experience the fate of Cobb in his youth when he was shunned by teammates and had to learn to go it alone. That story, Sheridan lectured, "should make good reading for youngsters who desire to make good in baseball or in any other occupation."[44] Other journalists chimed in to agree. A contributor to *Baseball Magazine* told readers to follow Cobb's example because he "has a habit of making up his mind that he is going to learn how to do something . . . and then accomplishing his object by dint of his natural athletic ability, perseverance, and a certain amount of stick-to-itiveness." Even journalists from beyond the sporting pages got into the act. *Collier's* Dayton Stoddart suggested Cobb was worthy of fans' idolatry because he modeled that singularity of focus that bred success. When

Stoddart asked Cobb how he maintained his drive after twenty years in the majors, Cobb responded in language that echoed the creed of the self-made man: "I've always been intensely interested in trying to do what I'm doing better than anybody else," Cobb claimed. No matter the challenge, "I try to improve on what I'm engaged in and to improvise" when he felt cornered or stifled.[45] Grantland Rice, probably the most widely read sports columnist of the era, seemed singularly obsessed with presenting his friend as a role model for businessmen. In articles with such telling titles as "The Durable Cobb," "The Winner's Way," "You Can Win If . . . ," and "They Laugh at the Years," Rice explained the secret to Cobb's success with each piece repeating the same essential point: others may have been more talented than Cobb, but no one matched Cobb's work ethic. Cobb "built upon the hardest sort of work, practicing . . . long after others quit," Rice asserted. Equally important, he remained committed to self-improvement even after he became the game's best player, never taking "it for granted that he was beyond mistakes." Instead, he built up a "human machine" that has become the "marvel of all time."[46]

Thanks to the labors of sportswriters like Sheridan and Rice, corporate America took notice of Cobb as an exemplar of occupational success. Eager to link themselves to such a popular figure, corporate leaders employed Cobb's services in an array of businesses. Articles in professional journals as diverse as the *Bulletin of the National Association of Credit Men, Advertising and Selling, Industrial Service, Pipeline and Gas Journal*, and *Personal Efficiency* drew from Ty Cobb lore to motivate and instruct readers. In a typical piece, William Ganson Rose of the National Laundry and Dry Cleaners Association encouraged his fellow dry cleaners to follow Ty Cobb's example—that is, "eliminate losing plays" so they could become "winning players" just like Ty. In another, a contributor to the *Pipeline and Gas Journal* encouraged his fellow kitchen appliance salesmen to find inspiration in Cobb to "steady your nerves and get . . . into the hustling habit." Those who followed his example could not fail to find greater success.[47] Meanwhile some organizations—including the Chicago field agents of Washington Life and Accident and the Wholesale Coal Association—found Cobb's message so inspirational, they invited him to address their meetings. Accolades for Cobb came from all over the business community. In a how-to primer for aspiring businessmen, *Certain Success*, sales guru Norval

Abiel Hawkins credited Cobb for "masterly salesmanship" and bid his readers to follow Cobb's example to escape the "bush leagues." National Lamp Works' executives thought so highly of Cobb as an inspiration for their sales team, they offered "Ty Cobb trophies" as incentives during their 1919 sales campaign.[48]

Corporations also attached themselves to Cobb's success through advertising. For several years, Cobb had used his celebrity to endorse a variety of products, from cigarettes to men's suits to Coca-Cola. Most such ads simply traded off Cobb's celebrity. That is, they featured an image of Cobb and perhaps identified him as one of the game's best players, but rarely mentioned the reasons behind his success. During the 1920s, advertisers began to provide the details: they explicitly paid homage to Cobb's values as the source of his accomplishments. In a 1922 advertisement REO Motor Car Company likened its continued success to Cobb's remarkable longevity. "No one, looking at the consistently brilliant record of Tyrus Raymond Cobb over a period of sixteen years would attempt to single out any one year as a 'Ty Cobb year,'" the ad's copy began. "And so it is with REO . . . . It is the consistency of its success . . . which accounts for the very unusual public confidence which Reo automobiles enjoy." Simmons Mattress—a company that also featured business titans like Henry Ford and John D. Rockefeller in their ads—paid tribute to—and took partial credit for—Cobb's self-discipline in an advertisement that ran in the early 1920s. "Sound sleep has kept 'Ty' Cobb in the great game for 19 years," the banner announced. The great Cobb, the text reminded interested shoppers, "has retained his speed and remarkable batting skill because he has made it a rule to sleep at least ten hours every night." So, too, "champions in *all* pursuits of life realize that a wide-awake mind and rested body are essential to conspicuous success."[49] So close was Cobb's identification to business success, some said the aging star had begun to resemble a new symbol of manhood—the business executive. Photos of Cobb in the national press often presented him in three-piece business suits of understated though formal stylings. This prompted one journalist to write that Cobb looked "more like a well-dressed broker in his early thirties than the usual conception of the aging ball player." Another suggested Cobb gave the appearance of a "florid-faced business executive." Small wonder a men's clothiers association asked Cobb to wear their goods as a kind of product placement. In making its offer, the association told Cobb, "You are the idol of the boys today and your opinion and guidance would make a lasting impression on the men of tomorrow. America needs you to make the nation better dressed and, therefore, better equipped to handle the affairs of life."[50]

These profiles reveal how much Cobb's public reputation had changed by the end of his career. To the mass media, Cobb was no longer the intemperate Southerner or the brash sporting dandy. Rather, he was a model of understated and conservative reserve—the very character traits his go-for-broke, pugnacious, and even malevolent on-field demeanor dramatically defied. At least to the purveyors of popular culture, Cobb had not simply grown up; he had ascended to the revered status of senior business partner. The ironies of this are manifold, not so much because he did not deserve such adulation but because he—no less than Ruth—owed his reputation to ballyhoo advertising and public relations. Moreover, the evolving reputation of this man so wedded to the traditions of honor gave witness to the pliability of the public persona in this emerging age of mass media and celebrity.

Cobb himself embraced the new image. "When I went into baseball," he told the *Detroit Free Press* in 1921, "I said to myself that baseball was a business and that like any other business, it was a matter of push and fight every instant."[51] For Cobb, part of that ethic entailed making his baseball income work for him. Playing ball in Detroit expanded his horizons. Cobb wisely took advantage of the opportunities to meet and learn from some of the age's greatest industrialists and entrepreneurs. During this time, he gained appreciation for the business culture of the modern city and adopted many of its values. By the 1920s, he had become quite the shrewd capitalist. Though he rarely talked specifics about his business dealings with the press, he made everyone aware that he was doing quite well. He invested wisely, purchasing General Motors and Coca-Cola stock before either was a national sensation. He then watched his stocks soar in value as both blanketed the consumer landscape. In 1917, Salsinger estimated Cobb's investments boosted his earnings to about $50,000 annually, the equivalent to about $1,000,000 today. Cobb continued to invest during the postwar stock market boom. By the time he retired in 1928, he was a multimillionaire—perhaps the only millionaire ballplayer until at least the 1960s.[52] Obviously, Cobb appreciated American business and relished his identification with modern capitalism. He saw no inconsistencies between this world and the ethic of honor. Nor should he have: after all the titans of the New South were every bit as Southern and as ambitious.

Cobb played an active role in the construction of his new persona. He consistently drew parallels between the values needed to succeed in sports with the values needed to succeed in all professions—commitment, determination, ambition, and self-discipline. As always, he infused his public utterances with a heavy dose of manly self-assertion. Cobb believed the successful professional must determine his fate or he risked annihilation by his competitors. In this, business values dovetailed with the code of honor. His mantra from the start of his career to the end was simple: "I must get ahead of the others and keep ahead of the others." He believed each individual had it within his power to succeed; it was just a matter of will. For this reason, he often emphasized the role self-discipline played in his success. In his various writings, Cobb persistently admonished readers to get plenty of rest and to be temperate with intoxicants. Cobb was particularly careful about his diet—not so much what he ate, but how much and when. His was the diet of a Spartan. As he told one interviewer, "Two meals a day is plenty." This diet was nothing new for Cobb; he has adopted it years before on the advice of his minor league manager and mentor George Leidy. Now he identified it as an essential part of his success. Too much food in the stomach, he maintained, makes the individual sluggish and dull-witted. When the *New York Evening News* asked Cobb to write a series of articles to commemorate twenty years with the Detroit Tigers, he devoted an entire column to diet. Here he claimed "knowing when and how to eat" was one of the most important factors to success on the ball field. [53]

Cobb probably had an ulterior motive in making such claims. He understood that personal discipline set him apart from his ever-looming nemesis, Ruth. As Ruth gained a disreputable reputation for his excesses, Cobb doubled down on the importance of self-discipline in ways that accentuated the differences between himself and the Big Bam. Once, while discussing the importance of diet, he offered the aside that he had recently witnessed an opposing player wolf down five hot dogs and two bottles of sarsaparilla under the grandstand during a game. To make the player pay for his gluttony, Cobb instructed his team to hit balls in his direction all afternoon. Was Ruth the guilty party? Cobb did not say. He did not have to: readers would have seen the resemblance and drawn their own conclusions.[54]

That was one thing about Cobb that had not changed. Underneath his Brooks Brothers three-piece suits, he retained a conception of manhood that embraced aggression and personal autonomy. On the field, he still acted the tyrant. In 1921, he had his bloody postgame altercation with umpire Billy Evans. A year later, he intentionally stomped on the toes of umpire Frank Wilson. A year after that, he got himself ejected from an exhibition game in his hometown of Augusta for throwing dirt at an umpire. Cobb ended up arguing so vehemently in that one, the head umpire ended up forfeiting the game to the opposing team. According to Detroit second baseman Charlie Gehringer, Cobb made a practice of sharpening his cleats on the dugout bench just to intimidate rookies. And, of course, he continued to apply the professional teach to any infielder who dared block him on the base paths. During an exhibition against a college team in Georgia, Cobb came flying with his spikes high against a young collegian. In retaliation, the infielder pounded Cobb hard with the ball as he applied the tag. Not to be outdone, Cobb threw dirt in the young man's face as he got up. A riot nearly erupted as shocked fans came to the collegian's defense. Cobb retained this kind of fierceness to the very end of his playing career. When rookie infielder Leo Durocher got in his way during a game in 1928, Cobb's last year in the majors, Cobb snapped, "You get in my way again, you fresh busher, and I'll step on your face." Off the field, it was much the same story. Usually courtly and congenial, he still erupted when crossed. After the 1924 off-season, he had an altercation with a waitress over a lunch bill that devolved into a slugfest as Cobb threw blows at both the restaurant manager and a policeman. Cobb was a recidivist mauler if ever there was one.[55]

It hardly seemed to matter. Journalists now began to treat Cobb's tantrums and violent encounters as either old news or as an unavoidable by-product of Cobb's hard-driving success ethic. The *Sporting News* took this latter stance when it praised Cobb for twenty years of stellar play. In a long testimonial, editor Spink praised behavior he once criticized. Yes, he admitted, "men have criticized [Cobb] because of his aggressiveness on the field." But that was just Cobb being Cobb. "If you are going to stay out in the right field corner of professional baseball and look moodily at the fence, and expect the manager will send you in a wheeled chair to get back to the bench," Spink offered, "you will never be a Ty Cobb." Cobb had learned how to take matters into his own hands; who could argue with the results? "Cobb stands forth today (as) one of the finest athletes in our history of professional athletics. He has a charming family. He is well to do. He has earned it."[56] Neither Spink nor anyone else had much to say about Cobb's frequent displays of bad temper, poor judgment, and violent behavior. Apparently, Cobb was now so successful, criticizing him would simply be in bad taste. Then too, the press had a new bad boy to obsess about—Babe Ruth.

Conveniently for Cobb, the Bambino gave the press all the scandal, gossip, and "color" it needed. For this reason, Ruth found himself constantly in and out of the doghouse during the 1920s, despite the best efforts of Christy Walsh. Indeed, Cobb owed some of his sustained popularity to Ruth. During the first half of the twenties, the Babe was a problematic idol at best. Even though the mavens of popular culture celebrated Ruth as a symbol of the age, the personification of the unbridled lust for pleasure that flourished in the Jazz Age, public perception of Ruth was not uniformly favorable. What practitioners of ballyhoo journalism defined as colorful—his uninhibited behavior, his insatiable appetites for sensual pleasures, and his irresponsible treatment of others—struck many as deeply troubling. During the early twenties, many considered him more a tragic figure than a hero because of his inability to control himself. Not everyone appreciated the lifestyle Ruth personified. Even as American culture slid into a world of consumerism, fads, and instant gratification, many Americans continued to extol values that ran counter to the enticements of excess.

Thanks to Ruth's many scandals, the press did not need Cobb scandals to sell newspapers anymore. Instead, they turned to Cobb for something else—a benchmark by which to measure the Bambino's many shortcomings. Most of the time, the press made the comparisons between the two implicit, as when they played up Cobb's dedication to fitness, his devotion to a strict diet, and his constructive use of the off-season to look after various business interests. Sometimes, however, events compelled journalists to go further. One such event occurred on August 31, 1925—the twentieth anniversary of Ty Cobb's major league debut. The city of Detroit marked the day by honoring Cobb with a gala banquet and naming him "First Citizen" of the city. Meanwhile Ruth was making headlines of another sort, receiving a stiff fine and a suspension from manager Miller Huggins for conduct unbecoming a baseball star. Apparently, Ruth missed batting practice because he was still recovering from a bender the night before. The coincidence of feting one star and fining the other on the same day was a contrast too pregnant with meaning for some journalists to ignore. In an editorial entitled "Two Heroes," the *New York Times* used the occasion to chastise Ruth for his inability to handle celebrity. Where most sports heroes fail, the newspaper observed in an obvious reference to Ruth, "is in remaining modest, in properly judging the fleeting nature of their fame, in keeping in good bodily trim, and of saving something for the rainy day." The true baseball star, the *Times* asserted, "ought to have a strong character" as well as ample physical skill. Cobb, the *Times* suggested, possessed such qualities and was "of the highest eminence"; Ruth's character paled in comparison.[57]

A few weeks later, the *Literary Digest* drew upon various newspaper accounts to give its take on the divergent paths the two stars had taken. Ruth, the unnamed writer suggested, was baseball's "baby," and a colicky one at that. If Ruth did not learn to control himself soon, the writer predicted, he might very well become "the Behemoth of Bust." Conversely, the author offered Cobb nothing but praise. Ignoring Cobb's well-documented shortcomings, he called Cobb baseball's "good boy" and its "paragon." "The story of Cobb," the writer summarized, "is the story of a determination to succeed, to be first in the chosen endeavor of life." In making its case, *Literary Digest* referenced a number of journalists and baseball men. Typical was the assessment of *New York Sun* sportswriter Joe Vila: "Cobb's wonderful record as a player never has been tarnished by fines or suspensions for violating the rules of dissipation." Instead, Cobb was an exemplary role model: "one of the builders of Detroit," a hero who offered "to the youth of the country a mark to shoot at on the diamond or in business life."[58]

Cobb must have been pleased with this turn of events. Unable to embarrass, let alone defeat, Ruth on the field, he could at least take solace in knowing he could hold his own in the public relations war. Sports history remembers the twenties as the Age of Ruth. For good reason: Ruth ushered in a new approach to the game and did so with a larger-than-life personality that dominated headlines and drew hundreds of thousands of new fans to the ballpark. Yet for all his popularity, he never completely overshadowed Cobb. Cobb remained a popular draw during the 1920s. Though the Tigers never competed for a championship during the first half of the 1920s (in their best season they finished second, a distant sixteen games behind the Yankees), they attracted more fans on the road than every team but the Yankees. Obviously, Cobb had a great deal to do with this. Cobb also remained an influential voice in baseball—despite his anxieties about being overtaken by Ruth and other hard hitters. Thanks to a sympathetic press, Cobb was able to garner more than a few headlines and feature columns for himself. As he had always done through the press, he crafted a projection of self that he hoped would have a broad appeal. No longer the young and impetuous insurgent, he now offered the perspective of the baseball sage—the wizened voice of authority and tradition. It was a role he was uniquely qualified to assume. By the early 1920s, he had become the longest tenured player in the major leagues. He drew upon this role often over the next several years, taking every opportunity to discuss the state of professional baseball in major newspapers and national magazines. His tone in these pieces was almost always reflective and reasonable, perfectly complementing the reverential treatment he received from the press.

Cobb had three goals when working with the press during these years. First, he wanted to show that his style of play was not only superior to the slugging craze, but more exciting. Second, he wanted to retain his popularity and his reputation by reinforcing the press's favorable presentation of him. Third, he wanted to take Ruth down a peg—without sounding overly desperate or petty. He nearly always began by asserting that the current fascination with home runs was a fad and that like all fads, it would not last. "The game runs in cycles," he cautioned. During his time, Cobb had seen baseball adopt only to abandon any number of fads—and now the fad was home runs. It has gotten so "to be in the limelight these days a batter must make home runs, and lots of them," he commented—apparently without bitterness. Even so, he underlined just how fickle baseball strategy could be, reminding fans that just "a few years ago, a batter would have been fined for swinging as they do nowadays."[59]

Cobb was confident fans' and players' desire for excitement would eventually kill the home run craze. As he saw it, the home run mania made the game far less enjoyable to watch. "Baseball today is a massing of heavy artillery. Everything is sacrificed to piling up runs," he observed. The game had become a "sort of free-for-all slugging match in which the heaviest slugging, bunched at the proper time wins out." It was all "biff-bing-bang." Boring. Cobb saw no drama, no risk-taking in this style of ball. "Outfiguring the other fellow," what old-timers called inside baseball, "is no more." Instead, the ruling "principle of baseball now is: play safe." He was particularly disappointed in the dramatic decline in base stealing that accompanied the advance of the long ball. "With the sluggers of today, base stealing is a back number," he observed. It had become "a lost art." "I may be wrong," he told a reporter, "but I believe the folks who pay to watch ball games enjoy a clever steal just as much as they do a home run." What was true for base stealing was true for daredevil base running—the plays of nerve and skill that had made Cobb famous. "There is no room for the things I used to do in the game as it is played today," he remarked. Cobb expected it would all change soon. Fans wanted excitement and what was more exciting than the risk-taking ventures he championed. With that, Cobb took a few swipes at the younger generation of ballplayers. He claimed modern players lacked the fire and combativeness of the players of his generation. Although the players might be stronger, bigger, and faster, they failed to use their abilities as completely as they should. He blamed the home run for this. Players waited for the long ball to save them rather than fight and scrap for runs; he hinted this mentality made them disengaged and even lazy. "It's about time the ball players got back to life and manifested something on the bases" beyond "a willingness to amble around in front of a home run," he told a reporter for the *Sporting News*.[60]

Cobb had added incentive to defend his style of play during the later years: in 1921, he replaced Jennings as manager. Naturally, he determined to rebuild the team in his image. Cobb wanted the Tigers to demonstrate the superiority of his style of play. The situation was this: In 1920, the Tigers finished in seventh place with a disappointing 60–94 record, thirty-seven games behind the champion Indians. Manager Hughie Jennings received much of the blame for the weak showing. Once an effective and inspiring leader, he now seemed tired and listless. Jennings found solace in the bottle, an addiction that further compromised his ability to manage. Two weeks after the season ended, Jennings resigned under pressure from Navin. Although Navin floated a number of names as possible replacements, including former White Sox manager Clarence "Pants" Rowland, current White Sox manager William "Kid" Gleason, and recently fired Braves manager George Stallings, his top choice was Cobb, who had taken on many managerial responsibilities as Jennings lost touch with the team. Cobb, however, was not at all sure he wanted the job, telling inquisitive sportswriters that he preferred to concentrate on his own performance without having to worry about the team's.[61]

In short order, Cobb changed his mind. He had many reasons for doing so, but the most important was prompted by honor-infused hubris. That is, Cobb found the opportunity to create the team in his image far too seductive to pass up. Cobb embraced the task of rebuilding the Tigers as a referendum on his style of play. He told the press he wanted a team of "fighters" and promised to "replace every member of the team," if need be. Although he confessed the team might not finish higher than sixth place, he was confident his players would compete with bold determination. Cobb also promised to assemble a team that would play the game as he played it—aggressively and intelligently. Whereas Jennings had come to rely upon heavy hitting, Cobb promised a more diversified approach. "We are going to make the other clubs try to figure out what they can expect instead of letting them feel secure in the belief that we cannot vary our attack," he told reporters. For this reason, he promised fans that his Tigers would value speed. Just before spring training opened, he ordered dozens of sheepskin sliding pads so he could teach his players how to run the bases and how to slide. All players—even pitchers—would "pound the earth" every day during practice. "Going into the bags standing upright will be regarded henceforth as a crime," the *Detroit Free Press* reported. As a player, Cobb sacrificed his body without consideration of injury; as manager, he expected his players to do the same. He also wanted the Tigers to master the war of nerves: "Beat them one day with a lot of stuff they didn't believe we had, they'll come out the next day wondering what we will do next, and consequently, their confidence is shaken." Reporters understood exactly what Cobb had in mind: he meant to have the team play the game as he played it. So personal was his stamp upon the team that sportswriters across the country began to refer to the team as the "Cobbmen" and the "Tygers."[62]

Initial results were encouraging. During the first year or so, players welcomed Cobb's leadership, even Harry Heilmann, a big-hitting outfielder whose taste for good times off the field sometimes compromised his ability to put forth his best efforts on the field. In 1921, Heilmann had a breakout year, hitting .394—seventy points higher than his previous personal best—to lead the league. Heilmann would eventually end up in the Hall of Fame, thanks in part to a lifetime .342 batting average. Although the Tigers remained a second division team that year, finishing sixth with a record of 71–82, experts agreed that Cobb was getting results. The team that seemed so apathetic in 1920 now played with heart and fire. Cobb was especially effective in working with young recruits like first baseman Lu Blue, outfielder Bob Fothergill, catcher Johnny Bassler, shortstop Topper Rigney, infielder Fred Haney, and—a bit later—outfielder and another future Hall of Famer Heinie Manush. These players became the foundation for one of the most dynamic offensive teams of the early 1920s—batting over .300 as a team and among the leaders in runs scored each of the first three seasons under Cobb. With so many prolific hitters, they were an entertaining group to watch: at home, they drew record crowds, topping one million for the first time in 1924; on the road, they trailed only the Yankees in drawing fans to the park. More important, their record steadily improved, topping out with a .558 winning percentage in 1924.

Journalists took note and gave much of the credit to Cobb. As early as 1922, experts identified the Tigers as a team to watch. They look "like a real contender," a Washington sportswriter declared. Grantland Rice was more effusive. Cobb had made the Tigers "the big sensation" of the season because he "has got 100 per cent out of the material" and proved what "the winning type of leadership can do with only average material." The following year, Hugh Fullerton called Cobb "a real manager, a real leader." Under Cobb, the Tigers were "one of the greatest hustling and fighting aggregations in the game, on its toes all the time, inspired by the spirit which has carried Cobb along at the top so many years." What's more, they played smart—"the best team ball" in the league with a "finer understanding of why they are doing smart plays." When the Tigers finished the season in second in 1923, their best showing since 1915, local correspondent Sam Greene of the *Detroit Free Press* announced Cobb had "silenced his critics" by exacting "startling" results from his young team. In 1924, Yankees manager Miller Huggins declared that "Cobb and his fighting players" were the Yankees' most dangerous rivals.[63]

Cobb often boasted of his skills as a manager. He was proudest of the combative spirit he instilled in his team. "I saw to it that we kept intact a tradition as old as old-fashioned baseball. . . . Namely you don't go in for a lot of hearts-and-flowers fellowship with other teams." He demanded a "go-to-hell-with-you-guys" attitude from his players, ordering them "to fight to the limit," even during spring training games.[64] An avid student of military history, he imagined himself a field commander leading a battle charge, confident that his devoted foot soldiers would follow close behind. All he had to do was find players who were man enough to follow his leadership. Once he had the right players, they would naturally fall in line, mesmerized by the force and power behind his commitment to the game. Players wanted to win and Cobb knew how to win. Why would they not follow him?

Yet for all Cobb's determination and guile, he was never able to push the Tigers to the pennant. After making steady progress for the first four years, the Tigers stalled, finishing fourth in 1925 and sixth in 1926—Cobb's last year as manager. They finished above .500 in these years, but this hardly satisfied—not after the promise of those first years. The pundits who had supported Cobb early in his tenure turned on him. 1925 and 1926 were years of tension, strain, and remorseless criticism for Cobb. Even old allies like John Sheridan and the Detroit beat writers harped at Cobb for failing to deliver.

What happened? In his final autobiography, Cobb deflected all criticism: it was all President Navin's doing; he "sabotaged" the team. Cobb rattled off a list of talented players Navin refused to acquire—first baseman Johnny Neun, ace reliever Si Blankenship, future Hall of Famer Paul Waner, future twenty-game winner Ray Kremer. Had the Tigers obtained those players, Cobb maintained, they would have won the Series during his tenure—maybe more than once. When Cobb demanded pitchers, the best Navin would do was sign players waived by other clubs or unproven minor leaguers. Cobb claimed Navin wasn't just cheap, he was afraid of success. He possessed a "negative, defeatist attitude," the antithesis of what Cobb had labored so hard to instill in his charges. In the end, Cobb maintained, he had willed his players to be champions, but he could not impress his will upon the club's principal owner because the owner lacked the capacity for true manhood. Instead, he made Cobb and the Tigers victims of his cowardice.[65]

Like many Cobb narratives, this one possesses some truth—Navin was notoriously tight with the dollar—but overlooks important details. In this case, Cobb failed to mention that his vaunted tactics alienated many of his players during his tenure as manager. He did not mean for this to happen, of course. Once he took over the team, he tried very hard to establish himself as a player's manager. Entering his first spring training, he promised to ban the 7:30 wake-up calls and "fatiguing" morning practices that every other manager used. Players should be rested and fresh for the late afternoon game, Cobb counseled. He intended to let his players sleep as long as they wanted, "until noon, if they so desire." Practice would not begin until 1:00 and continue for three to four hours. If a player looked sluggish, Cobb would insist he sit out the rest of the day's practice. After all, "fatigue is poison to the system." He also promised to not waste players' time with useless meetings. Skull practice was out. Why ruminate about hypothetical situations for an hour? He wanted his players to be quick-thinking attackers, not methodical by-the-book minions. Finally, he would do all he could to preserve the self-respect and confidence of each player. For pitchers this meant moving the bullpen's warm-up area behind the grandstand so that the starting pitcher could not see if someone was warming up to replace him. That sort of thing was disheartening to the starting pitcher, Cobb observed. "Here he is . . . working his hardest. The opposition bunches a few hits and the relief hurlers are rushed out to warm up. If that pitcher ever needed to concentrate, it is at that particular moment." But "how can he concentrate when every time he turns around he sees two or three of his teammates pitching merrily away to come to his rescue?" He promised to be equally sensitive to hitters. He would not change a hitter's style, so long as he produced. If a player slumped, Cobb promised to "coach" the player along without fiddling with his overall approach. Cobb, the dedicated individualist, promised to respect the individuality of his players.[66]

Cobb was confident this approach would make the team better—and make him a popular leader in the process. He knew what worked for him and now he was in position to give his teammates the advantage of his knowledge and experience. "I played ball for fifteen years and I know players thoroughly," Cobb said. "I know what I wanted and what they wanted and I know just what ballplayers will do and what they should do. I am simply keeping in mind all the things that benefited me and I am sure the same methods can benefit others." Finally, he seemed to be saying, he would have a chance to reveal his genius to the rest of baseball.[67]

Cobb was a big part of the problem. As a manager, Cobb had two weaknesses. First, he lacked patience for certain kinds of players—namely players who lacked his intelligence, athletic ability, or will to win. That is to say, almost everyone. As one journalist observed, Cobb chalked up to "dumbness" players who could not think as fast as he could, players who could not pull off the sorts of gambits he executed, and players who did not learn from their mistakes as quickly as he did. He became more impatient the longer he managed. By the time Charlie Gehringer became a regular in 1926, Cobb had alienated just about everyone. "Nobody liked him as a manager," Gehringer recalled. His impatience was his undoing: "He was such a great player himself, he figured that if he told you something, there was no reason why you couldn't do it as well as he did."[68] He could be especially short-tempered with pitchers. Gehringer remembered that when Cobb relieved a pitcher, he would "just grab the ball away from him," often without comment. When Bill Moore made his major league debut in 1925, he walked the first three batters he faced. After he started the next batter off with a ball, Cobb angrily waved Moore back to the dugout without bothering to visit the pitching mound. Interviewed forty years later, Moore still seethed. "I never had any use for Cobb," he said. He was convinced that Cobb and Navin buried him in the minors, refusing to let him sign with another team. That lone appearance was the sum of his major league career.[69]

Cobb's second weakness concerned his emotional makeup. He allowed the stress of losing to affect his relationships with players. Granted, winning matters in professional sports, but Cobb allowed defeat to affect him in ways that damaged the well-being of the team. He fretted and worried constantly, reaching a level of anxiety he probably had not experienced since the trauma of his first full year in the majors. He was quite candid about this when he wrote his autobiography years later. "Temperamentally, I was always on edge, unable to take things easy, once the bell rang on Opening Day," he wrote. "I always figured every play to be too close, and shot the works, which was both successful and a terrible physical drain." He likened himself to a steel spring, cryptically noting that "the slightest flaw causes an overworked spring to fly apart, and then it is done for." Observers believed Cobb was rapidly approaching that stage of psychosis. Gehringer said Cobb changed dramatically in the short time he played under him. Cobb was "super the first couple years I was up," Gehringer recalled. "Golly, he was like a father figure to me. He took care of me, coached me, rode with me on the train and all." Then he suddenly, and without explanation, turned on him. Gehringer assumed he had ticked Cobb off about something, but never figured out what. "Weird," was the future Hall of Famer's assessment. "He was a hard fellow to figure, to say the least." Batboy and clubhouse boy Eddie Forester witnessed Cobb become increasingly dictatorial as the team stalled during his last years as manager. "I'm the manager, you do what I tell you. . . . I send you up there to bunt, you bunt," Forester recalled Cobb telling the players. "When he said he wanted you to do something, you'd do it." Forester claimed Cobb was the meanest man he ever met; "he was always mad."[70]

The press first reported significant unrest in early 1923. With the team mired in a slump, Cobb determined it was time to crack the whip. He benched some players and fined others for what he called "chirking" and "breaking training." Desperate to right the team, he lost patience with players who—in his view—lacked his iron will. He took to bawling some players out in front of the whole team, believing that shame might be the best tonic for reluctant learners. When umpires and the press complained that Cobb delayed play by taking his players to task, Cobb responded that he believed in immediate and honest feedback. Waiting until after the game to reprove a player "would mean the loss of the moral effect of that which he had in mind." Players believed Cobb's pedagogy was more than a little ineffective. Why, they complained to the press, couldn't Cobb be equally expressive when players did something right? Why couldn't he praise as well as criticize?[71]

Equally problematic, the manager who vowed to let players go their own way off the field began to impose strict rules of conduct. He banned golf during spring training, pointing out that the purpose to going South was to train, not to play. When he learned some of his players were enjoying themselves a bit too much late at night at dance halls and speakeasies, Cobb imposed a curfew, a decision that quickly alienated two of the team's best players and indigenous leaders, drinking buddies Harry Heilmann and pitcher George "Hooks" Dauss. One can hardly blame Cobb; both players made a habit of showing up to games still reeling from late-night drinking binges. After one long night of drinking Heilmann was still so gassed at the start of a game, he collapsed at third and vomited on the bag after legging out a triple. A disgusted Cobb kept Heilmann in the game to both dry him out and embarrass him. On another occasion, he forced a red-eyed and wobbly Dauss to take his usual turn in the rotation, even though he was in no condition to play; Dauss was hammered (literally and figuratively) for seven runs in the first inning before Cobb took him out.[72]

The ethic of honor, which had propelled Cobb to excel as a player, ultimately hurt his effectiveness as a manager. As he understood it, the ethic dictated that he gauge his self-worth by his won-lost record. So long as the Tigers improved, he could claim his venture into managing enhanced his reputation. As the team stalled, however, his self-esteem must have taken a beating; after all, he created the team in his image. Even worse, Cobb, the master of the baseball diamond who willed everyone to do his bidding, could not control his fate. Instead, he had to depend upon the performance of his players. Their lack of success was untenable to Cobb, who defined dependence as a form of servitude and failure as a form of dishonor. Reflexively, he responded by doing what he had always done—assert control. This time, the effects were disastrous. When Navin fired Cobb at the end of the 1926 season, he explained he had to do so because Cobb so over-managed he had left the team "badly demoralized." In a very thoughtful post mortem, *Detroit News* sportswriter Sam Greene explained that Cobb became "a martyr to his own temperament as a manager." The "great zeal" that made him the greatest ballplayer "handicapped him as a manager." Cobb was so intent on winning, "he tried to direct every play" and "desired to take the game entirely in his own hands and run it strictly according to his ideas." He even tried to do the players' "thinking for them." As a result, they became embittered and alienated. Cobb failed, Greene concluded, because he "tried too hard."[73]

Cobb was not a bad manager, finally. Six straight seasons above .500 is an impressive accomplishment. So, too, is an overall winning percentage of .519. By comparison, such notable pilots as Connie Mack, Tony

LaRussa, Joe Torre, Bucky Harris, Casey Stengel, Gene Mauch, Jack McKeon, Clark Griffith, Tommy Lasorda, Whitey Herzog, and Dick Williams did just about the same, albeit over longer periods of time. Still, Cobb fell far short of the standards he set for himself. Honor could be a harsh and unforgiving taskmaster.

So was age. Cobb lied about many things, but he rarely lied about his declining physical skills. As he aged, he came to accept that this was one topic that deserved a unique degree of candor. In contrast to modern athletes who often refuse to accept the ravages of time, Cobb candidly explained how the aging process affected his play. As he reached his mid-thirties, he began to complain about fatigue, especially in his legs. He admitted that he now relied far more on stealth than speed and was unable to gamble on the bases as he once had because risk-taking took too much out of him. He became a defensive liability as his gait slowed and his arm weakened. Meanwhile, he began to show his age. Although he still kept himself in excellent shape, he looked irrevocably middle-aged. His waistline expanded. He developed jowls, lines in his forehead, and crow's feet around the eyes. His hairline receded. He admitted to vision troubles because of cataracts and underwent at least two surgeries to correct the problem. He complained of stomach troubles and was briefly hospitalized with influenza.[74]

Cobb made little effort to disguise his feelings as the end approached. Instead, he often talked to writers about his future—as if he were testing out possible scenarios to see if he liked the sound of what he said. He discussed retirement with a candor born of his realization that time now controlled his fate. As early as July 1924, he told reporters he would quit playing at the end of the year so he could devote his full attention to managing. He subsequently changed his mind, but he had set a precedent. Henceforth, he no longer talked about if he would retire, but when. The next year, Cobb claimed he was ready to take himself out of the starting lineup. He only needed to find and train a replacement. That came in 1925 with the emergence of Bob Fothergill. "Fats" was slow but a steady .350 batting average helped compensate for his defensive shortcomings. With an outfield of Fothergill and Heinie Manush and Harry Heilmann, there was no room for Cobb. He appeared in only seventy-nine games the following year, his fewest since becoming a regular. He started just over sixty of those games and most of those were in the first half of the season. Even so, he was still exhausted from the responsibilities of managing. On the road, he went straight to his hotel room after the game, called room service for his dinner, and then read in bed until he fell asleep. He often didn't rise until it was time to leave for the game. The end was near.[75]

That end—or the beginning of the end—came on November 3, 1926, when the Detroit Tigers announced that Cobb had resigned as manager and retired as a player. Baseball fans, players, and journalists may have mourned the end of an era, but could hardly have been surprised by the announcement. He was just a month shy of forty and could no longer play the game as he believed it should be played. "I'm about as good as I ever was," he believed, "but the time has come for me to quit taking chances and that means that it is time for me to get out," he told the press. "I don't want to be one of those men who fade or have to be pushed out." He assured everyone that his decision was final. Once he had dreamed of staying on as manager after he retired as a player, but that was no longer a possibility. It had been a bad year. The Tigers had finished in sixth place, just four games above .500. Cobb later admitted that he was about used up as a manager. "I could see a growing and dangerous flaw in me," he confided in his final autobiography. "I was thoroughly tired, no longer baseball-wedded, and I had to have a rest."[76] It sounded very much like the familiar and sad rite of passage that comes to every major league player at the end of his career. A few weeks later the rite was repeated—this time in Cleveland where Tris Speaker, the great outfielder and manager, announced his retirement. To most observers it looked as though the two best outfielders left over from the Dead Ball Era had decided to end their careers together.

And then came the bombshell via the machinations of a former Tiger named Hubert Leonard.

"Dutch" Leonard was a left-handed pitcher—and a very good one. He came up with the Boston Red Sox in 1913 and became an integral part of their pennant-winning teams. In 1914, he posted a 19–5 record with a all-time record low ERA of 1.01. Prior to the 1919 season, Boston traded him to the Tigers. Over the next two years he lost his effectiveness and the Tigers let him go at the end of the 1921 season. By the end of 1924, however, Cobb was desperate for pitching. He talked Leonard out of retirement and placed him in the starting rotation. It was a decision Cobb regretted almost immediately. Though Leonard pitched well at the start of the 1925 season, he whined, whimpered, and groused. He complained Cobb did not know how to handle pitchers and was in danger of permanently ruining his arm because he used him too much. When Leonard protested, Cobb blew up. "Don't you dare turn bolshevik on me. I'm the boss here," Cobb told his pitcher. As punishment, Cobb left Leonard in a game against Philadelphia, forcing him to absorb a twelve-run drubbing. It got so bad, opposing manager Connie Mack tried to intervene. "You're killing that boy," he told Cobb. Cobb just laughed. Leonard refused to pitch during the next series so Cobb released him. Leonard figured someone would sign him, but no one did—not even former teammate and current Cleveland player-manager Tris Speaker. Leonard believed Cobb had blacklisted him and vowed revenge. When Dickie Kerr of the White Sox met Leonard the following winter in California, Leonard confided to him that he planned to "get even with Cobb or die in the attempt."[77]

Leonard meant it. He believed he had the goods to ruin Cobb and Speaker—evidence that both men along with former pitcher-turned-outfielder "Smoky" Joe Wood fixed a game near the end of the 1919 season. According to Leonard, the four of them plotted their misdeed under the grandstand at Detroit's Navin Field after a game on September 24. The Indians had just clinched second place and the Tigers were desperately trying to hold onto third and a share of the World Series money. Speaker, a notorious gambler, suggested that perhaps his club could help the Tigers out—and the four of them could all make several hundred dollars in the process. Why shouldn't the Indians "slough off" a bit and allow the Tigers to win the next day's game? Meanwhile, the four would pool together several thousand dollars to bet on the game through a local bookie, using park attendant Fred West to place bets for them. The following day, Leonard left the team and headed home to his farm in California, confident he would make a hefty sum to begin the winter hiatus.[78]

The pitcher possessed two letters, one from Wood and one from Cobb, which seemed to corroborate his accusations. Wood wrote his letter shortly after the game. In it, he explained to Leonard that West was only able to bet $600 of the $5,500 the four had raised and only at rather unfavorable 10 to 7 odds at that. He also enclosed a certified check for $1,630—a sum that included Leonard's share of the winnings plus the share of what West had not been able to bet. Wood's conscience bothered him not at all. Indeed, he told Leonard, "If we ever get another chance like this we will know enough to try to get down early" so they could bet a larger sum. In his letter, Cobb explained what Wood must have meant by this final statement. Apparently, West arrived too late for the bookie to clear such a large sum with his agents in Chicago. Or as Cobb put it, "they refused to deal with us, as they had men in Chicago to take the matter up with and they had no time." Like Wood, Cobb expressed disappointment that they were not able to get a better haul from the bet, noting he and Wood were "disappointed in our business proposition." Unlike Wood, Cobb seems to have acquired no taste for backroom shenanigans, telling Leonard, "I don't care to do it again, I can assure you."[79]

Confident that he could ruin Cobb and Speaker just as they had ruined him, Leonard had only to decide the best way to exact his revenge. In May 1926, he traveled east from California with the two letters and a story to tell. Along the way, he talked to a number of individuals—including Navin, American League president Ban Johnson, Washington manager Bucky Harris, and various reporters. All along, he tried to figure out the best way to press his advantage and perhaps earn some serious change in the process. Finally, Navin and Johnson came through with an offer he liked: They agreed to purchase the incriminating letters for $20,000. No doubt, they also made clear to Leonard that they would force the two stars out of the game. And indeed at the end of the season, Johnson met with both men, telling them "whether . . . guilty or not," they were "through in the American League." It worked; both men announced their retirements within the next few weeks, eager to save face, even if it meant cutting their careers short.[80]

That might have been the end of it, if not for the intrigues of baseball commissioner Kenesaw Mountain Landis who decided to investigate the matter for himself. In the fall and early winter, Landis met with Leonard (traveling nearly two thousand miles to Leonard's farm to do so) and then with Cobb, Speaker, and Wood. Four days before Christmas, he dropped a bombshell by releasing the two letters and the transcripts of his various interviews to the press. He claimed this was all part of an exhaustive three-month investigation, but otherwise refused to state whether he believed Cobb and Speaker were guilty of betting on a game and if so what he planned to do to the guilty parties. He was, in fact, in no hurry to act. In part this was because all four were no longer in baseball (Wood retired in 1922). But that was the least of it. Scholars who have looked closely at the case believe Landis hoped to exploit the incident to discredit and humiliate Ban Johnson. Landis figured Johnson's reputation would take a beating once the public learned he had known about the Leonard accusations for over a year and tried to buy him off rather than clean house. Indeed, this is pretty much how it played out. When asked by the press, Johnson conceded Landis was in control of the situation and that he had failed to act decisively and for the good of the game. Diminished in power and stature, his health failing, the once powerful czar of the American League was forced to take a temporary leave of absence. He returned for a short time, and then retired for good in October 1927. Landis got what he wanted.[81]

What of Cobb and Speaker? While Landis was toying with Johnson, he left the two stars in limbo. As they waited, both tried to clear their names. Each vehemently denied that he had conspired to fix the game. The evidence seems to support them on this. Although the Tigers won 9–5, neither Cobb nor Speaker acted as though they were trying to ensure a Detroit win: Cobb managed only one hit in five at bats while Speaker belted two triples for Cleveland. That Cobb would intentionally fix a game seems highly unlikely given his understanding of baseball. He approached each game as a contest of wills and a test of his manhood. To adulterate the purity of that contest was simply not in keeping with the ethos he lived by for over two decades.[82]

The accusation of gambling is a bit more problematic. Before major league baseball prohibited gambling in the wake of the Black Sox scandal, players often wagered on games they played. Many placed side bets as a way to express their manly self-assurance. Since players often bet in groups, they also saw gambling as an extension of their sociability ethos—a way to demonstrate their loyalty and confidence in one another. More practically, small wagers offered players a chance to earn a little extra cash at very little risk. Opportunities to gamble abounded in the urban neighborhoods that surrounded most ballparks. Coming to and from games, players passed any number of saloons, cafes, billiard halls, and other establishments where gamblers congregated. Finally, both Cobb and Speaker were from the South (Speaker was a Texan) where gambling held a central place in male culture. Dating back to the eighteenth century, Southern men of honor placed high stakes on horse races, cockfights, card games, and whatever else struck their fancy to demonstrate their manly courage. Speaker, in fact, was a notorious gambler and Cobb most certainly was exposed to this element of Southern culture as a youth playing town ball with the Royston Reds and semi-pro ball with the Anniston Steelers. Still, Cobb was raised a Baptist and seems to have rejected this element of the South's manly culture. When interviewed by Landis, Cobb claimed the only time he had bet was during the 1919 World Series when he bet the Chicago White Sox would win.[83]

For the game in question, Cobb solicited the cooperation of Wood and West, both of whom stated that Cobb and Speaker were not involved. Perhaps the most likely scenario regarding all this is the one offered by Cobb biographer Charles Alexander. Alexander posits that Cobb was probably in on the bet early, but later pulled out because he simply did not like to gamble. In the end, he may have helped broker the deal for friends, but otherwise stayed clear. Cobb appreciated the value of a dollar, after all. As a young man, he learned the importance of frugality when his father's death and the resulting trial of his mother for murder nearly bankrupted the family. Thereafter, he remained extremely careful about how he spent his money. Babe Ruth, the reigning expert of Cobb-baiting, told teammates the most effective way to needle Cobb was to call him a "penny pincher."[84]

Whatever Cobb's actual involvement, he moved quickly to clear his name and reestablish his reputation for honest play. Shortly after news reports hit of the "Cobb-Speaker scandal," the two visited Cobb's well-placed friends on Capitol Hill, including senators William H. Harris and James E. Watson of Georgia and Pat Harrison of Mississippi. Though the senators could do little for the two former ballplayers, they told the press they believed both men were innocent. When Cobb returned home to Augusta for the Christmas holidays, he participated in a very public "testimonial meeting" on his behalf at the foot of the Augusta Confederate Monument, a massive seventy-six foot high obelisk of granite and pure Italian marble, capped with a statue of a Rebel soldier and surrounded by statues of four legendary Confederate generals. There, under the eternal gazes of Stonewall Jackson, Robert E. Lee, William H. T. Walker, and Cobb's distant relative Thomas R. R. Cobb, town fathers gave testimony to the moral purity of their favorite son. No doubt, they chose this site to link Cobb to the South's heritage of courage, defiance, and resolve in the face of injustice from arbitrary power. L. S. Arrington, president of the city's chamber of commerce, even nominated Cobb for mayor, much to the delight of the several hundred citizens in attendance. Cobb humbly declined. "Boys, I'm a baseball player, not a politician," he reminded them.

These events did more than simply buoy Cobb's confidence; to Cobb, these were essential public rituals, the purpose of which was to give testament to his manly honor. If the lords of baseball would not clear his name, he would have to act on his own by asking men of stature and reputation to swear to his character. As Cobb saw it, Leonard, Johnson, and Landis were inferiors who out of spite and jealousy were determined to soil his reputation; he could not allow this. He had expected as much from Leonard and Johnson, but Landis's behavior truly bothered him. Shortly after Landis released the damning documents, Cobb condemned the commissioner via a public letter. "Is there any decency left on Earth? I am beginning to doubt it," he stated. "I know there is no gratitude. Here I am, after a lifetime in the game of hard, desperate and honest work forced to stand accused without ever having a chance to face my accuser. It is enough to try one's faith." Cobb believed Landis should have taken him at his word; he was Ty Cobb, after all. Instead, Landis delayed and the longer he delayed, the angrier Cobb became. When Landis called Cobb back to his office to testify again—this time with reporters present—Cobb seized the opportunity to chasten Landis. He declared flatly, "There never has been a baseball game in my life that I played in, that I knew was fixed." He then glowered at Landis and asked, "Want to swear me?" He meant this as an insult, insinuating that Landis did not know enough to recognize a man of honor when he saw one. Essentially, he dared Landis to give him the lie.[85]

Meanwhile, people in and out of baseball offered Cobb and Speaker enthusiastic support as they waited for Landis to act. The sincerity of their concern testified to Cobb's continued popularity, Age of Ruth or not. The *Chicago Tribune* observed, "Baseball fans refused to be silent while the magnates pondered what to do. . . . These admirers of Ty and Tris almost unanimously rise to the defense of their favorites." Hyperbolic, but not off by much. While all baseball waited for Landis to act, the newspaper published a series of letters from fans protesting the poor treatment Cobb received from Landis. In the *Sporting News*, both Spink and Sheridan penned columns questioning Leonard's motives and praising Cobb for his honesty. In Detroit, the city council passed a unanimous "resolution of confidence in Cobb and Speaker." Meanwhile, Detroit citizens began a petition drive to exonerate Cobb of all charges; organizers expected at least 250,000 to sign. A Detroit merchant advertised a $500 reward "to anyone proving that Ty Cobb has ever been in any conspiracy to throw a ball game or injure the great national game." In Philadelphia, the local chapter of the Baseball Writers Association told Cobb by telegram that this scandal "in no way lowered you from the pedestal as the greatest ball player of all times." Even schoolboys got into the act. In downtown Detroit, kids started a petition drive in hopes of pressing Landis to give Cobb a fair hearing. In Chicago, the American Boys' Commonwealth Club sent telegrams of encouragement to Cobb and Speaker. "Buck up and fight, we're with you," the boys told the two stars. Cobb also found allies deep in the Land of Ruth. Westbrook Pegler, one of the New York ballyhoo journalists who rarely evinced much love for Cobb, defended the two maligned stars in a series of syndicated columns, arguing Landis should let the matter drop because he had no case.[86]

What impact all this had on Landis is unclear. By mid-January, he must have realized that he could take the case no further. No one else came forward to corroborate Leonard's testimony and Leonard himself remained too afraid to testify further. When Landis urged him to return to Chicago to confront the men he accused, Leonard refused. "They bump off people once in a while around there," he told the commissioner. Once Johnson took his leave of absence, Landis apparently decided he had gotten as much out of this affair as he was going to get. On January 27, he released a statement to the press in which he fully exonerated Cobb and Speaker. He also rescinded the releases of the two players and instructed the owners of both teams to grant them free agency within the American League.[87]

Cobb might have quit the game at this point, riding out on a wave of good will into retirement. But that was not his style. He believed Landis, Navin, and Johnson had conspired to soil his name and he was not about to quit so long as there was any hint of scandal. Although touched by the outpouring of support from fans and the press, Cobb believed that redemption, like vengeance, was best experienced viscerally. He wanted to prove his innocence on the playing field, just as he had proved his manhood and his honor there. Equally important, he wanted to demonstrate he was, to the very last, his own man. He would not allow Navin, Johnson, or Landis to have final control over his fate as a ballplayer. They had left him twisting for two months. He intended to show that he was back in control: "Even if I appeared in only one more major league game—on my own terms—I would have proved for the all-time record and generations of youngsters to come that baseball wanted Ty Cobb right to the last," he explained in his final autobiography.[88]

With something to prove, Cobb shopped for a new employer. He later claimed that he was pursued by several teams. In fact, only three teams showed much interest in the now forty-year-old outfielder—Washington, St. Louis, and Philadelphia. In the end, Philadelphia offered Cobb the most money—$70,000 and 10 percent of all exhibition gate receipts. Cobb liked the idea of playing for the venerable Mr. Mack, now the Athletics' club owner as well as manager, because of his reputation for moral purity and integrity. Surely, Cobb believed, playing under Mack would prove to the baseball world he was a clean player. For his part, Mack believed he had the makings of a champion caliber team. After over a decade of finishing at or near the bottom of the American League, he had retooled with young hitters like Mickey Cochrane, Al Simmons, and Jimmie Foxx, and pitchers Bob "Lefty" Grove and George Earnshaw. The Athletics had finished third the previous year; Mack hoped the addition of a few veteran bats (he also signed Eddie Collins that winter) might bring the Athletics a pennant.

It didn't happen. The Athletics finished second to the Yankees, who put together one of the greatest seasons in the history of the game, with a winning percentage of .714. Even so, Cobb had a truly remarkable year. In 133 games he hit a robust .357, fifth best in the league. He also knocked in ninety-three runs, good for second place on the club and tenth in the league, stole twenty-two bases, and led the team in runs scored with 104. He enjoyed the season so much he decided to come back for one more year, in what everyone realized would be his final campaign.

For the most part, Cobb played the game under Mack as he always had. He still quarreled with umpires, baited adversaries, and ran the bases aggressively—when his legs allowed him to. Off the field, however, he exhibited a lightness he had rarely shown before. He especially enjoyed playing alongside Al Simmons. Indeed, he liked Simmons so much he consented to be his roommate on some road trips—the first time Cobb roomed with anyone in over fifteen years.[89] Probably the biggest adjustment he made during these years was to learn how to take orders from the meticulous Mack. Both men claimed they got along splendidly. Perhaps Cobb believed embracing his new team would help in his vindication. Perhaps he was happy to let go of the reins a bit after managing for the past six years. Whatever got into him, Cobb did in fact obey Mack's directives with considerable grace. In their respective autobiographies, manager and player each recounted with both relief and satisfaction the first time Mack waved his scorecard at Cobb to position him in the field. Good-naturedly, Cobb saluted Mack "as a soldier salutes a general and followed orders." Happily, Mack's instructions were spot on: the ball went directly to Cobb on a fly for an easy out. Cobb later recalled Mack used the scorecard many more times "and not once did he err in moving me left or right, or deeper or tighter." Cobb confessed he "sometimes deeply questioned" Mack's thinking, but the manager was never wrong: "the man was uncanny," Cobb recalled.[90]

Cobb called these years the happiest of his baseball career. Mack, realizing Cobb wanted validation as much as vindication, lavished praise on his aging star. Accusations that Cobb only played for himself were "bunk," Mack asserted at the close of the 1927 season. "I never handled a finer baseball man," nor "one who gave me less trouble than Cobb."[91] So Cobb's career began to wind down with a rather ironic twist: he had played his career obsessed with protecting his personal autonomy only to end his career by voluntarily submitting to one of the most authoritarian managers of the era. Cobb probably saw no inconsistency in his behavior. To explain his admiration and devotion to Mack, he drew upon the language of honor and deference. He admired Mack as both a "baseball genius" and a "man of great character." For this, Mack was worthy of the fealty and loyalty Cobb bestowed upon him. In the Cobb narrative of his life, it had taken him a quarter of a century to find a man who rivaled his father and grandfather in both intelligence and moral fiber; once he found him, he happily deferred to his leadership. In this, Mack compelled Cobb to do something no man besides his father had ever been able to achieve—he persuaded Cobb to do his bidding.[92]

Cobb's major league career ended with nearly as little fanfare as it began. By late July he had lost his starting spot in the outfield. He could still hit, but he was much too slow afoot to do an adequate job in the field. His last plate appearance occurred on September 11 in New York, pinch-hitting for Jimmy Dykes to lead off the ninth inning. He hit a weak popup behind third that shortstop Mark Koenig caught for an easy out. Before the game that day, he made no intimation that this might be the end. Still, Yankee fans must have sensed it as they cheered ardently whenever they caught a glimpse of him. Six days later, with the team now in Cleveland, Cobb decided he had had enough. He called the press together to make the announcement: he would retire at the end of the season. When reporters wondered if he really meant it this time, Cobb was unequivocal. "Never again," he responded. Though his average was well over .300, he confessed he found it too difficult to continue. He was "baseball tired" and wanted to spend more time with his children before they "grow up and leave me." In the meantime, he wanted to be part of this pennant race. With the Athletics only a few games out of first, he was optimistic. He had never been with a world champion team and hoped his time had finally come. "Don't mistake this as any selfish motive on my part, for it is not," he cautioned reporters. "I would want the Athletics to win whether a member of the team or not, simply because the squarest man ever connected with baseball is managing the club."[93]

The Athletics stayed in contention for another ten games. Remarkably, Cobb made no more plate appearances, not even during a three-game series in Detroit. On September 28, with two games to go, word came that the Yankees had clinched the pennant. Rather than stay until the end, Cobb left the team, traveling first to Detroit to see his dentist and then home to Augusta. It was an anticlimactic finish for one of the most extraordinary and exciting players in baseball history. Cobb could at least take comfort that his two years with Connie Mack had redeemed and perhaps even enhanced his reputation. At last, his legacy seemed secure.

Tributes to Cobb began almost immediately in the press. Nearly everyone offered the same assessment: Cobb—not Ruth, Wagner, Hornsby, Lajoie, or Sisler—was the greatest player of all time. The *New York Times* noted simply that since 1907 Cobb has been "the greatest all-around player in the history of the pastime." The *Chicago Tribune* observed, "one watches with anticipation when Babe Ruth is at bat. One watched with anticipation when Ty Cobb was at bat, in the field, or on the bases. If one didn't watch, one was likely to miss something worth seeing." This was exactly as Cobb wanted it. The decade might have belonged to Babe Ruth, but baseball belonged to Cobb. His career was over, but he left the game more respected and—at least in some quarters—adored than at any point in his career. The man who had played for honor left the game under his terms, his status as the game's greatest player seemingly unassailable.[94]

NOTES

1. *New York Tribune*, December 19, 1918, 15; *New York Times*, December 17, 1919, 14; *New York Sun*, December 17, 1918, 3; *Washington Times*, December 18, 1918, 12.

2. *Detroit Free Press*, December 17, 1918, 13.

3. *Sporting News* (December 4, 1919): 2; *Sporting News* (December 25, 1919): 3; *Sporting News* (August 21, 1919): 1.

4. Harry Hooper in Lawrence S. Ritter, *The Glory of Their Times: The Story of the Early Days of Baseball Told by the Men Who Played It* (New York: Perennial, 1966), 145. Ruth biographies are numerous; I relied primarily upon Leigh Montville, *The Big Bam: The Life and Times of Babe Ruth* (New York: Anchor Books, 2006) and Marshall Smelser, *The Life That Ruth Built: A Biography* (Lincoln, NE: Bison Books, 1975).

5. Paul J. Zingg, *Harry Hooper: An American Baseball Life* (Urbana: University of Illinois Press, 1993), 82, 114, 124–25, 135–37; Timothy M. Gay, *Tris Speaker: The Rough-and-Tumble Life of a Baseball Legend* (Guilford, CT: Lyons Press, 2007), 146–50; Montville, *Big Bam*, 41–52; Kahn quoted in Harold Seymour, *Baseball: The Golden Age* (New York: Oxford University Press, 1971), 429.

6. Zingg, *Harry Hooper*, 135–37, 160–62; *Chicago Tribune*, November 17, 1918, A4.

7. *New York Times*, September 9, 1919, 27; *Detroit Free Press*, August 24, 1919; *Chicago Tribune*, August 5, 1919, 17; *New York Times*, September 21, 1919, 101; Montville, *Big Bam*, 86–89; *Sporting News* (October 30, 1919): 4.

8. Charles L. Ponce de Leon, *Self-Exposure: Human-Interest Journalism and the Emergence of Celebrity in America, 1890–1940* (Chapel Hill: University of North Carolina Press, 2002), 242–44; Frederick Lewis Allen, *Only Yesterday: An Informal History of the 1920s* (1931; repr., New York: Perennial

Classics, 2000), 161–69; Silas Bent, *Ballyhoo: The Voice of the Press* (New York: Boni and Liveright, 1927); Marshall Hunt in Jerome Holtzman, ed., *No Cheering in the Press Box* (New York: Henry Holt, 1973), 23.

9. *New York Times*, June 3, 1920, 19.

10. Hunt in Holtzman, *No Cheering*, 15–33; Montville, *Big Bam*, 165–71.

11. "The Baseball Hero," *New York Times*, October 8, 1926, 22; Hunt in Holtzman, *No Cheering*, 17.

12. Montville, *Big Bam*, 156–57.

13. Richards Vidmer in Holtzman, *No Cheering*, 105.

14. Smelser, *The Life That Ruth Built*, 208–209; Montville, *Big Bam*, 267–68; Ford Frick in Holtzman, *No Cheering*, 210–11.

15. Dan Daniel in Holtzman, *No Cheering*, 6.

16. For transformation of American culture during the late teens and early twenties, see Jackson Lears, *Rebirth of a Nation: The Making of Modern America, 1877–1920* (New York: HarperCollins, 2009); William Leach, *Land of Desire: Merchants, Power, and the Rise of a New American Culture* (New York: Vintage Books, 1993); Loren Baritz, *The Good Life: The Meaning of Success for the American Middle Class* (New York: Knopf, 1989), 72–85; Lynn Dumenil, *The Modern Temper: American Culture and Society in the 1920s* (New York: Hill and Wang, 1995), 76–97; Paul V. Murphy, *The New Era: American Thought and Culture in the 1920s* (Lanham, MD: Rowman & Littlefield, 2012), 43–72.

17. "The Inquiring Reporter," *Chicago Tribune*, July 31, 1921, A1; W. R. Hoefer, "The Reign of the Wallop," *Baseball Magazine* (July 1923): 366; Albert Theodore Powers, *The Business of Baseball* (Jefferson, NC: McFarland, 2003), 50.

18. Ty Cobb, with Al Stump, *My Life in Baseball* (1961; repr., Lincoln, NE: Bison Books, 1993), 266; Ty Cobb, edited by William R. Cobb, *Memoirs of Twenty Years in Baseball* (Marietta, GA: Self-published, 2002), 132–38; Ty Cobb, *Busting'Em and Other Big League Stories* (1914; repr., Jefferson, NC: McFarland, 2003), 95.

19. *Chicago Tribune*, September 2, 1918, 9; *Sporting News* (February 13, 1919): 8; *Detroit Free Press*, September 19, 1922, 17; "Our Letter Box," *Baseball Magazine* (February 1923): 422; F. C. Lane, "Who is the Greatest Player in Baseball?" *Baseball Magazine* (June 1923): 291; *Sporting News* (November 2, 1922): 3; "Editorial Comment," *Baseball Magazine* (July 1923): 344.

20. Fred Lieb in Holtzman, *No Cheering*, 54; Cobb, *My Life*, 214–16; Al Stump, *Cobb* (Chapel Hill, NC: Algonquin Books, 1994), 329; Charles C. Alexander, *Ty Cobb* (New York: Oxford University Press, 1984), 159. On Southern whites' understanding of appearances, see Kenneth S. Greenberg, *Honor and Slavery: Lies, Duels, Noses, Masks, Dressing as a Woman, Gifts, Strangers,*

Humanitarianism, Death, Slave Rebellions, the Proslavery Argument, Baseball, Hunting, and Gambling in the Old South (Princeton: Princeton University Press, 1996), 7, 23, 47–48.

21. *Sporting News* (March 15, 1923): 5.

22. *Columbus Enquirer-Sun*, December 7, 1919, 14.

23. *Miami District Daily News*, January 15, 1920, 3.

24. Ty Cobb, "Who Will Win My Batting Crown?" *Baseball Magazine* (September 1920): 472.

25. Cobb, *My Life*, 214–15.

26. All data compiled from baseball-reference.com. The data also reveals that Cobb did not "consistently hit for a higher average when Ruth was anywhere on the same field" as one recent biographer (Charles Leerhsen, *Ty Cobb: A Terrible Beauty* [New York: Simon and Schuster, 2015], 327) has contended. For the years 1920 to 1928, Cobb's average against the Yankees exceeded his yearly average only three times. See Sports Reference LLC, "Baseball-Reference.com," http://www.baseball-reference.com/ (accessed July 10, 2014). For Cobb's batting average against Ruth, see Tom Stanton, *Ty and the Babe: Baseball's Fiercest Rivals: A Surprising Friendship and the 1941 Has-Beens Golf Championship* (New York: St. Martin's Press, 2007), appendix.

27. *New York Times*, June 13, 1921, 9; *New-York Tribune*, June 13, 1921; *Detroit Free Press*, June 13, 1921, 9; *Chicago Tribune*, June 13, 1921, 18; *Detroit News*, June 15, 1921, 28; *Sporting News* (June 23, 1921): 1.

28. *New York Times*, June 12, 1924, 13.

29. *New York Times*, June 14, 1924, 1; *Sporting News* (June 19, 1924): 1; *Chicago Tribune*, June 14, 1924, 18; Stanton, *Ty and the Babe*, 94–108; Alexander, *Ty Cobb*, 172.

30. *New York Times*, June 21, 1924, 9.

31. Stanton, *Ty and the Babe*, 115–16; Alexander, *Ty Cobb*, 173; *New York Times*, October 8, 1924, 13.

32. Grantland Rice, "Joe Jackson Given 'Needle' by Ty Cobb," *Miami News*, April 6, 1955, 13A.

33. John B. Sheridan, "The Back of the Home Plate," *Sporting News* (March 8, 1923): 4; Sheridan, "Back of the Home Plate," October 5, 1922, 5; Sheridan, "Back of the Home Plate," November 11, 1926, 4.

34. *Sporting News* (July 31, 1924); *Sporting News* (November 11, 1926): 4.

35. *Sporting News* (May 26, 1921): 4; *Sporting News* (November 3, 1921): 4; *New York Evening World*, June 22, 1922, 20; *San Jose Evening News*, September 13, 1920, 13; *Twin Falls Daily News*, July 13, 1920, 3; *Dallas Morning News*, December 5, 1920, 2.

36. *Sporting News* (November 25, 1920): 2; Sheridan, "Back of the Home Plate," June 22, 1922, 4; Sheridan, "Back of the Home Plate," July 27, 1922, 4.

37. Quoted in Smelser, *Life That Ruth Built*, 112–13; *Philadelphia Inquirer*, June 6, 1920, 12; Ernest Lanigan, "Casual Comment," *Sporting News* (February 12, 1920): 4; "Billy Evans Says," *Salt Lake Telegram*, March 10, 1922, 14.

38. Lanigan, "Casual Comment," *New York Times*, December 18, 1925, 27.

39. "Editorial Comment," *Baseball Magazine* (May 1923): 534; F. C. Lane, "Completing a Record Baseball Career," *Baseball Magazine* (October 1922): 483; J. G. Taylor Spink, "The Perennial Tiger," *Sporting News* (May 11, 1925): 4; Paul Gallico, *The Golden People* (New York: Doubleday, 1965), 203.

40. Quoted in Dumenil, *Modern Temper*, 31; Earnest Elmo Calkins, *Business the Civilizer* (New York: Little, Brown, and Company, 1926), 232–33, 294–95; Edward Earle Purinton, "Big Ideas From Big Business: Try Them Out for Yourself!" *Independent* 105 (April 16, 1921): 395–96.

41. "Editorial: Playing the Game," *Rotarian* 7 (October 1915): 327.

42. Frank Weaver, "He Takes Care of Himself," *Young Men* 47 (1921): 344, 363.

43. Ted Hathaway, "Cobb as Role Model: Ty Cobb in Juvenile Periodical Literature: 1907–1929," *Nine: A Journal of Baseball History and Culture* 11 (Spring 2003): 64–72; "The Georgia Peach," *Youth's Companion* 49 (December 9, 1926): 966.

44. *Sporting News* (January 21, 1926): 4.

45. Sheridan, "Back of the Home Plate," January 21, 1926, 4; Ed Banks, "When Ty Cobb Visits the Traps," *Baseball Magazine* (April 1922): 802; Dayton Stoddart, "What Baseball Has Taught Ty Cobb," *Collier's* 74 (July 19, 1924): 7.

46. Grantland Rice, "The Durable Cobb," *Collier's* 77 (April 3, 1926): 24; Rice, "You Can Win If . . ." *Collier's* 75 (July 4, 1925): 15; Rice, "The Winner's Way," *Collier's* 78 (July 10, 1926): 10; Rice, "They Laugh at the Years," *Collier's* 76 (August 8, 1925): 17–19; *New York Tribune*, June 6, 1922, 14.

47. William Ganson, "Playing the Game Called Business," *National Laundry Journal* 86 (November 1, 1921): 36; J. B. Dillon, "Two Queens in the Kitchen: Milady and a Gas Range," *American Gas Engineering Journal* 116 (March 4, 1922): 209. See also "Ty Cobb Embarks on a New Venture," *Hardware Review* 25 (October 19, 1919): 61; Norval A. Hawkins, "The Credit Salesman," *Bulletin of the National Association of Credit Men* 21 (1919): 721–22.

48. "News and Comment From the Field of Life Insurance," *Standard* 88 (May 14, 1921): 635; "Wholesalers Plan for Annual Meet," *Coal Review* 2 (May 18, 1921): 45; Norval Abiel Hawkins, *Certain Success*, 3rd edition (Detroit: Self-published, 1920), 109, 164.

49. *Chicago Daily Tribune*, April 8, 1922, 10; *Chicago Daily Tribune*, August 26, 1923, B6.

50. Stoddart, "What Baseball Has Taught Ty Cobb," 21; Prosper Buranelli, "Ty Cobb Talks About Baseball," *Detroit Free Press*, September 25, 1921, E1; Hawkins, *Certain Success*, 164; "Another Sales Contest Booming Business," *Advertising and Selling* 29 (August 9, 1919): 32; *New York Times*, February 22, 1928, 38.

51. Buranelli, "Ty Cobb Talks Baseball."

52. Alexander, *Ty Cobb*, 136; Gallico, *Golden People*, 212–13; John D. McCallum, *Ty Cobb* (New York: Praeger, 1975), 102–103: *Detroit Free Press*, April 23, 1922, A3.

53. Cobb, *Memoirs*, 29–32.

54. Cobb, *Memoirs*, 31.

55. Ossie Bleuge in Donald Honig, *Man in the Dugout: Fifteen Big League Managers Speak Their Minds* (Lincoln, NE: Bison Books, 1977), 151, 152; *New York Times*, May 9, 1926, S1; Harry Johnson, *Standing the Gaff: The Life and Hard Times of a Minor League Umpire* (Nashville: Pantheon Press, 1935), 51–54; Charlie Gehringer in Richard Bak, *Cobb Would Have Caught It: The Golden Age of Baseball in Detroit* (Detroit: Wayne State University Press, 1991), 193; Bill Moore in Bak, *Cobb Would Have Caught It*, 168; Leo Durocher with Ed Linn, *Nice Guys Finish Last* (New York: Simon and Schuster, 1975), 48–49; Alexander, *Ty Cobb*, 174; *New York Times*, May 31, 1922, 26; *New York Times*, February 28, 1925, 2; *New York Times*, March 1, 1925, 10.

56. Spink, "Ty Cobb's Party," *Sporting News* (September 3, 1925): 4.

57. "Editorial: Two Heroes," *New York Times*, August 31, 1925, 14.

58. "Spanking Baseball's Baby and Petting Its Paragon," *Literary Digest* 86 (September 19, 1925): 59–66.

59. Cobb, *Memoirs*, 64–65.

60. John B. Foster, "Cobb Says He'll Revive a Lost Art of Baseball," *Sporting News* (August 3, 1922); *Sporting News* (March 15, 1923): 5; F. C. Lane, "When Sensational Base Running was Worth While," *Baseball Magazine* (October 1923): 485–87, 515; Stoddart, "What Baseball Has Taught Ty Cobb," 21; *Portland Oregonian*, July 3, 1921, 4; *Bay City* (Michigan) *Times*, July 20, 1922, 10.

61. *Detroit Free Press*, December 6, 1920, 11.

62. *Detroit Free Press*, March 6, 1921, 22; *Detroit Free Press*, March 14, 1921, 14.

63. *Sporting News* (June 22, 1922): 6; Grantland Rice, "The Sportlight," *New York Tribune*, July 1, 1922, 8; Rice, "The Sportlight," *New York Tribune*, August 12, 1922, 6; *Chicago Tribune*, April 1, 1923, A3; *Sporting News* (June 5, 1924): 1.

64. Cobb, *My Life*, 197, 198; *Sporting News* (April 12, 1923): 1.

65. Cobb, *My Life*, 200–204.

66. *Sporting News* (February 10, 1921): 3; Sheridan, "Back of the Home Plate," May 17, 1923, 4.

67. *Sporting News* (February 10, 1921): 3.

68. *Sporting News* (November 11, 1926): 1; Charlie Gehringer in Bak, *Cobb Would Have Caught It*, 191–93.

69. Charlie Gehringer in Bak, *Cobb Would Have Caught It*, 192; Bill Moore in Bak, *Cobb Would Have Caught It*, 168, 170, 172–73; "Scribbled by Scribes," *Sporting News* (March 26, 1925): 4.

70. Cobb, *My Life*, 240; Charlie Gehringer in Bak, *Cobb Would Have Caught it*, 192; Richard Bak, *Peach: Ty Cobb in His Time and Ours* (Ann Arbor: Sports Media Group, 2005), 129–130.

71. *Sporting News* (March 26, 1925): 4; Bak, *Peach*, 129–130; Bill Moore in Bak, *Cobb Would Have Caught It*, 169; *New York Times*, March 8, 1923, 11.

72. *Sporting News* (March 6, 1924): 3; *Sporting News* (May 10, 1923): 4; *Sporting News* (May 31, 1923): 1; Bak, *Peach*, 130; Eddie Wells in Bak, *Cobb Would Have Caught It*, 153–54.

73. *Sporting News* (November 11, 1926): 1.

74. *Sporting News* (January 18, 1923): 6; *Sporting News* (December 18, 1924): 4; *Sporting News* (April 1, 1926): 7; Alexander, *Ty Cobb*, 163, 170, 175, 179–80.

75. Alexander, *Ty Cobb*, 181–82.

76. *New York Times*, November 4, 1926, 30; Cobb, *My Life*, 240.

77. Alexander, *Ty Cobb*, 186–87; *Chicago Tribune*, December 23, 1926, 19.

78. Alexander, *Ty Cobb*, 186–87; *Chicago Tribune*, December 23, 1926, 19; Leerhsen, *Ty Cobb*, 340–43, 344–48; Tim Hornbaker, *War on the Basepaths: The Definitive Biography of Ty Cobb* (New York: Sports Publishing, 2015), 229–38.

79. *Sporting News* (December 30, 1926): 1.

80. Alexander, *Ty Cobb*, 189–95; Charles C. Alexander, *Our Game: An American Baseball History* (New York: MJF Books, 1991), 143–45; Seymour, *Baseball: The Golden Age*, 382–87.

81. Alexander, *Ty Cobb*, 190–91, 193–94.

82. *Sporting News* (December 30, 1926): 1.

83. On gambling in baseball, see Seymour, *Golden Age*, 176–77; Alexander, *Ty Cobb*, 190–91. On Southerners and gambling, see Greenberg, *Honor and Slavery*, 115–46; T. H. Breen, "Horses and Gentlemen: The Cultural Significance of Gambling among the Gentry of Virginia," *William and Mary Quarterly* 34 (1977): 239–57; Ted Ownby, *Subduing Satan: Religion, Recreation, and Manhood in the Rural South, 1865–1920* (Chapel Hill: University of North Carolina Press, 1990), 48, 53, 84–87.

84. Alexander, *Ty Cobb*, 188–93; Durocher, *Nice Guys Finish Last*, 49.

85. Cobb, *My Life*, 245; Cobb's letter is quoted in *My Life*, 244; Alexander, *Ty Cobb*, 193.

86. *Chicago Tribune*, January 2, 1927, A1; *Chicago Tribune*, December 30, 1926, 15; *Sporting News* (December 30, 1926): 4; Evans as quoted in Cobb, *My Life*, 243; *New York Times*, January 1, 1927, 16; *New York Times*, January 2, 1927, 14; *New York Times*, December 20, 1926, 16; *New York Times*, December 23, 1926, 16; *New York Times*, December 25, 1926, 8; *Chicago Tribune*, December 24, 1926, 13; *New York Times*, December 24, 1926, 12; *New York Times*, January 15, 1927, 6; *Chicago Tribune*, December 26, 1926, A3.

87. Bak, *Peach*, 151; Alexander, *Ty Cobb*, 188, 193–94.

88. Cobb, *My Life*, 245, 246, 248–49.

89. Leerhsen, *Ty Cobb*, 358.

90. Cobb, *My Life*, 250.

91. *Philadelphia Inquirer*, November 1, 1927, 27; quoted in Alexander, *Ty Cobb*, 203.

92. Cobb, *My Life*, 251.

93. *New York Times*, September 18, 1928, 24; *Chicago Tribune*, September 18, 1928, 21.

94. *New York Times*, September 18, 1928, 24; *Chicago Tribune*, September 23, 1928, A2.

9

PROTECTING A LEGACY

On the day Ty Cobb announced his retirement, he showed a side of his personality he usually kept hidden from the public—trepidation. He told reporters that he would "be leaving baseball with a lot of regrets." After all, baseball had raised him "to a place of prominence and affluence." But perhaps even more than that, the game had allowed him to express himself in ways that he found deeply satisfying. "It's hard to pull away from a game to which one has given a quarter century of his best manhood," he confessed.[1] The question Cobb must have asked himself as he contemplated life after baseball was what could he do to display and express manhood now that he could no longer play the game. What, if anything, could fill the void that retirement had created?

He tried to avoid answering the question for the first year by taking his wife Charlie on an extended tour of Europe, timing the trip perfectly so he would miss the first several months of the baseball season. But when he learned Connie Mack and the Athletics were to play the Cubs in the World Series, he made a point of being there. When interviewed, he told the press he hoped to rejoin major league baseball as either an executive or as a field manager. Since returning to the states just 48 hours earlier, he discovered that he could not "spend 24 years in baseball, then forget it." True, he had not felt a "yearning for the game" while he was in Europe, but that was "because there was no baseball all about me as there would be if I had stayed at home, but now that I am back it is different. . . . Tentative offers have been made," he announced; "I believe I will be back in the game next year."[2] It never happened. Whether the offers never materialized or did not meet Cobb's asking price is unknown. Regardless, he never returned to baseball in a formal capacity.

Thereafter, Cobb busied himself in a variety of activities that—from all appearances—brought him a great deal of personal satisfaction. Similarly to modern-day retired stars, his wealth enabled him to live a life of at least semi-leisure. He spent much of his time between golfing trips and hunting expeditions. When home, he sequestered himself in his office for hours at a time, managing his investment portfolio, responding to fan mail, and reading military histories and biographies. He also attached himself to a diverse array of charitable ventures. The two most ambitious were of his own creation. In 1950, he donated funds for the construction and maintenance of a modern twenty-five-bed hospital for his hometown of Royston. Three years later he established and endowed the W. H. Cobb Educational Fund, a scholarship fund to help needy Georgian youths attend college. The program was founded on a strict ethic of self-help: only those who made it through their freshman year without assistance could apply. He was especially eager that the scholarship would attract "Lincolnesque characters, boys and girls out of the fields and mountains." In other words, he wanted youths very much like his father as a young man.[3]

The low profile Cobb kept during the first two decades after his retirement seems to have done wonders for his public image. Even in retirement, sports journalists and former ballplayers could not stop talking about his sensational plays and numerous accomplishments. Now and again, journalists and fans alike confessed that they yearned for another Cobb to make the game more vital and exciting. Meanwhile, Cobb harvested a string of awards and honors. In 1936, the 226 members of the Baseball Writers' Association of America announced that Cobb received the most votes for the newly created Baseball Hall of Fame at Cooperstown, New York—falling just four votes short of unanimity. Essentially, this made Cobb the first "immortal" to be inducted into what has become professional baseball's greatest shrine. Cobb's peers were no less complimentary. In 1942, the *Sporting News* asked one hundred former ballplayers, managers, and umpires to name the greatest player of all time. Sixty voted for Cobb; the remaining forty divided their votes among fourteen different players with Honus Wagner finishing a very distant second with seventeen votes. To *Sporting*

News editor Taylor Spink, who by now had become one of Cobb's closest friends, the vote offered an obvious point: "the men who know baseball best pick Cobb." Throughout the forties, fifties, and into the sixties, the *Sporting News* interviewed a steady stream of players, writers, umpires, and executives—each of whom affirmed Cobb's superiority. Cobb might be gone from the game, but those who knew him best refused to let his greatness be forgotten.[4]

Ever mindful of his reputation, Cobb cherished these testimonials and kept scrapbooks of his press clippings well into his retirement. Yet for all the accolades, a troubling underside often accompanied tales of Cobb's—and his peers'—exploits. As the years passed, more and more reporters began to view the Dead Ball Era as the dark age of professional baseball. Rather than highlight the tactical superiority of the age—as encompassed in "scientific ball"—writers highlighted the rough and tumble elements of the game: the fights and donnybrooks, the disreputable methods ballplayers sometimes used to gain advantage, and the questionable characters who made their living from the game. For every laudatory article about Cobb's batting and base-running exploits, there seemed to be another that rehashed his violent run-ins with fans, his squabbles with teammates, and his presumed vicious spiking of some hapless infielder, most notably Frank "Home Run" Baker. Journalists loved to retell these stories because they were colorful tales. But there was more to it than that: such stories allowed the guardians of baseball to offer a narrative of the game that appealed to socially conservative America. They repeated and often sensationalized Cobb's violent encounters as a way to contrast the past with the present. The modern game, they claimed, had reached an unprecedented level of civility and sportsmanship. The barbarism of the past—now conveniently personified by Cobb and seemingly Cobb alone—was dead. Sure, it was fun to read about the old days, but the modern fan had an aversion to that sort of vulgarity.

Public memory of Cobb's career shifted in ways that dovetailed neatly with major league baseball's efforts to rebrand itself. In the years immediately after World War II, the major league game was in a bit of trouble. The once-imposing big league ballparks built during the teens and twenties were beginning to show their age. At the same time, the neighborhoods in which they once thrived also began to decline as middle- and upper-working class families moved to brand new suburban communities. True, the infusion of African American ballplayers, beginning with Jackie Robinson in 1947, opened up baseball to an entirely new demographic, but at the risk of alienating those whites who viewed integration with considerable ambivalence. As a result, attendance floundered. After drawing over 20 million fans in 1949, major league attendance began to decline; it would not top 20 million again until 1962, thanks in part to the addition of two new teams, the Houston Colt .45s and the New York Mets. Faced with such challenges, the keepers of the game decided it was time to spruce up its image. During the 1950s, baseball established itself as the sporting expression of the American Way, embodying the superiority of American customs in an otherwise dangerous and capricious world. The game that had once likened itself to war now claimed it embodied civility, order, democracy, fair play, and good will. To spectators, baseball was no longer a man's game; it was a family man's game, a sport equally suitable for fathers, mothers, and children. Ballplayers still argued with umpires and fans still booed bad calls and poor play, but such moments were less frequent and less venomous than what transpired in the ballpark in Cobb's heyday. Baseball strove for a cheery decorum at the ballpark that was completely foreign to the ballplayers and fans of the Dead Ball Era.

Postwar sports journalists accentuated the change in culture by once again shifting the rhetorical style in which they presented the game's heroes. The stars of Cobb's age—men like Wagner, Evers, Chance, Lajoie, Collins, Mathewson, and McGraw—were described as sagacious, iron-willed, savvy, weathered, and severe: blood-and-guts battlers in a game that aspired to replicate war. The heroes of the modern era rarely acquired such descriptions. Rather, the players who dominated the headlines in the forties and fifties—DiMaggio, Ott, Snider, Mantle, Mays, Berra, Campanella, Banks, Musial, Feller—were invariably celebrated for their relative youth (at least early on), exuberance, good cheer, and charm. There were exceptions, of course: Ted Williams struck everyone as aloof, cold, and humorless and Jackie Robinson eventually drew comparisons to Ty Cobb for both his daring play and intense combativeness. But they were anomalies, the exceptions that proved the rule, so different from the pack the press often likened them to the stars of the past.[5]

Cobb had a difficult time understanding just what was afoot here. Much of it rankled him, especially the way the press seemed to play up his violent encounters. No matter that journalists praised Cobb for his determination, genius, and—seemingly—invulnerable offensive records, Cobb smarted at what he perceived to be overly harsh, unwarranted, and inaccurate criticisms of his style of play. Though he had heard such complaints throughout his playing career, he still took criticism personally. "I find little comfort in the popular picture of Cobb as a spike-slashing demon of the diamond with a wide streak of cruelty in his nature," he complained in his final autobiography. He defended himself with all the old arguments: he usually received worse than he had dished out; he intentionally spiked only a handful of players; he always played within the rules. In addition, he now had an opportunity to add something new. Because his argument was now with a new generation of baseball fans, he tried to turn the tables on his critics, arguing that the problem was not so much that he and his compatriots were overly combative and aggressive; the problem was that the modern ballplayers were not combative enough. Modern ballplayers, Cobb asserted, simply did not measure up to the standard that the players of his generation had established.[6]

Cobb articulated this argument several times during the last years of his life, but most fully and forthrightly on two occasions. The first was a two-part article he penned for *Life* in 1952. The magazine offered Cobb $25,000 for his opinion of modern baseball and he came out firing. The first of the articles was provocatively titled "They Don't Play Baseball Any More." The title may have been the creation of *Life*'s editors, but the sentiment was entirely Cobb's. In this and the second piece, titled "Tricks That Won Me Ball Games," Cobb excoriated modern players. "The most publicized hitters of recent years"—Cobb refused to use complimentary adjectives like "best" or even "most productive"—"have limped along on one cylinder," he boldly proclaimed. They were so enamored with hitting the ball as far as they could that they failed to practice the "science" of hitting, much less develop the full spectrum of baseball skills. "Nobody in the major leagues today . . . is a first-class base runner," Cobb stated in one of his many viciously candid accusations. And fielding? Players were too ignorant of the fundamentals to field properly. In all, Cobb believed only two modern players could "be mentioned in the same breath with the old-time greats"—Stan Musial and Phil Rizzuto.

The problem, Cobb suggested, was that the players of the modern era were simply not man enough to play the game as it should be played. He was particularly critical of the game's two biggest stars, Ted Williams and the recently retired Joe DiMaggio. Both personified the distinct failings of the modern ballplayer. To begin, they were far too enamored with power to take full advantage of their natural talents. Williams was a "marvelous natural hitter," Cobb allowed, but that was about it. Because Williams failed to learn the fundamentals of place hitting, opposing teams simply shifted their defense to his power alley to neutralize him. DiMaggio was even worse. Not only did he fail to hit to the opposite field, he suffered from another problem common to modern ballplayers: he was lazy. DiMaggio "hated physical exertion," Cobb complained; "as far as I know, he never took a lick of exercise from October until March." As a result, "his muscles weakened and naturally got hurt a lot" so he had to retire at the relatively young age of thirty-seven. Had he taken care of himself, "he could still be out there this summer, gobbling up long fly balls and hitting .350." Of course, DiMaggio was not alone; the entire generation of ballplayers struck Cobb as "a particularly fragile lot." Overpaid and spoiled from the mass media's adulation, modern ballplayers spent their winters glad-handing and cashing in on their celebrity rather than training their bodies and minds for the upcoming season. They bastardized the profession by becoming little more than "part-time athletes." Cobb called them an anathema, "contrary to all the laws of nature." He lectured, "No athlete, if he wants to live up to his potentialities of greatness, has any business spending nearly half the year in an armchair or a ribbon-clerk job." In an obvious challenge to their masculinity, he offered them this bit of advice: "if you have to make some extra money, go work in a warehouse or deliver yourself some ice."

Cobb also contended ballplayers lacked the requisite fighting spirit. Case in point, modern infielders now allowed themselves to be mauled by advancing base runners. In the old days, Cobb claimed, infielders knew how to take care of themselves. When a runner tried to take out an infielder to break up a double play, the infielder immediately retaliated by intentionally "coming down with both sets of spikes planted firmly in the runner's ribs." If that didn't work, an infielder would wait until the next time the runner was on base and then "calmly" make "his throw in the exact direction of the runner's face." Brutal, but effective, Cobb asserted; he had the spike wounds to prove it.

In contrast to the milquetoasts who made up major league rosters in the modern age, the players of Cobb's era—at least according to Cobb—were real men. Old timers, Cobb claimed, were "a strange, hard-bitten and ambitious crew—up from the small towns and by no means eager to go back, trained at nothing but that one profession and battling to hang on to it to their last breath." Cobb then launched into a lengthy tribute to his generation of ballplayers, highlighting their resolve, fight, ingenuity, and commitment. The game they played was "rougher," less "polite," and "an endless battle of wits." Theirs was a primitive world—one that forced them to exert their manhood or get out. Playing with crude equipment on playing fields that looked more like washboards than the neatly manicured lawns of the modern era, players learned to steel their bodies and minds. Old-time catchers and infielders learned how to field with their bare hands and use their bodies to stop careening liners and sharp grounders. Ballplayers suffered through overnight train rides, hotels without air-conditioning, and rudely abusive fans. Neglected by the magnates, they nursed their wounds without aid of proper medical attention. Yet they never complained and they certainly never begged to be taken out of a contest. Far from it. All players believed it was their duty as men to finish what they started. "Nothing short of mayhem could keep some of the old-timers out of the game," Cobb maintained. They played when they were bruised, battered, and exhausted. Pitchers were especially unwavering in their commitment to stay in the game and considered it an insult to be taken out. Cobb fairly ridiculed the pampering modern players received, even suggesting many players faked illness and injury just so they could "paint the basement" or "take in a couple theater matinees." Meanwhile, Cobb was convinced the way management coddled players only sapped them of their emotional and physical strength and weakened their manhood. For this reason, modern players lacked the nerve, fortitude, and dedication to do what they needed to do—play (at least) nine innings each and every game for the entire season. Old-timers never rested, Cobb asserted. "They studied, practiced, lived baseball every minute except when they were sleeping," but "even then they dreamed about it at night." In short, they were "lean and hungry, and they played the game for keeps."[7]

Cobb was not the complete curmudgeon during his final years. In one remarkable way, he demonstrated a willingness to stay with the times—sort of. The man who steadfastly refused to play with or against African Americans now accepted the racial integration of professional baseball. Just weeks before he made a ruckus with his *Life* pieces, Cobb told the press "the Negro has a right to compete in sports in every section of the country, so long as his deportment is genteel and unchallengeable." He then praised black baseball players "not only for their deportment but their ability." In subsequent interviews, Cobb spoke highly of such black stars as the Dodgers' Roy Campanella, the Braves' Hank Aaron, and the Giants' Willie Mays. The latter he praised as "the only player I'd pay money to see" and even consented to be photographed standing alongside him.[8]

Although Cobb's endorsement of black athletes was indeed commendable, it may not have reflected a radical shift in his thinking. After all, Cobb came a bit late to the party. He did not address the issue of sports integration until five years after Jackie Robinson crossed the color line. Once he did speak, he largely failed to advocate; neither his *Life* pieces nor his final autobiography address the subject of baseball's integration. In addition, Cobb's caveats that blacks must be "genteel" in their on-field behavior is more than a little ironic considering not only his own behavior but his general approach toward baseball—that players should approach it as the moral equivalent of war. Did he mean to hold black athletes to a different standard than whites? Probably not, but the comment is an odd one. Finally, Cobb's overall assessment of black baseball players came—as we have seen—at a time when he had an extremely low opinion of contemporary ballplayers of all races. As much as he liked Mays, he did not include him—or any other modern ballplayer—in his all-time all-star team. For that matter, he ignored the great stars of the Negro Leagues entirely in all his writings and interviews. The obvious conclusion is that he believed black players inferior to the white players of his generation. Again, Cobb deserves credit for changing his views on such an important matter, but he remained something less than the enlightened egalitarian that one recent biography has portrayed him to be.[9]

Cobb's views on race aside, his spirited defense of the game could not have been more tone deaf to the tenor of modern baseball culture. Postwar sports-loving Americans took their idols seriously and resented having their stars ridiculed by some old codger whose feats they had only read about. The press and fans alike not only denounced Cobb's criticisms of modern players, they called into question the superiority of the Dead Ball Era. "Those old guys make me sick," the ever-candid Leo Durocher exclaimed. "Always talking about how good it was in the old days"; the truth was "they played with a ball that you couldn't hit across the room." Writing to *Life*, a fan noted "Sports, like other forms of human endeavor, move on to higher standards, leaving a disconsolate 'Georgia Peach' marooned on his little island bemoaning bygone days of diamond rowdyism, bare-knuckled pugilism and the 5¢ glass of beer."[10]

Some criticized Cobb directly. Long-time Chicago sportswriter Irving Vaughan admitted Cobb was a "good player a long time ago," but hastened to add that he was also "an individualist" who was "strictly for Cobb." The *Life* articles proved he had not changed a bit, Vaughan maintained: "In the Cobb viewpoint it would seem to be that he was the only big leaguer that ever made the grade." Cobb was no sage, Vaughan concluded; he was an embittered old man who "hasn't kept up with the times" and still craves attention. Rogers Hornsby used the occasion to settle an old score with Cobb, calling him selfish and a poor teammate. As an added insult, Hornsby left Cobb off his all-time all-star team, placing the Georgian behind contemporaries Speaker, Ruth, and Jackson, and modern stars DiMaggio and Williams. Even old friend Clark Griffith belittled Cobb, suggesting that his comments "sound senile." The Old Fox even maintained Cobb was no better at place hitting than Ted Williams. "Ty Cobb couldn't hit to right field on a bet," the Washington owner asserted. Griffith's former infielder and current manager Bucky Harris was more direct: "Cobb is nuts," he told the press.[11]

Cobb offered little rebuttal. Interviewed by the *Sporting News*, he dismissed his critics as overly sensitive. He claimed he did not mean to indict modern players, but the culture of major league baseball itself, what he termed the "new way of life" ballplayers lived. Owners, managers, the media, and even fans all coddled modern players, Cobb explained, and this enabled them to remain unaware in their spoiled ignorance. "I certainly don't imply that players of my time were superior physically to those of today. But we studied and applied ourselves." In other words, Cobb conceded nothing: the players of his generation were simply a more manly lot. Cobb could see it no other way. To the very last, he remained entrenched in the ideals and mentality of the early twentieth century. His critics were right on one point: Cobb failed to change with the times. But they were wrong on another: he was neither embittered nor frustrated. He was incredulous. When Cobb heard Clark Griffith's criticism of his *Life* piece, he replied that his old friend was either lying or "talking with his tongue in his cheek." Others were lying so as to remain friendly with modern players; in other words, they were part of the problem. Only he—the noble Cobb—was capable of speaking the truth, it seems.[12]

Cobb always believed time would vindicate him, if only baseball fans knew the truth about the way he and his generation played the game. He often talked about writing his autobiography to "set the record straight," but put off all publishers' queries, complaining to one longtime friend that most writers would not treat him fairly. By the end of the 1950s, however, he began to reconsider. The passing of friends and peers weighed on him; he nearly broke down completely when Connie Mack died in February 1956. "I loved Mr. Mack," he told the press. "You know a man can love another man. I'm pretty old myself, and I just can't help crying at hearing that he's gone." Meanwhile, his own health began to decline. He suffered from chronic back pain, caused, he believed, by either his kidneys or liver. By 1958, he had developed both diabetes and hypertension. In late 1959, a thorough examination at Emory University Hospital revealed he had an aggressive form of cancer that had already taken his prostate and was rapidly spreading to other organs. The doctors at Emory removed most of the damaged organ and prescribed cobalt radiation treatments to keep the cancer at bay. Cobb understood he had little time left.[13]

In these final days and months, Cobb also battled depression and loneliness created in part by two failed marriages, the premature deaths of his two oldest sons—Herschel to a heart attack in 1951 and Ty Jr. to a brain tumor in 1952—and often tense relations with two of his three surviving children. He began to drink heavily. Alcohol sometimes loosened his explosive temper, but also made him melancholy and reflective. He began to think more seriously about the autobiography. This would be an act of redemption for both himself and the game he loved. He envisioned this as a magnum opus, the definitive account of his life and times. In 1960, a now terminally ill Cobb finally settled on sports and pulp magazine writer Al Stump to help with the project. The two worked intermittently for about a year, as Cobb's health allowed. They completed the manuscript just weeks before Cobb died. *My Life in Baseball* hit the bookstores two months later.

The final product stands as a seminal work of sports autobiography. Cobb biographer Richard Bak has called it "one of the finest sports autobiographies ever" while sports historian Charles Alexander has termed it "the best book of its kind ever published . . . remarkably candid, revealing, and faithful to its subject." Both were right. True, Cobb offered no new revelations here and stayed clear of those subjects that were painful to him—most notably the death of his father and relations with family members. Moreover, because he had written several previous autobiographies and been interviewed extensively, most of the stories he told were quite familiar to baseball aficionados of the day. Some, including Cobb biographers Don Rhodes and Charles Leerhsen, have also criticized the autobiography for its many inaccuracies regarding specific events and people.[14] Nevertheless, as a work of self-presentation—and self-creation—*My Life* is a masterful achievement. Cobb wanted the baseball public to know that his playing style and achievements were manifestations of his character. He accomplished so much because he subscribed to a superior ethic of manhood. For this reason, he packed the narrative with the values that guided—or so he claimed—his every action: personal and family honor, will, self-reliance, and nerve. For good measure, he rooted these attributes in the lessons he learned as a child from the men he revered, most notably his father and grandfather. Several times in the narrative, he literally lectures the reader with advice his father passed on to him: "Beware an Entrance to a Quarrel" is the title of one chapter; "But Being in It—Let Them Beware!" is the title of the next. Alexander rightly notes that Cobb revealed himself in the autobiography as "sensitive, distrustful, often arrogant, and sometimes mean." We might also add aggressive, uncompromising, and vindictive. That is to say, he displayed all the qualities that had made him the most popular player of his era. During his prime, the public saw Cobb as an ideal man, a model to follow because of his ambition, determination, fortitude, and daring. Through the autobiography Cobb made one last attempt to remind Americans why this was so. Throughout his narrative, he displayed a cunning and brutal toughness that was a hallmark of the Dead Ball Era. He ends (or nearly so) with one of the most pitilessly frank descriptions of baseball ever offered:

> When I played baseball, I didn't play for fun. To me it wasn't parchesi [sic] played under parchesi [sic] rules. Baseball is a red-blooded sport for red-blooded men. It's no pink tea, and mollycoddles had better stay out. It's a contest and everything that implies, a struggle for supremacy, a survival of the fittest. Every man in the game, from the minors on up, is not only fighting against the other side, but he's trying to hold onto his own job against those on his own bench who'd love to take it away. Why deny this? Why minimize it? Why not boldly admit it?

This was Cobb's peroration—a congealed recapitulation of who he was and why he found baseball so compelling. He hoped his autobiography, especially these final words, would be inspirational. He wanted to compel the baseball establishment to return the game to its former glory. This was the redemption Cobb hoped to effect: for baseball and for himself.

That redemption never came. Baseball continued to follow the trajectory it had followed since Babe Ruth supplanted Cobb as the game's most popular player: station-to-station baseball that prized power and trivialized speed and guile; larger crowds and larger stadiums, yes, but more passive and generally less astute fans. Cobb articulated his understanding of the game with grace and power. What of it? People found Cobb's autobiography no more compelling than his 1952 *Life* articles. To many of those who bothered to read it, Cobb seemed bombastic, given to occasional tirades, and pathetically obsessed with settling old scores. Moreover, by presenting himself as a child of the turn-of-the-century South, he probably struck many readers as disturbingly atavistic. The Civil Rights Movement rekindled Northerners' and Westerners' prejudices that Southern whites of a certain generation were rubes at best, dangerous ruffians at worst. Cobb hoped readers would find his story compelling; instead many found it odd and disturbing. As the years passed, more and more people gravitated toward this sentiment.

Still, Cobb was not his own worst enemy. That distinction belongs to Al Stump, Cobb's coauthor. Stump had not been Cobb's first choice. Throughout the 1950s, Cobb was on the lookout for a writer to help him tell his story. Veteran Tigers' beat writer Harry Salsinger, a faithful Cobb ally, had the inside track, but bowed out because of poor health (he died in 1958). In 1955, Cobb worked with another Detroit sportswriter, John McCallum, but neither enjoyed the experience. McCallum eventually produced a sort of "how to" biography of Cobb, a useful work, but not the edgy, no-feelings-spared tell-all that Cobb was hoping to write. Sometime in the late 1950s, he contacted veteran writer Gene Fowler, biographer of John Barrymore, Jimmy Durante, Jimmy Walker, and Mack Sennett (among others). Daughter Shirley was hopeful. "I figured if he could take John Barrymore and make him lovable, he could do it for Mr. Cobb," she remarked. Unfortunately, Fowler was terminally ill by the time Cobb contacted him and thus refused the gig. Finally, in June 1960, Cobb told the *Sporting News* he was working with Clem Boddington, an obscure New York writer, illustrator, and promoter who had been reduced to writing for stag magazines, on the project. This, too, came to naught. Finally, Doubleday publishers recommended Stump, a freelance sportswriter who produced most of his work for pulp magazines. The two split the $6,000 advance and got to work.[15]

Cobb, who rarely made a bad business decision, made an egregiously poor one when he agreed to tell his life story to Stump. Stump was handsome (some said he looked like a dark-haired version of Hollywood actor Alan Ladd) and could be charming, or at least ingratiating, when he needed to be. He was also a very able writer. Unfortunately, he proved to be a pilfering opportunist when it came to Ty Cobb and his family. According to grandson Hersch Cobb, many of the Cobb clan were suspicious of Stump from the beginning. Shirley told Hersch that Stump had hounded Cobb for years to get his story. Once he got the job, he began to pry and prod family members, neighbors, and Cobb employees for whatever dirt they cared to offer. He once used his car to block Cobb's ex-wife Charlie from leaving her driveway. He then rapped on her window, yelling all sorts of questions in a vain effort to get her to talk to him. He also tried to bribe Cobb's gardener for information and encouraged him to go through the old man's garbage. When Hersch dropped by his grandfather's house, Stump tried to get the young man to tell him all about his grandfather's family secrets, drinking bouts, violent temper, and even his sex life. Cobb was distrustful of Stump, but continued to work with him because he desperately wanted to tell his story. The family believed Stump wanted to exploit Cobb's loneliness and vulnerability so he could get write a tell-all biography that would make him wealthy and famous. Never one to mince words, daughter Shirley called Stump "an old-fashioned weasel" and "the biggest louse I know." Many of the Cobb children and grandchildren shared—and, for those still living, continue to share—this opinion. "My grandfather's biographer was interested only in what was negative about Ty Cobb's family," Hersch Cobb has recently written.[16]

The truth of this assessment seems confirmed by subsequent events. In December 1961, just five months after Cobb's death, Stump published an account of his collaboration with Cobb in *True*, a men's pulp magazine, entitled "Ty Cobb's Wild Ten-Month Fight to Live." Stump presented himself as innocent and naïve, a good guy who somehow found himself intimately embroiled with a madman. Yes, he had heard all the stories about Cobb's volcanic temper, but he assumed the stories were exaggerations. He was incredulous when two Cobb associates—an in-law and a former teammate—urged him to back out of the book deal. "You'll never finish it and you might get hurt," they allegedly warned him. Later, he admitted he was just too starstruck to heed their warning. The great Cobb had chosen him to help write his memoir and he felt "distinctly honored to be named his collaborator." Stump survived the encounter and successfully helped Cobb write his life's story, but only because he displayed remarkable fortitude, patience, and courage. According to Stump, he drove with Cobb on a harrowing car ride through a dangerous Sierra Mountain pass during a torrential snowstorm. He listened in horror as Cobb admitted to killing a mugger during a 1912 altercation. He watched Cobb flash his Luger—and at least on one occasion fire it—at people who crossed him. He was there when Cobb stormed at nurses and doctors, threw a saltshaker at a waitress, accused a dietitian of conspiring to poison him, threatened the great Ted Williams, and bullied casino card dealers, various bartenders, a hapless one-armed butler, and—on more than one occasion—Stump himself. Stump was also there to watch league officials and club owners recoil every time Cobb showed up for a ball game or other league event. They "hated" him, Stump claimed, because he incessantly harped on how utterly inferior the modern game was compared to the ball they played in Cobb's era. Cobb so alienated family, friends, associates, and peers, he died lonely and nearly forgotten. Stump understood their reluctance to associate with the former star. He said his time with Cobb was almost torturous. "I'm not proud of it," Stump confessed, but "he scared hell out of me most of the time I was around him."[17]

Stump explained that long after Cobb had driven off every family member, friend, associate, and personal employee, Stump endured. In the process, the journalist claimed he became Cobb's constant companion and confidante for the final ten months of Cobb's life. He stuck to him "like court plaster." As their relationship grew, he helped Cobb keep track of his medications and even helped him administer his insulin. He steadied Cobb when he was too dizzy and weak to walk and picked him up when he fell down. He went everywhere with the dying man—to specialists, to visit old friends, and to visit his parents' Royston grave one last time. Perhaps most affecting, Stump offered a sympathetic ear as Cobb contemplated his own mortality; by staying with him during one particularly mournful night, Stump speculated that he may have saved Cobb from blowing his brains out. By the end, Cobb became convinced that he and Stump "were born pals, meant for each other." Together, they would "complete a baseball book that would beat everything ever published." In the end, Cobb had no one else he could turn to, only Stump.[18]

Stump's article severely damaged Cobb's reputation, of course. In essence, Stump presented Cobb as a pathetic, paranoid, and hateful loner, confirming the worst suspicions of Cobb's critics. But that wasn't all of it. Stump didn't want to just expose Cobb as a vicious and unrepentant bully. Many baseball folks had already made such claims. Stump wanted to add something new to the mix: the source of Cobb's furies. According to Stump, the death of Cobb's father at the hands of his mother left him emotionally unhinged. Until this time, writers had refused to write about the incident, out of respect for Cobb's right to privacy. Not Stump; he gave the incident primacy, alluding to it in the first installment and giving it full coverage in the final. According to Stump, Cobb let loose the family secret when the two visited his parents' crypt: "My father had his head blown off with a shotgun when I was eighteen years old—*by a member of my own family* (Stump's italics). I didn't get over that. I've never gotten over that." Stump believed this revelation explained everything:

I think, because [Cobb] forced upon me a confession of his most private thoughts, along with the details of his . . . I know the answer to the central, overriding secret of his life. Was Ty Cobb psychotic throughout his baseball career? The answer is yes.[19]

An emphatic yes, in fact. According to amateur psychologist Stump, the memory of that event "menaced his sanity" and left him with a "badly disturbed personality." What's more, Cobb knew it, feared what might happen if he snapped, but still refused treatment. "I was like a steel spring with a growing and dangerous flaw in it," Stump claims Cobb told him. "If it is wound too tight or has the slightest weak point the spring will fly apart and then it is done for."[20]

The article caused an immediate sensation. Provocative and forcefully presented, the narrative reads as though Stump was Cobb's most intimate associate, someone who truly knew this enigmatic and difficult man. Here, at last, was a journalist willing to tell the truth. The Associated Press awarded it the best sports story of the year. Veteran sportswriter and biographer Bob Considine called it "possibly the best sports story I have read." E. P. Dutton included it in the prestigious anthology *The Best Sports Stories of 1962*. The article has continued to find its way into important collections, including *The Greatest Baseball Stories Ever Told* (2001), *A Literature of Sports* (1980), *The Best American Sports Writing of the Century* (1999), and *The Art of Fact: A Historical Anthology of Literary Journalism* (1998). Largely on the strength of the article, Stump's popularity soared: he published three more books during the 1960s, including a collaborative effort with golfing immortal Sam Snead. In 1994, the article served as the basis for the Warner Brothers feature film *Cobb*, directed by Ron Shelton (of *Bull Durham* fame) and starring Tommy Lee Jones as Cobb and Robert Wuhl as Stump. That same year, Stump finally published his tell-all biography of Cobb, hailed by some as the definitive sports biography. Roger Kahn, author of the best seller *The Boys of Summer*, gushed that it was "the most powerful biography I have read." The *New York Times* listed it as one of their Notable Books for the year. Meanwhile, that other book—Cobb's *My Life in Baseball*—experienced only lackluster sales, 16,000 before quietly going out of print in less than a decade.[21]

Seldom has a single sports article had such a powerful impact on its subject matter's reputation. Thereafter, published narratives of Cobb changed dramatically. Now, nearly all focused as much on his supposedly fragile psyche as on his professional achievements. Perhaps Cobb's death had something to do with this: since he was gone, acquaintances felt more comfortable discussing his mental state. More than likely, however, many felt compelled to make their own assessments; once Stump went down that road, how could they not? Moreover, Stump gave credibility to those who wanted to disparage Cobb, regardless of motives. Hadn't Cobb confessed to Stump that he actually killed a man? Didn't Cobb admit that his father's death traumatized him? Stump was there, Cobb's critics could say; he saw and recorded the rage, his emotional instability, and his paranoia.

It seemed nearly early every profile of Cobb published after Stump's article included words like "troubled," "psychotic," and "disturbed." To Paul Gallico, Cobb was the greatest player the game ever produced, but also cruel, vengeful, and "highly neurotic." In an oblique reference to Stump's revelations, Gallico suggested Cobb was "weighed down with the then unsuspecting burden of weaknesses, insecurities, and compulsions." Branch Rickey described Cobb as a "paranoiac" who was "competitively unbalanced, and sadistically ruthless on and off the field," largely because of a "tragic event" in his life (discreetly unstated by Rickey). Even veteran writer Fred Lieb took a turn as amateur shrink. For many years, Lieb had offered positive assessments of Cobb, even defending him in the *Sporting News* after the *Life* debacle. Now he presented Cobb as racist, belligerent, egocentric, friendless, and pathologically cruel, even to his prized hunting dogs.[22]

In essence, Stump's article changed the debate about Cobb. The question was no longer "Was Cobb emotionally unstable?" but "How long was he unstable?" Since Cobb was so clearly off his rocker as he approached death, what evidence did he show of mental illness earlier in his life? Granted, Cobb's volatile temper and occasional violent outbursts made such investigative searches remarkably easy. Still, this was hardly sound historical scholarship: the pundits rarely considered the context of Cobb's actions nor paid much attention to the relatively calm periods between the violent outbursts. Regrettably, even some scholars fell victim to this approach. Esteemed baseball historian Harold Seymour made extensive use of Stump's article in his profile of Cobb for the seminal *Baseball: The Golden Age*. Drawing from Stump, Seymour concluded Cobb's mental illness was always apparent, but "became increasingly pronounced with age." Benjamin Rader also argued Cobb's "symptoms of insanity became more pronounced" after he retired, but were certainly present during his playing days. "Rarely has a more successful, more violent, and more maladjusted personality passed through the annals of American sport," Rader concluded.[23]

Stump cast a long shadow. That may have been the problem. He did more to obscure the meaning of Cobb's behavior than to illuminate and enlighten. Recent scholarship has determined that Stump was less than honest about his time with Cobb. Sometimes he distorted what Cobb told him; other times he lied and even falsified records. Start with some of the basics. Charles Alexander meticulously retraced Cobb's activities during his final months and concluded Stump could not have spent as much time as he has claimed with the dying star. According to Alexander, Stump probably spent only a month accumulative with him during a fourteen-month span. They probably only contacted each other intermittently and much of that by phone call and letter. Perhaps Stump still acted as confidante and confessor, but it seems unlikely their relationship was quite as intimate as he portrayed. Nor was Stump Cobb's only meaningful association during this period. Cobb remained in contact with his family during his final months. Daughter Beverly lived next door to Cobb in Atherton and checked on him often. According to Cobb's friend Pope Welborn, Ty visited Shirley at her Palo Alto bookstore frequently, though he avoided going to her home because ex-wife Charlie lived with her. Cobb's lone surviving son, Jimmy, drove up from Santa Barbara to visit during his final months. As Cobb lay close to death at Emory University Hospital in July 1961, his immediate family flew in from California to be with him. "It was a united family front," Beverly remembered. Even Charlie came. Although she had avoided talking to her ex-husband for nearly two decades, she was at the hospital the day he died and spoke privately with him shortly before he passed. Years later Beverly told a journalist, "There was never anyone else in my mother's life"; this "was something she wanted to do," that is to be with him at the end. Cobb's relationship with his family was often strained and contentious, but they were never completely estranged, least of all during Cobb's final months.[24]

Nor was Cobb forgotten or rejected by his former teammates and associates. Immediately after Stump's article appeared in print, the *Sporting News* counterattacked by interviewing several of Cobb's friends to rebut the pulp writer. Over the next several weeks, veteran writers, former players, and friends appeared in the pages of the *Sporting News* to praise the deceased's generosity, ambition, and graciousness. Many of these interviews were as saccharine as Stump's was sour—and thus nearly as unbelievable. One or two actually implied that Cobb never had a bad word to say about anyone. Though hardly accurate, the pieces nonetheless refute Stump's contention that Cobb died unloved and forgotten. More than a few liked Cobb well enough to protect his reputation by gilding the lily. Meanwhile, Ted Williams responded to Stump's accusation that he and Cobb had quarreled. Stump "was full of it" Williams asserted, implying Stump had lied. "Ty Cobb was a close friend of mine and we remained friends up until the time he died," the straightforward Williams told sportswriter Jim Prime.[25]

Cobb's final months were surprisingly active. Apparently , he was intent on visiting some of his favorite people and places before it was too late. In December 1959, he flew through Chicago on his way to Emory University Hospital so he could visit with old nemesis turned friend Ray Schalk, the former White Sox catcher. He made it to the Hall of Fame Reunion at Cooperstown in June 1960. A month later he was off to Rome to attend the 1960 Summer Olympics with Dr. Stewart Brown, the son of a childhood chum. In spring 1961, Cobb made it down to Arizona to watch the Giants, Indians, Cubs, and Red Sox practice. He held court in his hotel room as such luminaries as baseball commissioner Ford Frick, American League president Joe Cronin, and newly retired Ted Williams came to pay their respects. His body failing him and still self-medicating on pills and booze, Cobb battled depression along with cancer. Still, he found strength and resolve to make it to the April 27 Opening Day for the new Los Angeles Angels. Why? Because his old utility infielder Fred Haney was the team's general manager. Cobb told Haney he would throw out the first pitch and he was determined to make good on his promise. He lasted only two innings before exiting with the assistance of a park attendant who helped steady him as he walked from his seat to his car.[26]

Stump further claimed that Cobb was too egomaniacal to consider the feelings of others. To underline the point in the most dastardly manner possible, Stump claimed Cobb stripped the stamps off return envelopes from fans seeking Cobb's autograph so he could use them for his own mailings. In fact, Cobb's friends were genuinely impressed by the attention Cobb gave his fans. Throughout his playing career and through his retirement, Cobb boasted that he never neglected a fan's correspondence. Indeed, surviving letters suggest Cobb often wrote personal notes to fans who sought his attention. He was especially considerate of children, often stopping to chat with them as he signed autographs. True, Cobb was sometimes rude and callous toward waiters, nurses, bellhops, and the like; even his closest friends admitted to this. Yet he was also known to give large tips to those he had upbraided moments earlier. Cobb was often exceedingly generous financially and otherwise. He privately campaigned to have several former peers honored by the Baseball Hall of Fame, including at least two who never liked him very much during their playing days—Sam Crawford and Harry Heilmann. Cobb waged a letter campaign to get Crawford in, writing hundreds of letters to influential people on Crawford's behalf. When the news broke that Crawford was elected, Cobb was elated, but refused all accolades. When Spink told Cobb he planned to publish an article detailing the role Cobb played in helping Crawford get elected, Cobb rebuffed him. "Don't you dare do that," Cobb told his friend. "I want no publicity. If you do this, I'll never speak to you again as long as I live." Spink honored Cobb's wishes: Crawford did not learn of Cobb's efforts on his behalf until after Cobb died. Cobb took up Heilmann's cause in 1951 when news broke that the slugger was terminally ill, a victim of lung cancer. As he did for Crawford, Cobb wrote hundreds of letters to sportswriters—the one to the *New York Times* columnist Arthur Daley was four handwritten pages—urging them to vote for Heilmann before he died. Unfortunately, Heilmann passed away before the official vote was taken; even so, Cobb told the dying Heilmann he had just been elected to give him a bit of peace. Heilmann was elected posthumously six months later with 87 percent of the vote.[27]

None of this is to deny that Ty Cobb was a difficult person to live with, work with, and befriend. Subject to Homeric temperamental outbursts, petty jealousies, and egocentric impulses, Cobb estranged two wives, alienated countless teammates, and tested the affection of countless friends. Even Cobb's closest associates feared his Jekyll and Hyde personality. When drunk, he could be especially vicious. "He'd insult you right quick" and "didn't apologize to anybody," one friend recalled. Indeed, he was more likely to offend again than admit wrongdoing.[28] Cobb was also slow to forgive. For Cobb, petty grudges festered into all-out vendettas. Yet he could also be both generous and loyal to friends and even mere acquaintances. Equally important, his generosity and charisma elicited loyalty from others. Stump, for reasons known only to him, missed all this, preferring to present a simplistic and often petty portrait that in no way captured the complex personality of his subject. Here, as in so many other ways, Stump got Cobb wrong.

Stump ended his article with what may have been the cruelest misrepresentation of all—that the baseball world shunned Cobb at his own funeral. "From all of major-league baseball, three men, and three men only, attended his funeral," Stump reported. He then predicted Cobb would now slip into the same obscurity from which he rose. Cobb "had himself entombed in a chamber directly across from his father, Professor Herschel," Stump dutifully explained—omitting that Cobb's mother Amanda was buried next to William—"in dusty little Roystontown where it all began." Until recently, nearly every story about Cobb's death fully articulated what Stump implied—that the baseball world ignored the passing of their former star. Even the dispassionate and painstakingly professional Charles Alexander accepted Stump's presentation on this one. "Sid Keener was there representing the Hall of Fame. Ray Schalk and Mickey Cochrane had flown down together from Chicago, and Nap Rucker . . . had driven over from Alpharetta, north of Atlanta. Otherwise the world of baseball had no visible presence at the funeral for the man who had been possibly its greatest performer, certainly its most fiercely competitive spirit." With that, Alexander abruptly ends his narrative.[29]

In fact, many people wanted to attend. Several prominent friends, including Coca-Cola chairman Bob Woodruff and *Sporting News* publisher Taylor Spink, tried to persuade the Cobbs to hold a memorial service commensurate to Cobb's status, but the family refused. Rogers Hornsby, George Sisler, Ted Williams, and Casey Stengel told the family they wanted to attend but could not make travel arrangements on such short notice. Even General Douglas MacArthur expressed an interest in attending. Meanwhile, the family was overwhelmed by the hundreds, perhaps thousands, of letters and telegrams that began to pour in as soon as Cobb's death became public. For the next several weeks, tributes and reminiscences in honor of Cobb were published in newspapers and magazines across the country. The *Sporting News* treatment was especially expansive—a serialized biography of Cobb published over several weeks. Somehow one intrepid sportswriter failed to take notice.[30]

Had he bothered to ask, Stump would have learned the family wanted a small funeral; to ensure this, they scheduled the burial just two days after Cobb's death on July 17. Why the family wanted a quick and private funeral is not difficult to determine. Cobb had instructed family members to be wary of reporters for years; by keeping them at bay, the family may have believed they were acting in his interest. It also stands to reason they wanted it this way, too: to keep this most intimate and personal of occasions free of the annoyances that often accompanied their father's celebrity. This must have been a difficult time for Charlie and the children, steeped as they were in memories and emotions as they laid this dominating personality to rest. They may have concluded they needed privacy as they sorted out their feelings. Finally, some have speculated that the Cobbs did not want journalists in town for a more pragmatic reason: they did not want anyone to start rooting into the Cobb family's dark past, especially William Cobb's death. Whatever the reason, the Cobb family decided to bury Tyrus Raymond Cobb as quickly as possible and with little outside fanfare. Even so, some four hundred people showed up for the funeral, including some two hundred Little Leaguers who lined the path from the cemetery gates to the Cobb family mausoleum. As the twenty-six-car cortege made its way from the funeral service in Cornelia to the Royston Cemetery, passing motorists stopped their cars and stood along the road to pay silent homage to a man who they had once seen as the personification of American manhood. The ceremony lacked glamour and pretension; nevertheless, its simplicity befitted this Southern man of honor and blended well with the dignified solemnity of a small rural town.[31]

Ty Cobb, whose quest to excel drove him to play harder and longer than just about everyone, finally gave up the fight.

NOTES

1. *New York Times*, September 18, 1928.
2. *New York Times*, October 3, 1929, 42.

3. Charles Leerhsen, *Ty Cobb: A Terrible Beauty* (New York: Simon and Schuster, 2015), 394–95; Tim Hornbaker, *War on the Basepaths: The Definitive Biography of Ty Cobb* (New York: Sports Publishing, 2015), 262–64, 268–69. Quotation is in Charles C. Alexander, *Ty Cobb* (New York: Oxford University Press, 1984), 225.

4. Alexander, *Ty Cobb*, 217; *Sporting News* (April 2, 1942): 1; *Sporting News* (February 15, 1950): 3.

5. For baseball's post–World War II woes, see Charles C. Alexander, *Our Game: An American Baseball History* (New York: MJF Books, 1991), 217–45; Benjamin G. Rader, *Baseball: A History of America's Game* (Urbana: University of Illinois Press, 1992), 155–85. For the impact of suburbs on professional sports, see Steven A. Reiss, *City Games: The Evolution of American Urban Society and the Rise of Sports* (Urbana: University of Illinois Press, 1989), 231–51.

6. Ty Cobb, with Al Stump, *My Life in Baseball* (1961; repr., Lincoln, NE: Bison Books, 1993), 20.

7. Ty Cobb, "They Don't Play Baseball Any More," *Life* (March 17, 1952): 136–50; Cobb, "Tricks That Won Me Ball Games," *Life* (March 24, 1952): 63–80.

8. *Sporting News* (February 6, 1952): 4; Leerhsen, *Ty Cobb*, 304–305.

9. Leerhsen, *Ty Cobb*, 130–131. As evidence of Cobb's egalitarian ethos, Leerhsen observes that Ty came from a long line of Southern abolitionists, "rife with exceptions to the rule about Southern attitudes" toward race (189; see also: 29, 31–32, 130–31). Remarkably, the heritage-conscious Cobb never discussed the perspective of such heroic figures. Rather, he was far more enamored with those distant ancestors who played key roles in the Confederacy. In other words, Leerhsen seems more eager to highlight Cobb's antislavery heritage than Cobb himself. As I've pointed out earlier, Leerhsen overstates the Cobb family's egalitarian heritage. One wonders if Leerhsen regrets comparing William Cobb to Atticus Finch in light of the publication of *Go Set a Watchman*.

10. *Sporting News* (March 26, 1952): 12; Letters to the Editor, *Life* (April 7, 1952): 12.

11. *Chicago Daily Tribune*, March 30, 1952, A3; *Sporting News* (March 26, 1952): 12; *Sporting News* (April 23, 1952): 12.

12. *Sporting News* (March 26, 1952): 12; *Sporting News* (June 11, 1952): 1, 6.

13. Alexander, *Ty Cobb*, 229–30; Don Rhodes, *Ty Cobb: Safe at Home* (Guilford, CT: Lyons Press, 2008), 150–51, 153.

14. Rhodes, *Safe at Home*, 162; Leerhsen, *Ty Cobb*, 385–91, 399–400.

15. Alexander, *Ty Cobb*, 231; Rhodes, *Safe at Home*, 162; Richard Bak, *Peach: Ty Cobb in His Time and Ours* (Ann Arbor: Sports Media Group, 2005), 181.

16. Herschel Cobb, *Heart of a Tiger: Growing Up With My Grandfather, Ty Cobb* (Toronto: ECW Press, 2013), 255–56, 261–67, 270–72.

17. Al Stump, "Ty Cobb's Wild, Ten-Month Fight to Live," in *The Greatest Baseball Stories Ever Told: Thirty Unforgettable Takes from the Diamond*, ed. Jeff Silverman (Guildford, CN: Lyons Press, 2001), 55, 57.

18. Stump, "Cobb's Wild, Ten-Month Fight," 67.

19. Stump, "Cobb's Wild, Ten-Month Fight," 58, 67.

20. Stump, "Cobb's Wild, Ten-Month Fight," 72.

21. Bak, *Peach*, 204.

22. Paul Gallico, *The Golden People* (New York: Doubleday, 1965), 199–296, 207; Fred Lieb, *Baseball As I Have Known It* (1977; repr., Lincoln, NE: Bison Books, 1996), 53–66.

23. Harold Seymour, *Baseball: The Golden Age* (New York: Oxford University Press, 1971), 107–11; Rader, *Baseball*, 97, 98. Rader has since reconsidered this assessment. He now argues Cobb's violent behavior resulted from his devotion to the code of honor. Even so, Rader asserts Cobb "never had a close personal friend among the big-league players or managers." See Benjamin G. Rader, *American Sports: From the Age of Folk Games to the Age of Televised Sports,* 6th edition (Upper Saddle River, NJ: Pearson, 2009), 163, 164; Benjamin G. Rader, "'Matters Involving Honor': Region, Race, and Rank in the Violent Life of Tyrus Raymond Cobb," in *Baseball in America and America in Baseball*, edited by Donald G. Kyle and Robert F. Fairbanks (College Station: Texas A&M University Press, 2008), 189–222.

24. Rhodes, *Safe at Home*, 155, 172; Cobb, *Heart of a Tiger*, 273–74.

25. *Sporting News* (December 13, 1961): 3, 4, 10, 14; *Sporting News* (December 20, 1961): 10, 11, 12, 14; *Sporting News* (December 27, 1961): 11, 12, 13, 14; *Sporting News* (January 3, 1962): 17, 18; *Sporting News* (January 10, 1962): 13, 14, 15; *Sporting News* (January 17, 1962): 12, 15, 20; *Sporting News* (January 24, 1962): 11, 12, 15; Jim Prime and Bill Nowlin, *More Tales From the Red Sox Dugout: Yarns from the Sox* (Champaign, IL: Sports Publishing, LLC, 2002), 170.

26. Alexander, Ty Cobb, 233–34.

27. Alexander, *Ty Cobb*, 225; Bak, *Peach*, 176; *New York Times*, July 8, 1951, 116.

28. Rhodes, *Safe at Home*, 175.

29. Al Stump, *Cobb* (Chapel Hill, NC: Algonquin Books, 1994); Alexander, *Ty Cobb*, 235.

30. Bak, *Peach*, 199, 202, 203. *Chicago Tribune*, July 20, 1961, D2; *New York Times*, July 20, 1961, 20; *Sporting News* (July 26, 1962): 10, 11. See also *Chicago Tribune*, July 20, 1961, 10; *New York Times*, August 15, 1961, 32; *Sporting News* (August 9, 1961): 9; *Sporting News* (August 23, 1961): 18, 24; *Sporting News* (August 30, 1961): 12, 20; *Sporting News* (September 6, 1961): 16, 21; *Sporting News* (September 13, 1961): 13–15.

31. Bak, *Peach*, 199; Rhodes, *Safe at Home*, 155–56; Cobb, *Heart of a Tiger*, 273–74.

SELECTED BIBLIOGRAPHY

PRIMARY SOURCES

Journals

Baseball Digest
Baseball Magazine
Sporting Life
Sporting News

Newspapers

Atlanta Constitution
Atlanta Journal
Augusta Chronicle
Augusta Herald
Bay City Times
Birmingham News
Boston Gazette
Boston Herald
Boston Post
Carnesville (Georgia) Advance
Charlotte Observer
Chicago Daily News
Chicago Defender
Chicago Evening Post
Chicago Record Herald
Chicago Tribune
Cleveland Plain Dealer
Columbus (Georgia) Enquirer-Sun
Dallas Morning News
Detroit Free Press
Detroit News

Miami District Daily News (Oklahoma)
Mobile Register
New York American
New York Call
New York Daily News
New York Evening News
New York Evening World
New York Herald Tribune
New York Observer and Chronicle
New York Sun
New York Telegraph
New York Times
New-York Tribune
Pawtucket (Rhode Island) Times
Philadelphia Evening Bulletin
Philadelphia Inquirer
Philadelphia Press
Pittsburgh Gazette Times
Pittsburgh Press
Salt Lake Herald
Salt Lake Telegram
San Jose Evening News
Spartanburg (South Carolina) Herald-Journal
(St. Louis) Daily Missouri Republican
St. Louis Post-Dispatch
St. Louis Republic
St. Louis Star
Twin Falls Daily News
Washington Post
Washington Post and Times Herald
Washington Times

Books and Articles

"Another Sales Contest Booming Business," *Advertising and Selling* 29 (August 9, 1919): 32.
"The Baseball Bug," *Puck* (May 3, 1911): 19.
"Business Lessons from Fields of Sport: Jimmy Lavender, Who Was Supreme in Crisis," *Rotarian* (April 1913): 21–24, 38.
"Business Maxims and Suggestions Worthwhile," *Bankers' Magazine* 90 (March 1919): 329.
"Editorial: The Game of Baseball," *Rotarian* 8 (June 1916): 439–40.
"Editorial: Playing the Game," *American Architect* 117 (June 23, 1920): 791.
"Editorial: Playing the Game," *Rotarian* 7 (October 1915): 327–28.
"Editorial: Tyrus Cobb, Who Gets Home From Third," *Rotarian* 5 (July 1913): 36.
"The Georgia Peach," *Youth's Companion* 49 (December 9, 1926): 100.
"The New York-Atlanta Good Roads Tour," *Horseless Age: The Automobile Trade Magazine* 24 (October 27, 1909): 473–77.
"News and Comment from the Field of Life Insurance," *Standard* 88 (May 14, 1921): 635.
"Small People with Great Names," *Woman's Home Companion* 45 (December 1918): 43–46.
"Spanking Baseball's Baby and Petting Its Paragon," *Literary Digest* 86 (September 19, 1925): 59–66.
"Ty Cobb Embarks on a New Venture," *Hardware Review* 25 (October 19, 1919): 61.
"Wholesalers Plan for Annual Meet," *Coal Review* 2 (May 18, 1921): 45.
Allen, Frederick Lewis. *Only Yesterday: An Informal History of the 1920s.* 1931. Reprint. New York: Perennial Classics, 2000.

SELECTED BIBLIOGRAPHY

Barrow, Edward Grant, with James M. Kahn. *My Fifty Years in Baseball*. New York: Coward-McCann, 1951.
Bent, Silas. *Ballyhoo: The Voice of the Press*. New York: Boni and Liveright, 1927.
Bonner, M. G. *The Big Baseball Book for Boys*. Springfield, MA: McLoughlin Bros., 1931.
Braathen, Sverre O. *Ty Cobb: The Idol of Baseball Fandom*. New York: Avondale Press, 1928.
Browne, Junius Henri. "The Bread-and-Butter Question," *Harper's New Monthly Magazine* 88 (December 1893–May 1894): 273–74.
Bruce, H. Addington. "Baseball and the National Life," *Outlook* 104 (May 17, 1913): 104–107.
Calkins, Earnest Elmo. *Business the Civilizer*. New York: Little, Brown, and Company, 1926.
Camp, Walter. "Batter Up," *Boy's Life* (July 1924): 7.
Canfield, George T. "Competition: The Safeguard and Promoter of General Welfare," *Annals of the American Academy of Political and Social Science* 42 (July 1912): 89–97.
Claudy, C. H. *The Battle of Base-Ball*. 1912. Reprint. Jefferson, NC: McFarland, 2005.
Cobb, Herschel. *Heart of a Tiger: Growing Up With My Grandfather, Ty Cobb*. Toronto: ECW Press, 2013.
Cobb, Ty. *Busting 'Em and Other Big League Stories*. 1914. Reprint. Jefferson, NC: McFarland, 2003.
———. *Inside Baseball with Ty Cobb*. Edited by Wesley Fricks. Salt Lake City: Aardvark Publishing, 2007.
———. *Memoirs of Twenty Years in Baseball*. Edited by William R. Cobb. Marietta, GA: Self-published, 2002.
———. "They Don't Play Baseball Anymore," *Life* (March 17, 1952): 136–54.
———. "Tricks That Won Me Ball Games," *Life* (March 24, 1952): 63–80.
Cobb, Ty, with Al Stump. *My Life in Baseball*. 1961. Reprint. Omaha, NE: Bison Books, 1993.
Curtis, Henry. "Baseball," *Journal of Education* 83 (January 1916): 466–67.
Dillon, J. B. "Two Queens in the Kitchen: Milady and a Gas Range," *American Gas Engineering Journal* 116 (March 4, 1922): 209.
Dixon, Thomas. *The Clansman: An Historical Romance of the Ku Klux Klan*. New York: A. Wessels Co., 1907.
DuRocher, Kris. "Violent Masculinity: Learning Ritual and Performance in Southern Lynchings," in *Southern Masculinity: Perspectives on Manhood in the South since Reconstruction*, edited by Craig Thompson Friend. Athens: University of Georgia Press, 2009.
Durocher, Leo, with Ed Linn. *Nice Guys Finish Last*. New York: Simon and Schuster, 1975.
Elser, Frank B. "The Baseball Fan and the Box-Score," *Outlook* (April 19, 1913): 856–59.
Evers, John J. *Touching Second: The Science of Baseball*. 1910. Reprint. Danvers, MA: General Books, 2009.
Farrell, James T. *My Baseball Diary*. 1957. Reprint. Carbondale: Southern Illinois University Press, 1998.
———. *Young Lonigan*. 1932. Reprint. New York: Signet Classics, 2004.
Flatley, Nicholas J. "Baseball—The Play of the Nation," *National Magazine* 35 (November 1913): 501–13.
Fox, Edward Lyell. "Finding the Stars of Baseball," *Outing Magazine* 62 (August 1913): 530–40.
———. "The Hard Job of a Baseball Star," *Outing Magazine* 60 (1912): 359–69.
———. "What is 'Inside Baseball?'" *Outing Magazine* 58 (July 1911): 489.
Gallico, Paul. *The Golden People*. New York: Doubleday, 1965.
Goewey, Edwin A. "Youth Holds the Spotlight in Sport," *Association Men* 45 (February 1920): 348–49, 375–78.
Grey, Zane. *The Short-stop*. New York: Grosset and Dunlap, 1909.
Haney, Fred. "My Most Unforgettable Characters," *Reader's Digest* (June 1964): 99–102.
Hartt, Rollin Lynde. "The National Game," *Atlantic Monthly* 102 (August 1908): 220–31.
Hawkins, Norval Abiel. *Certain Success*, 3rd edition. Detroit: Self-published, 1920.

———. "The Credit Salesman," *Bulletin of the National Association of Credit Men* 21 (1919): 712–22.
Holliday, Carl. "The Young Southerner and the Negro," *South Atlantic Quarterly* 8 (1909): 17–31.
Holmes, Jr., Oliver Wendell. "An Address Delivered on Memorial Day, May 30, 1895, Called by the Graduating Class of Harvard University." *The Essential Holmes: Selections from the Letters, Speeches, Judicial Opinions, and Other Writings of Oliver Wendell Holmes, Jr.*, edited by Richard A. Posner. Chicago: University of Chicago Press, 1992. 88–89.
Holtzman, Jerome, ed. *No Cheering in the Press Box*. New York: Henry Holt, 1973.
Honig, Donald. *Baseball When the Grass Was Real: Baseball from the Twenties to the Forties Told by the Men Who Played It*. Lincoln, NE: Bison Books, 1975.
———. *The Man in the Dugout: Fifteen Big League Managers Speak Their Minds*. Lincoln, NE: Bison Books, 1977.
Hunter, George McPherson. *Morning Faces*. New York: George H. Doran Company, 1918.
Johnson, Clifton. *Highways and Byways of the South*. New York: Macmillan, 1904.
Johnson, Harry. *Standing the Gaff: The Life and Hard Times of a Minor League Umpire*. Nashville: Pantheon Press, 1935.
Jones, Ellis O. "Baseball," *Lippincott's Monthly Magazine* 82 (September 1908): 814.
Lardner, Ring. "Tyrus: The Greatest of 'Em All," *American Magazine* (June 19, 1915): 19–23, 78.
Lieb, Fred. *Baseball As I Have Known It*. 1977. Reprint. Lincoln, NE: Bison Books, 1996.
Luckman, Dick. "Notes of a Sportsman," *Town and Country* (September 2, 1911): 32.
Macfadden, Bernarr. "Editor's Viewpoint," *Physical Culture* 23 (June 1910): 515–20.
Mack, Connie. "Clean Living and Quick Thinking," *McClure's Magazine* 43 (May 1914): 53–62.
Mathewson, Christy. *Pitching in a Pinch: Baseball from the Inside*. 1912. Reprint. Lincoln, NE: Bison Books, 1994.
McGraw, John J. *My Thirty Years in Baseball*. 1923. Reprint. Lincoln: University of Nebraska Press, 1995.
Melendy, Royal. "The Saloon in Chicago," *American Journal of Sociology* 6, no. 3 (November 1900): 289–306.
Murnane, Timothy H. *How to Play Baseball*. New York: American Sports Publishing, 1914.
Northup, Solomon. *Twelve Years a Slave: The Narrative of Solomon Northup*. Auburn, NY: Derby and Miller, 1853.
Purinton, Edward Earle. "Big Ideas From Big Business: Try Them Out for Yourself!" *Independent* 105 (April 16, 1921): 395–96.
Rice, Grantland. "The Durable Cobb," *Collier's* 77 (April 3, 1926): 24.
———. "The Grand Old Batting Eye," *McClure's Magazine* 45 (June 1915): 19.
———. "They Laugh at the Years," *Collier's* 76 (August 8, 1925): 17–19.
———. "The Winner's Way," *Collier's* 78 (July 10, 1926): 10.
———. "You Can Win If . . ." *Collier's* 75 (July 4, 1925): 15.
Rickey, Branch. *The American Diamond: A Documentary of the Game of Baseball*. New York: Simon and Schuster, 1965.
Ritter, Lawrence S. *The Glory of Their Times: The Story of the Early Days of Baseball Told by the Men Who Played It*. New York: Perennial, 1966.
———. *Lost Ballparks: A Celebration of Baseball's Legendary Fields*. New York: Viking Studio Books, 1992.
Rosengarten, Theodore. *All God's Dangers: The Life of Nate Shaw*. New York: Alfred A. Knopf, 1974.
Salsinger, H. G. *Ty Cobb: Two Biographies*. Edited by William R. Cobb. Jefferson, NC: McFarland, 2012.
Sangree, Allen. "Fans and Their Frenzies," *Everybody's Magazine* 17 (September 1907): 378–87.
Sargent, Dudley A. "Physical Training as a Compulsory Subject," *School Review* 16 (January 1908): 42–55.

Spalding, Albert G. *America's National Game: Historic Facts Concerning the Beginning, Evolution, Development, and Popularity of Base Ball, with Personal Reminiscences of Its Vicissitudes, Its Victories, and Its Votaries*. 1911. Reprint. San Francisco: Halo Books, 1991.
Stoddart, Dayton. "What Baseball Has Taught Ty Cobb," *Collier's* 74 (July 19, 1924): 7, 21, 25.
Van Loan, C. E. "Baseball as the Bleachers Like It," *Outing Magazine* 54 (September 1909): 643–52.
Williams, Joe. *The Joe Williams Baseball Reader: The Glorious Game, From Ty Cobb and Babe Ruth to the Amazing Mets; 50 Years of Baseball Writing by the Celebrated Newspaper Columnist*, edited by Peter Williams. Chapel Hill: Algonquin Books, 1989.

Unpublished Sources

Ty Cobb materials, Baseball Hall of Fame Archives, Cooperstown, New York.

SECONDARY SOURCES

Alexander, Charles C. *Our Game: An American Baseball History*. New York: MJF Books, 1991.
———. *Ty Cobb*. New York: Oxford University Press, 1984.
Asinof, Eliot. *Eight Men Out: The Black Sox and the 1919 World Series*. 1963. Reprint. New York: Owl Books, 1987.
Ayers, Edward L. *The Promise of the New South: Life After Reconstruction*. New York: Oxford University Press, 1992.
———. *Vengeance and Justice: Crime and Punishment in the 19th-Century American South*. New York: Oxford University Press, 1984.
Babcock, Barbara A., ed. *The Reversible World: Symbolic Inversion in Art and Society*. Ithaca, NY: Cornell University Press, 1978.
Bak, Richard. *Cobb Would Have Caught It: The Golden Age of Baseball in Detroit*. Detroit: Wayne State University Press, 1991.
———. *Peach: Ty Cobb in His Time and Ours*. Ann Arbor: Sports Media Group, 2005.
Baritz, Loren. *The Good Life: The Meaning of Success for the American Middle Class*. New York: Knopf, 1989.
Bean, Jennifer M., ed. *Flickers of Desire: Movie Stars of the 1910s*. New Brunswick, NJ: Rutgers University Press, 2011.
Bederman, Gail. *Manliness and Civilization: A Cultural History of Gender and Race in the United States, 1880–1917*. Chicago: University of Chicago Press, 1995.
Bein, Michael. A Graphical History of Baseball, http://michaelbein.com/baseball.html (accessed August 26, 2015).
Beito, David. "To Advance the 'Practice of Thrift and Economy': Fraternal Societies and Social Capital, 1890–1920," *Journal of Interdisciplinary History* 29 (1999): 585–612.
Bingay, Malcolm W. "When Both Teams Won on the Same Error," *Baseball Digest* (October–November 1967): 21–22.
Breen, T. H. "Horses and Gentlemen: The Cultural Significance of Gambling among the Gentry of Virginia," *William and Mary Quarterly* 34 (1977): 239–57.
Bruce, Jr., Dickson. *Violence and Culture in the Antebellum South*. Austin: University of Texas Press, 1979.
Brundage, W. Fitzhugh. *Lynching in the New South: Georgia and Virginia*. Urbana: University of Illinois Press, 1993.
Burk, Robert F. *Never Just a Game: Players, Owners, and American Baseball to 1920*. Chapel Hill: University of North Carolina Press, 1994.

Burns, Ken, and Geoffrey C. Ward. *Baseball, Inning 2: Something Like a War.* DVD. Walpole, NH: Florentine Films, 1994.

Butler, Judith. *Gender Trouble: Feminism and the Subversion of Identity.* Revised edition. New York: Routledge Press, 1999.

Carnes, Mark C. *Secret Ritual and Manhood in Victorian America.* New Haven, CT: Yale University Press, 1989.

Charlton, Thomas, Lois E. Myers, and Rebecca Sharpless, eds. *Handbook of Oral History.* Plymouth, UK: AltaMira Press, 2006.

Cobb, William R. "The Georgia Peach: Stumped by the Storyteller," *The National Pastime* (2010), http://sabr.org/research/baseball-peach-state (accessed August 24, 2015).

Costantino, Maria. *Men's Fashion in the Twentieth Century: From Frock Coats to Intelligent Fibers.* New York: Costume and Fashion Press, 1997.

de Cordova, Richard. *Picture Personalities: The Emergence of the Star System in America.* Urbana: University of Illinois Press, 1990.

Deford, Frank. *The Old Ball Game: How John McGraw, Christy Mathewson, and the New York Giants Created Modern Baseball.* New York: Atlantic Monthly Press, 2005.

Dewberry, Eric. "'Imagining the Action': Audiovisual Baseball Game Reproduction in Richmond, Virginia, 1895–1935," in *The Cooperstown Symposium on Baseball and American Culture, 2003–2004,* edited by William M. S. Simons. Jefferson, NC: McFarland, 2005, 141–55.

Dickson, Paul. *The New Dickson Baseball Dictionary,* 3rd edition. New York: Harcourt Brace and Company, 1999.

Doyle, Andrew. "Turning the Tide: College Football and Southern Progressivism," in *The Sporting World of the Modern South,* edited by Patrick B. Miller. Urbana: University of Illinois Press, 2002.

Dreifort, John, ed. *Baseball History from Outside the Lines.* Lincoln: University of Nebraska Press, 2001.

Dumenil, Lynn. *The Modern Temper: American Culture and Society in the 1920s.* New York: Hill and Wang, 1995.

Dunaway, David K., and Willa K. Baum, eds. *Oral History: An Interdisciplinary Anthology,* 2nd edition. Plymouth, UK: AltaMira Press, 1996.

Dundes, Alan. "April Fool and April Fish: Towards a Theory of Ritual Pranks," *Etnofoor Jaarg* 1, Nr. 1 (1988): 4–14.

Edwards, R. A. R. "No Dummies: Deafness, Baseball, and American Culture," in *The Cooperstown Symposium on Baseball and American Culture, 2007–2008,* edited by William M. Simons. Jefferson, NC: McFarland, 2009, 120–31.

Elias, Norbert, and Eric Dunning. *The Quest for Excitement: Sport and Leisure in the Civilizing Process.* Oxford: Basil Blackwell, 1986.

Escott, Paul D. *Many Excellent People: Power and Privilege in North Carolina, 1850–1900.* Chapel Hill: University of North Carolina Press, 1985.

Felber, Bill. *A Game of Brawl: The Orioles, the Beaneaters and the Battle for the 1897 Pennant.* Lincoln: University of Nebraska Press, 2007.

Fischer, David Hackett. *Albion's Seed: Four British Folkways in America.* New York: Oxford University Press, 1989.

Fleitz, David L. *Ghosts in the Gallery at Cooperstown: Sixteen Little-Known Members of the Hall of Fame.* Jefferson, NC: McFarland, 2004.

Foote, Lorien. *The Gentlemen and the Roughs: Violence, Honor, and Manhood in the Union Army.* New York: New York University Press, 2010.

Foster, Gaines. *Ghosts of the Confederacy: Defeat, the Lost Cause, and the Emergence of the New South, 1865–1913.* New York: Oxford University Press, 1987.

Fredrickson, George. *The Black Image in the White Mind: The Debate on Afro-American Character and Destiny, 1817–1914.* Hanover, NH: Wesleyan University Press, 1971.

Friend, Craig Thompson, ed. *Southern Masculinity: Perspectives on Manhood in the South since Reconstruction.* Athens: University of Georgia Press, 2009.

Gallagher, Gary W., and Alan T. Nolan, eds. *The Myth of the Lost Cause and Civil War History.* Bloomington: Indiana University Press, 2000.

Gay, Timothy M. *Tris Speaker: The Rough-and-Tumble Life of a Baseball Legend.* Guilford, CT: Lyons Press, 2007.
Geertz, Clifford. *The Interpretation of Cultures.* New York: Basic Books, 1973.
Ginzburg, Ralph. *100 Years of Lynchings.* Baltimore: Black Classic Press, 1962.
Glover, Lorri. *Southern Sons: Becoming Men in the New Nation.* Baltimore: Johns Hopkins University Press, 2007.
Gmelch, George. *Inside Pitch: Life in Professional Baseball.* 2001. Reprint. Lincoln, NE: Bison Books, 2006.
Gorn, Elliott J. "'Gouge and Bite, Pull Hair and Scratch': The Social Significance of Fighting in the Southern Backcountry," *American Historical Review* 90 (February 1985): 18–43.
———. *The Manly Art: Bare-Knuckle Prize Fighting in America.* Ithaca, NY: Cornell University Press, 1986.
Gorn, Elliott, and Warren Goldstein. *A Brief History of American Sports.* New York: Hill and Wang, 1993.
Greenberg, Kenneth S. *Honor and Slavery: Lies, Duels, Noses, Masks, Dressing as a Woman, Gifts, Strangers, Humanitarianism, Death, Slave Rebellions, the Proslavery Argument, Baseball, Hunting, and Gambling in the Old South.* Princeton: Princeton University Press, 1996.
Griswold, Robert L. *Fatherhood in America: A History.* New York: Basic Books, 1993.
Gropman, Donald. *Say It Ain't So, Joe: The True Story of Shoeless Joe Jackson.* 1979. Reprint. New York: Citadel Press, 2002.
Halttunen, Karen. *Confidence Men and Painted Women: A Study of Middle-Class Culture in America, 1830–1870.* New Haven: Yale University Press, 1982.
Hathaway, Ted. "Cobb as Role Model: Ty Cobb in Juvenile Periodical Literature: 1907–1929," *Nine: A Journal of Baseball History and Culture* 11 (Spring 2003): 64–72.
Higham, John. *Strangers in the Land: Patterns of American Nativism, 1860–1925.* Revised edition. New York: Atheneum Press, 1967.
Hittner, Arthur. *Honus Wagner: The Life of Baseball's "Flying Dutchman."* Jefferson, NC: McFarland, 1996.
Hoganson, Kristin L. *Fighting For American Manhood: How Gender Politics Provoked the Spanish-American and Philippine-American Wars.* New Haven: Yale University Press, 1998.
Hornbaker, Tim. *War on the Basepaths: The Definitive Biography of Ty Cobb.* New York: Sports Publishing, 2015.
Huhn, Rick. *Eddie Collins: A Baseball Biography.* Jefferson, NC: McFarland, 2008.
James, Bill. *The New Bill James Historical Baseball Abstract.* Revised edition. New York: Free Press, 2001.
Johnson, Paul E. *Sam Patch: The Famous Jumper.* New York: Hill and Wang, 2003.
Kasson, John F. *Houdini. Tarzan, and the Perfect Man: The White Male Body and the Challenge of Modernity in America.* New York: Oxford University Press, 2001.
———. *Rudeness and Civility: Manners in Nineteenth-Century Urban America.* New York: Noonday Press, 1990.
Kasson, Joy S. *Buffalo Bill's Wild West: Celebrity, Memory, and Popular History.* New York: Hill and Wang, 2000.
Kaufman, Jason. "The Rise and Fall of Joiners: The Knights of Labor Revisited," *Journal of Interdisciplinary History* 31 (2001): 553–79.
Kidwell, Claudia Brush. "Gender Symbols or Fashionable Details?" in *Men and Women: Dressing the Part*, edited by Claudia Brush Kidwell and Valerie Steele. Washington: Smithsonian Institution Press, 1989, 124–43.
Kimmel, Michael. "Baseball and the Reconstruction of American Masculinity, 1880–1920," in *Baseball History from Outside the Lines*, edited by John Dreifort. Lincoln: University of Nebraska Press, 2001.
———. *Manhood in America: A Cultural History.* 2nd ed. New York: Oxford University Press, 2006.
Klein, Christopher. *Strong Boy: The Life and Times of John L. Sullivan, America's First Sports Hero.* New York: Rowman & Littlefield, 2013.

Koehlinger, Amy. "'Let Us Live for Those Who Love Us': Faith, Family, and the Contours of Manhood Among the Knights of Columbus in Late Nineteenth-Century Connecticut," *Journal of Social History* 38 (2004): 455–69.

Leach, William. *Land of Desire: Merchants, Power, and the Rise of a New American Culture.* New York: Vintage Books, 1993.

Lears, Jackson. *Rebirth of a Nation: The Making of Modern America, 1877–1920.* New York: HarperCollins, 2009.

Lears, T. J. *No Place of Grace: Antimodernism and the Transformation of American Culture, 1880–1920.* Chicago: University of Chicago Press, 1983.

Leerhsen, Charles. *Ty Cobb: A Terrible Beauty.* New York: Simon and Schuster, 2015.

Levine, Lawrence W. *Highbrow Lowbrow: The Emergence of Cultural Hierarchy in America.* Cambridge, MA: Harvard University Press, 1988.

———. *The Unpredictable Past: Explorations in American Cultural History.* New York: Oxford University Press, 1993.

Light, Jonathan Fraser. *The Cultural Encyclopedia of Baseball.* Jefferson, NC: McFarland, 1997.

Linderman, Gerald. *Embattled Courage: The Experience of Combat in the American Civil War.* New York: Free Press, 1987.

Litwack, Leon. *Trouble in Mind: Black Southerners in the Age of Jim Crow.* New York: Alfred A. Knopf, 1998.

Lowenfish, Lee. *The Imperfect Diamond: A History of Baseball's Labor Wars.* Revised edition. New York: Da Capo Press, 1991.

Lutz, Tom. *American Nervousness.* 1903. Reprint. Ithaca, NY: Cornell University Press, 1991.

Macht, Norman L. *Connie Mack and the Early Years of Baseball.* Lincoln: University of Nebraska Press, 2007.

Mansch, Larry D. *Rube Marquard: The Life and Times of a Baseball Hall of Famer.* Jefferson, NC: McFarland, 1998.

Masur, Louis P. *Autumn Glory: Baseball's First World Series.* New York: Hill and Wang, 2003.

May, Lary. *Screening Out the Past: The Birth of Mass Culture and the Motion Picture Industry.* Chicago: University of Chicago Press, 1980.

McCallum, John D. *The Tiger Wore Spikes: An Informal Biography of Ty Cobb.* New York: A. S. Barnes, 1956.

———. *Ty Cobb.* New York: Praeger Publishers, 1975.

McCurry, Stephanie. *Masters of Small Worlds: Yeoman Households, Gender Relations, and the Political Culture of the Antebellum South Carolina Low Country.* New York: Oxford University Press, 1995.

Miller, Patrick B. "The Manly, the Moral, and the Proficient: College Sport in the New South," in *The Sporting World of the Modern South*, edited by Patrick B. Miller. Urbana: University of Illinois Press, 2002.

———, ed. *The Sporting World of the Modern South.* Urbana: University of Illinois Press, 2002.

Montville, Leigh. *The Big Bam: The Life and Times of Babe Ruth.* New York: Anchor Books, 2006.

Mrozek, Donald J. *Sport and American Mentality, 1880–1910.* Knoxville: University of Tennessee Press, 1983.

Murphy, Cait. *Crazy '08: How a Cast of Cranks, Rogues, Boneheads, and Magnates Created the Greatest Year in Baseball History.* New York: Smithsonian Books, 2007.

Murphy, Paul V. *The New Era: American Thought and Culture in the 1920s.* Lanham, MD: Rowman & Littlefield, 2012.

Nisbett, Richard, and Dov Cohen. *Culture of Honor: The Psychology of Violence in the South.* Boulder, CO: Westview Press, 1996.

Okkonen, Mark. *The Ty Cobb Scrapbook: An Illustrated Chronology of Significant Dates in the 24-Year Career of the Fabled Georgia Peach.* New York: Sterling Publishing, 2001.

Ownby, Ted. *Subduing Satan: Religion, Recreation, and Manhood in the Rural South, 1865–1920*. Chapel Hill: University of North Carolina Press, 1990.
Owsley, Frank L. *Plain Folk of the Old South*. 1949. Reprint. Baton Rouge: Louisiana State University Press, 1982.
Pendergast, Tom. *Creating the Modern Man: American Magazines and Consumer Culture*. Columbia: University of Missouri Press, 2000.
Pettegrew, John. *Brutes in Suits: Male Sensibility in America, 1890–1920*. Baltimore: Johns Hopkins University Press, 2007.
Ponce de Leon, Charles L. *Self-Exposure: Human-Interest Journalism and the Emergence of Celebrity in America, 1890–1940*. Chapel Hill: University of North Carolina Press, 2002.
Powers, Albert Theodore. *The Business of Baseball*. Jefferson, NC: McFarland, 2003.
Powers, Madelon. "'Poor Man's Friend': Saloonkeepers, Workers, and the Code of Reciprocity in U.S. Bars, 1870–1920," *International Labor and Working-Class History* 45 (1994): 1–15.
Powers-Beck, Jeffrey P. *The American Indian Integration of Baseball*. Lincoln: University of Nebraska Press, 2004.
Prime, Jim, and Bill Nowlin, *More Tales From the Red Sox Dugout: Yarns from the Sox*. Champaign, IL: Sports Publishing, LLC, 2002.
Proctor, Nicholas. *Bathed in Blood: Hunting and Mastery in the Old South*. Charlottesville: University Press of Virginia, 2002.
Putney, Clifford. *Muscular Christianity: Manhood and Sports in Protestant America, 1880–1920*. Cambridge, MA: Harvard University Press, 2003.
Rader, Benjamin G. *American Sports: From the Age of Folk Games to the Age of Televised Sports*. 6th edition. Upper Saddle River, NJ: Pearson, 2009.
———. *Baseball: A History of America's Game*. Urbana: University of Illinois Press, 1992.
———. "'Matters Involving Honor': Region, Race, and Rank in the Violent Life of Tyrus Raymond Cobb," in *Baseball in America and America in Baseball*, edited by Donald G. Kyle and Robert F. Fairbanks. College Station: Texas A&M University Press, 2008.
Rasmussen, Susan J. "Joking in Researcher-Resident Dialogue: The Ethnography of Hierarchy among the Tuareg," *Anthropological Quarterly* 66, no. 4 (October 1993): 211–20.
Rhodes, Don. *Ty Cobb: Safe at Home*. Guilford, CT: Lyons Press, 2008.
Riess, Steven A. *City Games: The Evolution of American Urban Society and the Rise of Sports*. Urbana: University of Illinois Press, 1989.
———. *Touching Base: Professional Baseball and American Culture in the Progressive Era*. Urbana: University of Illinois Press, 1983.
Riley, James A., and Renwick W. Speer. *The Hundred Years of Chet Hoff*. Cocoa, FL: TK Publishers, 1991.
Ritter, Lawrence. *Lost Ballparks: A Celebration of Baseball's Legendary Fields*. New York: Viking Studio Books, 1992.
Roark, James L. *Masters Without Slaves: Southern Planters in the Civil War and Reconstruction*. New York: W. W. Norton, 1977.
Rossi, John P. *The National Game: Baseball and American Culture*. Chicago: Ivan R. Dee, 2000.
Rotundo, E. Anthony. *American Manhood: Transformations in Masculinity from the Revolution to the Modern Era*. New York: Basic Books, 1993.
Schlereth, Thomas J. *Victorian America: Transformations in Everyday Life, 1876–1915*. New York: HarperPerennial, 1991.
Seymour, Harold. *Baseball: The Early Years*. New York: Oxford University Press, 1960.
———. *Baseball: The Golden Age*. New York: Oxford University Press, 1971.
———. *Baseball: The People's Game*. New York: Oxford University Press, 1990.
Silber, Nina. *The Romance of Reunion: Northerners and the South, 1865–1900*. Chapel Hill: University of North Carolina Press, 1993.
Skipper, James K. *Baseball Nicknames: A Dictionary of Origins and Meanings*. Jefferson, NC: McFarland, 1992.
Smart, Barry. *The Sport Star: Modern Sport and the Cultural Economy of Sporting Celebrity*. London: Sage Publishing, 2005.

Smelser, Marshall. *The Life That Ruth Built: A Biography*. Lincoln, NE: Bison Books, 1975.
Sowell, Mike. *August 2, 1903: The Mysterious Death of Hall-of-Famer Big Ed Delahanty*. New York: Macmillan, 1992.
———. *The Pitch That Killed: The Story of Carl Mays, Ray Chapman, and the Pennant Race of 1920*. Chicago: Ivan R. Dee, 1989.
Stanton, Tom. *Ty and the Babe: Baseball's Fiercest Rivals: A Surprising Friendship and the 1941 Has-Beens Golf Championship*. New York: St. Martin's Press, 2007.
Stowe, Steven M. *Intimacy and Power in the Old South: Ritual in the Lives of the Planters*. Baltimore: Johns Hopkins University Press, 1987.
Studlar, Gaylyn. *The Mad Masquerade: Stardom and Masculinity in the Jazz Age*. New York: Columbia University Press, 1996.
Stump, Al. *Cobb*. Chapel Hill, NC: Algonquin Books, 1994.
———. "Ty Cobb's Wild Ten-Month Fight to Live," *True* 14 (December 1961). Reprint. *The Greatest Baseball Stories Every Told: Thirty Unforgettable Tales From the Diamond*, edited by Jeff Silverman. Guilford, CT: Lyons Press, 2001, 51–72.
Susman, Warren I. *Culture and History: The Transformation of American Society in the Twentieth Century*. New York: Pantheon, 1984.
Szalontai, James D. *Small Ball in the Big Leagues: A History of Stealing, Bunting, Walking and Otherwise Scratching for Runs*. Jefferson, NC: McFarland, 2010.
Tabor, Anna Belle Little. *History of Franklin County*. Carnesville, GA: Franklin County Historical Society, 1986.
Thomas, Henry W. *Walter Johnson, Baseball's Big Train*. Lincoln: University of Nebraska Press, 1995.
Thomson, Cindy, and Scott Brown. *Three Finger: The Mordecai Brown Story*. Lincoln: University of Nebraska Press, 2006.
Trachtenberg, Alan. *The Incorporation of America: Culture and Society in the Gilded Age*. New York: Hill and Wang, 1982.
Turner, Victor. *Dramas, Fields, and Metaphors: Symbolic Action in Human Society*. Ithaca, NY: Cornell University Press, 1974.
———. *From Ritual to Theatre: The Human Seriousness of Play*. New York: PAJ Publications, 1982.
Vaught, David. "'Our Players are Mostly Farmers': Baseball in Rural California, 1850 to 1890," in *Baseball in America and America in Baseball*, edited by Donald Kyle and Robert Fairbanks. College Station: Texas A&M University Press, 2008.
Waller, Altina L. *Feud: Hatfields, McCoys, and Social Change in Appalachia, 1860–1900*. Chapel Hill: University of North Carolina Press, 1988.
Wann, Daniel, Merrill J. Melnick, Gordon W. Russell, and Dale G. Pease. *Sports Fans: The Psychology and Social Impact of Spectators*. New York: Routledge, 2001.
Ward, Geoffrey, and Ken Burns. *Baseball: An Illustrated History*. New York: Alfred A. Knopf, 1994.
Wiebe, Robert. *The Search for Order 1877–1920*. New York: Hill and Wang, 1967.
Williamson, Joel. *The Crucible of Race: Black-White Relations in the American South Since Emancipation*. New York: Oxford University Press, 1984.
Wilson, Charles Reagan. *Baptized in Blood: The Religion of the Lost Cause, 1865–1920*. Athens: University of Georgia Press, 1980.
Woodward, C. Vann. *Origins of the New South, 1877–1920*. Baton Rouge: Louisiana State University Press, 1951.
Wyatt-Brown, Bertram. *The House of Percy: Honor, Melancholy, and Imagination in a Southern Family*. New York: Oxford University Press, 1994.
———. *The Shaping of Southern Culture: Honor, Grace, and War, 1760s–1880s*. Chapel Hill: University of North Carolina Press, 2001.
———. *Southern Honor: Ethics and Behavior in the Old South*. New York: Oxford University Press, 1982.
Young, Alfred. *The Shoemaker and the Tea Party: Memory and the American Revolution*. New York: Beacon Press, 1999.

Zeitz, Joshua. *White Ethnic New York: Jews, Catholics, and the Shaping of Postwar Politics*. Chapel Hill: University of North Carolina Press, 2007.
Zingg, Paul J. *Harry Hooper: An American Baseball Life*. Urbana: University of Illinois Press, 1993.
Zunz, Olivier. *Making America Corporate, 1870–1920*. Chicago: University of Chicago Press, 1990.

WEBSITES

Baseball Almanac. http://www.baseball-almanac.com/poetry/po_case.shtml (Accessed August 25, 2015).
Digital Scholarship Commons, "Georgia Lynchings Project," Emory Libraries. http://dev.emorydisc.org/galyn/lynchings/counties/ (Accessed August 31, 2015).
Heritage Quest Online, United States Manuscript Census. http://persi.heritagequestonline.com.ezproxy.gvsu.edu (Accessed August 31, 2015).
Historical Census Browser, Georgia, 1870–1910, Geospatial and Statistical Data Center, University of Virginia Library. http://mapserver.lib.virginia.edu/ (Accessed August 4, 2013).
Sports Reference LLC, "Baseball-Reference.com." http://www.baseball-reference.com/ (Accessed July 10, 2014).

INDEX

Aaron, Hank, 362
Alexander, Charles, 31, 365, 372, 375
American League, 57
Anniston Steelers, 13, 26
Anson, Cap, 47
Armour, William, 73, 91, 95, 96, 99, 175
Arrington, L. S., 341
Atlanta Race Riot of 1906, 151–152
Augusta, Georgia, 112, 152, 341
Augusta Tourists, 13, 25, 26–29
Austin, Jimmy, 69, 116, 183, 185, 188, 200, 201, 206
Ayers, Edward, 8

Bailey, Bill,, 114
Bak, Richard, 31, 184, 365
Baker, Frank "Homerun," 140, 194; public reaction to spiking, 272–275; spiked by Cobb, 271, 357
Baker, Newton D., 284
ballparks, 179, 224, 241; as male arena, 243–246
ballplayers: anxiety felt by, 63–66, 98, 248; baseball bats of, 88–89; celebrity culture and, 196; collegial ethic of, 163, 164–166; daily routines of, 163–164; defy middle-class Victorian values, 169, 172; ethnic diversity of, 92, 164–165; hazing rituals of, 83–89, 166, 168; honor and, 109, 118, 120, 163, 188, 194; managers and, 185–193; manhood and, 86, 118, 120, 178, 188; mutualist or "team play" ethos of, 185–215; "nerve" and, 178; nicknames of, 166–169; mistreated by owners, 59–62, 179–182; pranks played by, 173–178; rookies, 84–89; salaries of, 59, 61; sociability valued by, 169–172; toughness of, 181–184. *See also* names of individual ballplayers
ballyhoo journalism, 299–303
Baltimore Orioles, 47–48, 51
Banks, Ernie, 358
Barnes, Sammy, 139
Barrow, Edward Grant, 113, 188, 296
Barry, Jack, 274
baseball: creation myth, 58; gambling, 340; Hall of Fame, 356, 373; homerun epidemic in, 316; as homosocial experience, 239–241, 244, 246; "inside" or scientific style of, 66–67, 190, 315–316; as masculine drama of, 247, 248, 267; media coverage, 44, 63, 225–226; minor leagues, 41–43; National Agreement, 57, 60; National Commission, 57; popularity in early twentieth century, 41–45, 57–59, 223–224, 227–232; post-World War II culture of, 357–358; reserve clause, 60–62; as training ground for modern man, 232–236, 238–239; violence of early game, 1, 22, 46–50; World Series,

393

creation of, 58. *See also* ballplayers; American League; baseball attendance; baseball fans; baseball managers; baseball owners; baseball umpires; National League
baseball attendance: decline of in late nineteenth century, 51; increase of in early twentieth century, 57, 223
baseball fans, 59, 223–248; admiration for ballplayers by, 239–241; as aficionados, 242–243, 244, 273; ballpark behavior of, 243–248; booster clubs of, 246; intimate relationship with ballplayers of, 241–242; middle class as, 228–231; obsession with baseball of, 223–226; passion of, 242–247; rowdyism of, 47–49, 227; vacillating responses by, 275. *See also* baseball, popularity in early twentieth century; baseball attendance; Cobb, Tyrus Raymond "Ty," and baseball fans
baseball managers, 86, 175; growth in power, 66–71. *See also* Bezdek, Hugo; Bresnahan, Roger; Carrigan, Bill; Chance, Frank; Cobb, Tyrus Raymond; Jennings, Hughie; Mack, Connie; McGraw, John; Moran, Pat; Stallings, George
baseball owners, 50, 52–54, 57, 59, 70, 72
baseball umpires, 66, 130; early abuse of, 48–50. *See also* Evans, Billy; O'Laughlin, Francis "Silk"
Bassler, Johnny, 330
Beard, George Miller, 236, 265
Beckworth, Shirley Cobb (daughter), 2, 366, 367, 372
Bemis, Harry, 116, 136
Bender, Charles "Chief," 67
Berra, Lawrence "Yogi," 358
Bezdek, Hugo, 187
Blankenship, Si, 331
Blue, Lu, 330
Bluege, Ossie, 116
Boddington, Clem, 366
Bodie, Frank "Ping," 174
Boone, Dan, 266
Boston, 51, 255–256
Boston Braves, 69
Boston Red Sox, 84, 175, 295–296, 296, 297, 298
boy culture, 18–19
Bradley, Bill, 136
Bresnahan, Roger, 67, 182
Bressler, Raymond "Rube," 67, 114, 199
Breton, Jim, 116
Bridwell, Al, 84, 185, 188–190
Brook, Gilbert C., 265
Brooklyn, 240
Brooks Brothers (clothiers), 230
Brooks, Louise, 317
Broun, Haywood, 299
Brown, Joe E., 258
Brown, Mordecai "Three Fingers," 198
Brown, Stewart, 373
Browning, Pete, 169
Bruce, H. Addington, 45, 233, 236
Brush, John, 50, 70
Bryant, Bud, 21
Buranelli, Prosper, 263
Burroughs, Edgar Rice, 230
Bush, Donie, 126, 211
bushers. *See* ballplayers, rookies
Byrne, Bobby, 182

Caldwell, Ray "Slim," 266–267
Calkins, Earnest Elmo, 317
Campanella, Roy, 358, 362
Carey, Max, 171
Carpenter, William, 139
Carrigan, Bill, 186, 256
"Casey at the Bat," 49
Cravath, Gavvy, 297
celebrity culture: 1920s, 303; late nineteenth and early twentieth century, 125, 193. *See also* ballyhoo journalism; ballplayers, celebrity culture and; Cobb, Tyrus Raymond, celebrity of ; Ruth, George Herman "Babe," celebrity of
Chalmers Motor Car Company, 210, 211, 214
Chance, Frank, 166, 171, 182, 185, 188, 206, 358
Chapman, Ray, 206
Chase, Hal, 206
Chesbro, Jack, 71, 73, 167
Chevrolet, 259

INDEX

Chicago, 47, 57, 102, 126, 239
Chicago "Black Sox" scandal, 340
Chicago Cubs, 44, 64, 84, 223, 355
Chicago White Sox, 71
Chitwood, Caleb (maternal grandfather), 4, 93
Cicotte, Eddie, 117, 170
Cincinnati, xvii
Cincinnati, University of, 55
Cincinnati Reds, 50, 55, 84, 88, 192
Civil War, 3, 15
Clark, Fred, 173
Clarke, Jay "Nig," 177
Cleveland, 47, 57
Cleveland Indians, 175, 338
Cleveland Naps. *See* Cleveland Indians
Cobb, Amanda Chitwood (mother), xviii, 4, 13, 25, 29–30, 93, 94
Cobb, Charlotte Marion Lombard "Charlie" (first wife), 139, 208, 367, 372
Cobb, Florence (sister), 5, 29
Cobb, Hersch (grandson), 367
Cobb, Herschel (son), 364
Cobb, Howell, 8
Cobb, James "Jimmy," 372
Cobb, John (paternal grandfather), 14–17
Cobb, Ned (a.k.a. Nate Shaw), 148
Cobb, Paul (brother), 29
Cobb, Sarah Ann (paternal grandmother), 15
Cobb, Thomas Reade Rootes, 8
Cobb, Tyrus Raymond "Ty," 186; 1910 batting race and, 210–213; aggressive playing style of, 112–114, 181, 183, 271, 274, 324; assaults fan (Claude Lucker), 276–281; autobiographical writings, 9, 81, 91, 108, 141, 155, 331, 359, 361, 364–369; Baker, Frank "Home Run" spiking, 271–275; base running style of, 114–117; baseball records held by, 108, 317; baseball wisdom of, 308, 310, 326–329, 331, 332, 359–362, 365–366; baseball's appeal to, 1, 13, 22, 25; bravado of, 123–124, 268–269; celebrity of, 124–126, 129–130, 193, 196, 208, 256–258, 260, 293; charitable work of, 356; childhood of, 4, 9–13, 16–25, 93–94, 146–147, 340; childrearing practices of, 283; commercial endorsements by, 259, 321; competitive nature of, 20–22, 110–111; contract negotiations, 127–129; death and funeral of, 364, 375–376; ego, 125, 269; as elder statesman of the game, 315, 317, 326–328; as embodiment of 1920s business values, 318–323; as embodiment of modern professional man, 263–267, 270; as embodiment of primal manhood, 280–283, 365–366; father's death, response to, 30–35; feuds with opponents, 118–121, 136, 271, 308–313; feuds with teammates, 100, 103, 126, 203, 210–215; first major league season, 73–74, 79–83; hazed by teammates, 83–84, 89–96, 151; health, decline of, 364; homerun craze, responds to, 308, 329; inverts middle-class Victorian values, 270–271, 277, 283; manager of the Detroit Tigers, 311, 312, 328–336; masculine performance of, 1–2, 10, 79, 80, 82–83, 94, 109, 110, 113, 114, 270, 276, 280, 284, 285, 308, 361, 363, 365–366; minor league career of, 13, 25–28, 92; modern baseball, criticizes, 359–361, 363; "nerve," 193–194, 265–267, 365; neurasthenia and, 97–98; nicknames for, 166, 281; off-season activities, 93, 283; performance decline, 294, 304, 314–315, 336–337; personal autonomy, valued, 10–13, 163, 194, 215, 270, 293, 324, 332, 335, 345, 365; personality, 31–32, 94, 123, 261–262, 269, 333, 365, 369–370, 371, 373–375; Philadelphia, 224; Philadelphia Athletics, plays for, 344–346; physical appearance, 259; pitchers, intimidation of, 117–118; players' ethic, violates values of, 207–208; post-career activities, 355–367; post-career reputation, 356–359, 363; press, relationship with, 131–133, 133, 208–209, 257, 277, 315, 324, 325, 326–328, 342; race and, 282, 307, 362; retirement, 346, 355;

retirement rumors, 293; risk-taking by, 18, 20–21, 270; as role model for youths and adults, 262, 263–265, 317–323; self-discipline of, 323; significance to baseball, xx, 74, 83, 317; as Southerner, xx, xxi, 1–2, 10, 33–35, 92–94, 108–110, 120–123, 136–144, 145–155, 194, 270, 282–283, 307, 310–311, 335, 340, 341–342, 343, 345, 365, 366, 376; success narrative of, 107, 323; teammates' support of, 199, 276; violent behavior of, 21, 31, 122, 139, 150, 271, 276, 324; wealth of, 322; World War I military service, 284–287, 293. *See also* Cobb, Tyrus Raymond "Ty," and the ethic of honor; Cobb, Tyrus Raymond "Ty," and baseball fans; Cobb-Speaker gambling scandal; Ruth, George Herman "Babe"

Cobb, Tyrus Raymond "Ty," and baseball fans: fans' appreciation of, 242, 256, 263–267, 268, 273–275, 277–280, 283–284, 373; fans, feuds with, 134, 244, 255–256, 267–273, 276; fans, solicitous of, 133, 135, 244, 261–262, 269, 373; taunt Cobb, 255–256, 267–276. *See also* Cobb, Tyrus Raymond "Ty," and the ethic of honor, fans as arbiters of honor

Cobb, Tyrus Raymond "Ty," and the ethic of honor, xviii, xxi, 155, 194, 345; assumes superior status as a right of honor, 123–124, 125–126, 129, 130–133, 140, 149, 215; contract negotiations as an expression of, 127–129; gambling and, 340; fans as arbiters of honor, 135, 274–275, 307; father's death and, 34–35, 92–94; lying ("giving the lie") and, 136–143, 310–311, 342; as manager and, 335; racial attitudes and behavior influenced by, 143, 145–155, 277; reared according to, 2, 8, 108–110; responds to perceived attacks upon his honor, 138–139, 144, 341–342, 343, 365–366; rivalry and, 83, 123, 139–143, 304–306; vengeful behavior and, 81, 81–82, 100, 120–123

Cobb, Tyrus Jr. (son), 283, 364

Cobb, William Herschel (father), 4–13, 93–94, 121, 136, 365; child-rearing practices, 9–13; death, xviii, 25, 29–30, 32–35, 369, 376; racial views, 145

Cobb-Speaker gambling scandal, 337–343

Coca-Cola, 259, 322

Cochrane, Mickey, 344, 375

Cohan, George M., 258

Cole, Bert, 312

Collins, Eddie, 88, 198, 235, 268, 304–305, 344, 358

Collins, Fred, 153

Comiskey, Charles, 55, 56, 124, 167, 238

Coolidge, Calvin, 317

Corriden, John "Red," 212

Corridon, Frank, 167

Coughlin, Bill, 100, 175

Coveleski, Stanley, 65

Crawford, Sam, 91, 164, 167, 175, 176, 183, 200; Cobb, Ty, and, 163, 203, 209, 210–211, 214, 373

Criger, Lou, 136

Cronin, Joe, 373

Cunningham, Joe, 20

Curtis, Henry S., 46

Dana, Charles A., 231

Daniel, Dan, 298, 302

Daubert, Jack, 199

Dauss, George "Hooks," 334

"Dead Ball" era, 71–72, 88, 179–181, 357, 361, 363. *See also* baseball, "inside" or scientific style of

Delahanty, Ed, 169

Dell, Bill "Wheezer," 167

Detroit, xvii, xix–110, 225, 244, 297, 325, 338, 342

Detroit Tigers, 89–92, 95–102, 125, 176–177, 181, 207–208, 209–215, 244, 271, 276, 294, 311–312, 326, 328–337

DiMaggio, Joe, 358, 360, 363

Dixon, Thomas, 230, 281–282

Donahue, Francis "Red," 176

Donlin, Mike, 168

Donovan, "Wild" Bill, 101, 169

Doubleday, Abner, 58

Doubleday publishers, 367

Doyle, "Dirty" Jack, 195

Doyle, "Laughing" Larry, 172, 185, 195

INDEX

Dudley, Bide, 315
Durant, William C., 317
Durocher, Leo, 324, 363
Dykes, Jimmy, 67, 87, 346

Earnshaw, George, 344
Elberfeld, Arthur "Kid," 201, 206; gives Cobb "the professional teach," 79–83, 103, 113
Elser, Frank B., 226
Evans, Billy, 116, 193, 212, 296, 316; assessment of Cobb, 125, 262; fights Cobb, 138, 324
Evers, Johnny, 61, 64, 167, 170, 185, 203, 248, 262

fans. *See* baseball fans
Farrell, James T., 239–240, 243
Feller, Bob, 358
Ferris, Hobe, 136
Fitzgerald, F. Scott, 317
Fitzgerald, Zelda, 317
Fletcher, Art, 118
Flick, Elmer, 102
Flood, Curt, 127
Ford, Henry, 317
Forester, Eddie, 333
Foster, John B., 131
Fothergill, Bob "Fats," 184, 330, 336
Fowler, Gene, 366
Foxx, Jimmie, 344
Frazee, Harry, 296
Freud, Sigmund, 238
Frick, Ford, 298, 302, 373
Frisch, Frankie, 190
Fullerton, Hugh, 44, 173, 190–191, 232, 235, 262, 330

Gainor, Del, 110
Gallico, Paul, 30, 298, 371
gambling, 340. *See also* Cobb-Speaker gambling scandal
Gehringer, Charlie, 333
General Motors, 322
Gibson, George, 173, 182
Gleason, William "Kid," 328
Gmelch, Mark, 169
Golsin, Leon "Goose," 164, 167
Grand Rapids, 55, 57

Greenberg, Kenneth, 120
Greene, Sam, 330, 335
Grey, Zane, 45, 45–46
Griffith, Clark, 139, 336, 363, 364
Grimes, Burleigh, 186, 191
Grimm, Charlie, 167
Groh, Henry, 183
Grove, Bob "Lefty," 344
Grudzielanek, Mark, 168

Hall, G. Stanley, 231, 283
Hamilton, "Sliding" Billy, 190
Haney, Fred, 112, 123, 330, 373
Harding, Howard, 139
Harding, Warren G., 258
Hargrave, Eugene, 167
Harris, Raymond "Bucky," 335, 339
Harris, William H., 341
Harrison, Pat, 341
Harrison, Ulysses, 148, 149
Hartt, Rollin Lynde, 239
Hawkins, Norval Abiel, 262
Hayne, Paul H., 144
Hearst, William Randolph, 317
Heilmann, Harry, 214, 330, 334, 336, 373
Hendrix, Jack, 198
Herrmann, August, 57
Herzog, Charles "Buck," 118–120, 143, 167, 190
Herzog, Dorrel "Whitey," 335
Hicksville Academy (North Carolina), 4
Hoff, Chet, 188
Holmes, Oliver Wendell, Jr., 191–192
honor. *See* ballplayers, honor and; Cobb, Tyrus Raymond "Ty," and the ethic of honor; Southern culture, honor and
Hooper, Harry, 84, 197, 199, 295
Hopper, De Wolf, 49
Hornsby, Rogers, 346, 363, 375
Hoy, William "Dummy," 167, 202
Hoyne, Thomas T, 233
Huggins, Miller, 311, 330
Hughes, Charles Evans, 257
Hunt, Marshall, 298, 300–302
Hunter, George McPherson, 262

"inside" baseball. *See* baseball, "inside" or scientific style of
Isbell, Frank, 136

Jackson, Joe, 139–143, 198, 241, 296, 304–305, 310, 363
James, Bill, 66
Jeffries, Jim, 125
Jennings, Hughie, 47, 178; as manager of Tigers, 99, 186, 203, 328, 329; on Cobb as a player, 114, 265; relationship with Cobb, 126, 203, 207, 210, 214, 270
Jim Crow Era, race relations in, 143–145, 147, 151
Johnson, Byron Bancroft "Ban," 169, 212, 213–214, 227, 312; and Cobb-Speaker gambling scandal, 339, 342, 343; disciplines Ty Cobb, 280; early career of, 54–57
Johnson, Ernie, 312
Johnson, Syd, 312
Johnson, Walter, 42, 61–62, 166, 200, 241
Jones, Bobby, 258
Jones, Davy, 89, 91, 96, 126, 165, 176–177, 211, 246
Jones, Ellis O., 225
Jones, "Sad" Sam, 188
Jones, Tom, 181
Joss, Addie, 238

Kahn, Roger, 296
Keeler, William "Wee Willie," 102
Keener, Syd, 375
Kerr, Dickie, 337
Kieran, John, 299
Koenig, Mark, 346
Kremer, Ray, 331
Krichell, Paul, 117
Ku Klux Klan, 282

Lajoie, Napoleon, 57, 175, 176, 304–305, 346, 358; 1910 batting race and, 212, 213
Lane, F. C., 44, 67, 131, 132, 231, 239, 247, 261, 264, 283, 315, 317
Landis, Kenesaw Mountain, 339–340, 342–343
Lanigan, Ernest, 316
Lardner, Ring, 44, 131, 262, 298
LaRussa, Tony, 335
Lasorda, Tommy, 336
Lavender, Jimmy, 239

Leach, Tommy, 176, 181
Leerhsen, Charles, 365
Leever, Samuel, 167
Leidy, George, 27–28, 323
Leitner, George, 167
Leonard, Hubert "Dutch," 118, 136, 337; gambling accusations made by, 337–343
Lewis, George "Duffy," 175, 199
Lieb, Fred, 44, 131, 206, 262, 299, 315, 371
Lobert, Hans, 84, 88, 174, 179, 180, 201, 246
Lodge, Henry Cabot, 258
London, Jack, 230, 284
Lopez, Al, 200
Los Angeles Angels, 373
"Lost Cause," 3, 7–8, 24
Louisville, 48
Lowe, Bobby, 107
Lucker, Claude: assaulted by Cobb, 276; harasses Cobb, 276, 277; public condemnation of, 277–280

MacArthur, Douglas, 375
Mack, Connie, 67–69, 139, 170, 188, 202, 227, 235, 271, 335, 337, 344, 344–345, 355, 364
Magee, Sherwood "Sherry," 196
magnates. See baseball owners
manhood: baseball promotes, 1–2, 231–236, 244–248; Cobb as embodiment of masculine ideal, 263–267, 270–271, 277–280, 283–284; nineteenth-century conceptions, 230; new middle-class conceptions of, 230–231, 233, 234, 238; Southern male child rearing, 7, 9–13, 24–25, 93–94; Southern conceptions of, 2–3, 8–9, 16–20, 281–283. See also ballplayers, manhood and; boyhood culture; Cobb, Tyrus Raymond, masculine performance of; middle class, manhood and;
Mantle, Mickey, 358
Manush, Henry "Heinie," 330, 336
Marietta College, 55
Marquard, Richard "Rube," 108, 186

Mathewson, Christy, 66, 67, 71, 84, 85, 128, 164, 167, 171, 172, 193, 358; as celebrity, 196, 198; describes McGraw as manager, 191
Mauch, Gene, 335
Mays, Carl, 205, 362
Mays, Willie, 358
McCallum, John D., 120, 127, 136, 147, 366
McCormick, Cyrus, 257
McCreary, Bob, 11–12, 20
McFadden, Bernarr, 236
McGeehan, W.O., 299
McGinnity, Mike, 169
McGraw, John, 48, 65, 86, 168, 358; feuds with Ty Cobb, 118–120; as manager, 66, 69, 70–71, 181, 185–186, 188, 189, 191, 315
McIntyre, Matty: feuds with Ty Cobb, 89–91, 95–96, 100, 100–101, 103
McKeon, Jack, 335
McLaren, Beverly Cobb (daughter), 372
Mellon, Andrew, 317
Mensor, Edward, 167
Merkle, Fred, 64
Meusel, Bob, 312
Meyers, John "Chief," 185, 189
middle class: Babe Ruth as embodiment of, 303; baseball appeals to, 231–233; manhood and, 230–231, 233, 234–235, 238; transformation of, 228–229, 303; Ty Cobb as embodiment of, 263–267; values of, 229–231. *See also* baseball fans, middle class as
Milan, Clyde, 305
Moore, Bill, 155, 333
Moran, Pat, 192–193
Morgan, Cy, 118, 136
Moriarty, George, 181
Morris, Ada, 154
Mullin, George, 100
Murnane, Timothy Hayes, 44, 47, 238
Murphy, Charles, 171
Murphy, Herbert, 167
Musial, Stan, 358
Mutt and Jeff, 277
My Life in Baseball. See Cobb, Tyrus Raymond, autobiographical writings; Stump, Al

The Narrows (Georgia), xvii, 4
National League, 49–54, 55–57, 71
Navin, Frank, 99, 102; relations with Cobb, 127–129, 328, 331–332, 335, 339
nerve: baseball as contest of, 238–239; baseball as tonic for, 247; modernity's strain upon, 236; and neurasthenia, 236–238. *See also* Cobb, Tyrus Raymond, "nerve" of
Neun, Johnny, 331
neurasthenia. *See* Cobb, Tyrus Raymond "Ty," neurasthenia and
New South, 3, 144–145
New York City, 276, 293, 297–300, 301
New York Clippers. *See* New York Yankees
New York Giants, 64, 65, 70–71, 80, 118, 170, 181, 195, 223, 304
New York Yankees, 73, 84, 241, 276, 298, 304, 311–312, 326, 346
North Georgia Agricultural College, 5
Northup, Solomon, 122
Nunamaker, Les, 266–267

O'Conner, Jack, 212
O'Doull Francis "Lefty," 183
O-Laughlin, Francis "Silk," 267
Oldfield, Barney, 258
Ott, Mel, 358
Overall, Orvie, 179
Ownby, Ted, 19

Page, Thomas Nelson, 281
Pape, Larry, 256
Patten, Simon, 228
Pegler, Westbrook, 298, 302, 342
Peters, Madison C, 235
Phelon, William, 85
Philadelphia, 51, 272–275, 342
Philadelphia Athletics, 67–68, 87, 170, 271, 344, 346, 355
Pittsburgh Pirates, 181
Pulliam, Harry, 53, 58, 60

Rader, Benjamin, 371
Raskob, John J., 317
Raymond, Arthur "Bugs," 170
Reconstruction, 3, 15–16

Rhodes, Don, 365
Rice, Grantland, 26, 44, 131, 136, 262, 298, 314, 319, 330
Richter, Francis, 52, 54, 67
Rickey, Branch, 114, 133, 143, 209
Rigney, Topper, 330
Ritchey, Claude, 175
Rivers, Alexander George Washington "King," 149
Robinson, Jackie, 357, 358, 362
Rockefeller, John D., 257, 317
rookies. *See* ballplayers, rookies
Roosevelt, Theodore, 45, 230, 231, 257, 283–284
Roth, Andy, 26–28
Roth, Robert "Braggo," 198
Roush, Edd, 188, 199
Rowan, Jack, 99
Rowland, Clarence "Pants," 328
Royston (Georgia), xviii, 5–6, 18, 19, 366
Rucker, George "Nap," 110, 375
Runyan, Damon, 298, 315
Ruth, George Herman "Babe," 133, 155, 168, 179, 183, 199, 346, 363; appetites of, 295; ballyhoo journalism and, 298–302; celebrity of, 297; Cobb jealous of, 304–308; Cobb criticizes, 307, 310; Cobb makes peace with, 313–314; as Cobb's rival, 311–312, 323; critics of, 315–316; hazed by teammates, 296; as hitter, 294, 296–298, 299, 310, 311; as fan attraction, 297; masculine performance of, 294–295; personality of, 295, 300–302, 303; as pitcher, 296; scandals involving, 325–326; traded to New York Yankees, 298
Runyon, Damon, 131

Salsinger, Harry, 209, 214, 311, 315
Sanborn, L.E., 236
Sangree, Allen, 242–243, 246
Schaefer, Herman A. "Germany," 148, 176–178, 182
Schalk, Ray, 114, 305, 375
Schlereth, Thomas, 230
Schmidt, Charlie, 90, 152, 181
Schwab, Charles, 317

scientific baseball. *See* baseball, "inside" or scientific style of
Sewell, Luke, 84–85
Seymour, Harold, 45, 240, 371
Shannon, William "Spike," 201
Sheridan, John, 131, 315, 319, 342
Siever, Ed, 99; fights with Ty Cobb, 100–101
Simmons, Al, 344, 345
Sims, P. Hal, 137
Sisler, George, 297, 304, 306, 310, 313, 346, 375
Slocum, William, 302
Smith, Harry, 173
Smith, Hoke, 145, 151
Snider, Donald "Duke," 358
Snodgrass, Fred, 71, 84, 170, 188, 196, 201, 202
southern culture and society: baseball, unpopularity of in nineteenth century, 113; child-rearing practices and, 9–13, 16–17, 283; fatalism, 32–34; gambling and, 340; honor and, 2–3, 33–35, 93–94, 120, 122; hunting and, 17; lying (giving the lie) and, 135–136; northerners' fascination with, 281–283; violence and, 21, 22–25, 122. *See also* New South; southern manhood
southern manhood, 1–3, 9–13, 16–25, 340. *See also* Cobb, John; Cobb, Tyrus Raymond; Cobb, Tyrus Raymond and the ethic of honor; Cobb, William Herschel; southern culture, honor and
southern race relations, 7, 10, 143–144; "negro problem" and, 144; racial moderates and, 145; racial radicals and, 144, 146, 151. *See also* Jim Crow Era, race relations in; Ku Klux Klan, New South
Spalding, Albert, 46, 58, 223, 232, 316
Speaker, Tris, 175, 197, 203, 296, 304–305, 310, 363; accused of gambling, 338–343; as manager, 180
Spencer, Edward "Tubby," 170
Spink, Alfred, 44
Spink, J. G. Taylor, 74, 121, 214, 315, 324, 342, 373, 375
Spooner. F. Ed, 260

INDEX

sportswriters. *See* ballyhoo journalism; Frick, Ford; Fullerton, Hugh; Gallico, Paul; Hunt, Marshall; Lane, F. C.; Lanigan, Ernest; Lieb, Fred; McCollum, John; Murnane, Timothy Hayes; Runyan, Damon; Sheridan, John; Spalding, Spink, Alfred; Spink, J. G. Taylor; Stump, Al; Vidmer, Richards; Vila, Joe; Wheeler, Joe; Wray, Ed
Stallings, George, 69, 185, 186, 188, 328
Steinfeldt, Harry, 184
Stengel, Casey, 335, 375
St. Louis, 101, 107
St. Louis Browns, 100, 170, 306
St. Louis Cardinals, 67
Stoddart, Dayton, 319
Stone, George, 100
Stovall, George, 177
Strang, Sammy, 70
Street, Charles "Gabby," 206
Stump, Al, 30, 98, 364, 366–372; authors "Ty Cobb's Wild Ten-Month Fight to Live," 368–372
Sullivan, Bill, 136
Sullivan, John L., 125

Taft, William Howard, 258
Taylor, Charles H., 236
Taylor, Frederick, 229
Taylor, Luther "Dummy," 202
Thaw, Harry K., 225
Thayer, Ernest Lawrence, 49
Tinker, Joe, 171, 203
Torre, Joe, 335
Tumulty, Joseph, 285
Tuthill, Harry, 126
twenties culture, 298–303, 317
"Ty Cobb's Wild Ten-Month Fight to Live.". *See* Stump, Al

Uhle, George "The Bull," 180

Vanderbilt, William, 231
Vaughan, Irving, 363
Veach, Bobby, 214
Vidmer, Richards, 299, 302

Vila, Joe, 131, 326
Von Der Ahe, Chris, 50

Waddell, George "Rube," 68, 170
Wagner, Honus, 124, 128, 171, 173, 175, 176, 183, 201, 241, 304–305, 346, 358
Walker, James J., 301–302
Walsh, Christy, 301–302, 313
Walsh, Ed, 71, 239
Waner, Paul, 331
Warner, Jack, 175
Washington, Booker T., 145
Washington Senators, 61–62, 313
Watson, James E., 341
Webb, Bill, 121, 143
Welborn, Pope, 372
Wells, Eddie, 184, 197
West, Fred, 338, 341
Western League, 55–57. *See also* American League
Wheeler, John, 66, 140, 197, 263
White, Stanford, 225
Willett, Edgar, 95
Williams, Dick, 335
Williams, Joe, 117
Williams, Ted, 358, 363, 368, 372, 373, 375
Williamson, Ned, 296
Wilson, John "Chief," 181
Wilson, Woodrow, 257, 258
Wister, Owen, 230, 281
Wood, "Smoky" Joe, 42, 180, 241; accused of gambling, 338, 339
Woodruff, Bob, 375
Wray, Ed, 131

yannigans. *See* ballplayers, rookies
Yawkey, Bill, 128
Young, Denton "Cy," 57
Young, Nicholas "Nick," 49–50, 53–54, 55, 56–57
Young Men's Christian Association, 236

Ziegfeld, Florenz, 257
Zimbalist, Efron, 257
Zimmerman, Henry "Heinie," 206

www.ingramcontent.com/pod-product-compliance
Lightning Source LLC
Chambersburg PA
CBHW021937240426
43668CB00036B/74